UNIVERSITY OF NORTH CAROLINA AT CHAPEL HILL

DEPARTMENT OF ROMANCE LANGUAGES

NORTH CAROLINA STUDIES
IN THE ROMANCE LANGUAGES AND LITERATURES

Founder: URBAN TIGNER HOLMES

Editor: MARÍA A. SALGADO

Distributed by:

UNIVERSITY OF NORTH CAROLINA PRESS

CHAPEL HILL

North Carolina 27515-2288

U.S.A.

NORTH CAROLINA STUDIES IN THE
ROMANCE LANGUAGES AND LITERATURES
Number 230

GOD, THE QUEST, THE HERO:
THEMATIC STRUCTURES IN BECKETT'S FICTION

GOD, THE QUEST, THE HERO:
THEMATIC STRUCTURES IN BECKETT'S FICTION

BY

LAURA BARGE

CHAPEL HILL

NORTH CAROLINA STUDIES IN THE ROMANCE LANGUAGES AND LITERATURES
U.N.C. DEPARTMENT OF ROMANCE LANGUAGES

1988

Library of Congress Cataloging in Publication Data

Barge, Laura Inez Deavenport.
God, the quest, the hero: thematic structures in Beckett's fiction / by Laura Barge.
p. cm. – (North Carolina studies in the Romance languages and literatures; 230)
Originally presented as the author's thesis (Ph. D.) – University of Alabama, 1985.
Bibliography: p.
Includes index.
ISBN 0-8078-9235-1
1. Beckett, Samuel, 1906- –Fictional works. 2. God in literature. 3. Quests in literature. 4. Heroes in literature. I. Title. II. Series: North Carolina studies in the Romance languages and literatures; no. 230.
PR6003.E282Z5647 1988
843'.914–dc19 88-6904
CIP

ISBN 0-8078-9235-1

DEPÓSITO LEGAL: V. 2.609 - 1988 I.S.B.N. 84-599-2536-6

ARTES GRÁFICAS SOLER, S. A. - LA OLIVERETA, 28 - 46018 VALENCIA - 1988

CONTENTS

FOREWORD

This book explores ideas of God and the nature of the quest in Samuel Beckett's fiction, dealing specifically with *Assumption, More Pricks than Kicks, Watt, Malone Dies, The Unnamable* (with *Murphy*), *How It Is, Still, Sounds, Still 3, As the Story Was Told, La Falaise,* and *Company.* Although Beckett's claim that he is neither a philosopher nor a purveyor of philosophical systems of thought adorned in literary guise is valid, his writings – particularly his fiction – involve themselves with philosophical questions that lie at the very center of human experience. Indeed, this involvement is one of the two foremost reasons (the other being Beckett's incredible craftsmanship as a poet in all genres in which he has chosen to write) for the persistent and universal appeal of his works.

Numerous books on Beckett's fiction have dealt with his metaphysics, including the motifs – ideas of God and the nature of the quest – that are the major concerns of this study. But adequate definition and focused analysis have not been applied directly to the responses made by various protagonists to the sensing of a divine presence/absence. Instead, critics have approached these responses only indirectly, and on the occasion of analyzing other motifs or rhetorical structures. Furthermore, the apparent strategy of much criticism on Beckett's metaphysics has been a divorce between philosophical questions and the narrative movements of the quest. My intention is to define, analyze, and integrate the philosophy of the God-idea with basic thematic structures which support the entire fictional canon.

I do not intend the above justification for my work to imply any degree of arrogance or uniqueness on my part. The approaches, both possible and profitable, to Beckett's work are multiple and many-faceted. Furthermore, I make no pretense to have definitively unraveled the matters of God and the quest in the fiction – such a task would be, by definition, impossible. My purpose is to pose and elucidate certain questions that bear greatly on Beckett's "fundamental sounds," – and to enlighten my readers concerning them. Besides, I have not simply chosen to write about Beckett's metaphysics: I am compelled. From the moment, as a first-year, graduate student working on an MA in English, I read on assignment that incredible play *Waiting for Godot,* I have been awed and fascinated by Beckett's vision of life and of art. Also, like the writer Malone, I was born, not "syphilitic," but with the "disease" (dis-ease) of "earnestness" or graveness. Hopefully, my composition, unlike that of Malone, will not be an "incomprehensible indulgence," but one that will prove valuable to those of us who read and vastly enjoy the offerings of this giant of modern literature.

My choices of the particular pieces of fiction dealt with rest on the dual premise that these works represent the entire fictional canon, and that they exhibit both the development and unity apparent in tracing the paradigmatic patterns I describe through pivotal junctures in this canon. *Assumption* and *More Pricks than Kicks* are two of Beckett's earliest pieces, dating from 1929 to 1934. *Watt* (1944) is pivotal, not only because it is Beckett's last major fiction written originally in English before he began to write primarily in French, but also because its characterization of the hero, movements and goals of the quest, and obsession with the matter of language set the stage for all the subsequent fiction. *Malone Dies,* written in French in 1947 and 1948, and first published in 1956, is the middle novel of the trilogy. This novel is also the point in my descriptions of the quest where the hero first moves from level one to engage in the artistic quest of level two. The importance of the trilogy as a progression of three major novels which together form the apex of Beckett's ficitional achievement makes appropriate an explanation of the positions of *Molloy* (1951) and *The Unnamable* (1953) as they precede and follow *Malone Dies.* The emphasis in this explanation is on the linking of concepts of the self and language with the God motif in *The Unnamable.* Because the earlier novel *Murphy* (1938) provides particularly relevant comparisons to certain thought processes of the Unnamable as hero, it is included in this explanation also.

How It Is (1964) is distinctive in that it exhibits for the first time Beckett's setting as being definitively that of the microcosm rather than the macrocosm or a vague blending of the two. These terms, as is common in Beckettian criticism, refer to the "little" world of the human mind or imagination as opposed to the "big" world of the outer sphere of ordinary human movement and activity. *Still, Sounds,* and *Still 3, La Falaise,* and *As the Story Was Told* are examples both of Beckett's offerings of the seventies and of his many quintessential "briefs" – very short fictional pieces exhibiting an uncanny skill at compressing intense content into stripped form. *Company* is the first major long work to follow *How It Is* and introduces the group of novels – *Company, Ill Seen Ill Said,* and *Worstward Ho* – that some critics refer to as a second trilogy. Thus, my selections span the time period of Beckett's composition of fiction, deal with lengthy works and "briefs," and focus on significant transition points in his development as a writer of fiction.

The second chapter, "Paradigms of Heroes and Quests," is an analytic description of the two levels of the quest as they are disclosed in the fiction, and of the heroes' motivations for and responses to the undertaking of this quest. The first chapter, "Beckett, God, and their Critics," is an examination of and interaction with critical ideas concerning the question of God in Beckett's literature as a whole, but particularly in the fiction. Exploring the quest structures of the selected pieces of fiction dealt with in the remaining chapters becomes the method of elucidating this question.

I wish to express my gratitude to several persons and institutions that have aided me in this project. Professor Dwight Eddins, of the University of Alabama at Tuscaloosa, and Professor William McClung, of Mississippi State University at Starkville, have been of inestimable assistance in guiding me in the development of my understanding of the matters about which I write. Professor Lawrence Graver, of Williams College, Williamstown, Massachusetts, is due a word of thanks for reading portions of the manuscript and providing valuable insight and direction.

I am grateful to the Beckett Archive of the Library of the University of Reading, England, for making available to me copies of Beckett's pieces *As the Story Was Told* and *La Falaise.* I wish to thank Syble Bottrell and Linda Herbst for help in translating French and German criticism. A strong word of thanks is due Margaret Weir and Susan Russell, whose patience and typing skills produced the typescript of this work. And I am grateful to Norma Flora, that most excellent of proofreaders.

I especially want to express my appreciation to the University of Alabama Graduate School for the financial aid provided by two Graduate Council Research Fellowships, and to many librarians – particularly those of interlibrary loan – of this university.

Excerpts or chapters from this study have been previously published in *Romance Notes,* 25 (1984), 109-20; and in *Cithara: Essays in the Judaeo-Christian Tradition,* 24 (1985), 49-58.

The dedication of this book is to the memory of Maudie Ivy, who died at the age of sixty, in July of 1985. Maudie, my friend and helper for many years, was the person most responsible for making available to me the time to undertake the studies that have led to the completion of this work.

If there had anywhere appeared in space
Another place of refuge, where to flee,
Our hearts had taken refuge in that place,
And not with Thee.

For we against creation's bars had beat
Like prisoned eagles, through great
worlds had sought
Though but a foot of ground to plant our
feet,
Where Thou wert not.

And only when we found in earth and air,
In heaven or hell, that such might
nowhere be
That we could not flee from Thee
anywhere,
We fled to Thee.

Richard Chenevix Trench

Poem 281, p. 394, in the *Oxford Book of Christian Verse.* Chosen and edited by Lord David Cecil, Oxford, at the Clarendon Press, 1940.

BECKETT, GOD, AND THEIR CRITICS

Belacqua Shuah contemplates the inscrutable justice of Dante's God. Moran remembers that he had once been taught to "ascribe my angers, fears, desires, and even my body" to God. Hamm, in one breath, calls God a bastard and claims that "He doesn't exist!" The voice of *Company* ironically questions, "God is love. Yes or no?" and answers with a decisive "No."[1] From beginning to end, Samuel Beckett's *œuvre* is permeated with the various protagonists' perceptions of and responses to the idea of God. A survey of the attempts critics have made to analyze this permeation reveals the astonishing complexity of the God-idea in Beckett's writings. It is probably safe to claim that in no writer's work, modern or otherwise, is the spectrum of ways of perceiving and responding to the idea of God any wider. Critical opinion has defined a gamut ranging from Christian orthodoxy to Christian existentialism to humanistic immanentism to Zen (and other modes of Buddhism) to Manichean dualism to agnosticism to atheism to nihilism to blasphemy. What is incredibly true is that each of these attitudes or ways of thinking about God does appear, although only as part of a whole, at some point somewhere in the canon.

Any critical effort to put a definitive label on Beckett in order to fit him into some particular religious or philosophical system is

---

[1] See *More Pricks than Kicks* (1972), p. 21; *Molloy*, in *Three Novels: Molloy, Malone Dies, The Unnamable* (1965), p. 174; *Endgame* (1958), p. 54b; and *Company* (1980), p. 52. References to these works by Beckett are to the separate editions published by Grove Press, New York. Specific references are designated by titles and page number(s) in the text.

obviously futile. That Beckett cannot be pigeonholed in a system, however, does not necessarily mean that efforts to do so serve no purpose at all. Investigation of many perspectives – if they are recognized as merely perspectives – can aid us in comprehending the total picture. Of course, the use of any phrase such as "total picture" must itself be strongly qualified. In Beckett's works, we are not dealing with theological, philosophical, or even literary statements, formulas, or propositions which purport to say what God is like or even that God is or is not. Instead, what we are confronted with is a given hero's experience of what he senses as God, or of what he senses as the absence of God. It is possible, however, to differentiate between critical assessments of this sense of God in Beckett's work and to focus on those assessments that will force us toward definition, analysis, and critical judgment. Such differentiation and focusing will provide a certain degree of orientation as we proceed into the works themselves – in this case, the fiction – in order to arrive at some understanding of how different perspectives fit together into one whole.

Because Beckett's use of Christian imagery and symbolism is so persistent[2] and because his work is permeated by a religious quality that causes John Pilling to refer to him as a "God-haunted man,"[3] it is possible, in any given period of time, to find critics who attempt to connect the writer or his various protagonists with a positive attitude toward orthodox Christian belief. One of the earliest and best-known of such attempts is G. S. Fraser's piece on *Waiting for Godot,* which appeared in the *Times Literary Supplement,* 10 February, 1956.[4] An analysis of the deficiencies of this essay – which Beckett has called a poor piece of work – can help to

---

[2] Beckett has claimed that his use of Christian symbols is due merely to his familiarity with the Christian system: "Christianity is a mythology with which I am perfectly familiar. So naturally I use it" (Colin Duckworth, *Angels of Darkness: Dramatic Effect in Samuel Beckett with Special Reference to Eugene Ionesco* [New York: Barnes and Noble, 1972], p. 18).

[3] Pilling, *Samuel Beckett* (London: Routledge and Kegan Paul, 1976), p. 1.

[4] Fraser, *"Waiting for Godot",* in *English Critical Essays: Twentieth Century,* 2nd ser., ed. Derek Hudson (London: Oxford Univ. Press, 1958), pp. 324-32; rpt. from *Times Literary Supplement,* 10 Feb. 1956, p. 84; rpt. in *Casebook on* Waiting for Godot, *The Impact of Beckett's Modern Classic: Reviews, Reflections, and Interpretations,* ed. Ruby Cohn (New York: Grove, 1967), pp. 133-37. References to this essay given by page number(s) in the text are to the copy in *English Critical Essays.*

reveal why traditional Christian interpretations have never, in spite of their continued appearance, gained reputable critical recognition. Fraser first of all makes certain claims which are obviously valid and which, in a sense, substantiate the plausibility of his position. "The fundamental imagery of *Waiting for Godot* is Christian" (p. 326). Vladimir and Estragon are spiritually superior to Pozzo and Lucky in that their relationship is more charitable, as defined from a Christian perspective (p. 327). The tramps' attitude toward Godot consists of the two basic human emotions felt in regard to the traditional Christian God – "hope and fear" (p. 327). But these claims are not tied together thematically, and, in their isolated validity, do not support any interpretation of the play, orthodox Christian or otherwise.

Fraser proceeds to insist that Godot stands for an "anthropomorphic image of God" and that each tramp has "an overmastering concern with the other's salvation" (p. 328). At this point, the critical remarks become presumptive: Fraser's claim that Godot represents the Christian God can neither be proven nor disproven, and, even if Godot does, the resultant interpretation of the play is more likely anti-Christian. Neither Fraser nor the play offers evidence that Vladimir's and Estragon's comradeship involves unselfish concern for each other's salvation, especially salvation as defined by Fraser. Instead, each is obsessed with his own salvation – as defined by Beckett – and the concern of either tramp for the other focuses on a physical, not a spiritual, need. The lesson or Christian moral that Fraser finds in *Godot* – that we should avoid both presumption and despair – is one that the tramp-heroes themselves do not, and, given the conditions of the play, cannot learn. Fraser ends by reading his own philosophical inclinations into Lucky's speech – "The Nietzschean and the Liberal hypotheses" are "put out of court" (p. 332) – and leaves his readers wondering exactly how the "message" of *Godot* comes close to being one of "religious consolation" (p. 325). Any effort to read any of Beckett's works as Christianly orthodox is marked by some of the characteristics of this essay on *Godot* – an over-reliance on a prevalence of Christian imagery and symbolism, a failure to tie isolated facts together, the making of unfounded assumptions, a tendency to read one's own philosophical ideas into the work, and, above all, a failure to recognize irony.

We can learn from such critical efforts what not to do with Beckett's use of Christian elements, but the problem of what we should do with them remains. Nor does the fact that these elements are nearly always used ironically relieve us of the necessity of confronting them critically. A random sampling of the corpus of Beckett's fiction reveals that the hero's metaphysical condition and need are very frequently portrayed in orthodox Christian symbols, language, and logic. An example of such portrayal is Beckett's use of the supreme symbol of orthodoxy – the Eucharist, which embodies or represents Christ, sacrificed and raised from the dead by the power of God that he might provide for the spiritual needs of man. Parodies of the Eucharist surface from *More Pricks than Kicks* through the very latest prose. A hero continually engages in some way in a "partaking" of the sacred feast but never realizes any benefits from doing so. Thus these parodies conform to a basic pattern of Christian imagery in all Beckett's work, a pattern of offering, response, and failure. Four examples lifted from the continuum of the fiction will reveal this pattern and show the prevalence of such symbolism in Beckett's work.

In "Dante and the Lobster," the Eucharist is symbolically contained in Belacqua's sandwich or bread – the cheese for the sandwich is offered him by a Pilate-like grocer in a "wild crucified gesture." Also, Belacqua refers to the lobster as a "fish" or "Jesus Christ, Son of God, Saviour," and, as he and his aunt view the lobster as their meal, it forms an "exposed cruciform on the oilcloth." Belacqua, however, gains no knowledge or experience of "mercy and Godliness" in this particular "stress of Sacrifice" (*More Pricks than Kicks,* pp. 14, 19-20, 21-22). In *Malone Dies,* the "celebrated sacrifice" exists in the form of a yellowed, rotting tooth in Moll's mouth – and in Macmann's as he and Moll kiss. When Moll loses the symbolic tooth, she puts it "away in a safe place" rather than making Macmann a present or offering of it. The paragraph that relates this last bit of information also introduces Lemuel, who heads up the Easter weekend excursion that ends in hell rather than any kind of life for both Macmann and Malone.[5]

---

[5] *Malone Dies,* in *Three Novels: Molloy, Malone Dies, The Unnamable* (New York: Grove, 1965), pp. 263-64, 266, 287. All other references to *Malone Dies* are to this edition. Citations in the text are referred to by title and page number(s).

Each of the multitudes of sacks deposited along the way of the mud-crawler in *How It Is* contains a "celestial tin" of "miraculous sardines" or fish, which, as Belacqua has explained, can mean "Jesus Christ, Son of God, Saviour." The voice of Part Three of *How It Is* assures us that the only possible logical source of these sacks is the "one not one of us an intelligence somewhere a love." That this "intelligence" vanishes in his own illogicality, leaving the mud-crawler (unless he has vanished also) as needy as ever, is a matter of small importance: as the voice concludes, there is "more nourishment in a cry" "than sardines can ever offer."[6]

For to End Yet Again contains language and imagery that can be read as allusive to Christ offered to man in his death. The setting – "last place of all" – is connected with some skull (a microcosmic Golgotha as the Place of the Skull), and the piece begins with a figure "alone in a dark place pent bowed on a board." If this "expelled" hero is a crucified Everyman/Christ, the dwarfs may nonetheless carry a relic of a non-resurrected Christ on their "dung litter of laughable memory." There are two dwarfs – Beckett's everlasting couple, an image always resonating with allusions to the two thieves. The dwarfs appear exceedingly white, even from the "crowns of their massy skulls" – two angels or men in shining white attend the tomb of Christ (Luke 24:4). "Crown" and "skull" echo the Passion, and the litter the dwarfs carry is covered with a "bone-white" sheet, has "'shafts fore and aft,'" and holds a pillow marking the "place of the head." The narrator gives no indication that the figure staring at the dwarfs can "decipher" this offered "whiteness" as an image of the body of Christ.[7] Our defining of the image in this manner rests in part on a knowledge of similar jumbled but very significant references to crucifixions, ruined landscapes, and fathers' refusals to offer bread to their sons in *Endgame.* The more closely we read and compare *For to End Yet Again* with other works by Beckett, the more we appreciate John

[6] *How It Is* (New York: Grove, 1964), pp. 48, 137-38, 143. All other references to *How It Is* are to this edition. Citations in the text are referred to by title and page number(s).

[7] *For to End Yet Again,* in *Fizzles* (New York: Grove, 1976), pp. 55-59. All other references to *For to End Yet Again* are to this edition and are cited by title and page number(s) in the text.

Pilling's assigning of "infinite nuances" to this short piece.[8] At any rate, nearly all of Beckett's fictional heroes, in their early or late guises, appear to be obsessed with promises contained in the symbolic language of orthodox Christianity and destitute because of their non-fulfillment.

Another highly orthodox element that must be accounted for, found in the hero's spiritual questing or response to life, is his sensing of a transcendent power outside himself as the potential source for the meeting of his metaphysical needs. Such a reliance on transcendence is, of course, not uniquely Christian, orthodox or otherwise. It is a common element in nearly all religions, both Eastern and Western. In fact, the word "religion" implies a system of thought and experience that acknowledges some reality beyond and above the boundaries of man's material and empirical existence. It is the biblical trappings of what we may call Beckett's "figures of transcendence" that connect the concept of transcendence in his writings with orthodox Christianity.

One such figure is Belacqua's "mysterious pedlar," who appears to him as a "sign" in "Ding-Dong," hawking "seats in heaven" (*More Pricks than Kicks,* pp. 44-46). This woman is a welfare or social worker, a type of woman who appears also in *Molloy* (pp. 23-24), where she is disdainfully compared to charitable workers of the Salvation Army. The description of the woman in *More Pricks than Kicks* confronts us once more with overt Christian symbolism. The narrator presents her as a "sign," a common biblical term used especially in the gospel of John (see, for example, chapter 4:18-22) for some kind of supernatural evidence of God's intervention in human affairs. The woman lifts "up upon him [Belacqua]" a "countenance . . . full of light." This particular phrase – the lifting up of a countenance of light – occurs throughout the Old Testament in reference to Jehovah's spiritual disclosure to favored persons, four times in the Psalms – 4:6, 44:3, 89:15, and 90:8. Belacqua responds to this "radiance" (which is "luminous, impassive, and serene") as if it implies the impartial favor of deity toward "the just and the unjust." The awareness of the narrator as

---

[8] Pilling and James Knowlson, *Frescoes of the Skull: The Later Prose and Drama of Samuel Beckett* (London: John Calder, 1979), p. 190.

he records Belacqua's response is ironic: in Beckett's world all persons are equally guilty of both justice and injustice, but at a loss to understand why this universal condition merits the fate of a life of suffering in a universe arranged by a supposedly just God who is also love. The idea of impartial favor on both "the just and the unjust" is lifted directly (and distorted' a la Beckett) from Jesus' terminology in Matthew 7:45: "he [God the Father] maketh his sun to rise on the evil and on the good, and sendeth rain on the just and on the unjust." The final blessing of the woman on the astonished, but strangely impressed, Belacqua that "Jesus . . . and his sweet mother preserve yer honour" erases any doubt as to what "heaven" the woman thinks her "seats" are situated in.

The welfare worker in *Molloy* is not a figure of transcendence, but she is part of a Kafkaesque authority group that makes up a system that holds Molloy's immediate destiny in its hands. This system resonates subtly with allusions to the first-century system that rationally and logically, under the governance of a just and loving God, would have delivered and vindicated Jesus, who claimed to be God's Son and who had spent the thirty-three years of his life in innocence and goodness. Molloy's treatment at the hands of the system he is forced to rely upon is a clumsy parody of the crucifixion of Jesus, who was relying on his Father/Gods. The social worker offers Molloy what, to anyone aware of Beckett's subtle nuances in the use of symbolism, is a sloppy Eucharist. The mug and saucer holding the "greyish concoction" of green tea and powdered milk and the "thick slab of dry bread" form a "little pile of tottering disparates, in which the hard, the liquid and the soft [the bread, the wine, and Christ's body] were joined." Other members of the system the woman represents are "malefactors [the two thieves and Barabbas], policemen [the Roman soldiers] . . . priests [the Jewish religious leaders] and journalists [those later responsible for the recording of the crucifixion event in the gospels]." The food being offered to Molloy in order "to hinder you from swooning" reminds us of the potion offered Christ as he swoons on the cross. Molloy contemplates, at this point, the guilt he carries in regard to "the long confused emotion which was my life" and attempts to "judge" his condition as he has been told that God will one day judge him "with no less impertinence" (*Molloy,* p. 23). As readers, we are not at all surprised, a few paragraphs further on, to find Molloy encountering along the river a barge with a "cargo of nails and timber," manned by a boatman with a "long white beard," that is on "its way to some carpenter I suppose." We also see this hero lying down on the earth "with outspread arms" and watching a horizon "burning with sulphur and phosphorus" (*Molloy*, pp. 26-27).

Like the inhabitants of Kafka's world, Beckett's people must rely on mysterious persons from higher realms for the help they so desperately need and never receive. As Josephine Jacobsen and William R. Mueller point out, when the Beckett hero bends

> "an ear toward some dimly perceived supernatural redemption, he does not find the slimmest skein of hope in the natural man; if man can look only to himself, he should wisely cut the thread of life with utmost dispatch. There may or may not be hope, but if there is, it is of supernatural initiation."[9]

More often than not, Beckett's narrators describe such sources of hope in orthodox Christian terminology. Major figures so described are Watt's Mr. Knott and Godot. No one can prove that Godot represents any God, Christian or otherwise. But he is certainly a personage who transcends the habitation and experience of Vladimir and Estragon. And he has two servant boys, one of whom keeps sheep and receives beatings from Godot and one of whom keeps goats and does not receive beatings. Also, as everyone knows, Godot has a long white beard, and Estragon has all his life compared himself to Christ.

There is no point in multiplying proofs that only the event of Godot's coming will "save" Vladimir and Estragon and all their reincarnations throughout the prose. Nor is there any point in repeating the by-now-commonplace critical remark that Beckett's man finds no comfort or hope in all the bright promises of humanism from the Enlightenment on. Stephen of Joyce's *A Portrait of the Artist* may find the darkness falling from the desolate air of earth changing to a brightness as luminous as that of Nashe simply because of the ecstasy of the artist's response to a girl

---

[9] Jacobsen and Mueller, *The Testament of Samuel Beckett* (1964; rpt. London: Faber and Faber, 1966), p. 105.

walking through an evening.[10] But for the Unnamable, if "brightness" ever comes to Worm, "little by little, or rapidly, or in a sudden flood," it will be from whatever source first decreed that light should be.[11] Of course, the inexistence, impotence, or cruel indifference of this mysterious source renders highly improbable any significant increase of metaphysical light for Worm. Also, as Murphy would remind us, how can anything new (like transcendence) enter a closed system? Whatever positive qualities are connected with transcendence by the hero's reliance upon some such power are cancelled or contradicted by the negative qualities associated with it. Thus the sense of transcendence, like the symbols of the Eucharist we have examined, is reduced to irony. Although we can therefore define any positive, Christian, orthodox interpretation of a given work as a failure to recognize subtle levels of irony, we cannot escape the critical task of accounting for the irony itself.

The orthodox perspective is not the only Christian vantage point from which critics view Beckett's writings. In fact, the vantage point of Christian existentialism is more widely employed than that of Christian orthodoxy. From this modified view of traditional Christian thought, critics make repeated efforts to account for the Christian elements and the heavy irony that, as we have noted, is associated with their use. Richard N. Coe is the best example of such a critic. In the book *Samuel Beckett* and in the lengthy article "God and Samuel Beckett," Coe explores Beckett's use of Christian symbols and terminology.[12] The thrust of Coe's argument is that Beckett is pointing in a particular Christian direction by having his characters' "indictment" of God "as conceived by the orthodox" turn into a "pilgrimage in search of a new and more acceptable version of God."[13] Both literary and bio-

---

[10] James Joyce, *A Portrait of the Artist as a Young Man* (1916: rpt. New York: Viking, 1964), pp. 232-34.

[11] *The Unnamable*, in *Three Novels: Molloy, Malone Dies, The Unnamable* (The York: Grove, 1965), pp. 361-62.

[12] See Coe, *Samuel Beckett* (New York: Grove, 1964); first printed as *Beckett* (Edinburgh and London: Oliver and Boyd, 1964). "God and Samuel Beckett," in *Twentieth Century Interpretations* of Molloy, Malone Dies, The Unnamable; *A Collection of Critical Essays,* ed. J. D. O'Hara (Englewood Cliffs, N. J.: Prentice-Hall, 1970), pp. 91-113; rpt. from *Meanjin,* 24 (1965), 66-85.

[13] "God and Samuel Beckett," pp. 99, 98, and 100.

graphical support exists for attempting to solve the problem of God in Beckett's writings by formulating such an approach. The typical Beckettian hero – certainly in the work published before 1962 – seems obsessed with the idea and need of God. At the same time, he is appalled by what seem to be evidences – cruelty, injustice, suffering, death – that God, as he is conceived of by man (the hero), must be either malign, indifferent, impotent, dead, or nonexistent. Perhaps Beckett is suggesting that the ideas or notions of traditional, orthodox Christianity that define a Godot-like God, visualized with a long, white beard, who has created and now controls the disordered affair of human history, should be abandoned in favor of a more enlightened, less rigid concept of deity. It is common knowledge that Beckett turned early on from the traditional Irish Protestantism of his childhood, but that he has remained, in Pilling's terms, a "God-haunted" man.[14] Is Beckett redefining man's continuing need of God in modern Christian existential terms?

Coe claims that the God of the Preacher (a term lifted from *All That Fall*) – the anthropomorphic God of Western tradition – is caricatured in Beckett's writings as being "concocted out of human words and reflecting human evil." The "true God," who, because he is outside of time and cannot be spoken of in language, "must necessarily exist and yet equally necessarily can never be known." Such a God is "a macrocosmic equivalent of the microcosmic Void of the 'true self.'" This true God is not responsible for the suffering, absurdity, and death of the created order that men (such as Beckett's heroes) have heretofore assigned to God. Coe concludes that whatever possibility exists for reaching the true God rests on the communicating power of words or perhaps of music as a symbol of love.[15] He identifies the quality of love as "one of

---

[14] Pilling, *Samuel Beckett*, p. 1.

[15] "God and Samuel Beckett,", pp. 107-108; 110-12. One apparent contradiction or at least an assertion of confusing claims is the description of the new or true God as being one beyond language or the verbal constructs men have devised to hold him ("God and Samuel Beckett," pp. 107-08) and yet as the one who ultimately reveals himself in the existence of human language because he is the universal listener who hears human speech ("God and Samuel Beckett," pp. 110-12). These claims are probably paradoxical rather than contradictory, but Coe does not resolve them even as paradox.

the most persistent ideals in Beckett's writings."[16] Coe understands Beckett to be saying that to imprison God in words and in the logic of time and space (the reality of human evil) is to distort the true God, or the Absolute, into a pseudo-God.

Jeffrey G. Sobosan follows Coe closely, citing him twelve times in "Time and Absurdity in Samuel Beckett" and agreeing that Beckett rejects "the mythical representation of God as a false view." This critic is a bit more theologically oriented than Coe as he laments his belief that Beckett, having rejected the false view of deity, is left with nothing "to hold as a divine and personal God." The term used by Beckett that most closely approximates the idea of the true God is that of the Void or the Nothingness of the Self. Sobosan agrees with Coe on what these critics see as Beckett's emphasis on the need for love in human relationships: "Beckett's people revile the love they do know, and by doing so hint of a love which they have never known and cannot know."[17]

The French critic Louis Barjon echoes similar ideas in his analysis of Beckett's God, an analysis which is essentially a contrast between *Waiting for Godot* and *Happy Days.* Barjon sees Beckett's portrait of Godot as the false image of God projected in the catechism and in traditional religious pictures. Such a God is rejected because he never fulfills the expectations men have of him. *C'est celui qui s'annonce toujours et qui ne se montre jamais:*

> Il est clair que toute représentation de Dieu, toute définition en formules de son être insaisissable, apparaît au regard de Beckett comme anthropomorphique et suspecte.[18]

Barjon sees *Happy Days* as offering a *radicale modification d'optique.* What he interprets as Winnie's courage and gaiety in the face of great adversity are evidence enough that some kind of God-force, coming from a source other than her own personality and yet also from within her, is sustaining her. This God-force is a *présence*

---

[16] Coe, *Samuel Beckett,* p. 104.

[17] Sobosan, "Time and Absurdity in Samuel Beckett," *Thought,* 49 (1974), 192, 188-89, and 194.

[18] Barjon, "Le Dieu de Beckett," *Etudes,* 322 (1965), 656.

amicale that *seule demeure réelle et fidèle* in Beckett's otherwise Godlesss world.[19]

In *The Shape of Chaos,* David Hesla applies Heideggerian terminology to Beckett's works: Watt and Godot represent "Being" which is "the Absolute Essence of the contingent Ego's existence, the Ground and Authentication of its decisionful life, the purpose and very Basis of its thought."[20] Hesla sees Beckett's proposed remedy for the absence of this Absolute Ego from the human scene, however, in Christian existentialist terms. Vladimir and Estragon are waiting "to be given something which only they themselves can supply." From the "frozen wasteland of the spirit," man must reach out to "touch the hand of his neighbor."[21] Given a God who is beyond meaning, man must supply his own religious meaning to life, a meaning that can be derived only from the love of interpersonal relationships.

Eugene Combs is surveying Beckett from a similar perspective when he notes that Beckett's "use of the term 'God' is confined to sardonic references to conventional facile piety; the 'God' of his catechetical, middle-class Protestantism":

> This 'God is abhorrent to Beckett because he is definable, is knowable through the constructs of man's mind, is the 'creation' of man. The language about this God is man-made and refers only to the reality of man's constructs. . . . But Beckett is deeply conscious of Being that lies outside man and is beyond man, that is not knowable, but remains mystery.[22]

Combs notes that the Unnamable denotes the "unnamableness of God . . . that is, the impenetrable mystery of deity" and asserts that Beckett is attempting, in his art, to "reinstate into modernity" the "contemplation" of this God.[23]

---

[19] "Le Dieu de Beckett," pp. 658-59.

[20] Hesla, *The Shape of Chaos: An Interpretation of the Art of Samuel Beckett* (Minneapolis: Univ. of Minnesota Press, 1971), p. 224.

[21] *The Shape of Chaos,* pp. 164 and 158.

[22] Combs, "Impotence and Ignorance: A Parody of Prerogatives in Samuel Beckett," *Studies in Religion/Sciences Religieuses,* 2 (1972), 125.

[23] See "Impotence and Ignorance," p. 120.

Gabriel Vahanian is like Combs in assigning to Beckett the active intent of awakening a culture still shackled to outmoded, orthodox religious ideas to a truer vision of deity. In *The Death of God,* Vahanian claims that *Waiting for Godot* "is an invitation to shake off the fetters that still link Western man to a past Christian culture." This critic sees *Godot* as entirely "constructed around the irrelevance of Christian concepts" that are "based on the belief that there is a God who particularly cares for man and is ever loving and concerned enough to enter the scene of man's destiny." Beckett is pleading with his readers to abandon "all atavistic attachment to a deity." We are intended to see Godot as being "even stupider than God – he is what Christians have made of God."[24] In "The Empty Cradle," Vahanian explains that *Waiting for Godot* represents the climate of the "darkness" which the "light of the Christian heritage" was "addressed to but has failed to overcome in the practical lives of men."[25]

Hélène L. Webner exemplifies this company of critics as she also writes on what she interprets as the meaning of *Waiting for Godot.* The "anthropomorphic God of western tradition, the old man with the white beard . . . is no longer accessible to modern man." A "more reliable insight into the nature of the Divine can be found at the foot of that Tree by which Vladimir and Estragon wait." The person symbolized by this tree or cross is "Jesus as the Man for Others": Beckett is pointing his readers in the religious direction formulated by Dietrich Bonhoeffer and Trillich.[26] Reading such criticism as Webner's, we are made suddenly aware of how great our critical distance has become from Beckett's Estragon, Vladimir, and Godot. Webner's suggestion that perhaps Beckett read some of Bonhoeffer's thought in the popular press because both he and Bonhoeffer worked for the underground resistance, although in different countries, during World War II,[27] signals a departure into speculation.

---

[24] Vahanian, *The Death of God: The Culture of Our Post-Christian Era* (New York: George Braziller, 1950), pp. 120-23.

[25] Vahanian, "The Empty Cradle," *Theology Today,* 13 (1957), 525.

[26] Webner, "*Waiting for Godot* and the New Theology," *Renascence,* 21 (1968), 3-4, 9.

[27] "*Waiting for Godot* and the New Theology," p. 4.

Christian existentialism is as good a term as any to designate the theological perspectives implied by criticism such as the above. There is no feasible way to know – nor any reason to seek to know – exactly where each of these literary critics is coming from religiously and where he or she is attempting to situate Beckett. Obviously, some of them can be taken much more seriously than others. The milieu common to all of them is that associated with religious thinkers such as Kierkegaard, Tillich, Bonhoeffer, Gogarten, Niebuhr, Bultmann, and, to some extent, Brunner and Barth. These theologians do not constitute a unified group – no creeds or organizational structures hold them together. In fact, in regard to doctrine, massive and significant differences separate them. For instance, Both Tillich and Bultmann depart radically from historic Christology, whereas Brunner, Barth, and Bonhoeffer are defenders of more or less historically orthodox concepts of Christ. They, except for Kierkegaard, share the common heritage of having been influenced by secular existentialism, particularly that of Heidegger. Furthermore, from a theological perspective, they can all be said to be reacting against, and yet simultaneously assimilating, certain aspects of the nineteenth-century Protestant liberalism of Schleiermacher and others. Fereanc Morton Szasz defines Protestant liberalism as characterized by the following affirmations:

> (1) God is immanent in human affairs, causing history to evolve toward the realization of a good and ideal society. He should be thought of as immanent rather than transcendent.
> (2) "Love" is emphasized over "Justice," and "Character" matters more than "Grace."
> (3) The Bible is to be interpreted by the scientific method – in this case, by the analysis of higher criticism – rather than by lower criticism or an examination of content as revealed by God to man.
> (4) The Social Gospel is more expressive of God's dealings with mankind than ideas of individual salvation.[28]

[28] Szasz, *The Divided Mind of Protestant America, 1880-1930* (University, Ala.: Univ. of Alabama Press, 1982), pp. 68-69.

The Christian existentialist would probably have inherited (2) and (3) but not necessarily (1) and (4).

Neoorthodox is an adjective that can be applied to many Christian existentialists, but not all of them. This term is a loose one used to designate various forms of twentieth-century Protestant theology which, while claiming the desire to recover certain perspectives and interpretations of the Reformation, have nonetheless radically restated these perspectives. Emphasis is put on the absolute otherness of God, man's weight of sin, guilt, and responsibility as a creature, the uniqueness of Christ – even if stated only in human terms – and personal encounters with God in existential revelation.[29] Certainly we cannot assign this adjective indiscriminately to the critical interpretations we have just surveyed, although some of the religious ideas that are brought to bear on Beckett's writings are neoorthodox in that they are related to the Dialectical Theology of Barth. Coe's ideas of God as the Wholly Other who is not to be identified with anything in our world, even our Christian ideas of him, and of our use of language making God more distant than accessible, seem Barthian or neoorthodox. Sobosan and Hesla's emphases on the primacy of interpersonal love in human relationships as a means of participating in divinity bring to mind Brunner's I-Thou relationship. Hesla and Combs' usage of the terms "ground" and "being" echoes Tillich's ontological Ground-of-Being God. Barjon's admiration of Winnie's courage and gaiety – surely a failure to recognize Beckett's subtle levels of irony – parallels Tillich's courage to be in the face of non-being. Vahanian, who is himself a theologian, brings to bear on Beckett's works his belief in a God who is wholly other, a God so transcendent that he cannot be objectified in human terms. Both Combs and Vahanian, in their interpretations of *Waiting for Godot,* assign to Beckett intentions similar to Bultmann's purpose of the necessity of calling men to authentic spiritual decision.[30] Surveying this particular segment of religiously-oriented

---

[29] For formulations of neoorthodox thought, see "Neoorthodoxy" in *The New International Dictionary of the Christian Church,* ed. J. D. Douglas, et al. (Grand Rapids: Zondervan, 1974), pp. 697-98.

[30] For additional information on specifics of the thinking of such theologian/philosophers, see Eugene B. Borowitz, *A Layman's Introduction to Religious*

criticism on Beckett's writings, we can speak of critics with a plethora of ideas ranging the gamut from Barth's resurgence of orthodox emphases to Heidegger's "atheistic" insistencie in the interview published after his death that "Only a God Can Save Us."[31]

Although these critics point out some obvious facts concerning Beckett's portrait of God, they do not succeed in establishing their premises in regard to the intent and/or content of his writings. Certainly, in work after work, Beckett not only caricatures but has his heroes reject and curse the God concocted of human words and reflecting human evil. The problem is that this anthropomorphic God appears to be the only one referred to by the heroes or the narrators throughout the canon. Watt explains the blatant anthropomorphism of Beckett's people: "the only way one can speak of God is to speak of him as though he were a man" (*Watt*, p. 77). The God responsible for the creation of a world that traps man in suffering, absurdity, and death is not only ridiculed but also relentlessly blasphemed. But where in Beckett's work is there one clear and indisputable reference to a God who is not responsible for the creation of the world, not to mention man's unwilling entrance into this world? If there is a true God – different from the one caricatured and blasphemed – who exists entirely outside of time and apart from human language and evil, Beckett's people cannot discover or locate him, much less relate to him by engaging in profoundly loving relationships. Surely Vladimir and Estragon are not satirized or held up as examples of what not to do because they do not spiritually deepen their relationship and courageously leave the site where they think Godot is to meet them. They are together precisely and only because they are both waiting for Godot. It is true that the void or nothingness that the various heroes seek as the essence of the self or the ultimate reality of human experience can easily be equated with the actuality of God.

Existentialism (Philadelphia: Westminster Press, 1966) and John MacQuarrie, *Studies in Christian Existentialism* (London: SCM Press, Ltd., 1966).

[31] Martin Heidegger, "Only a God Can Save Us," *Philosophy Today*, 20 (1976), 267-84. This article is a translation by Maria P. Alter and John D. Caputo of an interview between Heidegger and *Der Spiegel*, 31 May 1976, issue No. 23, pp. 193 ff. (Spiegel-Verlag, Brandstwiete 19/Ost-West Strasse, 2000 Hamburg 11, West Germany.)

But there is no suggestion anywhere, to the best of my knowledge, that this reality can be seized upon existentially by abandoning false, outmoded ideas of divinity and embracing new ones.

The question of Beckett's knowledge of Christian existentialism must also be confronted. From all the evidence at hand, Beckett shares in the religious skepticism of his *Zeitgeist,* but there is little evidence of his familiarity with the particular religious solutions of Protestant liberalism, neoorthodoxy, or Christian existentialism. One has only to read any summary of the dominant intellectual and philosophical influences on his writings to realize that his understanding of what constitutes Christian thought has been shaped not only by the orthodox Protestantism of his childhood but also by his extensive reading of Augustine, Duns Scotus, and Dante.[32] Beckett himself has pointed out the strong influence of Samuel Johnson on his thought and writings: "They can put me wherever they want, but it's Johnson, always Johnson, who is with me. And if I follow any tradition, it is his."[33] Such a statement does not, of course, limit Beckett's definition of Christianity to that of Johnson, but it does reinforce the case for asserting that Beckett does not work with modern reinterpretations of the Christian faith. Beckett rejects the God of Christian orthodoxy, but this God is the only Christian one that he and his people seem to be familiar with.

Another difficulty with this approach is assigning to Beckett an interest in theological definitions and distinctions that would result in his pointing in some particular religious direction. Such assignation has yet to be critically proved, and, as I have claimed earlier, Beckett's hero has little, if any, interest in fabricating philosophical or theological formulas. Beckett's works contain and deal seriously with multiple philosophical ideas, but their author's repeated assertion that he is no philosopher is valid. The hero's sole concern with philosophical formulas is their failure to define human experience, or, more precisely, to define his experience. In like

[32] See, for instance, "The Intellectual and Cultural Background to Beckett" in Pilling's *Samuel Beckett,* pp. 110-31.

[33] This assertion is recorded by Deirdre Bair in *Samuel Beckett: A Biography* (New York and London: Harcourt, Brace, Jovanovich, 1978), p. 257. Her date and place for the remark are April 13, 1972, Paris.

manner, although the works contain and deal seriously with multiple perceptions of God (as Coe says, Beckett "takes God as seriously as nuclear warfare," "God and Samuel Beckett," p. 98), neither Beckett nor his hero is a theologian, either Christian existentialist or orthodox. The hero is not concerned with wrong ideas that people have about God that need to be straightened out and exchanged for right ones. Nearly all the ideas that people have about God are wrong, not because the ideas are theologically obsolete but because they are invalid – they do not work or hold true in life. As Alice and Kenneth Hamilton point out, Beckett "ignores . . . the fashionable claim that twentieth-century man . . . has made irrelevant the beliefs and values of former ages."[34] The problem with Christianity, for Beckett, is not that its God needs to be redefined in modern existential and psychological terms but that God does not do what a God is supposed to do on the human scene. God matters only at points where he touches human life.

The most religious or theological of all Beckett's heroes is Moran, with his compulsion to take communion and his pseudo-interest in theological questions. These sixteen nonsense questions about Adam, Mary's conception, and the ascetic habits of saints serve two purposes. One, they are an acknowledgment, however weighted with irony, that Moran has been trying to make some kind of philosophical/theological sense out of his "journey home" with "its furies and treacheries" (*Molloy,* p. 166). Second, they serve as a preamble, or as pointers, to the questions that follow the theological speculations – questions that concern Moran "perhaps more closely" (*Molloy,* p. 167). These seventeen interrogations follow the sixteen theological questions in parallel form, and deal with the matters of greatest interest or importance to Moran – his recent life-journey and its meaning. Ironically asking about the possibility of meeting certain other persons in heaven one day in question ten from the group of seventeen, Moran is not bothered about theological concepts of life after death but about human consciousness as it is and the horrible possibility (to him) of its continuing beyond physical death. Question seventeen states the

[34] A. and K. Hamilton, *Condemned to Life: The World of Samuel Beckett* (Grand Rapids: Eerdmans, 1976), p. 40.

essence of all the questions: "What would I do until my death? Was there no means of hastening this, without falling into a state of sin?" (*Molloy*, pp. 166-68). The acute awareness of the Beckett hero that life and death merge in their mystery and meaninglessness into a continual "state of sin" is implicit in this query.[35] Thus Lawrence Harvey's categorizing of the targets of Beckett's "artistic arrows" in regard to Christianity is exactly backward. Beckett is not out to assault the habits and conventional patterns of Christianity because they deserve condemnation as being habitual in the Proustian sense, or, as Coe would claim, because they are theologically obsolete. Nor is he sympathetic toward Christianity "insofar as it makes contact with the realities of the human condition and man's fate."[36] This is exactly the point where Beckett is most unsympathetic toward Christianity. In the interview with Driver, Beckett explains that the religious dimension in his writing is due to the fact that religion is supposed to deal with what he writes about – human distress – but that it does not. Beckett's evidence is very personal: "My brother and mother got no value from their religion when they died. At the moment of crisis it had no more depth than an old school tie."[37] The hero is not concerned with redefining God but with understanding life as it is offered to him by whatever God is or may be in charge.

Much less critical attention has been directed toward elements of Eastern mysticism in the *œuvre* than toward Christian elements. In fact, no serious critic has built a systematic reading of Beckett on Eastern philosophy.[38] Nevertheless, the Eastern elements are

---

[35] See my article "Life and Death in Beckett's Four Stories," *The South Atlantic Quarterly*, 76 (1977), 332-47, for a study of how Beckett uses metaphors to merge life with death in *Stories*, including *First Love*.

[36] See Harvey, "Art and the Existential in *En attendant Godot*, *PMLA*, 75 (1960), 142.

[37] Tom F. Driver, "Beckett by the Madeleine," *Columbia Univ. Forum*, 4 (1961), 23-24.

[38] In unpublished dissertations, Stuart Lee Coonin ("Samuel Beckett: The Eastern Influence," Michigan State Univ. 1974) and Charles M. Wells ("The Transcendence of Life: The Positive Dimension in Samuel Beckett," Univ. of New Mexico 1960) both make extravagant claims that reveal the folly of attaching Beckett's "philosophy" as a whole to that of Eastern mysticism. Coonin sees the canon as subtly espousing a renunciation of Christian Occidental values in favor of finding the "void-self of Nirvana." Wells recognizes the mystical

obviously there for the critic to deal with. Although, as we have noted, Coe's emphasis on Beckett is in the area of Christian existentialism, he also, in his *Samuel Beckett,* writes of Beckett's "toying" with Oriental thought and notes what he sees as a positive and spiritual dimension (a plenum Void) to Beckett's nothingness. Furthermore, in his article "God and Samuel Beckett," Coe cites Murphy as seeking a kind of Nirvana and, at times, actually achieving it. Coe is careful to note, however, that the inner state for Beckett's hero usually consists more of torture than of bliss and that the nothingness sought is a "negative which constitutes his [Murphy's] inner Self."[39] In *Structures in Beckett's Watt,* John C. Di Pierro attempts an innovative application of Eastern religious thought to Beckett's work. Rejecting critical understandings that define *Watt* as a negative portrayal of the breakdown of man's rational and linguistic cultures, Di Pierro contends that Watt's search in Western rationalistic terms ends in the chaos of the asylum but that Watt is reincarnated as a new Watt at the "end" of the novel, as he searches "for an escape" of the "self into a higher reality" (in Hindu and Buddhist terms). Such reincarnation may be the "ultimate meaning of *Watt* as a novel."[40] John Pilling, explaining that Beckett is "far from being a Buddhist," sees whatever sympathy Beckett exhibits for negative mysticism as resulting from his fascination with its "basis in contradiction," that is, that the self, to exist, must escape from physical or fleshly existence. Pilling correctly situates this theme, altered a la Beckett, in Beckett's first published short story, *Assumption,*[41] where the hero loses the bodily macrocosmic self in efforts to realize a microcosmic, artistic/spiritual self. Pilling also comments on Beckett's response to related theories of history as a continuing cycle and the reincarnation of selves or spirits in matter. For a Buddhist,

---

failure of the heroes and claims that what Beckett is doing is to indict them for their existentialist habits of seeking authentication of the self. The heroes *should* renounce such habits and recognize the wisdom of Buddhist thought in its insistence on the "total loss of self."

39 *Samuel Beckett,* pp. 25-26 and "God and Samuel Beckett," p. 103.

40 Di Pierro, *Structures in Beckett's Watt* (York, South Carolina: French Literature Publications, 1981), pp. 90-93.

41 *Assumption, transition,* Nos. 16 and 17 (1929), pp. 268-71. All other references to *Assumption* are to this edition. Citations in the text are referred to by title and page number(s).

such notions offer hope: because time is continually recycled, the self is given, through repeated reincarnations, the opportunity to eventually escape whatever negative imprisonment is inherent in matter and realize oneness with Being or Non-Being. For Beckett, however, as Pilling explains, the concept of recurring time is as gloomy and futile as it appears to the writer of Ecclesiastes because only a permanent death offers any promise of release, and such a death is mere illusion in Beckett's hero's world.[42]

Pilling's observations open up other discrepancies between the hero's ascesis and any bona fide Eastern mysticism. The hero's flight inward from a macrocosmic self trapped in time and space, although exhibiting the structure of religious mysticism, is more aesthetic than mystical.[43] Beckett has not departed essentially from an early stance shared with other poet-critics in "Poetry is Vertical" that the primary reason for seeking the "inner life over the outer life" or any sort of "mystic-gnostic trance" is to receive an "ecstatic revelation" of images to use in the artistic "construction of a new mythological reality."[44] Beckett reasserts this motivation for ascesis, defined here as withdrawal from the material world to the realm of the spiritual, directly in *Proust,* "Dante . . . Bruno. Vico . . . Joyce," and the interview with John Gruen,[45] and indirectly in the prose, at least from *Malone Dies* onward. In fact, Murphy – the most purely mystical hero of all – does well enough in the first and second zones of his mind, where he fictitiously rearranges life and enjoys contemplation, but ceases any kind of being at all in the depths of the third zone. And Watt journeys to Mr. Knott's so as to learn how to use words – the elementary task of the literary artist. There are aesthetic nuances to the inward journeys of even these early heroes. Another disruptive factor in

---

[42] *Samuel Beckett,* pp. 122-23, 145.

[43] Pilling points out this fact; see *Samuel Beckett,* pp. 122-23.

[44] "Poetry is Vertical," *transition,* No. 21 (1932), pp. 148-49. Although Beckett did not write this manifesto and may have signed it only reflexively, the reappearance of its basic stance in numerous critical remarks by Beckett lends weight to its significance.

[45] *Proust and Three Dialogues with Georges Duthuit* (London: Calder and Boyars, 1965), pp. 65-66. "Dante . . . Bruno . . . Vico . . . Joyce," in *I Can't Go On, I'll Go On: A Selection from Samuel Beckett's Work,* ed. and introd., Richard W. Seaver (New York: Grove, 1976), pp. 108, 116. John Gruen, "Samuel Beckett Talks About Beckett," *Vogue,* 154 (1969), 210.

any smooth analysis of the hero's flight from the material world as pure spiritual mysticism is something I wish to mention now and develop at length later. The hero may *wish* to escape the materialism of the flesh, but the very nature of his task makes such escape impossible. No matter how far the artist/hero retreats into the microcosm of the mind, his art must be formed of landscapes, men, and words – all elements cementing him to the macrocosm. In spite of his abhorrence of the flesh, Beckett's man's existence is Heidegger's *Dasein:* he is dependent for being on the material world. Flight from this world toward the inner self is certainly a basic narrative structure in Beckett's prose, but such flight never achieves pure abstraction.

Other apparent similarities between Eastern mysticism and Beckett's work can be noted.[46] The Hindu doctrine of rebirth or *sansara* as a reincarnation – not of the identical, permanent self, but of residual, fleshly matter, from one body to another – reminds us of Beckett's heroes, different but made of the same substance, from Belacqua of *More Pricks than Kicks* to the barely breathing figures of the later fiction. The state of this substance, however, is not determined, as it is in Buddhist belief, by whether a "good" or "bad" life has been lived. Beckett's world is similar to that of Proust, which he himself describes in *Proust* as detached from "moral considerations" such as "right" and "wrong."[47] A careful look at the first two of Buddhism's Four Noble Truths reveals a close affinity between the assumptions of these truths and the hero's mind-set. The first truth – that life is suffering – describes a condition in which birth is the beginning of a painful life: man is a victim of sickness, old age, death, separation from what he loves, desire for what he is unable to get, and bondage to what he dislikes. Furthermore, this suffering is "basically mental," exhibiting itself as "sorrow, despair, or anxiety." That this condition is very similar to that of Beckett's hero is so obvious as to need no proof. The second truth – that desire is the cause of suffering – is also peculiarly relevant to life in Beckett's universe. Murphy and

---

[46] My information concerning Eastern religions used in these comparisons is from S. Vernon McCasland, et al., *Religions of the World* (New York: Random House, 1969), pp. 545-46, 551-53, 679-80.

[47] *Proust,* p. 66.

the person addressed in *Heard in the Dark 2* are heroes who realize that desire, especially when experienced in regard to a loved person, is often a precursor to loss and loneliness.

An interesting comparison (or contrast) at this point is to note that Beckettian man embraces the Buddhist concept of the suffering involved in the risk of love but is tormented by an inability to achieve the Eastern religious detachment from loved persons or desirable objects. True, Murphy is the only fictional hero whom we could describe as actually involved in a loving relationship, but nearly all the heroes seem agitated and frustrated with compulsive needs to gain some kind of bonding with another. The hero would agree that to love one is to endure one agony, to love fifty, fifty agonies, and to love none, no agony. But he cannot refrain from his repeated and ludicrous attempts to bond with another. Thus we can say that his theory of love is Buddhist, but his actual practice is a reluctant caricature of repeated attempts at bonding. Indeed, the prevailing tone of the fiction as a whole betrays an empathy for and identity with the suffering of others (from which the reader is carefully distanced by irony and Beckett's hilariously funny but dismal humor) more Christian than Buddhist.

The Buddhist concept of desire, termed *tanha,* implies "intensity" and "encompasses the concept of persistence and insatiability." Not descriptive of an ordinary desire such as hunger, that can be satisfied by eating, *tanha* is linked with *anicca* or impermanence, which defines the unstable nature of all things (both physical things and thoughts or ideas) as they change and decay, and with *anatta* or no-self, which holds any entity to be of a composite nature, with any separate part of its composition being dissoluble. Thus the self is not an ego, personality, or soul but only a combination of five entities – "body, feelings, perceptions, dispositions, consciousness" – in constant flux. *Anicca* brings immediately to mind Molloy's "leaning things, forever lapsing and crumbling away, beneath a sky without memory of morning or hope of night" (*Molloy,* p. 40), and *anatta* the procession of the "no-selves" of the heroes, who suffer acutely from a lack of identity or selfhood, throughout the canon.

The relevance to Beckett ceases, however, in Buddhism's third and fourth Noble Truths. Beckett's hero knows of no method for eliminating this suffering-producing desire; certainly he has found no course of "right" conduct and meditation leading ultimately to an "extinction of craving" that would eliminate desire as the cause of suffering." The influence of Schopenhauer on the Beckett hero's desire for elimination of the will is evident at this point. Beckett and his hero would agree with Schopenhauer that the more completely we negate the will, the more we escape suffering. Although the hero would long for such negation and strongly endorse any possible method of achieving it, he would consider the occurrence of actually silencing the clamorous human will to be highly unlikely. As Murphy's friends Wylie and Neary remind us: "The syndrome known as life is too diffuse to admit of palliation. For every symptom that is eased, another is made worse. The horse leech's daughter is a closed system. Her quantum of wantum cannot vary."[48] Also, in spite of the hero's longing for the cessation of an existence that he experiences as suffering, the goal of his quest cannot be defined as annihilation of the self.[49] The hero of *Stories* speaks very generally but nonetheless truly when he claims that his "soul writhed from morning to night, in the mere quest of itself."[50] Beckett's use of the term "the Unnamable" suggests its counterpart in Taoism. Equated with Nonbeing in Eastern thought, this term designates the power or source that produces the Namable or Being, with the latter depending on the former for its existence. We move closer to Heidegger than to Beckett, however, when we understand that this Taoist power "conceals its essence from man" and mystifies him with its presence, which is "eternal, absolute, and unchanging," the basis of all else. Beckett's Unnamable may be searching for some source definable by such a term, but whatever mystical selfhood he realizes, to the best of his knowledge, is not this essence. If Beckett's hero can be described as an Eastern mystic, it must be as

---

[48] *Murphy* (New York: Grove, 1957), p. 200. All other references to *Murphy* are to this edition and are cited by title and page number(s) in the text.

[49] See the argument between Ethel Cornwell and myself on this matter in "Forum," *PMLA*, 92 (1977), 1006-008.

[50] *The Expelled* (pp. 9-25); *The Calmative* (pp. 27-46); *The End* (pp. 47-72), in *Stories and Texts for Nothing* (New York: Grove, 1976), p. 11. All other references to these *Stories* are to this edition and are cited by title and page number(s) in the text.

a very confused one. As with any philosophy or religious system, Beckett borrows and alters as he pleases.

The last religious system that I will examine in relation to Beckett's theological milieu is the Manichean doctrine or tradition, a tradition that – as we shall see when we examine *Assumption* – Beckett became familiar with early on in his writing career. Manicheanism is a highly mythological account of the world as a dual cosmos made up of two opposing forces of good and evil, or of light and darkness. This tradition, which died out as an active religion after the eighth century, has third-century origins in the aristocratic Mani of Persia. The opposing forces represent two eternal principles – God and Matter. When the principle of evil or darkness invaded the realm of good or light, Primeval Man undertook to repossess the light lost to matter. But some of his substance (light) remained imprisoned in matter after his return to the spiritual realm. Adam, although demon-born, possessed elements of light or spirit imprisoned in his earthly being or flesh. Redemption – effected by "Jesus the Brilliant Light" – involves the freeing of man's spirit from the prison of his earthly body. This Jesus is different from the traditional Jesus of the gospels, who was only an example of man suffering from the imprisonment of light in matter.[51]

Certainly, critics who explore the relevancy of this tradition to Beckett's writing would join Edouard Morot-Sir in his intention not to be "snared" in the "trap" of "making Beckett a devotee of Mani and his works Manichean experiences."[52] Nevertheless, this system describes quite well the religious orientation of Beckett's hero. Therefore, we are reminded once again that we are not trying to devise or discover religious or philosophical abstract formulas to use as categories but to describe and analyze the experience of the hero's sensing of God.

Any critic who focuses on the weighty gnostic element in Beckett's works is skirting Manicheanism, whether he mentions the

---

[51] See "Manichaeism" in *The New International Dictionary of the Christian Church*, pp. 624-25.

[52] Morot-Sir, "Samuel Beckett and Cartesian Emblems," in *Samuel Beckett; The Art of Rhetoric*, ed. Edouard Morot-Sir, Howard Harper, and Dougald McMillan, Carolina Studies in the Romance Languages and Literatures, Symposia, No. 5 (Chapel Hill: Univ. of North Carolina Press, 1976), p. 85.

term or not. Gnosticism, as a system, also defines the created, material world as being so characterized by darkness that even its luminaries are "dark light." The transcendent, spiritual world of light is in radical contrast to the world of matter. Because man has a soul (his "spark of light"), he is capable of gaining enlightenment by means of *gnosis* (knowledge). Thus darkness, in gnostic thought, is not only whatever is material (and therefore evil) but also ignorance or *agnoia,* which hinders man's salvation. Simply because he has a body, man is more or less locked in this sphere of ignorance/darkness. Unlike Beckett, the gnostic sees salvation for man as possible by a turning from the earthly darkness of ignorance to the spiritual light of knowledge.[53] Beckett's gnostic ideas are nearly always developed into the principles of the Manichean system. When Colin Duckworth describes Beckett's "view" as "a simple gnostic ambiguity" structured on two gods, one of whom is a "demiurge who created this imperfect and suffering world" and one of whom is a "Redeemer who may set all things to rights when he chooses,"[54] he is describing gnostic belief that parallels quite closely Manichean dogma. The most dominant trait of the God who inhabits Beckett's world is cruelty, and Manichean doctrine boasts a fixed dualism that includes, in addition to the good God of light, a God of darkness, who is completely evil. Jean Onimus, in a book-length study of Beckett that focuses on the question of God, describes such a God under the heading *Le Dieu du Mal:*

> Si l'on admet l'existence d'un créateur responsable, il faut donc se le representer comme un sadique qui ne suscite la pensée – et la liberté – que pour en jouer cruellement et pour satisfaire une sorte d'instinct de domination et de destruction. Celui qui crée pour assister ensuite à la lente agonie d'un corps et d'une intelligence ne peut être que l'esprit du Mal.[55]

---

[53] See "Darkness" in *The New International Dictionary of the Christian Church,* p. 422. For elaboration on Beckett's use of gnosticism, see "Samuel Beckett and the Gnostic Vision of the Created World," Alice and Kenneth Hamilton, *Studies in Religion/Sciences Religieuses,* 8 (1979), 293-301.

[54] *Angels of Darkness,* pp. 90-91.

[55] Onimus, *Beckett* (Paris: *Desclee de Brouwer,* 1968), p. 100.

Although Onimus does not use the term "Manichean" to describe this evil God, the God is decidedly Manichean. Lawrence E. Harvey notes a Manichean influence on Beckett's views of women and procreation, and John Fletcher connects the Manichean doctrine of reincarnation with Beckett's continually reappearing characters.[56]

Four critics who connect Beckett directly and at some length with the Manichean tradition are Kenneth and Alice Hamilton, John Pilling, and Edouard Morot-Sir.[57] A synthesis of their views reveals the close affinity of Manichean beliefs to the religious orientation of the hero. Any system of thought that allows for a God with evil or harmful designs on humanity can so easily be associated with the perception of the Beckettian hero that the offering of evidence for such a claim seems superfluous. The often-quoted conclusion of Mahood/Worm/Unnamable that the "essential is to go on squirming forever at the end of the line, as long as there are waters and banks and ravening in heaven a sporting God to plague his creature" (*The Unnamable*, p. 338) remains a succinct statement concerning man's condition. Manicheanism shares with Christian existentialist interpretations the advantage of being able to describe one God as evil and rejected by the hero while salvaging a good God to connect with positive facets of his consciousness. A possible reason that neither the Hamiltons, Pilling, nor Morot-Sir deals with the good God – of light or of the spiritual world – in their discussions of Manicheanism in regard to Beckett is their emphases on what they see as a fixed mingling of light and darkness, of good and evil, in the Beckettian universe. Because any separation of forces or qualities remains only a possibility, the hero never perceives clearly anything beyond what Pilling calls a "precarious . . . balance of forces"[58]

[56] Harvey, *Samuel Beckett: Poet and Critic* (Princeton: Princeton Univ. Press, 1970), pp. 78-79. Fletcher, *The Novels of Samuel Beckett* (London: 1964; rpt. New York: Barnes and Noble, 1970), p. 229.

[57] See *Condemned to Life*, pp. 51-58; *Samuel Beckett*, pp. 118-21; "Samuel Beckett and Cartesian Emblems," pp. 81-103. As the page listings suggest, Morot-Sir offers the most detailed and in-depth (but also the most enigmatic) study of the place of Manicheanism in Beckett's writings.

[58] *Samuel Beckett*, p. 120.

and Morot-Sir, "repetitive experiences of light and darkness."[59] Nevertheless, Manichean dualism can account not only for dual primary sources or causes (two Gods) but also other dualities that structure the hero's experience. Basic orientation in existence for Beckett's protagonist may be either macrocosmic or microcosmic, and, within each of these worlds, further dual fragmentation occurs. The outer world consists, as Beckett tells Driver, of both darkness and light,[60] and the microcosm of the infinitely splitting self. Beckett's particular concept of the dialectical nature of language (i. e., that language is not allegorical but a continual reversal between affirmation and denial, both of which are equally valueless as truth-statements) is basic in his structuring of the hero's dual universe.[61] Basics other than these dualities that can be identified with Manichean belief are the flight inward from the material world toward the core of the self and the horror with which activities of the flesh – eating, sex, birth, and life itself – are regarded. Such horror explains and includes the antipathy toward women, connected in Manichean doctrine with the darkness of the material world and the inability to deliver the spiritual light of the human psyche from its imprisonment in fleshly matter due to continued procreation. It also explains antipathy toward the human body and the idea of the Incarnation as God present in fleshly matter.[62]

In spite of its close affinity with the hero's perception, however, Manicheanism is used, not embraced, by Beckett. There is no recognition of the virtues associated by Mani with the spiritual Christ – Beckett's Christ, as we shall see later, is almost completely of the flesh – and any notion of salvation achieved by finally escaping the flesh and becoming totally spirit will not work for Beckett's hero. As Morot-Sir explains, the effort of Beckettian man to free the light or spirit imprisoned in the material world of the macrocosm and secure this liberated light as pure spirit within the

---

[59] "Samuel Beckett and Cartesian Emblems," p. 103.

[60] "Beckett by the Madeleine," p. 23.

[61] For a detailed study of Beckett's language dualism as Manichean, see "Samuel Beckett and Cartesian Emblems," pp. 92-104.

[62] Pilling explains (*Samuel Beckett*, pp. 119-21) how Manichean doctrine concerning women and procreation influences Beckett's concept of incarnation (of spirit housed in flesh) in general and in regard to the Incarnation of Christ.

microcosm is futile. Descartes' simple dualities of outer and inner worlds become a more complex duality of the macrocosmic self continually perceived by the microcosmic self within the confines of the human consciousness.[63] Thus Beckett's concept of the split inner self is Manichean in that it remains a duality, but is non-Manichean in that the self of the material world continues to exist in the inner realm of the spirit. In fact, a reversal of Manichean values occurs in that whatever is light or good and desirable to the hero is inescapably attached to the macrocosm. In our examination of orthodox Christian elements in Beckett's work, we noted that the symbols that seem to promise some kind of fulfillment or salvation are often presented in terms of the Eucharist – as embodied in the material substances of the bread and wine. In spite of the hero's asceticism, if he ever finds Paradise, it will be a Paradise for the body as well as for the spirit. Murphy's awareness of the good cannot be separated from the "music" he experiences with Celia, and when he loses all memory of that music in death (*Murphy,* p. 252), he loses everything. The flashes of light that invade the subterranean hell of *How It Is* are from "up above" (p. 8), and whatever the inhabitants of *The Lost Ones* are searching for exists in some form outside the cylinder in a world of nature (pp. 18, 21).

If the hero, in spite of his asceticism, cannot embrace Manicheanism to the extent of surrendering the material world, neither can Beckett the artist do so in the exercise of his craft. It is true that Beckett speaks for himself as well as for Proust when he defines the necessity of asceticism for the artist:

> The only fertile research is excavatory, immersive, a contraction of the spirit, a descent. The artist is active, but negatively, shrinking from the nullity of extracircumferential phenomena, drawn in to the core of the eddy.[64]

Nevertheless, Beckett is also speaking for himself – as well as for Vico – when he insists that

[63] See "Samuel Beckett and Cartesian Emblems," pp. 82-83, 97.
[64] *Proust,* pp. 65-66.

> Poetry is essentially the anithesis of Metaphysics: Metaphysics purge the mind of the senses and cultivate the disembodiment of the spiritual; Poetry is all passion and feeling and animates the inanimate.

And he speaks for himself as well as for Joyce in his admiration of Shakespeare's "fat, greasy words to express corruption" – words which are like Joyce's in that they "are alive" and "elbow their way on to the page, and glow and blaze.[65] Neither Beckett's hero nor Beckett the artist can wholly adopt Mani's code – the material world must maintain its materiality even when imprisoned in the spirit, and light cannot be defined as complete separation of flesh from spirit. The little figure of *Lessness,* who, suspended in the skull-world of the mind, flees toward the abstractness of the non-materiality of the inner self, nevertheless longs for the "blessed days face to the open sky" when he curses God in the "passing deluge" of the macrocosmic earth.[66]

Not all critics who explore ideas about God in Beckett's works relate these ideas to a particular religion or even to a theological position or definition. Harvey, in both his article on *Waiting for Godot* and in his book on the poetry and criticism, comments on the ambiguity of the question of God in Beckett's work as a literary convenience that is best left unresolved. "Beckett's ambiguous treatment of Christianity suggests that such a subject matter is simply useful as a way of bringing up . . . existential themes" such as hope and despair.[67] If we admit that the idea of God is used primarily to write about hope and despair, we must still ask why Beckett uses this idea so extensively for this purpose. In his book, Harvey goes on to connect Beckett's religious ambiguity more directly to the question of God:

> No one, not Beckett himself, can presume to assay the nature of his relationship to the God who is absent yet everywhere

[65] "Dante . . . Bruno . . . Vico . . . Joyce," pp. 113, 119.

[66] *Lessness* (London: Calder and Boyars, 1970), p. 20. All other references to *Lessness* are to this edition, and are cited by page number(s) in the text.

[67] "Art and the Existential in *En Attendant Godot,*" p. 142.

> present in his writing... whose shadowy presence heightens the sense of his absence.[68]

Many matters, other than this basic question of God's presence or absence, are best couched in statements or descriptions that do not aspire to resolution,[69] and some of the most thorough critical descriptions of attitudes toward God on the part of Beckett or of his hero remain deliberately ambiguous. Three such descriptions are interwoven in the general content of Jacobsen and Mueller's *The Testament of Samuel Beckett*, Michael Robinson's *The Long Sonata of the Dead*, and Jean Onimus' *Beckett.*[70] The fact that none of these critics (with the possible exception of Onimus) is attempting to resolve or even to synthesize ideas or perceptions of God allows greater freedom in describing Beckett's religious climate than critics of more focused aims enjoy. Thus God can be absent yet present, the object of the hero's quest and the power from which he flees, the instigator of promises of salvation and the annulment of these promises. Man can suffer for his own "sin" and guilt and yet also be the victim of a malignant God of evil; he can exist simultaneously in a state of freedom and of determinism; he can search for an entity known as the true self which is described as opposition to nothingness and also as eternal oblivion. It is interesting to note that each of these studies that rest content with ambiguity raises provocative questions that force us toward a

---

[68] *Samuel Beckett: Poet and Critic*, p. 412.

[69] Ruby Cohn offers for consideration the conflict between the mother and daughter in the "story" the mother tells in *Footfalls:* a mother (Mrs. Winter of the "story") insists that she has heard her daughter (Amy of the "story") say "amen" to an evening prayer – "The love of God, and the fellowship of the Holy Ghost be with us all, now and evermore." When daughter Amy contends that she was not even present on the occasion her mother is remembering, the mother cannot understand, but Cohn explains in a statement that exploits ambiguity. "In Beckett's world... you *can* be absent from love and redemption, and yet you can say 'Amen' to hope, embodied in Christian faith" ("Outward Bound Soliloquies," *Jorunal of Modern Literature*, 6 [1977], 37). In a single paragraph defining Beckett's "attitude to God," John Fletcher joins words and phrases ("languish for the lack of any God to save," "loathing and fear," "humorous irreverence") which, although they contradict each other, fuse in a meaningful ambiguity to anyone familiar with Beckett's works (*The Novels of Samuel Beckett*, pp. 231-32).

[70] I refer to these three studies by title and page number(s) in the text. Robinson's study is *The Long Sonata of the Dead: A Study of Samuel Beckett* (New York: Grove, 1969).

search for more definitive answers concerning major motifs related to the question of God. If, as Robinson claims, the hero's self is opposed to the nothingness in the void (supposedly macrocosmic) about him and, at the same time, is the "final and eternal oblivion" of the microcosm (*The Long Sonata of the Dead,* pp. 26, 3), how shall we define the self? How shall we conceive of the void or nothingness?

Mueller and Jacobsen's basic contention in regard to the motif of the quest is that the hero is torn between answering the hypothetical imperative in the macrocosm and withdrawing from the macrocosm in a microcosmic descent toward nothingness (*The Testament of Samuel Beckett,* pp. 144-45). This description is of movement that is not simply ambivalent but obviously dual. Is the hero's quest, then, a dual one of opposite intentions, motivated, on the one hand, by hope (in responding to the hypothetical imperative) and, on the other hand, by despair (in withdrawing inwardly) (*The Testament of Samuel Beckett,* pp. 147-48)? If so, how can we equate Beckett's quest – as is almost certainly the case – with a quest for the true self? If the "Other" or God offers the macrocosmic hypothetical imperative, then he must be defined as the object of the quest and the descent toward the self as a merely negative movement away from this object. Also, if, at this point, we insist that the movements constitute separate quests, we deny the sense of unified structure that reputable critics, including Mueller and Jacobsen, agree ties the various works together. Onimus echoes an apparent contradiction in Coe's "God and Samuel Beckett" when the French critic depicts God as being beyond language and yet as revealed by his involvement in language.[71] The suspicion that these assertions do not really contradict each other, however, may motivate us to examine more carefully whatever links between the idea of God and function (or non-function) of language exist. In short, it is precisely at the point of ambiguity defined in studies such as these that a search for more definitive formulations must begin.[72]

---

[71] See Onimus, *Beckett,* p. 111 and Coe, "God and Samuel Beckett," pp. 107-08, 110-12.

[72] My contribution to the criticism describing the ambiguity inherent in the matter of God in Beckett's canon is "The Empty Heaven of Samuel Beckett," *Cithara: Essays in the Judaeo-Christian Tradition,* 15 (1976), 3-19.

Critics who perceive the ambiguity that Beckett invests in the idea of God as almost completely negative and ridiculous in tone cite it as evidence that the writer's religious position is one of blasphemy. Numerous passages from the drama or prose are undoubtedly blasphemous. Perhaps the funniest of these is Nagg's story of the Englishman and the tailor and God's making of the world in six days (*Endgame,* pp. 22-23). The image of the dog as what Mueller and Jacobsen call "the reversal of the principle of a God" appears again and again throughout the fiction.[73] Certainly Beckett's hero hurls not only insults and expressions of contempt but also anguished cries of outrage toward whoever or whatever is responsible for human existence. Most critics who assess Beckett's stance as blasphemous also describe him as nihilistic. The French critic Danielle Bajomée speaks of Beckett's *"vigoureux blasphèmes"* and *"dérision flamboyante"* against the notion of God and concludes that Beckett is nihilistic to the extent that he subversively denounces all Western ideology in favor of *"la rédemption grâce a l'écriture."*[74] Since Bajomée assumes that Beckett's blasphemy is actually a satiric denunciation of Christian or Western ideas of God, the word "satire" is more in line with his understanding of Beckettian attitudes than is "blasphemy." In Hersh Zeifman's study of "Religious Imagery in the Plays of Samuel Beckett," instances of blasphemy are interpreted as evidences of nihilism. The hero's "bitterly outraged and frequently outrageous indictment of the extent of divine malevolence" reveals the conviction "that man is the victim of a heartless metaphysical ruse, trapped in the midst of an alien and hostile world, his life a protracted and painful crucifixion without hope of transcendence." Thus man's understanding of God guarantees the "impossibility of salvation."[75]

Alice and Kenneth Hamilton contend, like Bajomée, that the hero's blasphemy is an attack against mythical and preposterous ideas of God. The early works, especially, are intended by Beckett to expose "the cardinal error of Christianity" – belief in an omnipo-

---

[73] See *The Testament of Samuel Beckett,* pp. 18-19, for instances of such appearances.

[74] Bajomée, "Beckett devant Dieu," *Les Lettres Romanes,* 25 (1971), 351, 357.

[75] See Zeifman's essay in *Samuel Beckett: A Collection of Criticism Edited by Ruby Cohn* (New York: McGraw-Hill, 1975), pp. 93-94.

tent God who is also "righteous and loving." Thus these works contain "explicit anti-Christian polemic." Because Beckett also rejects the philosophy and values of any "humanistic vision of existence" – all the "theories of evolutionary progress dating from the Enlightenment" – he portrays a hero who finds in human experience an "absolute absence of the Absolute."[76] The process of life has "no rational foundation for its being, and no final end toward which it moves." Nothing in life can be judged as "good or bad" because we lack the justification for "any scale of values." The Hamiltons mention Beckett's "own vision of reality" as rendering "unnecessary" the viewpoint and values he rejects – a vision that defines art "as the means to escape the desolation and lonelines of the cosmic prison."[77]

Both in general book-length studies and in his book *Samuel Beckett,* Nathan A. Scott, Jr. deals with the "malediction and blasphemy" found in Beckett's works in regard to the hero's awareness of divinity as being "polemic against Christian premises."[78] Beckett's "agnosticism" is so deep that he cannot even be said to share Kafka's assurance "that there *is* no God and that there *must* be God." Instead, Beckett "sticks to zero" (*Samuel Beckett,* p. 100), finding a universe minus God to negate any values, even those of literature or art (*Samuel Beckett,* p. 82). Scott does not leave Beckett in such a vacuum, however. Using Paul Tillich and Heidegger as aids, he pulls the writer, on the basis of a "certain metaphysical vastness . . . *felt* [my italics] in his work" (*Samuel Beckett,* p. 124), into company with religious "waiters" such as

---

[76] This term, used by Beckett in "Dante . . . Bruno . . . Vico . . . Joyce," pp. 125-26, in reference to Joyce's works is often applied by critics to Beckett's own writings. With the meaning Beckett intends in his essay, it is applicable to his own writings (i. e., that experience is portrayed in Joyce's art as being neither hell nor paradise, but a "conjunction of the two elements" in a purgatory). With the meaning the Hamiltons give the term (i. e., as defining a state of nihilism), the phrase is only partially applicable to Beckett.

[77] *Condemned to Life,* pp. 37, 39, 35, 195.

[78] Scott, *The Broken Center: Studies in the Theological Horizon of Modern Literature* (New Haven: Yale Univ. Press, 1966), p. 185; *Samuel Beckett,* Series of Studies in Modern European Literature and Thought (London: Bowes and Bowes, 1965), pp. 98-99. To gain a comprehensive summary of Scott's evaluation of Beckett, it is necessary to examine not only these two books but also his *Modern Literature and the Religious Frontier* (New York: Harper, 1958), pp. 84-90. See references to these works given by title and page number(s) in the text.

Eliot, Auden, M. Gabriel Marcel, Heidegger, Simone Weil, and Bultmann (*Modern Literature and the Religious Frontier,* pp. 87-90). Once more we find Beckett placed in the Christian existentialist tradition, although Scott's placing of the writer in this tradition is not as focused as the categorizing of critics such as Coe. For Scott, Beckett's nihilism may be a "purgation" that makes possible a "renewal" of some kind of faith (*Samuel Beckett,* p. 129).

Wylie Sypher is focusing on the nothingness of the self or of human identity, not on God, when he claims that "Beckett's nihilism is a last phase of anti-literature." This bankruptcy is poorer than suicide in the existentialist tradition because there is not even an identifiable self to engage with life and choose self-annihilation. The problem for Beckett's hero is that the extinguishing of identity does not cause existence to cease, however much he may desire such cessation. Sypher's discussion of Beckettian blasphemy is limited to comments on indictments of the Old Testament God in the person of Pozzo in the first act of *Waiting for Godot,* whose victim is the New Testament Christ in the person of Pozzo in the second act. Godot, who never appears, may confer meaning on Vladimir and Estragon's otherwise meaningless situation, but either he will not appear, cannot be known, is irrelevant, or is one "whom we are too stupid to worship."[79] We may conclude that both Beckett and Sypher are writing within a sphere which Sypher assigns to Beckett – a "logic of contradiction."[80]

The confusion apparent in these four summaries of criticism appraising Beckettian attitudes as blasphemous and/or nihilistic is not entirely – or even primarily – the fault of the critics: it is a confusion apparent, at least on the surface, of Beckett's writings themselves. What shall we do with Hamm, who, in what is obviously intended to be a true extremity of human need and distress, insists on praying to his Father/God only to exclaim moments later, "The bastard! He doesn't exist!" – a Hamm who longs for the ending of all things because all things mean

---

[79] Sypher, *Loss of the Self in Modern Literature and Art* (New York: Random House, 1964), pp. 1512-57, 148.

[80] Sypher uses this term in regard to Beckett on p. 15 of *Loss of the Self.*

nothing?[81] Is Beckett satirizing the act of prayer as words addressed to a nonexistent being, or is he blaspheming a God who will not answer prayer? How shall we define a writer who ironically and blasphemously mocks Mrs. Saposcat's frantic prayer-pleas for her dull-witted son to pass his examinations (*Malone Dies,* p. 210) and who, in the same novel, has Malone lament, with a seriousness of tone worthy of Augustine, that his great trouble and sorrow are that he does not know "what my prayer should be nor to whom" (*Malone Dies,* p. 226)? Were we to analyze all the prayers found in Beckett's works, we would not escape the basic duality posed by the comparisons of these questions. An acceptance and formulation of paradox at this point, however, can clarify the direction our efforts should take. Any critic who does not recognize the blasphemy implicit in a large majority of Beckett's religious allusions or images is failing to identify ironic tone.[82] Beckett far surpasses insult and a surface irreverence in assigning to his heroes attitudes of malicious mockery and utter contempt for God.

The weakest component of blasphemy, however, that of irreverence, seems strangely misassigned to a writer who, as both Coe and the Hamiltons claim, considers the question of God to matter more than atom bombs and nuclear warfare.[83] Whatever nihilism Beckett exhibits is likewise locked in paradox. Certainly the heroes deny all traditional values and find human experience to be senseless and futile. But, as Linda Ben-Zvi brings to our attention, the quality that she finds in Fritz Mauthner's thought and that which Beckett assigns to Joyce's works – a total denial of absolutes – is not actually asserted in Beckett's works. "Godot," "the

---

[81] *Endgame* (New York: Grove, 1958), p. 55. All other references to *Endgame* are to this edition and are cited by title and page number(s) in the text.

[82] Coe's observations on Sucky Molly's having the two thieves as earrings and Christ as a "long yellow canine" in her mouth (*Malone Dies,* pp. 263-64) reveal such failure to recognize irony (see "God and Samuel Beckett," p. 100), as does Louis Barjon's definition of *Happy Days* as a religious turning point in Beckett's dramatic canon. The title of this play – in French (*Oh! les beaux jours*) as well as in English – is weighted with irony. Barjon's assigning of a *"flamme spirituelle"* to Winnie and his claim that she becomes, with the passing of each dramatic minute, *"plus joyeuse, apaisée"* ("Le Dieu de Beckett," *Etudes,* 322 [1965], 658) misses not only the basic tone but also the basic theme of the play.

[83] "God and Samuel Beckett," p. 98; *Condemned to Life, p. 40.*

end," "salvation" never come, but neither we nor the heroes can *know* that such an epiphany or *parousia* will never occur. As Ben-Zvi claims, the "color of the Beckett world is not black but gray."[84] Beckett is a religious nihilist in that his God is not, but we remember Molloy's resignation to the fact that the only way to speak of God is "in terms of what he is not" (*Molloy*, p. 39) and Watt's answer to Sam's inquiry as to how he has arrived at the state of crucifixion he exhibits in the asylum garden:

> Why, Watt, I cried, that is a nice state you have got yourself into, to be sure. Not it is, yes, replied Watt.[85]

Watt's answer is easily rearranged into "Yes, it is not," meaning "Yes, it is Knott who is responsible for my state." Such dialogue echoes with the "screaming silence of no's knife in yes's wound" and underscores the conclusion of this screaming voice in text 13 of *Texts for Nothing:*

> It's not true, yes, it's true, it's true and it's not true, there is silence and there is not silence, there is no one and there is someone, nothing prevents anything.[86]

Thus a consideration of critical assessments of Beckettian blasphemy and nihilism simply raises further questions. If Beckett can be said to "believe" in God at least to the extent that he blasphemes him, or has his hero blasphemne him, why is he so obsessed with the expression of blasphemy? Such an obsession seems too theological and limited to serve as a major impetus for a body of work such as Beckett's. Surely Beckett does not intend his art to be primarily a polemic against the Christian God or any other God. Any polemic is essentially negating in nature. Granted that a "nothing" underlies the entire Beckettian *œuvre*, is it possible

---

[84] Ben-Zvi, "Samuel Beckett, Fritz Mauthner, and the Limits of Language," *PMLA*, 95 (1980), 192.

[85] *Watt* (New York: Grove, 1959), p. 159. All other references to *Watt* are to this edition. Citations in the text are referred to by title and page number(s).

[86] Text 13 in *Stories and Texts for Nothing* (New York: Grove, 1976), p. 139. All other references to *Texts* are to this edition and are cited by title and page number(s) in the text.

this "nothing" is truly negative in its essence? On the other hand, if Beckett does not "believe" in God and is, like many of his fellow twentieth-century writers, satirizing obsolete notions of divinity, why is his hero so intense and agitated about the matter? Why is the hero's religious consciousness not cast more in the mold of that of Joyce's Stephen and Mr. Bloom? Also, satire presupposes an alternative offered in lieu of what is being satirized. Joyce offers human experience itself restructured by art into a sacred profanity. What alternative is Beckett offering? Ben-Zvi convinces us,[87] if the Unnamable has not already done so, that art, including Beckett's own art of literary language, will not serve as such an alternative. C. J. Bradbury Robinson admires Beckett for having the "courage and honesty to see that, if nothing matters, then the saying of this doesn't matter either," for Beckett's including of "himself and his work in his own condemnation."[88] If this condemnation is a rejection of life and all its realized values, including art itself as a value – and, in one sense, it is – how can we absolve Beckett of a nihilism that makes the very practice of his art illogical?

Harold Clurman's observation on Beckett's "rejection of life" leads to consideration of a final religious perspective of the hero:

> His rejection of life is something other than that. It is a vast, insatiable hunger, a yearning, an immense ache and regret which is at the core of living.[89]

Clurman's *his* refers to Beckett, but we can easily, without distorting the critic's meaning at all, transfer the pronoun to the hero. Beckett's hero cannot pray, as the persona of Eliot's tenth chorus from "The Rock" does, "And we thank thee that darkness reminds us of light,"[90] because no hero (except perhaps Moran for a brief

---

[87] "Samuel Beckett, Fritz Mauthner, and the Limits of Language." See the article as a whole, especially pp. 197-98.

[88] Bradbury Robinson, "A Way with Words: Paradox, Silence, and Samuel Beckett," *The Cambridge Quarterly*, 4 (1971), 258.

[89] Clurman, *The Divine Pastime; Theatre Essays* (New York: Macmillan, 1974), p. 123.

[90] T. S. Eliot, "Choruses from 'The Rock,' X" in *The Complete Poems and Plays, 1909-1950* (New York: Harcourt, Brace and World, 1971), p. 114.

season) entertains any delusions that prayer is heard. But, for Beckett's hero (as for Eliot's persona), the darkness, however blasphemed and rejected, is precisely a reminder of light. From this perspective, the nothingness that undergirds the hero's world is not a minus sign but a zero, empty of the light that should fill it.

The need for a missing transcendence in human experience, is, of course, exceedingly common in nineteenth- and twentieth-century thought, whether philosophical, religious, or literary. Sartre reiterates Nietzsche's announcement that God is dead, Heidegger claims he is absent, and Martin Buber explains that he is in eclipse. F. Thomas Trotter cites Rilke, Kafka, Camus, Proust, Graham Greene, Gide, Faulkner, and Mann as witnesses "to a world in which God is 'silent,' 'absent,' 'disappeared,' or 'dead,'"[91] and J. Hillis Miller has written a book on nineteenth-century writers of literature entitled *The Disappearance of God.*[92] Numerous critics reflect on the metaphysical emptiness of Beckett's hero and connect this emptiness with some kind of absence or lack of God. Coe describes as an "irreducible contradiction" the fact that, in Beckett's world, "God is that Being whose non-existence is the only conceivable evidence of his existence."[93] Colin Duckworth sees Beckett as depicting what such non-existence entails by writing plays that may cause us to "comprehend traumatically what a Godless universe means."[94] David H. Hesla stresses the great need of the heroes (his examples are Watt, Estragon, and Vladimir) for the Other:

> Without him, nothing in the world is valuable or meaningful. Without him, thinking leads merely to madness, living to the grave. In him and for him they [the heroes] live and move and have whatever little Being they have.[95]

---

[91] Trotter, "Variations on the 'Death of God' Theme in Recent Theology," in *The Death of God Debate,* ed. Jackson Lee Ice and John J. Carey (Philadelphia: Westminster, 1967), p. 99.

[92] Miller, *The Disappearance of God: Five Nineteenth-Century Writers* (Cambridge: Belknap Press of Harvard Univ. Press, 1963).

[93] *Samuel Beckett,* p. 94.

[94] *Angels of Darkness,* p. 111.

[95] *The Shape of Chaos,* p. 224.

Günther Anders, in writing on *Waiting for Godot,* goes so far as to claim a *proof ex absentia* in regard to the heroes' concept of God: for Beckett's characters (Günther is careful to distinguish between the characters and Beckett himself), God's absence is "made into a proof of His being."[96] Onimus defines the God-void in Beckett's work as that of an absentee – *"D'un absent."* Such an absent one can be responded to: *"on l'attend, on le désire, on ressent même sa présence comme un manque, un vide pénible, une blessure."*[97] Michael Robinson wraps the hero's response to God up in the questions of Dostoevsky's Ivan Karamazov, which he phrases as, "can I forgive God for not existing, and if He did exist, could I forgive Him for all the suffering He has caused?" The "fundamental cause" of the hero's suffering – his *"angoisse"* – is his experience of the absence or want of God.[98] I have stated, in earlier criticism, that "God may not exist, but we cannot escape the conclusion that Beckett's void that houses the ultimate reality is God-shaped, and thus could be filled only by a God."[99]

Critics surveying the hero's void or need from a distinctively Christian perspective have noticed the similarity of what the hero needs and expects from a transcendent power outside himself to the promises offered in the Christian faith.[100] An editorial appearing in *The Month* soon after Beckett's receiving of the Nobel Prize for Literature defends him against writing only of "disintegration" by pointing out that Beckett can serve to make Christians "better aware of a world as it would be without Christ," that Beckett agrees with the Christian that "dereliction is the natural state of grace-less man."[101] Edouard Morot-Sir fabricates a linguistic confrontation between Wittgenstein, Beckett, and Pascal. Wittgenstein and Beckett's ideas of the failure of language (an emptiness of varying degrees of meaninglessness) can be overcome by recourse

---

96 Anders, "Being Without Time: On Beckett's Play *Waiting for Godot,*" in *Samuel Beckett: A Collection of Critical Essays,* ed. Martin Esslin (Englewood Cliffs, N. J.: Prentice-Hall, 1965), p. 145.

97 *Beckett,* p. 75.

98 *The Long Sonata of the Dead,* pp. 26-27.

99 "The Empty Heaven of Samuel Beckett," p. 17.

100 My contribution to this body of criticism is "Light in a Dark Place," *Christianity Today,* 18 (1973), 345-48.

101 *The Month,* Second New Series, 1 (1970), 8.

to Pascal's structuring of human words on the Christ/Word or the Logos.[102] From such a perspective, it is tempting to compare Beckett's void with Pascal's "infinite abyss" that "can only be filled by an infinite and immutable object, that is to say, only by God Himself."[103] Helmut Thielicke, in his book *The Hidden Question of God,* perceives God as the missing entity accounting for Beckett's meaningless situations and empty words. Thielicke qualifies this viewpoint, however, by defining Beckett's missing "x" as "a final reality beneath our lives" and by claiming that "religious themes" are not dealt with to any point of resolution but rather "introduced" by Beckett. Such qualification is needed because, as Thielicke emphasizes later in his book, the "experience of deficiencies does not lead necessarily to God. It may lead to the experience of absurdity. . . . Thus the experience of want is ambivalent. It may be either open or closed to God."[104]

Before assuming that Beckett's want or void leads toward God, certain hard questions have to be faced. Some of these questions have already been stated in essence but need to be posed again from this particular perspective. If the hero's need can be supplied only by God, is God the entity he is searching for and thus the object of the quest? If so, what shall we do with the generally established critical opinion – which we have already acknowledged as valid and which can hardly be gainsaid – that the object of the Beckettian quest is the self? From a perspective that equates God with the consciousness or spirit of man's highest state of selfhood, the question can be resolved, but, as we have seen in our survey of Beckett's works viewed from the standpoint of Christian existentialism, there is something inescapably theistic, something other-than-man, about the hero's notion of God. Another basic question derives from our knowledge of the blasphemous content of Beckett's work. The heroes blaspheme God because he either does not exist or, existing, he cruelly chooses not to meet their needs. Can we say of Beckett, as Eliot asserts of Baudelaire, that

[102] Morot-Sir, "Pascal versus Wittgenstein, with Samuel Beckett as the Anti-Witness," *Romance Notes,* 15 (1973), 201-16. See all pages.

[103] For Pascal's description of this "abyss," see *Pensées; The Provincial Letters* (New York: Random House, 1941), (4255), p. 134.

[104] Thielicke, *The Hidden Question of God,* trans. and ed. Geoffrey W. Bromiley (Grand Rapids; Eerdmans, 1977), pp. 10-11, 170-71.

his "satanism" is "genuine blasphemy" and thus at least partial belief or entrance "into Christianity by the back door"?[105] If we attempt this equation, we are brought up short by Beckett's words in his interview with Colin Duckworth to the effect that, because "Christianity is a mythology" with which he is "perfectly familiar," he naturally *makes use of it* (my italics).[106] This remark reminds us that, however strong or weak – and however distanced from the metaphorical element in orthodox Christian language – we may understand it to be, there is a very definite metaphorical dimension to the hero's perception of God. The hero may long for God to fill his voids, but what he is searching for is not, to the best of his knowledge, a purely mystical union with God, that is, God himself. God may not even exist, and if he does, he is a malignant God that no rational person would desire union with. Having arrived at this realization, we are immediately led to another major question: what exactly is the hero searching for (what is wrapped up in his search for the self), and what is the connection of this search or quest (and thus the void) with his experience of God?

Even a casual reading of almost any cross section of Beckett's fiction and drama taken together or separately strongly suggests that the distressful, negative condition of the hero – the void – is somehow connected essentially with the idea of God. A very simple statement of this suggestion – and a statement that will not lead us astray – is that the hero's need exists because God does not, for whatever reason, do what a God is supposed to do on the human scene. Such a statement does not by itself, however, posit the necessity of God in the sense that it assumes his existence or a need for him *per se*. Both Nietzsche and Sartre acknowledge that if there were a God who fitted man's expectations of him, man's metaphysical needs would be met. But for Nietzsche, God is dead, and should and will remain so, while man as Overman learns to fulfill his own needs. For Sartre, also, the existentialist premises work – aesthetic man can meet his own deficiencies, can authenticate himself. By comparison, we can note the obvious truth that the Beckettian hero does not and cannot fill his void left empty by

---

[105] T. S. Eliot, *Selected Essays, New Edition* (New York: Harcourt, Brace, 1950), p. 373.

[106] *Angels of Darkness*, p. 18.

the absence or cruelty of God. Again, to make this claim is not to assert that God fills the void – in fact, what is certain is that Beckett's God does not do so – but to see the void as something only a God could fill.

We must make a very needed and careful distinction here between the hero engaging in a genuinely mystical quest for spiritual union with God and the hero desperately responding to any symbolic God/promise (even though he is acutely aware of the irony of such a promise) that seems to offer fulfillment of his metaphysical needs. The Promethean myth is an excellent analogical framework for making this distinction.[107] Although numerous critics, including Coe, define Beckett's "philosophy" as being "at bottom that of the mystic,"[108] Beckett's hero would no more desire

---

[107] I am not claiming any kind of thoroughgoing comparison between Beckett's hero and Prometheus. Instead I am pointing out the analogy of their obsessions with divine gifts and their feelings of frustration and animosity toward a God who withholds these gifts from humanity. Mueller and Jacobson explain that, for Beckett, "no one could be further from the truth than the humanist, with his exaltation of man and his devotion to the Prometheus myth." Their claim that Beckett is "at the other pole" from Prometheus (*The Testament of Samuel Beckett,* p. 129) is valid in that Beckett's man entertains no hopeful illusions that man, cut off from God, can effect prosperity and happiness for mankind. A careful distinction would be that Prometheus successfulluy *steals* the gifts from Jupiter and Beckett's hero waits in vain for God to *proffer* the gifts. The comparison between the Beckettian hero and Prometheus has not been fully explained. In *The Unnamable,* the unnamed hero ends his preamble with the following disclaimer:

> The fact that Prometheus was delivered twenty-nine thousand nine hundred and seventy years after having purged his offence leaves me naturally as cold as camphor. For between me and that miscreant who mocked the gods, invented fire, denatured clay and domesticated the horse, in a word obliged humanity, I trust there is nothing in common. (*The Unnamable,* p. 303)

The disclaimer contains no ironic overtones, but there are certain points where the Unnamable and Prometheus do touch. Lawrence Graver once asked his students in a seminar on Beckett to react to the Unnamable's disclaimer, and they replied that it was "quite right." What the students failed to see was that, in Graver's words, by "the ferocious quest to discover a true self (with full knowledge that the quest is futile, isolating, and destructive), the Unnamable was bringing back a kind of fire and obliging humanity . . . indeed that the frightening quest was self-creating" (from a letter to me from Graver, dated Sept. 12, 1980). I have examined the Promethean aspects of the Beckett hero's quest to some extent in a paper entitled "The Promethean Quest of Beckett's Hero," that was presented at the First Annual Symposium in the Humanities, *Samuel Beckett: Humanistic Perspectives,* held at the Ohio State University, May 7-9, 1981.

[108] "God and Samuel Beckett," p. 112.

spiritual union with the God he senses as being in charge of things than Prometheus would want union with Zeus. The cruelty of Beckett's God (if this God exists) is quite similar to the cruelty of Zeus: both deities are evil because they withhold from the creature man those qualities necessary for the authentication of the human self which only a God can provide. From this perspective, we can understand the ambiguity of the Beckettian hero's rejection of God and his obsession with him. The hero rejects God because of his cruel non-existence or withholding of divine gifts; he is obsessed with God because only God can bestow the gifts. We can also understand the hero's joint obsession with the self and with God: only God can bestow the qualities needed for self-authentication. Just as Zeus holds in absolute control the sacred fire that is the sole means of sparking all progress for mankind, so Beckett's God holds the key to ultimate knowledge and significance in regard to the human experience.

This void of ignorance and insignificance in the experience of Beckett's hero is an updated version of man's ancient emptiness. Adrift in a world of finiteness, he hungers for infinity. Simply to be aware of the possibilities of a harmony between matter and spirit, of a place and identity that would establish a true self, of beauty, and of love makes life without these qualities a continuing crucifixion. The Beckettian hero never finds Paradise, but he is obsessed with an awareness or memory of it. But, unlike Augustine, he does not equate these qualities with the "happiness" of union with God.[109] Instead, like Prometheus, he is determined to wrest them from a God whom he despises and scorns. Thus J. Hillis Miller aptly applies the term "Prometheanism of the depths" to Beckett's writings.[110] How an evil God can be the source of these crucially desirable gifts remains a paradox that can be resolved only partially by recourse to a Manichean dualism. The Beckett hero's God may be double or have two faces (like Janus), but the God who withholds the gifts is logically the only one who could supply them. Like Prometheus, the hero deals with a dark

---

[109] Augustine, *The Confessions of St. Augustine,* trans. F. J. Sheed (1943; rpt. New York: Sheed and Ward, 1965), Bk. 10, XX, p. 230.

[110] *The Disappearance of God,* p. 13.

God who holds his destiny – his authentication or non-authentication – in his hands.

Thielicke insists that "when God is a cipher for something other than himself he becomes superfluous and yields to that other."[111] In spite of the metaphorical dimension in Beckett's use of the God-motif, the hero's void is truly a God-void. Because the hero is seeking for a quality of experience that would be possible only in a godly, not godless, universe (with these terms used as defined by Beckett), the completion of the quest is dependent upon God. Therefore, God looms just beyond every horizon and is of vast importance. These claims will be illuminated by a detailed exploration of the point where God, the quest, and the hero coalesce in Beckett's fiction.

---

[111] *The Hidden Question of God,* pp. 133-34.

PARADIGMS OF HEROES AND QUESTS

A consideration of traditional literary patterns involving God, a quest, and a hero brings to mind immediately ideas of a purposeful hero with lofty or holy motives (such as finding the Holy Grail) braving the evil dragon or giant, and seizing and bearing away the treasure or the lady. Twentieth-century literature, more often than not, debunks such notions of a quest and defines the human endeavor in compromising terms more commensurate with the disenchantment of the present era. Beckett's fiction is unusual in that it also ironically debunks the possibility of the success of any such quest but nonetheless retains the high seriousness and intense purpose associated with such an effort. This combination of irony and high seriousness is precisely what makes the Beckettian quest so impervious to analysis. As critics, we are mystified by the incongruity of, for instance, Malone's humorously fatalistic efforts to play games with his stories, and simultaneous longings to use the construction of the stories as his only hope of self-authentication.

Hugh Kenner has recognized a strong element of mystery in Beckett's writings. In the "Preface" to the 1967 edition of *Samuel Beckett: A Critical Study,* he states that "the Beckett universe" is "permeated by mystery and hounded by . . . darkness." Kenner also tells us that Beckett has denied "the presence in his work of some hidden plan or key like the parallels in *Ulysses.*" As critics, therefore, we must take care not to "assail those qualities" of mystery and darkness by forcing our own interpretive schemes onto Beckett's writings. Instead, we should exercise our proper freedom "to note recurrences" and to "cherish symmetries."[1]

My efforts to "assail" the "mystery" of the matter of God in Beckett's fiction have convinced me of the validity of Kenner's observations. The identification, compilation, and careful critical examination of references to deity (by a narrator or a hero) occurring on the surface of any given text, or of the texts taken as a whole, lead, more often than not, to the stalemate of confusion and ambiguity so apparent in the body of criticism we have examined in Chapter One. Beckett's writings – like all writing that matters – certainly hold meanings, but these meanings are implicit rather than explicit, resonances that lie buried beneath the language and empty spaces of the text. Neal Oxenhandler refers to the necessity, in regard to Beckett's writings, of going "behind the verbal to that primordial psychic process where the work originates." He correctly points out that the critic's "tactics" must be "indirect" in order "to reach the nonverbal." Oxenhandler also comments on a common misconception among critics who focus on language as mere language – the confusion of "non-verbal psychism" with "mysticism."[2] While, as I have claimed, Beckett's writings are not genuinely mystical, they are profoundly mythical, and myth is always structured on skeletal patterns of repetition. It is, then, in these repeated patterns lying beneath the surface of the text or, to use Kenner's language, these recurrent symmetries, that I shall search for some cohesive understanding of the God-idea as it occurs throughout Beckett's fiction.

The first pattern or symmetry that I shall describe and examine is the religious aspect of the consciousness of the Beckett hero. Whether the protagonists are taken as being different personae or as being one persona in different guises, the persons, voices, or observed figures of the various pieces of fiction share – for the most part – a common theological orientation. An analysis of this orientation into its particular components yields the following

---

[1] Kenner, *Samuel Beckett: A Critical Study* (New York: Grove, 1967), pp. 9-10.

[2] Oxenhandler, "Seeing and Believing in Dante and Beckett," *Writing in a Modern Temper: Essays on French Literature and Thought in Honor of Henri Peyne,* Ed. Mary Ann Caws, Anma Libri, 1984, Saratoga, Calif., p. 219.

four-point pattern or paradigm of almost any given hero's religious consciousness:

1. An awareness that to be is to be perceived by some other, an other conceived, if not as a person or persons, at least in terms of personhood.
2. A conviction that some power or force other than man or chance is in charge of human life and that human freedom is decidedly limited by the determinism of this power(s).
3. A sense of guilt or "sin" based, in somewhat the same manner as the Greeks reasoned, on the fact of suffering as presupposing failure or wrongdoing.
4. An experiencing of "eternal life," in the sense of a continuation of consciousness that does not cease even, most probably, in death.

I am ascribing a religious dimension to these components. Other ways of examining them are, of course, possible – for instance, from a psychological or Freudian perspective. Or, the first point of my paradigm could easily be explored from the Sartrean existentialist perspective that a person exists as he is perceived by other persons. To choose the theological is, however, not only suited to my purposes but also particularly applicable to Beckett as a writer. He portrays his heroes as obsessed with a sense of a cosmic other who determines the limits of their freedom, positions them as guilty "sinners," and punishes them with a consciousness of finitude, non-fulfillment, and alienation that never ends. Such an obsession is obviously theological. To locate God in this pattern is not to situate God, however defined, as existing objectively in Beckett's fictional world but to explore his phenomenological existence in the consciousness of a given hero. Therefore, we will need no working definition of the word "God" other than the definitions we devise as we examine this consciousness. God will be defined in terms of whomever or whatever a given hero perceives him to be or not to be. As we shall see, Beckett's contradictory references to divinity often embrace the negative, describing voids that the hero senses should be filled, but which remain empty.

What is the connection between this particular theological perception and the hero's undertaking of a quest toward God?

There would seem to be none. In fact, given a hero with such an orientation, we might surmise that he, like Jonah, would flee from the face of a stern Jehovah. But we must remember that this cosmic perceiver who determines the limits of the "guilty" hero's freedom is also the holder of the qualities considered necessary for self-authentication. Therefore, there is no other logical direction toward which to quest. Furthermore, the components of the theological orientation suggest a Being who, if he should choose, could easily arrange matters so that the hero's needs are met. If human existence is dependent on this Being's act of perception, if he is in charge of human life and freedom, if the experience of guilt or suffering is "sin" against him, and if the continuation of consciousness is at his disposal, then this Being (or non-Being, or absent Being) is the one with whom the hero must interact. Like the mindless Immanent Will of Thomas Hardy's *The Dynasts,* he is the Power toward whom man must direct his philosophical questions and needs.

The hero's questing in the direction of such a perceived deity can, like his perception of this deity, also be analyzed into distinct structural patterns or paradigms. This structural pattern of the direction(s) of the quest, that I shall describe and proceed to examine in the fiction, is much more complex than the phenomenological pattern of the hero's consciousness. This pattern is found in what I shall describe as the levels or dimensions of the quest. The first level is the macrocosmic quest undertaken by the protagonist or hero as what I shall call the self-as-character. The second level is the microcosmic quest undertaken by the protagonist as the self-as-artist. The two quest levels are sequential in that the first is dominant in the fiction preceding *Malone Dies,* and the second in *Malone Dies* and the fiction following this novel. However, the levels are also static in that they can exist simultaneously, and sometimes do, in a given work. This quest pattern, occurring on one or both levels in Beckett's fiction, is so pervasive that it can be defined as a basic structural skeleton in these writings. In fact, those few works of fiction in which this pattern cannot be clearly discerned are the ones of least literary merit.[3]

---

[3] *Mercier and Camier, Fizzles One* through *Six,* and *All Strange Away* are examples of such works. For critical evaluation of *Mercier and Camier,* see Kenner,

On the first level, the hero quests in macrocosmic, recognizable time and space – in the sphere that we can define as the ordinary world of nature and observable human activity – for certain qualities that have always been associated, certainly in Western literature, with authentication or fulfillment of the human self. These qualities appear as needs that the hero must fill, or have filled, for him to find happiness and purpose in life. The needs can be variously described; I shall define them in the following manner. The hero longs to establish a true identity of the self; to unite with another – or a community – in love; to find and reside in a place that is a true home – in Augustine's use of the word, a resting place for man's spirit; to gain a harmony with nature – or the system it represents; and to resolve the dichotomy or lack of unity that he experiences between his flesh and his spirit. Examples of heroes with these needs that throng to mind – Belacqua, Murphy, the protagonist of *Stories* – only state the obvious: these needs are the basic desires of all Adam's descendants since he lost Paradise. Fulfillment of the needs is the Godot who never comes, referred to by Kenner as "the perpetual possibility of personal impingement on mechanism."[4] At this level of the quest, God appears as the point at which the hero and the granting of the needs meet, or, more precisely, fail to meet. A dominant narrative structure involves a protagonist responding to some God/sign or word/promise that appears to him to offer fulfillment of one or more of these needs. The sign or word, however, is a false promise; responding to it never results in fulfillment but, instead, in disillusionment and continual need. To say that Beckett is satirizing the needy hero and his response to the religious stimuli is to misread the quest structure. In fact, to insist on this perspective is to define almost all Beckett's protagonists as objects of satire. Vladimir and Estragon are not satirized for their waiting. Certainly Beckett is ironically debunking the stimuli, but he is indicting whoever or whatever offers the false promises, not his

---

Samuel Beckett; A Critical Study, pp. 70-77 and 186. For *Fizzles* and *All Strange Away*, see Pilling, *Frescoes of the Skull*, pp. 132-44. *From an Abandoned Work* can also be read as suitable for inclusion in this group.

[4] *Samuel Beckett: A Critical Study*, p. 186.

heroes. Vladimir and Estragon, and Everyman, watch trees sprout green leaves and wait endlessly on dark roads for Godot.

The macrocosmic quest as described above can be visualized as five voids or empty circles of need that must be filled. Such visualization suggests a second way to describe the quest on the macrocosmic level: as a reaching for the zero, that enigmatic symbol that Beckett uses to gather all the voids into one empty circle. Kenner offers mathematical examples of Beckett's metaphysical reaching toward zero:

> Twenty-two by 7 is the schoolbook approximation to pi, the circle squarer. And the 'true ciphers' are 3.142 857, 142857 . . . accumulating, to no definite end, invariable patterns that grow less and less significant. As their sum gradually approximates toward the secret of the circle, their importance gradually dwindles toward zero.

Kenner's second example is what he terms the "aboriginal surd, the square root of two," which he represents as follows:

$$1 + \cfrac{1}{2 + \cfrac{1}{2 + \cfrac{1}{2 + \cfrac{1}{2 + \dots}}}}$$

Such equations reveal "the denominator growing steadily emptier [nearer to nothing or zero] the further we carry it." When Kenner defines Watt's quest as the "curve of a function that approaches and turns around zero (Knott) before disappearing irretrievably off the paper," he is describing the asymptotic movement of a point along a curve so that it almost but never quite reaches zero distance from its associated straight line.[5] Zeno's pile of millet can be divided endlessly, but it never actually disappears, and the ceasing of words never diminishes into a final silence beyond language.

---

[5] *Samuel Beckett: A Critical Study*, pp. 105-06 and 109.

Zero or nothingness in Beckett's art becomes a symbol of the ever-beckoning but never-attained essence of knowledge and being in human experience. Linda Ben-Zvi is correct in claiming, contrary to much other critical assertion, that Beckett's work does not assume a "total denial of absolutes."[6] In fact, we can say that the Beckettian quest is structured on the possibility of attaining the absolute. Ruby Cohn's early observation that the hero is engaged in the "old Greek quest for the metaphysical meanings of the Self, the World, and God"[7] remains relevant. George Szanto sees completion of the quest as impossible because it is a search for "absolute knowledge, which, being one aspect of Godness, is, by definition, unavailable to man."[8]

This idea of the quest as a search for zero places it, in spite of its goal of self-authentication, at some distance from the concerns of Sartre, and certainly, of Camus. The quest of Beckett's hero is comparable to that of Kafka's, but to go further and define the quest for zero as genuine mysticism is to overstep boundaries. Unlike Meister Eckhart, the hero is not searching for a God *per se,* although he is seeking for something that is possible only at the disposition of a God. Like Prometheus, he is a rebel frustrated with his ignorance who wants to invade God's domain, discover the secret fire, and appropriate it to his own use. Watt, Molloy, and Moran engage in the quest on the first level primarily as a search for zero. Each journeys into a twilight zone vaguely removed from ordinary time and space and searches for a mythical person – Mr. Knott, Molloy's mother, or Molloy as object. In each case, however, neither hero wants actually to find and unite in spiritual union with the person sought. Instead, the hero's attitude toward the person sought is a mixture of fearful dread, hateful loathing, and reluctant fascination. What is being desperately sought is mystical or divine knowledge that will unlock the riddle of life (an affair that Moran calls a "wretched existence," *Molloy,* p. 107), solve the puzzle of what human experience is all about,

---

[6] "Samuel Beckett, Fritz Mauthner, and the Limits of Language," p. 192.

[7] Cohn, "Philosophical Fragments in the Works of Samuel Beckett," *Criticism,* 6 (1964), 33-43. Rept. in *Samuel Beckett: A Collection of Critical Essays,* ed. Martin Esslin (Englewood Cliffs, N. J.: Prentice-Hall, 1965), p. 176.

[8] Szanto, *Narrative Consciousness: Structure and Perception in the Fiction of Kafka, Beckett, and Robbe-Grillet* (Austin: Univ. of Texas Press, 1972), p. 186.

and authenticate or create the selfhood of the searcher. The quest on level one as a search for zero also fails. No answer, meaning, or identity is ever found.

On level two of the quest pattern, the hero descends into the realm of the imagination or mind. This level is Beckett's microcosm, that complex area without discernible boundaries, the soulscape of the human consciousness, that Beckett visualizes as encased in the human skull. This microcosm, with its surreal landscapes and pantomimes of ghosts is the most real of Beckett's worlds. In *Proust,* Beckett insists that "the world" is "a projection of the individual's consciousness."[9] Beckett joins Proust in the view that the outer world or macrocosm assumes reality only as it is assimilated into the microcosm. This place within the human consciousness is the world of the imagination, but *it is not an imaginary world:* it alone defines reality.

The quest on this level becomes the task of constructing a literary artifact that will serve as evidence to confer identity upon the self as an artist. Intimations of the development of the quest pattern from the macrocosmic level of the outer world to the microcosmic level of the inner world or imagination are present in embryo in Beckett's fiction as early as the writing of *Assumption.* This quest pattern of the artist/self becomes overtly dominant in *Malone Dies* and continues as the dominant pattern as late as *Worstward Ho.* For Beckett, no other development could be possible. Self-authentication or a realization of the absolute – call the goal of the quest what you will – is theoretically possible only through art. We must be careful, having made this statement, not to align Beckett or his hero with Schopenhauer or Proust as a believer in salvation or redemption through art. Beckett's hero cannot attain to such experience and becomes a skeptic, finding art to be as valueless as other supports of Western culture. But, in spite of this skepticism, the hero's ideal does not change. The quest on level two, the descent into the microcosm of the imagination, is an artistic quest for the word or story that will create the self.

The quest on level one can be said to hold the quest on level two much as one Chinese box holds another. The artist/self splits

---

[9] *Proust,* p. 8.

from the character/self of the macrocosm and descends into the imaginative realm of the microcosm. Here the goal of the quest becomes to tell or write a story; needless to say, Beckett's artist/self is always literary. Just as the macrocosmic hero could finish the quest only by having the empty circles of need filled or by arriving at the zero of the ultimate essence of being, so the microcosmic artist/hero must construct a story of this finished quest. Only in this manner can the artist/self authenticate his artistic selfhood and "find the self" by achieving identity as a person. He cannot, of course, tell a story of a finished or successful quest, since he has no knowledge of such fulfillment. Therefore, his story can never end or complete itself. Beckett's fiction structured on the quest pattern at level two does not contain such incompleted stories; it consists of them. What is the exact connection between the failure of the quest in the macrocosm and the failed or abortive stories of the microcosmic artist/hero? How is the failure of life reflected in the failure of art? Certainly this failure is peculiarly Beckettian; it is not a manifestation of any artistic or literary principle. Literature is replete with successful, completed stories of human experience that must be described as failure. Stories as old as that of Samson in the Book of Judges and as recent as Hemingway's *The Old Man and the Sea* are tragic but artistically successful and completed accounts of human failure. In fact, tragedy is a profoundly moving type of literature precisely because it is a story of human frailty and failure.

An examination of the almost unvarying method that Beckett's artist/hero employs in fabricating his would-be stories offers enlightenment on this matter. The only material for art, for the subject matter of the stories, consists of personal or biographical memories of macrocosmic life. From *How It Is* onward, there is almost no question but that the fabricated stories are abortive accounts of the narrator's or observed figure's "life above in the light." But even as early as *Malone Dies,* the first work that is overtly structured on a narrator/hero telling himself stories, the tales told exhibit an underlying dependence on the narrator's previous life. Trying desperately (and futilely) to describe his planned storytelling as only a "game" that he is "going to play," Malone takes a "good look all round" and begins to "play with what I saw." He plans that his projected four stories shall feature a man, a woman, a thing, and "an animal, a bird probably" (*Malone Dies,* pp. 180-81). The stories turn out to be the confused and dismal accounts of Saposcat, Macmann, and Lemuel – his "creatures." These accounts, however, contain material that is not only personal or biographical in regard to Malone but also to Malone's creator, Beckett. The hills where the stonecutters live, flickering with the faint lights of gorse fires at night, appear here (pp. 206, 286-87) as they do throughout the fictional canon. These hills are the Dublin Mountains, their slopes interspersed with stonequarries, which remain indelibly imprinted in the literary memories of Beckett and Malone. As a boy, Beckett had heard, from his home near Dublin, the barking dogs and ringing hammers of the stonecutters living in these hills. At night he had watched the lights of the burning gorse flickering from the slopes.[10] Malone's predecessor (Beckett's narrators are often reincarnations of each other), the hero of *The End,* remembers this burning gorse. He had watched it from a high window, after climbing into bed at night, having often set the fires himself during the day (*Stories and Texts for Nothing,* pp. 71-72). The "vast continuous buzzing" which Malone hears in his mind's ear and translates into his stories is "of nature, of mankind and even my own . . . all jumbled together in one and the same unbridled gibberish" (p. 207). Writing about Sapo, Malone acknowledges that "I write about myself with the same pencil and in the same exercise-book as about him" (p. 207). The final vision of Malone's story is of Lemuel, tangled with his victims "in a heap" in the boat, while the "faint fires of the blazing gorse" burn on in Malone's literary memory. The blood will never dry on Lemuel's hatchet, Malone says, a hatchet that changes easily into Malone's stick, or his pencil (*Malones Dies,* pp. 287-88).

The artist/hero's literary strategy, then, is to fabricate stories out of the memories of his own macrocosmic life. Because these memories are invariably of the failed macrocosmic quest (conceived of in one fashion or another), the fabricated stories reproduce in various forms the nonfulfillment, disappointment, and loss of the macrocosmic hero's experience of this quest. Malone

---

[10] Vivian Mercier, *Beckett/Beckett* (New York: Oxford Univ. Press, 1977), p. 58.

valiantly announces, "I shall not speak of my sufferings" (p. 186), but his sufferings are precisely what he does speak of:

> But it was not long before I found myself alone, in the dark. That is why I gave up trying to play and took to myself for ever shapelessness and speechlessness, incurious wondering, darkness, long stumbling with outstretched arms, hiding. (*Malone Dies,* p. 180)

The last six nouns of this passage – "shapelessness," "speechlessness," "wondering," "darkness," "stumbling," and "hiding" – form a precise mini-lexicon of the experiences and stances fabricated by Beckett's various artist/selves. Like their creator, Beckett, the artist/selves do not or cannot transcend in art the pain and bewilderment of life.

To arrive at this conclusion is to raise the complex question of what Beckett intends by his application of the adjectival noun "failure" to his own literary effort. In Chapter One and in the pages that follow this second chapter, I refer, directly and indirectly, to Beckett's infamous claims – claims so often quoted that to repeat them leads to redunancy *ad nauseam* – that not only is his art an art of "failure," but that any art (whether painting, literature, or what have you) worthy of note is also, of necessity, a "failure,"[11] Beckett has unquestioningly written an extremely significant body of literature. What is the Beckettian meaning of the failure of art?

In his essay on Beckett's artistic theory, David Read explores the relations of selfhood and language in regard to art.[12] Considering Beckett the writer and also the struggling narrator/writers whom Beckett creates, Read describes the artistic dilemma as resulting from a lack of being or personality on the part of the artistic self (or the no-self) and from the limitations of language. Perceived only by the others that its own perception has created,

---

[11] Beckett has described van Velde as a pioneer in producing painting that admits "that to be an artist is to fail, as no other dare fail, that failure is his world." See "Bram van Velde," the third dialogue in *Proust and Three Dialogues with Georges Duthuit,* p. 125.

[12] Read, "Artistic Theory in the Work of Samuel Beckett," *Journal of Beckett Studies,* No. 8 (1982), pp. 7-22. Particular quotations from this article are referred to by specific page numbers in the text.

the self lacks conclusive evidence that it even exists and can only intuit its being (p. 11). Unexpressed, the self cannot consider itself an agent of expression, artistic or otherwise, because "expression requires personality" (p. 14). As for language, it is merely a game, locked in the confines of its own causality: "The subject implies a verb, which, in turn, implies an object" (p. 18). The artistic self cannot express, nor, if it could, has it language with which to express. Thus Beckettian artistic failure is failure to realize being or to find a "form for being" (p. 22).[13] By his formulations of Beckett's theory, then, Read defines the Beckettian *œuvre* as "failure" because it is composed of language (not the "unword") and is produced by the pseudo-self or the "êtré manque" (not the actual or real self).

From a slightly different perspective, we can say that Beckett's problematic subjective self produces art that is a "failure" because it is a mirror image of the self's non-being, an art permeated by the no-selves of the various heroes and consisting of the no-stories that these heroes enact or fabricate. The Unnamable is such a self – he "neither speaks nor listens" and "has neither body nor soul." Therefore, unable to tell "the story of the silence," he has no story, except of course, "my story" or *The Unnamable* (*The Unnamable*, pp. 413-14), which may be described as a no-story. The imaginative eye of *La Falaise*[14] is only an impersonal observing eye, and, as it penetrates the eye-sockets of the skull that it fabricates, encounters only vacancy. The final vision of this "story" is also of emptiness or nothingness.

A simpler and more literal understanding of failure in regard to Beckett's work is the fact that he and his narrators appear unable to master even the rudiments of story-telling. Characters blend into each other (losing and exchanging names in the process); beginnings are indistinquishable from endings and endings from beginnings (the first paragraph of *The Calmative* begins exactly where the last paragraph of *The End* stops); and digressive

---

[13] The phrase, as Read acknowledges, is Beckett's own. See Harvey, *Samuel Beckett: Poet and Critic*, p. 249.

[14] All references to *La Falaise* are to the copy of MS 1396/4/40 in the Beckett Archive of the University of Reading. I quote no page numbers because the MS is a single page.

material becomes deliberately obscurant in regard to plot (notoriously and particularly in *Watt*). Such "failure" is, of course, ironically deliberate on Beckett's part.

Each of these perspectives on failure is a literary mode that Beckett experiments with, seeking for the elusive form that will accommodate being (individual and collective) or what he terms the "mess" of human experience.[15] Beckett will not practice the successful "classic" form of Kafka, with its "consternation . . . in the form" of the literature itself.[16] Nor will he concede that an artistic effort such as his is a successful allegory *expressing* the failure of art.[17] In the third dialogue with Duthuit, Beckett rejects the explanation that van Velde's painting is "expressive of the impossibility to express." He insists that van Velde's art (and, by implication, his own) "is inexpressive."[18] The artist's dilemma is not that being or the "mess" of human experience has no potential artistic form that could accommodate it. The problem is that no one has as yet discovered this form:

> Being has a form. Someone will find it someday. Perhaps I won't but someone will. It is a form that has been abandoned, left behind, a proxy in its place.[19]

In the Driver interview, Beckett pinpoints the finding of this form as the present "task of the artist."[20] If, following Beckett's lead, we agree that his art fails to "express" or to offer a "form for being," we must nonetheless insist that he has achieved an extremely successful rendering of artistic failure.

Beckett's narrating self-as-artist can more easily be defined as an unsuccessful artist than Beckett himself. The nearest the artist/

---

[15] Driver, "Beckett by the Madeleine," pp. 22-23.

[16] Israel Shenker, "Moody Man of Letters," *New York Times,* 6 May 1956, Sec. 2, p. X.

[17] Jonathan Culler suggests that by giving to Beckett's work "an allegorical relation to the world," we can take its "signifying" of "absurdity and chaos" as a meaningful "statement about the incoherence and absurdity of our own languages." See *Structuralist Poetics: Structualism, Linguistics, and the Study of Literature* (Ithaca: Cornell Univ. Press, and London: Routledge and Kegan Paul, 1975), p. 138.

[18] *Proust and Three Dialogues with Georges Duthuit,* pp. 120-21.

[19] Harvey, *Samuel Beckett: Poet and Critic,* p. 249.

[20] "Beckett by the Madeleine," p. 23.

self can come to a successful story is the Joe Breem or Breen of *The Calmative* and text 1 of *Texts for Nothing* (*Stories and Texts for Nothing*, pp. 30 and 78-79). Joe is a hero who braves the elements for a mighty cause with fortitude and bravery. Were this story successfully told, it would be one of "sheer heroism," of a hero overcoming the elements for a mighty cause. Unfortunately, neither the reader nor Beckett's narrator ever knows exactly what Joe is doing or why. The macrocosmic situation that holds the Joe Breem story like a Chinese box is of the speaker as a child in his father's arms, hearing his father's words under "that ancient lamp." This frame story contains in embryo a nostalgic desire or need for all the qualities that serve as objects for the macrocosmic quest on level one (*Stories and Texts for Nothing*, p. 79).

The reason for the failure of the quest by the self-as-artist in the microcosm, then, is that the unfulfilled God/promises and unmet needs that cause the quest to be defined as one of failure in the macrocosm invade the realm of the imagination also. The darkness that controls Malone's life invades his stories as well – a darkness that "accumulates, thickens, then suddenly bursts and drowns everything" (*Malone Dies*, p. 190). The suffering memories that afflict the artist/self of *How It Is* become the flashes of light that bring the macrocosm into the structures of the imagination pictured in *Imagination Dead Imagine* and which crucify the little figure of *Ping*.[21]

Morot-Sir explains how the darkness that renders the hero impotent in the macrocosm invades the imagination. Cartesian dualism develops into a phenomenological Manicheanism, a microcosmic consciousness of duality or "mingling." Thus the division of a dual universe enters the hero's "little world," and there is no resolution, no matter how far inward the hero journeys, from the continuing dialectics of yes/no, light/darkness, truth/untruth, and self/no-self.[22] The particular curse of this inner duality for the artist/hero is not only the darkness of the light/darkness dialectic but also the eternal contradiction of affirmation/negation inherent

---

[21] For elaboration of macrocosmic intrusion into the microcosms of these pieces, see my article " 'Coloured Images' in the 'Black Dark': Samuel Beckett's Later Fiction," *PMLA*, 92 (1977), 273-84.

[22] "Samuel Beckett and Cartesian Emblems," pp. 96-103.

in human language. Because of this contradiction, the hero must quest beyond the limits of language for the Unnamable's "real silence" or for what Mauthner calls a "godless mysticism."[23]

This "real silence" or the Word beyond language that the hero needs is the creative Logos, referred to in text 6 as the breath of the Eternal that once breathed on "slime" and created a world in spite of nothingness and darkness. Such a Word could create, in the microcosmic confines of the mind, an imaginative facsimile of a macrocosmic world in which the quest on level one could be completed – a world in which human existential needs could be met and ultimate riddles of being solved. In such an imaginative world as this, the artist/self could fabricate a story of a successful macrocosmic quest and thus accomplish the completion of the microcosmic quest – the authentication of his own artistic selfhood by means of the creation of art.

Nearly every piece of fiction that Beckett has written insists that the imagination, in order to create the story, must avail itself of life, of macrocosmic experience that is lodged in the memory. In *Still* such an experience is whatever once happened in the shade of the beech tree. This event, although barely mentioned (in comparison, for instance, with Krapp's experience with the girl in the boat) is the substance of the figure's reverie. In the companion pieces to *Still* – *Sounds* and *Still 3* – the "sound" that the figure responds to is a memory or memories associated with the tree, and the reason (in *Still 3*) that there is "nothing to tell" is that the response to memory has proved painful and non-productive, leaving the figure with an inner world almost as chaotic as Murphy's after his final encounter with Mr. Endon.[24] The artist/self's rebellion is against an outside world that controls his imagination rather than his imagination being able to shape the outside world: "The whiskey bears a grudge against the decanter."[25] Like Nietzsche's Overman, the microcosmic hero wants to drink up the sea – integrate the world into his mind and shape it

---

[23] Ben-Zvi, p. 197, quotes Gershon Weiler's *Mauthner's* Critique of Language (Cambridge: Cambridge Univ. Press, 1970), p. 294.

[24] *Still* is "Fizzle 7" in *Fizzles* (New York: Grove), pp. 47-51. See p. 49 for mention of the beech tree. *Sounds* and *Still 3* are in *Essays in Criticism,* 28 (1978), 155-57.

[25] *Proust,* pp. 21-22.

according to his own image. The failure of the quest on level two is described at the end of text 13: there is "not a speck of dust, not a breath, the voice's breath alone, it breathes in vain, nothing is made" (*Stories and Texts for Nothing*, pp. 103 and 138).

Northrop Frye writes of the Logos as the "eternal verbal symbol" that masters the macrocosm by being "no longer a commentary on life or reality, but containing life and reality in a system of verbal relationships."[26] It is precisely a commitment to this Logos of artistic integrity that insures the failure of Beckett's artist/self on level two of the quest. His story must be a true story – not "commentary" or a writing "*about* something" but a containing of *"that something itself."*[27] He finds this *"something itself"* – Frye's "life or reality" – to be a "mess" of darkness, contradiction, and nothingness.[28] Furthermore, he has not found available to him the divine Logos of Joyce or Proust that creates mythological universes *ex nihilo*. Instead, he must struggle in a universe silent except for Molloy's sound of "things forever lapsing and crumbling away" for the Logos that Molloy needs – a Word that will make it possible for "my story, so clear til now," not to "end" in "darkness" (*Molloy*, pp. 40 and 78). Thus God appears in the quest pattern on level two as he does on level one – as the maker of false promises and as the ever – receding zero. But he appears on the second level in profounder forms as well. He is the word beyond language, the creative Logos, that the artist/self forever seeks but never finds.

---

[26] Frye, *Anatomy of Criticism: Four Essays* (Princeton: Princeton Univ. Press, 1957), pp. 121-22.

[27] "Dante . . . Bruno . Vico . . Joyce," p. 117.

[28] See Driver, "Beckett by the Madeleine," p. 23.

BLUE FLOWERS AND BELACQUA'S GIRLS

Assumption

Although the unnamed hero of Beckett's earliest fiction is a literary artist, he appears, not in the role of self-as-artist on level two of the questing pattern, but in the role of self-as-character in the simpler pattern on level one. Thus he is seeking the fulfillment of his existential needs – needs that can be defined by the paradigm I have formulated in Chapter Two, but which have to do particularly in the earliest fiction with romantic or sexual love, pseudo-mysticism, and art. The complex of ideas on sexual love, mystical fulfillment, and artistic expression held by the early incarnations of the Beckettian hero [1] finds its origin in *Assumption*, Beckett's first published fiction. [2] The hero of this short story is frustrated – sexually, mystically, and artistically – although the frustration he is most aware of is artistic. He lives in ambivalent dread and longing in regard to a potential sound that is locked within his being. He longs to utter the sound, both as artistic expression and as mystical release. At the same time, however, he greatly fears

---

[1] These incarnations would include, along with the hero of *Assumption*, the heroes of the unpublished *Dream of Fair to Middling Women*, the episodic novel *More Pricks than Kicks* and the novel *Murphy*, although in *Murphy*, the hero's ideas on sexual love have undergone decided changes.

[2] *Assumption* was published in 1929 in *transition*, Nos. 16 and 17, Paris, pp. 268-71. As the story remains uncollected, my references are to this publication. Specific references are cited by page number(s) in the text of this chapter.

such utterance, convinced that the sound will prove to be "the torrent that must destroy him" (p. 270). The nameless hero's dread appears to be winning out over his longing, as he desperately chokes back the sound, speaking in whispers during the day and drugging himself at night lest the sound involuntarily escape him in sleep (pp. 269-70). Suddenly, into these extenuating circumstances of life, the Woman comes. He resents her intrusion and fears her influence on the precarious balance of his predicament, but eventually succumbs to her charm ("he thought he had never seen such charming shabbiness," p. 270). In fact, he begins to associate the possibility of sexual intercourse with her with the breaking of the dam of silence he is maintaining against the torrential release of the sound. Sure enough, after several sexual encounters occur, on a particular occasion, the "great storm of sound" is emitted, "shaking the very house with its prolonged, triumphant vehemence" (p. 271). On earlier occasions of sexual union, the hero has experienced some kind of mystical fulfillment: "each night he died and was God" (p. 271). Now, with the Woman continuing to act as a catalyst, he has achieved artistic expression as well. The aftermath of such expression, however, is, as he has feared, tragic: "They found her caressing his wild dead hair" (p. 271).

As literature, *Assumption* is terrible; as thematic foreshadowing, it is invaluable. This hero, obsessed with love, divinity, and art, is – in many respects – an embryo of a merging of Beckett's later fictional heroes. Like Belacqua, he associates mystical fulfillment and artistic expression with sexual experience. Like Murphy, he dies attempting to enter a mystical zone separated from the phenomenological world. Like Watt, he intuitively knows that the expression of sound constitutes the significance of life. Like the protagonist of *Stories,* he is one whose being is somehow dispersed into the elements of nature. Like Molloy, he associates a return to metaphysical origins with a turning to a woman (although, unlike Molloy, he is not seeking his mother). Like Malone, he learns of the close ties between artistic expression and death. Like the Unnamable, he has no name. Like the hero of *Texts for Nothing,* he is accustomed to the screaming silence of no's knife in yes's wound. And, like the narrator/narrated of *How It Is,* he is in conflict with and yet dependent upon some dreaded cosmic Power.

We will not continue *ad infinitum,* but the point is made: this hero is the rudimentary prototype of the heroes to come.

Categorized in regard to our questing patterns, the hero of *Assumption* is the self-as-character, searching on level one – in the macrocosm – for the fulfillment of his existential needs. A surface analysis of these needs and the hero's efforts to fill them, or to have them filled, is easily set forth. The identity he seeks is that of the artist, with the attempted art being the sound he both longs and dreads to emit. We must be careful to define this anticipated literary identity as rudimentary in comparison to that of later self-as-artist heroes who descend into the microcosm and function on level two of the quest pattern. As we have noted in Chapter Two, this descent on the second level does not appear as a developed theme or structural pattern in Beckett's fiction until the writing of *Malone Dies.* This early hero of *Assumption* is already successful with certain sounds: he is able to whisper "the turmoil down" in other persons (p. 268), but longs to emit the decisive sound that would be the articulation of his own artistic being. Almost against his will, he comes to desire to unite with the Woman (as other), if not in love, at least in sex, coming to associate union with her with the articulation of artistic being. Like Belacqua of *More Pricks than Kicks,* he senses nature to be a facade covering some kind of spiritual home or haven for man. He hungers "to be irretrievably engulfed in the light of eternity, one with the birdless cloudless colourless skies, in infinite fulfillment" (p. 271). Thus nature as haven becomes the system he is drawn toward. The conflict between flesh and spirit is evidenced by his body imprisoning the sound that would free his spirit artistically, and also by his physical desire for the Woman distracting him from the intentness of his obsession with uttering the artistic sound.

The exact way in which the promise of the fulfillment of these needs appears as a God/sign, however, is extremely complex. Jeri L. Kroll sees *Assumption* as "the story which opens Beckett's exploration of mystical experience and the way in which women may function as catalytic agents in artistic inspiration or catharsis." The story is the "initial formulation of Beckett's conception of women as givers of life, and bry implication, death, the thought that perhaps they can bridge the gap from womb to tomb."[3] Pilling also sees the woman as an active agent in the hero's attaining mystical and artistic expression. "Sexual ecstasy leads him to a religious ecstasy in which he becomes the Power that previously sought to thwart him; in this way he is liberated. . . . The sexual death of orgasm leads on to 'the blue flower, Vega, GOD.' "[4] In *More Pricks than Kicks,* Belacqua identifies whatever woman he is momentarily involved with as a Shekinah/sign of the promise of mystical/sexual fulfillment. Throughout this episodic novel, he attempts to overcome his sexual aberrations so as to pursue this fulfillment via sexual intercourse with a woman. In *Assumption,* however, the hero does not initially conceive of the Woman as offering any kind of fulfillment or release other than sexual. Only when he actually experiences sexual union with her does he "die and become God" (p. 271). Furthermore, it is questionable whether the Woman promises or gives any good experience of mysticism or divinity. Instead, the Woman, in spite of the fact that sex with her finally causes the hero to emit the sound, seems to function as part of the negative Power that works to inhibit and destroy the hero.

A close examination of ideas of divinity in *Assumption* leads us to detect a strong Manichean influence on the story.[5] In fact, the hero's religious consciousness is of a Manichean world order. The other who perceives him is a "Power" that not only exercises control over his individual life (it denies him, for a period of time, articulation of the sound) but also over "the cosmic discord" of the macrocosm (p. 269). The hero's "sin" is that his artistic and mythical consciousness is locked or imprisoned in his body or flesh, his guilt evidenced by his strong desire and yet great dread of allowing this consciousness to escape. By resisting articulation, the hero is "playing into the hands of the enemy," that is the "Power" (pp. 269-70). The final haven of escape from the body that the hero envisions is entirely spiritual or nonmaterial. He

[3] Kroll, "Belacqua as Artist and Lover: 'What a Misfortune,'" *Journal of Beckett Studies,* No. 3 (1978), p. 15.

[4] *Samuel Beckett,* pp. 122-23.

[5] For information on Manicheanism, see the sources referred to in notes 51 and 57 of Chapter One of this work.

wants to achieve unity with a sky without birds, clouds, or color, a sky that is thus conceived of as abstract and nonmaterial (p. 271). Upon the hero's death, the artistic sound fuses, not with the forest and the sea, but with the "*breath* of the forest" and the "*cry* of the sea" (my italics, p. 271). This analysis of religious consciousness is well-defined by the paradigm that I have constructed: the hero's being is defined and determined by the mysterious Power; his guilt is evidenced in his dread of articulating the sound; and some part of his being – if not his spirit, at least his artistic essence – continues as a part of nature after his death. The Manichean motifs of this particular hero's God-consciousness are obvious: a divine Power that is man's enemy, the condemnation of the bodily or fleshly and exaltation of the spiritual, and a world order that is cosmically disordered.

The Woman is also recognizably Manichean. She first approaches the hero in the dark, bringing disorder and chaos into the ordered intensity of his efforts to maintain balance in regard to the possible articulation of the sound. She is metaphorically compared to demons: "An irruption of demons would not have scattered his intentness so utterly." Her "sensuality" is described as a quality that is sinister, threatening, and destructive of the hero's well-being. Whenever she visits him, she seems to take from him vitality and strength: "When at last she went away he felt that something had gone out from him . . . something of the desire to live, something of the unreasonable tenacity with which he shrunk from dissolution" (p. 270). The experience of sex with her is to be "unconditioned by the Satanic dimensional Trinity"[6] and to die (p. 271). Although this sexual dying is to become "God," the meaning is clearly not the positive notion of sexual experience as a "death" found in seventeenth-century metaphysical poetry. Instead, the Woman, who has already been absorbing life from the hero, brings

[6] The exact meaning of this phrase is not clear, but it obviously refers to the Woman. Perhaps the Satanic trinity symbolized in Jesus' Temptation in the Wilderness and in the First Epistle of John, chapter 2, verse 16 – the world, the flesh, and the devil – is being referred to. Certainly Manichean doctrine would define the material world, especially the human body or flesh, as created and sustained by the devil or the evil God of Darkness. The human creature who would best exemplify such a blending of evil is, by Manichean definition, a woman.

him to a condition of great agitation and unrest. Although he is "spent with ecstasy," he is also "torn by . . . bitter loathing" and "battered with increasing grievousness." What the Woman has "overlaid" the hero with is "death" (p. 271). Almost every detail about the Woman resonates with allusions to the Manichean notions of women as begotten by and mated with Satan, and as being the chief means of preventing man from realizing the light (or goodness) within him and of trapping him (by sex and procreation) in the prison house of the flesh. The woman in Beckett's fictional canon who most closely resembles this Woman is Anna (or Lulu) of *First Love,* with her sexual aggressiveness and affiliation with death.[7]

The recognition of such obvious, overt Manichean characteristics leads to the question of Manichean influence on Beckett at or before the time of the composition of *Assumption.* Several critics point out the fact that Beckett's readings of St. Augustine and the Provençal troubadours could have been the early avenues through which he assimilated Manichean thought and perspective. Augustine wrote at length against the Manicheans, and the troubadours were associated with the Catharist Church, a religious group that perpetrated Manichean belief and practice.[8] Pilling sees an indirect Manichean influence on *Dream of Fair to Middling Women* (1932),[9] and Morot-Sir claims that Beckett has been familiar with Manicheanism since the writing of *Whoroscope* (1930).[10] The poem "Dortmunder" specifically uses Manichean terminology lifted from St. Augustine's polemics against this doctrine.[11] The Manichean

---

[7] For an analysis of this heroine's Manichean attributes, see Alice and Kenneth Hamilton, *Condemned to Life,* pp. 54-57.

[8] For speculation and information on Beckett's early contacts with Manichean thought, see Alice and Kenneth Hamilton, "Samuel Beckett and the Gnostic Vision of the Created World," p. 294; and *Condemned to Life,* pp. 57-58. Also see Harvey, *Samuel Beckett: Poet and Critic,* pp. 78-79. Harvey informs us that Denis de Rougemont has established connections between the poetic writings of the troubadours and the Catharist heresy, with its Manichean sources. His source for this information is *L'Amour et l'Occident,* 2nd ed. (Paris: Plon, 1956).

[9] *Samuel Beckett,* p. 119.

[10] "Samuel Beckett and Cartesian Emblems," p. 85.

[11] See note 6, p. 294, of the Hamilton's "Beckett and the Gnostic Vision of the Created World." "Dortmunder" is in *Echo's Bones and Other Precipitates* (Paris: Europa, 1935; rpt. in *Collected Poems in English and French: Samuel Beckett* [London: John Calder, 1977), p. 16.

motifs we have described in *Assumption* suggest that Beckett was familiar with this teaching before 1929, the year that *Assumption* was published.

The Manichean traits we have discovered in the Woman make her a negative figure, both for us as readers and for the hero, who can hardly be said to respond to her as a positive God/sign, although she is a manifestation of an evil divinity. Nor can we view the potential utterance of the sound as an unsullied God/sign of promise, beckoning the hero on his mystical/artistic quest. He seems fully aware, from start to finish, that union with the Woman and the emitting of the sound will lead to his death (pp. 270-71). The hero's quest on its most profound (or confused) level is best described as a longing to pass beyond the articulation of the sound (and the physical death the sound produces) to some kind of mystical unity with nature. To become "one with the birdless cloudless colourless skies" is to be "engulfed in the light of eternity" and to know "infinite fulfillment." The hero's "struggle for divinity" (p. 269) can best be equated with the desire for this kind of unity. The God/sign beckoning to such fulfillment in *Assumption,* then, is not the Woman, or the utterance of the sound, but nature itself. Upon first experiencing sex with the Woman, the hero mistakenly thinks that union with her is resulting in a mystical merging with nature. The heavy but extremely subtle irony of the hero's notions of union with the Woman in this regard is indicated by the narrator's statement that, "for the first time, he [the hero] was unconditioned by "the Satanic dimensional Trinity" (p. 271). Although Pilling reads this phrase as referring to a "three-dimensional world" that union with the Woman is supposedly liberating the hero from,[12] the phrase seems to refer to the Woman herself, who has "unconditioned" the hero. The exact sense in which this Manichean Woman is "the Satanic dimensional Trinity" is, as I have stated, not clear. Perhaps the reference is to her vital role as an agent in the kingdom of darkness or evil – a kingdom conceived of in the New Testament and in Manichean thought as composed of the world, the flesh, and the devil. At any rate, the voicing of this descriptive term must be assigned to the

---

[12] *Samuel Beckett,* p. 123.

narrator, not the hero. The hero seems to have momentarily forgotten the treacherous emanations of the Woman and, in the ecstasy of sexual feeling, believes himself to have been "released," to have "achieved, the blue flower, Vega, GOD" (p. 271).[13]

We as critics must be careful not to fall prey to the hero's delusions. Careful examination of these terms reveals them to be symbols of false promise that appear to usher the hero (via the sexual act with the Woman) into a mystical unity with nature or God, but which fail to do so. Pilling notes that the "blue flower" is mentioned again in Beckett's review of Rainer Maria Rilke's *Poems,* being taken from the first chapter of *Heinrich von Ofterdingen.*[14] Beckett is writing of self-deception, discontent, and disillusion in regard to Rilke's "blaue Blume."[15] In *Assumption,* Beckett uses the flower as an ironic symbol. Blue, of course, is the color of

---

[13] The ambivalent response of the hero to the Woman, not only at this point but also throughout the story, is typical of the early ambiguity concerning women and sexual love found in Beckett's fiction. This ambiguity is blatant in *More Pricks than Kicks* and *Murphy,* and can be detected at least as late as the writing of *Molloy,* whose hero journeys desperately toward the mother he loathes. Harvey writes of two girls that Beckett "knew and loved in real life" (in Germany, 1928; and in Ireland, 1929), and claims that Beckett "stylized [them] in his writing until they come to represent diametrically opposed possibilities. . . . one is a type of the physical and the other of the intellectual" (*Samuel Beckett: Poet and Critic,* p. 257). Although he acknowledges such psychological influences on Beckett the writer, Harvey defines the sexual conflict in the writings as primarily philosophical: numerous myths (reaching Beckett, according to Harvey, most significantly via Schopenhauer) contain the "universals of man's sexuality and his antisexuality, of action and contemplation, of the macrocosm and the microcosm" (*Samuel Beckett: Poet and Critic,* p. 269-70). The ambiguity in *Assumption* is distinctively sexual. One Catharist idea of the loved woman – which Beckett would have encountered in the poetry of the troubadours – defines heterosexual love as a form of mysticism embracing spiritual fulfillment. Such a loved woman is found in the gnostic myth of Sophia, or woman as *anima* (man's soul) and spiritual guide. This aspect of woman is a transcendence (or denial) of physical sexuality and procreation. (See "The Loved One" and "Sophia" in J. E. Cirlot, *A Dictionary of Symbols,* trans. from the Spanish by Jack Sage, 2nd ed. [1971; rpt. New York: Vail-Ballou Press, 1983], pp. 194 and 300.) The opposite mythical aspect of woman views her as Eve or Helen – an instinctive and emotional being who functions as a siren, lamia, or monstrous creature designed to entice and destroy man by trapping him in the transitory, fleshly world. (See "Woman" in *A Dictionary of Symbols,* pp. 375-76.) This second aspect of woman is, of course, also found in Catharist and Manichean thought. (See Morot-Sir, "Samuel Beckett and Cartesian Emblems," pp. 87-88).

[14] *Samuel Beckett,* note 51, p. 213.

[15] Review of *Poems* by R. M. Rilke, *The Criterion,* 13 (1934), pp. 705-07.

the Virgin Mary and of the sky or heaven where God is. The flower, particularly the rose or the lotus flower, is the symbol of the heart, the irradiating point or hidden center of the ultimate goal of true love – a goal defined in much literary symbolism as the elimination of dualism and separation in a mystical and biological unity. "The 'blue flower' is a legendary symbol of the impossible, and is probably an allusion to the 'mystic Centre' as represented by the Grail and other such symbols."[16] Vega is a reference to the constellation Vega in the Lyre, a constellation also referred to by Beckett in *Embers.*[17] In this drama, the reference occurs in the story of Bolton and Holloway. Bolton is an old man in some kind of great need, and Holloway is the friend (doctor?) who comes in the night to help him. No help is offered or received, and Vega in the Lyre (glimpsed as Bolton opens the door for Holloway) remains an ironic symbol of disharmony and isolation, not only for Bolton and Holloway but also for the father, mother, and daughter of *Embers.* The lyre, traditionally a symbol of the harmonious union of cosmic forces,[18] functions ironically in *Assumption* as a symbol of disharmony, both between individuals (the hero and the Woman) and between the individual and the cosmic system (the hero and nature). Beckett's sexual play on words is certainly comic:

> he was released, achieved, the blue flower, Vega, GOD . . . After a timeless parenthesis he found himself alone in his room, spent with ecstasy, torn by the bitter loathing of that which he had condemned to the humanity of silence. (p. 271)

But the dilemma of the hero – "torn, torn and battered with increasing grievousness" (p. 271) – is comically tragic. Union with the Woman has not resulted in any kind of mystical unity with nature, God, or anything or anyone else.

If the Woman is not the gateway to Nature/God, perhaps death is, but Beckett's ending to the story gives us no clear

---

[16] See "Love" and "Flower" in *A Dictionary of Symbols,* pp. 194 and 109-10.

[17] *Embers;* in *Krapp's Last Tape and Other Dramatic Pieces* (New York: Grove, 1957), p. 99.

[18] *A Dictionary of Symbols,* p. 195.

indication that such might be the case. Pilling remarks that "he [the hero] fuses 'into the breath of the forest and the throbbing cry of the sea,'" gaining the absolute freedom of Murphy's third zone of being.[19] Close examination of Beckett's pronouns, however, reveals that "it" (the sound) is what fuses into unity with nature (p. 271). Pilling correctly emphasizes that Beckett's "final focus" in the story is on the hero's dead body.[20] The question remains open as to exactly what has become of the hero's psyche or spirit. Only if we equate his spirit with the artistic sound, can we say that it continues to exist in unity with the breath of the forest and the cry of the sea. If, like Belacqua and Murphy, he is dead in spirit and body, then only his art (the sound) has survived the death of his body. If this is the case, then the hero's transcendence of death is a clumsy facsimile of that of Yeats as described by Auden in the poem "In Memory of W. B. Yeats." The day of Yeats' death was "his last . . . as himself." Only in the form of his art does he live on in the forests and the river. The reason for Yeats' artistic immortality is that, by his "farming of a verse," he has started a "healing fountain" in the "deserts of the heart" of the English people.[21] Such ideas of artistic immortality are present in Yeats and in Auden, but not in Beckett. We know of no Beckettian reason why even the "sound" of Beckett's hero should have survived his death. Certainly, in Beckett's world, art does not ordinarily cause the artist to survive as a vital and energizing force.

Thus the ending of *Assumption* leaves us with more questions than answers. As exactly as can be determined from an extremely close reading of the account of the hero's sexual experience, articulation of the sound, and death, the element that achieves immortality is the artistic expression or identity that is fused in some abstract way with nature. The fact that such artistic immortality does not occur elsewhere in Beckett's canon does not mean that it does not occur here, especially in such an early story, the writing of which is obviously an attempt on Beckett's part to arrive at literary stances in regard to sexual love, art, and mystical

---

19 *Samuel Beckett,* p. 123.

20 *Samuel Beckett,* p. 123.

21 W. H. Auden, "In Memory of W. B. Yeats," *Selected Poetry of W. H. Auden,* 2nd ed. (New York: Random House, 1970), pp. 52-54.

fulfillment and/or immortality of the human spirit. But, as is nearly always the case in analyzing any part of Beckett's tightly-woven *œuvre,* we gain understanding from a comparison with the heroes of other works. Belacqua's death is as final as Hairy and the Smeraldina would wish it to be (*More Pricks than Kicks,* pp. 189-91). Whatever of Murphy lives on must, of necessity, survive Cooper's scattering of his ashes on the floor of the pub in Dublin. The narrator is lucidly clear at this point concerning any kind of personal immortality for Murphy: "By closing time the body, mind, and soul of Murphy were freely distributed over the floor of the saloon" (*Murphy,* p. 275). The memory of Murphy, however, does survive – as artistically as that of any of Beckett's heroes – in the consciousness of Celia. The unusually devoid-of-irony and poignant description of this heroine's lifting her face to the sky to seek healing for grief from the "soft sunless light" of happy, pre-Murphy days in Ireland lets us know that the weight of her "tired heart" is the loss of Murphy (*Murphy,* pp. 280-82). She has remarked earlier to Murphy's ardent seekers that, "I was a piece out of him that he could not go on without" (*Murphy,* p. 234), and now Murphy has become a part of her. But Celia's memory of Murphy is not, *per se,* the continuation of Murphy himself, artistic or otherwise.

Beginning with *Watt,* we have the classic Beckettian portrayal of the hero's experience of death and "immortality." Watt "dies" as he watches his own approaching figure (in hallucination) grow fainter and fainter and finally disappear (*Watt,* pp. 225-28). But Watt is not "dead"; he appears later (in regard to chronological time although not in regard to plot sequence) in Sam's asylum garden and relates the strange occurrences of his sojourn at Mr. Knott's. In fact, to the best of our knowledge, Watt is yet alive – surviving in the tangled words he leaves with Sam and in the tangled trees and underbrush of his own particular garden where he disappears from view (*Watt,* p. 213). Like the hero of *The End,* who "ends" only to reappear in the opening paragraphs of *The Calmative* (*Stories,* pp. 71-72 and 27), Watt does not escape the burden of continued consciousness. He reappears by name in Beckett's *Mercier and Camier,*[22] and is apparently one of the

[22] *Mercier and Camier* (New York: Grove, 1974), pp. 111-18.

Unnamable's company of "puppets," who wheel about this nameless hero like planets about the sun as he sits "fixed and at the centre" of whatever place it is that he inhabits (*The Unnamable*, pp. 293-95).

Thus the typical experience of death by a hero is seldom a fulfillment of what he paradoxically appears to long for – an absolute ceasing of consciousness. His true or actual longing – to achieve unity with the nothingness or silence of absolute, atemporal being – is likewise ironically denied and parodied as he fails to escape the consciousness of continued literary existence in Beckett's world of frustration and distress. In *Assumption*, however, the hero seems to achieve the condition of his artistic essence being fused with an abstract nothingness of nature: the skies are "birdless, cloudless," even "colourless," and the fusion of the artistic sound is not into the organic life of the forest and the sea but into the "*breath* of the forest and the . . . *cry* of the sea" (my italics, p. 271).

The achievement of such complete abstraction of being into spirit is positive from a Manichean perspective, and should be clearly positive in this Manichean tale of Beckett's. But something in the tone of the conclusion of the story suggests the negative rather than the positive. If the hero's realization of artistic identity has indeed taken place, who is the Other that he is recognized by (certainly it is not the Woman), and what is the haven or home that is a habitation for his spirit? Can a system of nature that is utterly abstract be represented as such a habitation? Somehow we sense, at the story's close, not a healing of the dichotomy between the flesh and the spirit, but instead a colossal and destructive swallowing up of flesh by spirit. The significance of this short early piece is that it raises a problem endemic in Beckett's fictional canon – if man escapes the ravages and limitations of the flesh by absorption into the sterility and nothingness of abstract spirit, how shall he, as a being that is essentially both flesh and spirit, authenticate himself? Perhaps it is because Beckett never finds a solution to this problem that his later heroes wander forever in a no-man's land between the flesh and the spirit. As the voice of text 1 struggles with the dichotomy of body and "head" (or spirit), he laments, "I should turn away from it all, away from the body, away from the head, let them work it out between them, let them cease, I can't, it's I would have to cease" (*Stories and Texts for Nothing*, p. 75).

MORE PRICKS THAN KICKS

An apparently fixed dichotomy between the flesh and the spirit is also a problem for Beckett's first named fictional hero, who undertakes a quest both similar to and different from that of the nameless hero of *Assumption.* Certain characteristics of *More Pricks than Kicks* render problematical the assertion that this episodic novel is structured on the pattern of a serious quest of any kind. Beckett distances both himself as author and us as readers from the aspirations of the hero of this work – the unfortunate Belacqua Shauh.[23] The sardonic humor, the brittle tone of the prose, the enigma of Belacqua's personality, and the loose connections between the episodes that form whatever "plot" is present in the work cause us almost to agree with Hugh Kenner that "None of this [the novel as a whole] needs to be revived, though it is enlightening to know it exists."[24]

The fiction is a treatment of the hero as lover and as artist, and the quest can be defined as an account of his pilgrimage to realize himself in both these roles. Like the nameless hero of *Assumption,* Belacqua is a self-as-character who searches in the macrocosm – on level one of the quest pattern – for the fulfillment of his existential needs. As lover, this hero is a maladjusted male who is not at all certain just what he desires from the female objects of his affection. As artist, he is a student-poet, who studies Dante's *Divine Comedy* and offers as a gift to his best man "the original manuscript" of his *Hypothalamion,* "corrected, autographed, dated, inscribed and half-bound in time-coloured skivers."[25] *More Pricks than Kicks* is ob-

---

[23] Ruby Cohn remarks that the style of *More Pricks than Kicks* is polished "to a glossy veneer that effectively separates the reader from any sympathy with what lies behind it." See "Preliminary Observations," *Perspective,* 11 (1959), p. 121.

[24] *A Critical Study,* p. 41.

[25] *More Pricks than Kicks* (New York: Grove, 1972), pp. 9 and 123-24. Other references to *More Pricks than Kicks* are also to this edition and are cited by page number(s) in the text of this chapter. The first publication of this episodic novel was in 1934 by Chatto and Windus, London.

viously a satire on literature, and the characterization of Belacqua is a satire on the poet. Nonetheless, this hero's artistic aspirations are to be taken quite seriously: they merge with his confused efforts to function as a lover into an obsession with relationships with women that reveals the complex of ideas Belacqua holds on art and love. As we have understood from analyzing the quest pattern in *Assumption,* Beckett's early hero feels that sexual unity with a woman is the gateway into a physical/mystical experience that will authenticate his identity or selfhood and will simultaneously function as a catalyst in subsuming an ordinary level of consciousness into artistic madness or divine exaltation of being.[26]

In *Assumption,* also, as we have seen, sexual love is portrayed with profound ambivalence. The Woman who visits the unnamed hero is not only Sophia or the spiritual ideal of Woman but also Helen or Eve, the fleshly temptress/destroyer who finally "overlays" him with death. In *More Pricks than Kicks,* this latter aspect of the woman loved is weakened into a portrayal of a love partner who is simply too fleshly or artistically insensitive to serve as a catalyst into the kind of spiritual union that Belacqua wants sexual experience with a woman to be. If Belacqua's women share the Manichean traits of the Woman of *Assumption,* these traits are so overpowered as to be submerged by the brittle silliness of their alliances with Belacqua. Belacqua views them, not as evil or dangerous, but as disappointing because they cannot lead him into the sexual/artistic/mystical experience he is seeking.

The exact connections or sequence of the various elements or stages of such an experience is never made clear, either in *More Pricks than Kicks* or in the preceding fiction.[27] Is sexual consummation the means of artistic inspiration, heightened to a state of ecstasy? If so, what does the artistic ecstasy have to do with

[26] For a detailed exploration of Belacqua's attitudes toward women and his responses to them in this regard, see Jerri L. Kroll's excellent study "Belacqua as Artist and Lover: 'What a Misfortune,'" pp. 10-39. I am indebted to this article for insight into Belacqua's relationships with and ideas about women in *More Pricks than Kicks.*

[27] Between the publishing of *Assumption,* in 1929 and that of *More Pricks than Kicks* in 1934, Beckett worked on his first novel – the unfinished *Dream of Fair to Middling Women,* which still remains unpublished in its entirety. Belacqua is also the hero of *Dream,* and his escapades and attitudes are quite similar to those in *More Pricks than Kicks.*

mystical fulfillment or a sensing of the divine? Belacqua certainly does not know, and, if Beckett had clear ideas as to the answers to these questions as he wrote this early fiction, he does not communicate them to his readers. What is clear is that the quest on the first level, as we are examining it in *More Pricks than Kicks,* is capsulated in Belacqua's affinity for pseudo-sexual encounters with women that seem to offer him some promise of artistic and mystical fulfillment. The five needs that the hero, as character in the macrocosm, quests to fill or to have filled are expressed in the varied aspects of Belacqua's sexual/artistic/mystical desires related to women. In order to explore these needs, we must first examine the hero's sexuality, physically and psychologically.

Belacqua's name signals the fact that he is a composite of certain sexual aberrations and inadequacies. He is named Belacqua after Dante's Florentine, who is found in the fourth canto of the *Purgatorio.* Dante's Belacqua is the legendary procrastinator. On earth, he postpones repentance until just before his death; in the afterlife, he waits (by divine fiat) in Antepurgatory for a time equal to his earthly existence before being allowed to enter Purgatory proper and begin the long climb up the mountain to atone for his sins. The narrator of *More Pricks than Kicks* describes Beckett's Belacqua as "sinfully indolent, bogged in indolence" (p. 36), and subsequent references to his name in Beckett's later fiction – *Murphy, Molloy,* and *How It Is* – imply a passive indifference to and a loathing for positive actions of various kinds. Here, however, in addition to this general meaning, the name also suggests a hesitancy to engage in normal sexual relations. Belacqua's girlfriends and wives arouse him sexually, but his approach-avoidance responses lead, more often than not, to fantasizing (in "A Wet Night"), escape into drink ("Fingal"), voyeurism ("Walking Out"), or temporary impotence ("What a Misfortune"). We understand what the narrator means by "bogged in indolence" when we learn that Belacqua's wife Thelma (who "perished of sunset and honeymoon," p. 175) has the surname of bboggs.

Belacqua's surname is Shuah, a name which, as John Fletcher points out, probably refers to the maternal grandfather of the Onan of Genesis, chapter 38, who spills his semen on the ground rather than give children to his brother's wife.[28] Jerri L. Kroll notes that, in Beckett's "Sedendo et quiesciende" (*transition*, No. 21, March, 1932, p. 65), Belacqua's affinity for voyeurism is referred to as the "livid rapture of the Zurbarán Saint-Onan." She explains that Zurbarán was a Spanish baroque artist of the seventeenth century who is remembered for his depictions of mystical figures (saints or monks) in contemplation.[29] In "Walking Out," Belacqua stops in the woods to contemplate the sexual performance of Harold Tanzherr and the pretty German girl rather than keeping his tryst with Lucy, his intended bride. The terrible accident that befalls Lucy, in the meantime, cripples her for life (pp. 110-12) and makes marriage with her, for Belacqua, so comfortable that she is the girl he most looks forward to seeing in the afterlife (p. 181). Belacqua's auto-eroticism, manifesting itself as a confused sublimation in both the artistic and mystical areas of his life, does not rule out but blends with a persistent effort to become intimately involved with various women.

Our purpose of describing the quest as five existential needs to be filled can best be pursued by observing this hero's motivations for, and attempts to achieve, such relationships. To establish an identity of the self, Belacqua must function as lover and undergo the experience of self-recognition as a poet. Six of the ten episodes recounted relate his efforts to achieve intimacy with some woman, either Winnie, the Alba, Ruby, Lucy, Thelma, or the Smeraldina. Only once (with Ruby and full of whiskey) does Belacqua actually engage in sexual intercourse, but the narrator tells us, at the close of this episode (or escapade), "that at least on this occasion, if never before nor since, he [Belacqua] achieved what he set out to do" (p. 100).

As is common for a young man, Belacqua is seeking to identify and define himself sexually, but, like Joyce's "Young Man," he cannot do so on a merely sexual level. Belacqua is a poet. He studies poetry (p. 9), writes poetry (p. 124), and wants to be recognized by the women he pursues as a poet (pp. 119-20). His poetic ideal of love includes not only physical satisfaction but also

---

[28] *The Novels of Samuel Beckett*, p. 16.

[29] "Belacqua as Artist and Lover," p. 24.

certain notions of artistic and mystical communion. The manifesto "Poetry is Vertical," which Beckett helped to formulate, speaks of "ecstatic revelation" and a "stupor which proceeds from the irrational to a world beyond a world."[30] The self-identity that Belacqua is seeking is not so much the status of success as an artist but the experience of self-recognition as a poet. He wants his women not only to relate to him physically but also to authenticate his artistic self-awareness. Belacqua wants Winnie to enter into his mystical, poetic vision of the landscape of Fingal as a "magic land," a "land of sanctuary," but she proves to be insensitive to his mystical awareness (pp. 24-25). As the bridegroom of Thelma, he proposes to kneel in meditation in the Church of Saint Nicolas as they begin their honeymoon. Thelma, much to Belacqua's secret dismay, is interested – not surprisingly – in a "prospect" of the honeymoon much more "happy" (and carnal) than this plan (p. 125). The narrator is mocking both bridegroom and bride, but Belacqua's aspirations are both comic – he is avoiding sex with his new wife – and serious. His notion of physical intimacy includes some kind of metaphysical bonding between partners.

The "other" that I have defined as one object of the quest in the macrocosm is, then, for Belacqua, whatever woman seems to offer a chance for him to achieve identity of the self as lover and as artist. If we replace the word "other" with "community," the latter can be defined as those who see the world of sexual experience and communion with Belacqua's artistic vision. Belacqua would conceive of this community as consisting minimally of himself and the woman of his choice, whoever she might be at the moment. The narrator informs us, after Belacqua's demise, that he "had often looked forward to meeting" the women he had been involved with, as a group, in a life beyond death. Significantly, he had conceived of this group as "hallowed and transfigured beyond the veil." Ironically enough, death cures "him of that naiveté" (p. 181).

The hero's existential need to resolve the dichotomy between the flesh and the spirit, which is developed throughout the fiction,

[30] "Poetry is Vertical" was published in 1932. Beckett's signature appears with those of eight others.

appears in embryonic form in this early work. The prime reason (from a philosophical point of view, if not from a psychological) that Belacqua cannot manage mature sexual performance is because his obsession with spiritual unity handicaps him in his efforts at physical comsummation. Only when the whiskey deadens his mind or spirit sufficiently do the circumstances of privacy and the exposure of Ruby in her knickers bring about "the inevitable nuptial" (pp. 95-96, 99).

Kroll says that Belacqua seems to believe that intimacy with a woman "can somehow lead to a reunification of man with his essential nature or source." She also points out, however, that because Belacqua senses man's physical and spiritual natures to "exist in a continuum," each balanced against the other, he sees one nature fulfilling itself only by depleting the other.[31] This understanding leads to a new perspective on Belacqua's approach-avoidance tactics in regard to sex: sexual union would supposedly reunify his dual natures, but it would also deplete his artistic/spiritual self by fulfilling his physical desires. On the occasion of taking Winnie to Fingal, Belacqua is particularly aware of a weariness of the body and spirit. Winnie accuses him of being "sad and serious" (p. 24), and the narrator dubs him "a very sad animal indeed" (p. 23). Although Belacqua scoffs at "the idea of a sequitur from his body to his mind," he is attempting to use the "nature outside" to compensate for disquiet and disharmony in the "nature inside" (p. 29). Certainly Belacqua is approaching the "pretty, hot and witty" Winnie as solace for his jaded dual self, but he finally flees on a bicycle in order to avoid further intimacy with her. The thought of uniting his body with the body of a woman as insensitive as Winnie appears to be to the spiritual aspects of nature and life frightens Belacqua. Rather than a union of physical and spiritual fulfillment, sex with Winnie might prove to be a desensitization of Belacqua, both artistically and spriritually. She is not moved, as Belacqua is, by the beauty of the Fingal landscape, nor does she share his obsessions with conditions of consciousness such as insanity and the pre-natal state. Belacqua is interested in a resolving of flesh-spirit disharmony in his relationship with

[31] "Belacqua as Artist and Lover," pp. 22 and 15.

Winnie – as Kroll comments, "Belacqua feels he needs Woman to heal a division in himself,"[32] – but balks at the possibility of a physical union with her draining him spiritually.

The two remaining needs of this hero's quest – to find a true home and to gain a harmony with nature – coalesce into one. Belacqua's longings for a true home or haven for the spirit crystallize into efforts to escape his unhappy existence by retreating into the world of the insane, returning to a state comparable to the pre-natal condition, or experiencing death by committing suicide. Each of these three efforts takes place in a natural setting (the Dublin countryside), each time the natural setting is associated with the particular method of escape Belacqua is contemplating, and each time he fails to gain any kind of harmony with the setting involved. Thus we can say that Belacqua seeks his true home or place of belonging, not only through a relationship with some woman, but also through efforts to gain mystical entrance into states epitomized by various natural landscapes that serve as settings for his romantic exploits.

The landscape of Fingal, where Belacqua takes Winnie, seems to have a particular significance to this hero:

> "I often come to this hill" he said "to have a view of Fingal, and each time I see it more as a back-land, a land of sanctuary, a land that you don't have to dress up to, that you can walk on in a lounge suit, smoking a cigar." (p. 25)

His reason for being fascinated with this setting (and for his avowal to Winnie that this is where his heart is, p. 26) is made clear when we learn that the area of Fingal surrounds the Portrane Lunatic Asylum. Belacqua desires to escape into the undemanding bliss of the world of the insane. But his longing is also directed toward Winnie, the woman, and he tries to merge both desires by drawing Winnie into his longing for the state of insanity. He does so by attempting to communicate to her his fascination with the landscape, explaining to her that it is a "land for the sad and serious," a "magic land." Winnie refuses to respond, replies that

---

[32] Kroll, "The Artist's Mind in Samuel Beckett's Fiction," *Journal of the Australasian Language and Literature Association,* No. 55 (May 1981), p. 45.

she can "see nothing but three acres and cows," and crushes Belacqua with her remark that the view is "flat and dull." Belacqua despairs of reaching Winnie, concludes that she is a "clod," and decides that he will "drop the subject," that he will "not try to communicate Fingal" (pp. 24-26). Betrayed by his "magic land," unsuccessful in being admitted to the world of blissful insanity, and disappointed by Winnie, Belacqua resigns himself to the solace of "Taylor's public house in Swords, drinking in a way that Mr. Taylor did not like" (p. 35).

It is also to Winnie that Belacqua remarks that he would like "very much to be back in the caul, on my back in the dark for ever" (p. 29). But it is in another episode that Beckett develops this motif of Belacqua's longing for regression, for a return to a condition characteristic of the pre-natal state. The landscape around Leopardstown suggests such a regression, backward in time towards birth and before. The time of this particular episode is spring, and suggestions of birth are everywhere:

> These latter [legions of sheep and lambs] were springing into the world every minute, the grass was spangled with scarlet afterbirths, the larks were singing, the hedges were breaking, the sun was shining, the sky was Mary's cloak, the daisies were there, everything was in order. (p. 101)

A plantation of larches on the hillside is "Poignant and assuasive at once," carrying Belacqua back to the time when he had "climbed them as a little fat boy" (p. 102). And the "sun beamed down on this as though it were a new-born lamb" (p. 103).

The woman who might possibly serve as a catalyst between Belacqua and this landscape and the consciousness or state it epitomizes is Lucy, the Irish girl to whom Belacqua is currently engaged to be married. Lucy rides her black jennet out into this landscape suggestive of sexual love and birth in search of her betrothed. When she finds him, however, her anticipation of conjugal bliss is changed to disgust and horror. Belacqua does not desire Lucy's company just now; in fact, he has slipped away from her to engage in what he terms "sursum corda" or "private experiences," his own private brand of voyeurism. Lucy suddenly realizes the real reason for Belacqua's "baby talk . . . of her living with him like a music while being the wife in body of another" (pp. 107, 109). At this propitious moment, a car runs Lucy down, killing the jennet and leaving her "crippled for life and her beauty dreadfully marred" (p. 110). Belacqua later marries her anyway, secretly delighted with the perfect situation in which to continue his infantile sexual habits. Any peacefulness of regression suggested by the landscape, however, is ironic. The lover of the "pretty little German girl" that Belacqua spies upon spies Belacqua and beats him until he is "half insensible" and hardly able to crawl home. The narrator comments, "So much for his youth and vigour" (p. 113). Belacqua's desire for regression back towards the limbo of the pre-natal state, evidenced in this episode by his infantile sexuality, is unfulfilled. He remains in painful alienation from the woman, from the state he desires as bliss, and from the landscape. As Raymond Federman remarks, "Belacqua leads a schizophrenic existence which denies both physical and mental escape."[33]

In the chapter containing this episode, the narrator mentions three times (pp. 101, 107-108, and 111) the absence of the proverbial bird of spring and love, the cuckoo. After Lucy is maimed, but before Belacqua is aware of her accident, he hears another bird, the corncrake or quail, whose call ("crex-crex, crex-crex") he finds offensive because he has been longing to hear the cuckoo's call "with its promise of happiness," and he is offered instead the corncrake's, which seems to him a "death-rattle" (p. 111). Beckett's French character Molloy also hears the corncrakes' cries (Molloy, p. 17), and Dieter Wellershoff notes of this incident that Molloy's designation of these cries as "awful" is an allusion to the horror (for Beckett's heroes) of birth. Zeus, after transforming Leto and himself into quails, mates with her and begets Artemis, the goddess of birth, whose sacred bird is the quail.[34] In assigning such meaning to this allusion, Wellershoff is merging the early Greek Artemis (or Diana), the virgin goddess of

---

[33] Federman, "Beckett's Belacqua and the Inferno of Society," *Arizona Quarterly*, 20 (1964), p. 240.

[34] Wellershoff, "Failure of an Attempt at De-Mythologization: Samuel Beckett's Novels," in *Samuel Beckett: A Collection of Critical Essays*, p. 96; trans. from the German by Martin Esslin and rpt. from *Der Gleichgultige, Versuche uber Hemingway, Camus, Benn, and Beckett* (Cologne: Kiepenheuer & Witsch, 1963).

the moon, who is also the huntress of the mountains, with the Ephesian Artemis, who, with her clusters of breasts, is worshipped as a fertility goddess and thus as the goddess of birth. Of further significance is the fact that the Greek Artemis is also sometimes identified as a deity of the underworld such as Hecate or Persephone.[35] Thus the quail represents a mythological blending of birth and death and symbolizes for Belacqua a birth which is essentially a death. His concern with birth is different from the traditional association suggested by the spring countryside and the cuckoo. For him it is not birth into life, but a birth into death, a state described in *Dream of Fair to Middling Women* as "the shades of the dead and the deadborn and the unborn and the never-to-be-born, in a Limbo purged of desire."[36]

Belacqua's final attempt toward escape, this one also mixed with sexual love and a natural landscape, begins as a planned attempt at suicide. The co-conspirator in this project is Ruby Tough, a woman who in her prime (she is now "in the thirty-third or-fourth year of her age," p. 87) has been bypassed by love because she demands of such a relationship a solidarity ("that it should unite or fix her as firmly and as finally as the sun of a binary in respect of its partner," pp. 87-88) that her erstwhile suitors are uninterested in. Years of "erotic frustration" have produced in her a willingness to settle for almost any kind of man-woman relationship, even one as bizarre as Belacqua's notion of becoming united in death. Belacqua, of course, is exploring his third possibility of escape into the peacefulness of an alternate world as haven or home. That he thinks of death as a state other than one of annihilation is apparent from the narrator's remark that Belacqua "had often looked forward to meeting the girls" (who had preceded him in dying) after his death (p. 181).

Although this hero has made elaborate preparations for his dramatic departure from this world ("The revolver and balls, the veronal, the bottle and glasses, *and* the notice"), fate, or some such

[35] Michael Grant, *Myths of the Greeks and Romans* (World, n. d.; rpt. New York: New American Library, 1962), pp. 125; 225. The Ephesian Diana associated with fertility is mentioned in connection with St. Paul's preaching in Acts 19: pp. 23-41.

[36] Quoted by Harvey in *Samuel Beckett: Poet and Critic*, pp. 38-39. Harvey does not use this quotation from *Dream* in connection with *More Pricks than Kicks*.

power (Belacqua thinks that it may be the "finger of God") intervenes, and the suicide never comes off. Instead, Ruby's discarding of her skirt so as better to cross the fence, the romantic setting of the woods, and the contents of the bottle combine in bringing about the "inevitable nuptial" rather than death (pp. 93; 99).

The incident is grotesquely amusing, and most on display is Belacqua's consistent indolence, his inability to take decisive steps as planned. There are, however, undertones of Beckett's metaphysical anguish present in the tale. Belacqua's act of love is not a successful step into a secure haven; rather it is a mockery of the idea of love as a haven. In all of his work Beckett defines the tenuous strands which bind any two persons together in "love" as those of a common suffering and a shared despair. Other than this joint misery, only a selfish desire to use another person to alleviate one's own pain binds any person to another.[37] Vladimir and Estragon *(Waiting for Godot)* and Mercier and Camier *(Mercier and Camier)* are examples of couples joined in despair. Pozzo and Lucky *(Waiting for Godot)* and Hamm and Clov *(Endgame)* are couples of which it may be said that one or each of a pair uses the other for selfish purposes. In the later works (for instance, *How It Is*), such ties are further developed as outright sadism or masochism.

The narrator closes the tale of Belacqua and Ruby's romance with a quotation from Ronsard's Poem LXXVII of *Le Second livre des sonnets pour Hélène:*[38]

> *car . . . l'Amour et la Mort* – caesura – *n'est qu'une mesme chose.* (p. 100)

Beckett is satirizing the Renaissance concept of sexual love being a kind of exalted death. In his world, love is the same as death because all life is a dying, and man's idea of love an impossible dream.

---

[37] The only possible exception to this statement is Celia and Murphy in *Murphy.* Celia's love for Murphy seems particularly un-Beckettian, and his for her somewhat so.

[38] See Harvey's *Samuel Beckett: Poet and Critic,* p. 285.

Belacqua's failure to enter an alternate world as a haven (whether that world is conceived of as death or love) is symbolized here ironically by a description of the landscape. Belacqua and Ruby pause to admire the view. From the top of the hill they see

> The long arms of the harbour like an entreaty in the blue sea. Young priests were singing in a wood on the hillside. They heard them and they saw the smoke of their fire. To the west in the valley a plantation of larches nearly brought tears to the eyes of Belacqua. . . . (p. 95)

Larches are mentioned two other times (pp. 29; 183) in *More Pricks than Kicks,* and each of these times they are associated with Belacqua's childhood – a step backward in regression, a time of freedom from involvement in the demands of life. Of more significance in this passage is the mention of the "entreaty in the blue sea." David Hesla notes Beckett's use of the sea to suggest "the eternity from which he [man] has come and to which he will soon return." This critic describes Malone's fictional ego, Macmann, floating out to sea with the inmates of St. John of God's asylum just before Malone dies (*Malone Dies,* p. 287), and Molloy's mention of once having put out to sea and his uncertainty as to whether he ever returned (*Molloy,* p. 69).[39] The most definitive use of the sea as such a symbol occurs in *Stories.* In this collection, the narrator-protagonist both avoids and is drawn toward the sea, exhibiting man's fear of death and the Beckett hero's fascination with the uncertain hope that death may offer the haven for which he longs. In the last of these *Stories, The End,* the protagonist dies by drifting out to sea (*Stories and Texts for Nothing,* p. 72).

The setting of Belacqua's suicide attempt defines it as a sort of death-seeking ritual or ceremony. The "entreaty" of the sea, the singing of the priests, and the "smoke of their fire" suggest the mystical state which Belacqua associates with death. His failure to realize what the scene appears to promise is intensified by his later realization (related to us by the omniscient narrator, who apparently sees beyond death) when he finally does die that death is simply annihilation, a total negation of being. Thus the needs to find a

---

[39] *The Shape of Chaos,* p. 71.

true home or haven for the spirit and to gain a harmony with nature as epitomized by various landscapes are not fulfilled by Belacqua as a questing hero. Even as Beckett affords him the release of actual death, he remains in disillusionment and continual need.

Where, precisely, does God appear in this narrative structure of Belacqua seeking mystical and artistic fulfillment in pseudosexual relationships? What is the God/sign or word/promise that appears to offer fulfillment but becomes, instead, a sign or word of false promise? Kroll points out that the Belacqua of *Dream of Fair to Middling Women* claims that "'the true Shekinah . . . is Woman.'"[40] Although the word "Shekinah" does not occur in the Bible, it is used by Jews and Christians to describe the visible presence of Jehovah as a cloud, or light, or other manifestation of divine glory.[41] In *More Pricks than Kicks,* Belacqua's idea of Woman as offering passage into mystical/artistic fulfillment and ecstasy transforms her into a Shekinah/sign of false promise. The narrator informs us that Belacqua senses in his bride Thelma a Shekinah-like quality:

> Without going so far as to say that Belacqua felt God or Thelma the sum of the Apostolic series, still there was in some indeterminate way communicated to the solemnization a kind or sort of mystical radiance. . . . (p. 139)

The narrator is mocking his hero – the "mystical radiance" is "that [which] Joseph Smith would have found touching" (p. 139) – but nonetheless describing the actual sensitivity of Belacqua in regard to Thelma.

The most explicit appearance of a woman as the God/sign or false word/promise in *More Pricks than Kicks* is that of the "suffragette or welfare worker" of the "remarkable presence" and the countenance "full of light." As Belacqua sits slaking his thirst in a pub and waiting "for a sign" (p. 43), this "mysterious pedlar" of "seats in heaven" at "tuppence apiece, four fer a tanner" appears,

---

40 "Belacqua as Artist and Lover," p. 21.

41 See "Shekinah" in the *Zondervan Pictorial Bible Dictionary,* ed. Merrill C. Tenney (Grand Rapids: Zondervan, 1964), p. 782.

"luminous, impassive and secure" to offer him her wares. Again, Beckett's language suggests mockery and ironic humor; the woman certainly does not have the seats "on her" (p. 45). But the description of the woman offering Belacqua access into heaven becomes a symbol of Woman as the gate-way to God as she appears throughout the various episodes of *More Pricks than Kicks.* The sufferance woman is no Beatrice, for Belacqua's sixpence purchase nothing more than a benediction: "'Jesus' she said distinctly 'and his sweet mother preserve yer honour'" (p. 46). Although Beckett overlays this incident as heavily as possible with mockery and irony, so as to distance himself, the narrator, and us from any serious understanding of the event, certain profound undertones remain. From the perspective of our insight into Belacqua's notions regarding art, love (or sex), and mystical yearning, the welfare worker becomes an abortive epiphany of divine invitation.

The chapter "Ding-Dong," which tells of this "Shekinah" woman, is one of two (other than "Yellow" and "Draff," which relates Belacqua's death and burial, respectively) in the entire collection of episodes that does not deal with the hero seeking some sort of intimate relationship with a woman. The other chapter is "Dante and the Lobster," the opening story in *More Pricks than Kicks,* which, as Fletcher observes, gives "the earliest clear revelation of Beckett's talents as a writer."[42] The three women who figure prominently in this episode are not involved sexually with Belacqua: Dante's Beatrice is the guide and teacher whom Belacqua reads about in his Italian lesson, Signorina Adriana Ottolenghi is his Italian teacher (or teacher of Italian), and Belacqua's aunt is his cook and, inadvertently, his teacher also. These women do, however, serve as guides who, in a completely ironic sense, bring Belacqua nearer to God. Belacqua's approach toward God in this episode is a quest to gain some kind of understanding of the meaning of suffering, both human and creaturely, as apparently divinely instigated and sustained. Thus the story can serve as a quintessential vignette of nearly all of

---

[42] Fletcher, "Beckett's Debt to Dante," *Nottingham French Studies,* 4 (1965), note 9, p. 46.

Beckett's stories, stories which exhibit in some manner, explicitly or implicitly, a questioning of and rage against the pain and suffering of human experience and observation.

Although "Dante and the Lobster" is ostensibly merely an account of a typical day in the life of the student/poet Belacqua, it is also a collection of persons and creatures who suffer. Belacqua suffers with his feet: "Belacqua had a spavined gait, his feet were in ruins, he suffered with them almost continuously. Even in the night they took no rest, or next to none" (p. 15). McCabe, the assassin, waits in his cell, knowing he is to be hanged at dawn (p. 17). A "poorly dressed couple" stand gazing through a "pretentious gateway" of persons more wealthy than they, apparently suffering the deprivation of essential comforts of life (pp. 20-21).[43] A horse is "down" in the street, with a man sitting on its head, an action "considered the right thing to do" (p. 20). And the lobster Belacqua buys at lunch as dinner for himself and his aunt is nearly eaten by the French teacher's cat (p. 20) and finally boiled alive by Belacqua and his aunt. (p. 22).

The sufferer in "Dante and the Lobster" who is symbolic of all other endurers of pain, within the boundaries of Beckett's *More Pricks than Kicks,* Dante's *Divine Comedy,* and God's universe, is the Man in the Moon, fabled in Dante's Italy and alluded to by Beckett in "Dante and the Lobster" as Cain with his Bush of Thorns. The fable describes the dark spots on the moon's surface as shadow figurings of the wandering and exiled Cain. Belacqua is "stuck" in Canto II of *The Paradiso,* Beatrice's "scientific" explanation to Dante of the marking of the moon, a passage Belacqua finds to be "impenetrable" (p. 9). In this passage, Beatrice corrects Dante in his attribution of the dark traces on the moon's surface to differences in the density of the lunar matter which cause the moon to reflect light unequally. Beatrice's explanation is as difficult

[43] Beckett's inclusion of this couple in "Dante and the Lobster" is so overtly deliberate that it seems artistically flawed. His fiction, poetry, and drama, however, abound in such inclusions of irrelevant anguished figures. We are reminded of his comments in the Driver interview (p. 24) regarding the three signs for help posted in the taxi in London: "one asked for help for the blind, another help for orphans, and the third for relief for the war refugees." Beckett explains, "One does not have to look for distress. It is screaming at you even in the taxis of London."

for the modern reader as it is for Belacqua. The essence of her reasoning is that the flawed appearance of the moon's surface is the result of a special, mystical power of the Primum Mobile exerted on the moon.[44]

Belacqua (and Beckett) is not actually concerned with a scientific understanding of spots on the moon; he is concerned with understanding Cain and all subsequent sufferers, medievel or modern, on the earth:

> The spots were Cain with his truss of thorns, dispossessed, cursed from the earth, fugitive and vagabond. The moon was that countenance fallen and branded, seared with the first stigma of God's pity, that an outcast might not die quickly. (p. 12)

Ruby Cohn tells us that the paragraph from *More Pricks than Kicks* from which this quotation is taken is the only unrevised paragraph in the manuscript of "Dante and the Lobster." She notes the "tonal shift" from the mockingly comic account of Belacqua cooking the toast for his sandwich to the sensitive empathy of the allusion to Cain.[45] Just as Dante and Belacqua have difficulty understanding how and why the Primum Mobile causes flaws on the moon's surface, Beckett and Belacqua have trouble with Dante's Christian God, who is limited to "rare movements of compassion in Hell" (p. 19). Belacqua meditates on Cain and McCabe: "Why not piety and pity both, even down below? Why not mercy and Godliness together?" (p. 21).

Belacqua conceives of Woman as Shekinah promising some kind of knowledge of God, but none of the three women in "Dante and the Lobster" are able to fulfill such a promise by elucidating on suffering and Dante's God. Beatrice's explanations of "Cain" in the moon are obtuse in the extreme, and the teacher Ottolenghi can only promise her pupil Belacqua to look up the perplexing passage (which she describes as a "famous teaser") in

---

[44] See pp. 34-44 of John Ciardi's translated-into-English verse rendering of *The Paradiso* (New York: New American Library, 1970).

[45] Cohn, *The Comic Gamut* (New Brunswich, N. J.: Rutgers Univ. Press, 1962), p. 32.

her "big Dante" when she gets home (pp. 18-19). The aunt, who knows nothing of Dante and who is accustomed to boiling lobsters alive, serves as Belacqua's Beatrice, but offers only an object lesson that sharpens the questions at hand without supplying any answers. Together, Belacqua and his aunt descend into the kitchen in the basement, a descent the narrator describes as a going down "into the bowels of the earth." As Belacqua realizes that the lobster is still alive (and has been throughout the day, as it is carried about in the paper sack), he is moved to oaths:

> 'Christ!' he said 'it's alive.'
> 'My God' he whined 'it's alive, what'll we do?' (p. 21)

The lobster forms an "exposed cruciform on the oilcloth" during the last thirty seconds of its life. Belacqua, observing the crucifixion, thinks, "it's a quick death, God help us all." But the narrator reminds us – "It is not" (p. 22). Belacqua is questing for some understanding of why lobsters must be boiled alive, and Beckett is mocking and accusing Dante's God for arranging a world where such necessities exist. Beckett's method of mockery and accusation in *More Pricks than Kicks* is to create a hero who responds to Woman as Shekinah/sign only to experience disillusionment and bewilderment, and finally to suffer an ignominious death as he is "executed" like the assassin McCabe and the crucified lobster/Christ.

Thus Belacqua as hero charts a macrocosmic quest pattern that reappears over and over in Beckett's fiction, although only in Belacqua's quest does Woman appear (falsely) as the gateway to mystical experience and divine knowledge. To turn our attention from the quest pattern to the matter of Belacqua's religious consciousness is to confront the difficulty of assigning to this hero any serious awareness of divinity. Such direct awareness is limited to using the words "God" and "Christ" as curses (p. 21), impersonally pitying the suffering of all "the undead" (pp. 114-15), and waiting illogically for some unusual "sign" from another world (p. 43). Indirectly, Belacqua turns toward Woman as toward God and perceives of himself as worthy or blessed when some woman is unexpectedly gracious to him. He thinks that Winnie is going to get up and leave him when she notices the impetigo rash on his face. Her unexpected response – "Don't pick it darling . . . you'll make it worse" – comes to Belacqua "like a drink of water to drink in a dungeon" (p. 25). When Belacqua arrives disheveled and wet to the bone at the Frica's party, and the stunning Alba summons him to her, asking the admirers around her to make a place for him, Belacqua stumbles toward her call, finding it "like a pint of Perrier to drink in a dungeon" (p. 78). In the hospital, Belacqua is not concerned with having courage in the face of the operation. He is concerned that the people about him at the moment – the large majority of whom are women – perceive him as being courageous (pp. 160-61). Such dependence on the perception of others is adolescent male insecurity rather than Beckett's "to be is to be perceived by some other" consciousness developed in the later heroes. Nonetheless, Belacqua exhibits certain early traces of such a consciousness.

Point two of the paradigm of the hero's religious consciousness – a sensing of human affairs being determined by some power or force other than man or chance – can be discerned beneath the surface of certain random remarks Belacqua makes. Planning the events of his day, he is uncertain what will occur after the Italian lesson, but speculates that someone may have determined a schedule (p. 10). Lobsters are always boiled alive because (by God's decree?) they "must be" (p. 22), and the "finger of God" fires the bullet intended for him and/or Ruby harmlessly into the air (p. 99). Heavy irony is apparent in all such remarks, but particularly in the description of the little girl run down by the bus as she hastens toward her home carrying milk and bread. The child is killed, the milk is all over the road, and the loaf of bread, "which had sustained no injury, was sitting up against the kerb, for all the world as though a pair of hands had taken it up and set it down there" (p. 40).

All of Beckett's fictional heroes suffer from some sense of inexplicable guilt, and Belacqua is no exception. His guilt reveals itself in the condition of having the "fidgets": Belacqua "was pleased to think that he could give what he called the Furies the slip by merely setting himself in motion." Given to introspective brooding when motionless for very long, he believes "that the best thing he had to do was to move constantly from place to place" (p. 36). Lucy weights him with guilt in regard to his wandering, especially when she realizes that his walking in the woods is in hopes of undergoing one of his "private experiences" (p. 107). In his review of Rainer Maria Rilke's *Poems,* Beckett criticizes the German poet for having the "fidgets," for exhibiting changes of mood in his poetry and attributing these changes to "God, Ego, Orpheus, and the rest."[46] Beckett has his narrator criticize the restless Belacqua (p. 38), but the narrator himself seems as fidgety as Belacqua. He moves capriciously from episode to episode, never quite settling the hero satisfactorily into the novel until he is lowered into his grave, which has been lovingly upholstered with moss and ferns by Belacqua's present wife and his best friend (p. 182). Even then, the landscape about Belacqua is fidgeting – the moon is "on the job," the sea tosses and pants in her dreams, and the hills observe "their Attic vigil" (pp. 190-91). Only Belacqua is at rest and finally quieted, having been awarded the release later Beckett heroes long for but never (except for Murphy) attain – the ceasing of consciousness in death.

Nathan A. Scott writes of Belacqua's fidgets, claiming that this hero's restless wandering and "'waiting' is not an affair of expectancy and anticipation, but only of sheer nullity and unrelieved abeyance." Beckett's hero, unlike Dante's Belacqua, is not longing "for the time when the Gates shall be opened and the Secret unveiled."[47] Certainly Belacqua Shuah is a parody of Dante's Florentine, expecting no act of grace that will open some gate leading to ascent up the mountain of God. Nonetheless, he can be ironically defined as a quester for grace, for some understanding and quietude in the face of a bewildering and suffering world.

---

[46] Review of *Poems* by R. M. Rilke, p. 706.

[47] *Samuel Beckett,* p. 39.

WATT, KNOTT, AND A PILLOW OF WORDS

That Beckett's earliest fictional heroes should link notions of divinity with nature and romantic/sexual love is not surprising. Beckett was young when he wrote *Assumption* and *More Pricks than Kicks,* and such ideas are common to artistic, sensitive young men, especially poets. By the time of the writing of *Murphy,* however, intimations of the divine no longer restrict themselves to Celia and the "music" Murphy enjoys with her – although Celia is without question the most lovingly conceived and the most loved of all Beckett's heroines. Instead, the hero's questing for the sublime in this novel is for the guidance of the macrocosmic astrological system (a system that transcends nature *per se*) and for the peace of submersion into the microcosm of the "little world" of Murphy's multi-layered self. In all three of these early works – *Assumption, More Pricks than Kicks,* and *Murphy*[1] – the hero appears as the self-as-character and engages in the macrocosmic quest on level

[1] Fictional prose by Beckett, other than the ten stories collected in *More Pricks than Kicks,* written between *Assumption* and *Murphy* includes *Che Sciagura,* a satire written in 1929 and published in *T. C. D.: A College Miscellany,* 36 (1929), 42; the novel *Dream of Fair to Middling Women,* written in 1932 and still only partially published in *transition,* No. 21, The Hague, 1932, pp. 13-20; *New Review,* No. 2, Paris, 1932, p. 57; *New Durham,* Durham University, June 1965, pp. 10-11; and *Disjecta: Miscellaneous Writings and a Dramatic Fragment by Samuel Beckett,* ed., Ruby Cohn, John Calder, London, 1983, pp. 43-50 (the entire novel exists in typescript in the Baker Memorial Library of Dartmouth College, New Hampshire); *A Case in a Thousand,* written in 1934 and published in *Bookman,* 86 (1934), 241-42; and *Echo's Bones,* written in 1935 (the year *Murphy* was written) and still unpublished.

one as an effort to fulfill – or to have fulfilled – the existential needs that we have described. To categorize these works in this way is not to say that elements of the quest pattern on level one toward the goal of Beckett's metaphysical zero, and on level two as the artistic descent into the microcosm, do not surface in their pages at times. Murphy seeks, by withdrawing from the outer world, sensations of contact with "the accidentless One-and-Only, conveniently called Nothing" (*Murphy,* p. 246). The term "Nothing" here suggests a search for the metaphysical zero. And the nameless hero of *Assumption* and Belacqua are poets who associate any sort of subliminal retreat from the real world with an increased awareness of artistic consciousness.

Nevertheless, it is in Beckett's second published novel, *Watt,* that the full dimensions of the quest on level one as a search for the metaphysical zero are initially exploited. In fact, *Watt* and *Molloy* are the two novels in which this particular questing pattern is most explicit. This quest is a pattern on level one because no descent by the hero into the microcosm for artistic purposes takes place. Although Watt is a "university man" (p. 23), his only literary effort is to relate the account of his sojourn at Mr. Knott's to Sam, the narrator of the novel. And Sam undergoes no artistic ascesis as he offers us as readers the flawed account of Watt's story (we cannot be certain who flaws it – Beckett, Sam, Watt, or all three) that is the novel *Watt.* To undertand, however, that Watt does not seek to enter the microcosm of the inner self, even to the extent that Murphy does, is not to overlook the fact that his quest does take him into a twilight zone so removed from ordinary time and space that the landscape assumes decidedly mythical dimensions. In fact, never again in his fiction – even in the *Stories,* including *First Love* – does Beckett fabricate a landscape as "real" as those of *Assumption, More Pricks than Kicks,* and *Murphy.* From the writing of *Watt* onward, the fictional rooms, roads, gardens, cities, and bodies of water that Beckett creates are more like elements in a dream world than in the world of reality. This twilight-zone landscape prevails through *Stories,* the three novels of the trilogy, *Texts for Nothing,* and *From an Abandoned Work* only to be displaced in *How It Is* (and the subsequent fiction of the sixties) with Beckett's unique inner world of the microscosm with its surreal landscapes and pantomimes of ghosts.

In Chapter Two of this study, I briefly describe the quest for zero as a search for a mythical person, as an existential effort to authenticate the self, and as a Promethean effort to invade God's domain and appropriate the secret fire of divine knowledge and power. But the quest for zero in *Watt* is not contained in this description: spilling over from any descriptive formula, this quest becomes Everyman's search for the ultimate truth of being. Before attempting to analyze the quest on this more profound stratum of level one, we can connect *Watt* with the earlier fiction by noting that the quest on level one in the simpler form found in *Assumption, More Pricks than Kicks,* and *Murphy* – that of the hero to have his five existential needs fulfilled – is also present in *Watt.* Thus Watt's journey to Mr. Knott's establishment can be described from either or both aspects of the questing pattern on level one.

Watt's lack of distinctive identity is established early in the novel. As the tram moves on, having dislodged this hero as a single passenger, he makes his initial appearance, standing "on the pavement, motionless, a solitary figure." Tetty (Mrs. Nixon) cannot tell if he is a man or a woman, and Mr. Hackett is unsure whether he is human or a "parcel, a carpet ... or a roll of tarpaulin."[2] Although sometime prior to the beginning of the novel, Mr. Nixon has loaned Watt five shillings, he admits that he is in "Utter ignorance" of exactly who Watt is: he knows nothing concerning his "Nationality, family, birthplace, confession, occupation, means of existence" or "distinctive signs" (p. 21). The odd facts about Watt that the Nixons do know – for instance, that he is a "university man" and "drinks nothing but milk" (p. 23) – add little to the puzzle of Watt's actual identity. This identity becomes even more nebulous as we realize that the narrator, Sam (who is not present as a character at this time in the novel), is relating the perceptions and comments of Mr. Hackett and the Nixons, that they are standing some distance across the road from Watt, and that Sam is supposedly limited, in regard to his entire narration of events, to information given him by Watt. The question of Watt's

---

[2] *Watt* (New York: Grove, 1959), p. 16. Other references to *Watt* are also to this edition and are cited by page number(s) in the text of this chapter. This novel was completed in 1944 and first published in Paris by the Olympia Press in 1953. Written in English, *Watt* has never been translated into French.

lack of identifiable selfhood is internalized in section 11, when Watt, undergoing his servitude on the ground floor of Mr. Knott's, makes the "distressing discovery" that he can affirm nothing about himself as a man that does "not seem as false as if he had affirmed it of a stone." Unable to pronounce with any sense of conviction the basic statement that "Watt is a man," Watt takes to trying names on himself "almost as a woman hats," and finds what "semantic succour" he can by remembering that his mother had once called him a "good," "bonny," or "clever little man." This failure confidently to name himself (or the pot that stubbornly refuses to be named a "pot") causes Watt great distress: he is "more troubled perhaps than he had ever been by anything" (pp. 82-83).

The significant other that Watt searches for is, of course, Mr. Knott. The exact intent of Watt in regard to the person of Mr. Knott, however, is so complex as to perhaps be undecipherable. As I have stated in describing the quest as a search for zero, the hero's attitude toward the person sought is a mixture of need, reluctant fascination, and dread. Although Watt does not loathe Mr. Knott as Molloy does his mother, neither does he desire union with him as simplistically as Belacqua desires relationships with his women or as Murphy wants sexual union with Celia, or mystical union with Mr. Endon. Certainly Watt is obsessed with Mr. Knott. His interest in anything or anyone else (even Mrs. Gorman the fishwoman) pales by comparison with this obsession. The italicized paragraph that Sam offers as an example of Watt's passion is as intense an expression of one person's need for another as any appearing in the Beckett canon:

> *Of nought. To the source. To the teacher. To the temple. To him I brought. This emptied heart. These emptied hands. This mind ignoring. This body homeless. To love him my little reviled. My little rejected to have him. My little to learn him forgot. Abandoned my little to find him.* (p. 166)

But Sam also tells us that, although Watt wishes to see Mr. Knott "face to face," he nonetheless fears to do so, and that, in one sense, Watt is "sorry" he does not see Mr. Knott more often, but in another sense, he is "glad" (p. 146). Although we are told that

Watt suffers "neither from the presence of Mr. Knott, nor from his absence," being "content to be with him" and "content to be away from him," we are also informed that, as he departs from the Knott establishment, he bursts into tears (pp. 107-08). And Watt's failure to accomplish whatever he set out to do at this establishment is the direct cause of the subsequent disintegration of personality and intellect exhibited in the asylum garden.

The Knott establishment cannot be precisely defined as a community that Watt seeks to become a part of, in the sense that Belacqua wants mystical union with his group of sweethearts or Murphy with the inmates of the Magdalen Mental Mercyseat. Watt's relationships with Mr. Knott's other attendants – Vincent, Walter, Arsene, and Erskine – are merely perfunctory, locked into the sterile rationality of Watt's endeavors in general. As Ruby Cohn comments, the only "two human relationships upon which he erects no rational edifices" are those with Mrs. Gorman and Mr. Graves. And the meanings of these names – "gore man and grave" – reveal the emptiness of these relationships.[3]

Although we must, then, limit any community actually sought by Watt to the various aspects of Mr. Knott, we can nonetheless say that Mr. Knott's house is the place that Watt seeks as a true home, a resting place for his spirit. The reason for this claim is that this establishment is the place where Mr. Knott is to be found, and Mr. Knott, in spite of all Watt's ambivalent feelings toward him, is "harbour" and "haven" (p. 135). On the most superficial level, Watt conceives of Knott's house as a place of rest and warmth. The night that Micks arrives and Watt leaves, as Watt stands in the kitchen holding his bags, he longs simply to sit down at the table and bury his face in his arms, succumbing to the desire for the rest and warmth that he associates with this place (pp. 221-22). Watt learns from Arthur that the reason Arthur has been unable to finish the story of Mr. Nackybal and Louit is because the telling of it has mentally transported Arthur "far from Mr. Knott's premises" and has physically kept him so long in the garden that he feels a compulsion to reenter the house with its "mysteries," its "fixity." Arthur has "been absent longer from them, than he could bear."

---

[3] Cohn, *Back to Beckett* (Prnceton, N. J.: Princeton Univ. Press, 1973), p. 50.

No matter that one reason Arthur has become so engrossed in telling the story is a longing to escape the mystery and fixity; once thrust out, he is compellingly called back. Watt sympathizes with Arthur's predicament. He understands that this place where Mr. Knott lives produces both a longing to escape and a compulsion to return (pp. 198-99).

The fourth existential need of the hero can also be assigned to Watt. He longs to experience a unity with nature, or, more precisely, with the system that nature represents. Watt seems to have an intuition that, if he can obliterate the strangeness man experiences in regard to nature, he will be a step further along in conquering the obscurity of the universe as a whole. Before reaching Mr. Knott's, Watt experiences a disharmony with nature which is expressed in his stated dislike of the moon, the sun, the earth, and the sky (pp. 33 and 36). Eleanor Swanson attributes Watt's attitude toward these cosmic elements to his "dogmatic rationality." The sky is actually infinite space but appears as a half-sphere, and the spherical earth presents itself as a flat surface. Therefore, "Watt loathes them as perceptual illusions."[4] Arsene describes the state of disharmony common to questers traveling to Mr. Knott's and also the sensory anticipation of the harmony with nature which such a traveler hopes to gain on his journey:

> He feels it. The sensations, the premonitions of harmony are irrefragable, of imminent harmony, when all outside him will be he, the flowers the flowers that he is among him, the sky the sky that he is above him, the earth trodden the earth trodden the earth treading, and all sound his echo.

Arsene defines this "feeling of security" as a prediction that nature will become "exceedingly accommodating, on the one hand, and man, on the other," and accepts all "past trials and errors" as "mere stepping-stones to this!" (pp. 40-41).

Unfortunately for Watt, the relationship of the Knott establishment with nature precludes any chance of his finding any such

---

[4] Swanson, "Samuel Beckett's *Watt:* A Coming and a Going," *Modern Fiction Studies,* 17 (1971), 265.

cosmic harmony. Nature at the Knott household is embodied in the garden, and this garden mocks any notions of harmony by the fact that the men involved as caretakers are not able even to make the most simple statements concerning it. Neither Watt nor Erskine (who works the first floor during Watt's tenure on the ground floor) nor Mr. Graves (the gardener, who is sexually impotent), nor Mr. Knott (the owner) ever reduces the enigma of the garden to a clearly-understood concept logically stated in language. Instead, mystery, verbal contradiction, silence, and illogicality accompany all verbal efforts to describe, explain, or communicate this garden.

Watt's ministrations to the garden are those of mystery. He is instructed to empty the first floor slops on certain vegetables and flowers at specific times; he is given no instructions about the second floor slops, but is "formally forbidden" to mix the two. There are no reasons beyond the instructions themselves "offered to the understanding," but Watt is "not so foolish as to suppose" that these instructions are "the real reason" (pp. 67-68). Furthermore, the garden never appears the same to Watt, but is continually changing. The bushes, the light, and the clouds seem "to vary, from day to day, and from night to morning" so that they refuse to appear "in their ancient guise, and consent to be named, with the time honoured names, and forgotten" (pp. 83-84).

Erskine's apprehension and efforts at verbalization concerning the garden are not only mysterious, but also are characterized by contradiction and silence. We are informed that Erskine is the only person who can speak of the garden "usefully" to Watt, and that Erskine is the one who must explain Watt's duties to him. Such information is contradicted by the comment which follows that "Erskine never spoke" of the garden. That, in fact,

> Erskine never opened his mouth, in Watt's presence except to eat, or belch, or cough, or keck, or muse, or sigh, or sing, or sneeze.

And that the song he always sings is:

?

(p. 85)

All of Mr. Graves' dealings with the garden are illogical. This strange gardener arrives punctiliously each morning to pick up the key for his shed and returns it before leaving each afternoon. But when Watt leaves the key out, first overnight and then all the time, Mr. Graves never gets it but leaves it wrapped in a piece of blanket under a stone (pp. 142-43, 145). Does the key open the shed? Is there another key that opens the shed? Does Mr. Graves ever open the shed? The questions can be multiplied in Beckettian fashion *ad infinitum,* but we never ascertain a logical relationship between the key and the garden shed. Also Mr. Graves has forsaken the logic of cause-effect in his gardening efforts. He no longer believes the growth of his plants to be in any way dependent on the way they are sown. Once, using "a line, a measure, a plumb, a level," he had placed his seeds in careful lines and groups. Now his procedure is to "let fall the seed, absent in mind, as the priest dust, or ashes, into the grave, and cover it with earth." Mr. Graves no longer believes in the logic of careful planting resulting in a good harvest. Instead, he knows that if the seed grows well, "it will do so, and that if . . . not, it will not" (pp. 181-82). Watt's opinion is that the gardener cannot speak of the garden, that his "remarks" are simply not "evidence" (p. 85).

Mr. Knott himself often walks in the garden, where, the narrator comments, Watt occasionally encounters him. Once, in the garden, the master and the servant "stood together" with their "bowed heads almost touching" watching a worm and a flower (p. 146). But negating such an incident is the oft-repeated statement that Watt never really sees Mr. Knott, that, in fact, he finally abandons "all hope, all fear, of ever seeing Mr. Knott face to face" (p. 146). Obviously Mr. Knott can give Watt no information whatsoever, including any about the garden or nature.

In order to understand the system that nature represents in *Watt,* we need to examine a certain experience of Arsene's – the famous experience of falling into existence "off the ladder," of having his universe slip, just a little, but enough to thrust him into a totally new dimension of being. Before the fall – or the slip – Arsene experiences (or imagines that he experiences) the kind of harmony with nature that he has previously described as desirable. Sitting in the October sun on a Tuesday afternoon, Arsene

> was in the sun and the wall was in the sun. I was the sun, need I add, and the wall, and the step, and the yard and the time of year, and the time of day, to mention only these. (p. 42)

After the fall or slip occurs, "the sun on the wall" undergoes, for Arsene, "an instantaneous" and "radical change of appearance." The change is so pronounced that Arsene feels that he has "been transported . . . to some quite different yard, and to some quite different season, in an unfamiliar country" (pp. 43-44). Arsene's perception of a suddenly unfamiliar nature is almost exactly described by Camus:

> . . . strangeness creeps in: perceiving that the world is "dense," sensing to what a degree a stone is foreign and irreducible to us, with what intensity nature or a landscape can negate us. At the heart of all beauty lies something inhuman, and these hills, the softness of the sky, the outline of these trees at this very minute lose the illusory meaning with which we had clothed them, henceforth more remote than a lost paradise.[5]

As for Camus, the earth ceases to be in any way paradisical for Arsene. Instead, the description of the seasons he interpolates into his lengthy soliloquy at this point – a description revealing Beckett at his best poetically in its sensory and poignant language – is used by him to dub nature (as the earth) an "excrement," a "turd," and a "cat's flux" (p. 47).

As Arsene loses his habitual response to nature, he also loses his former hold on the reason and logic that Western man has assumed for centuries to be functional in making truth statements and value judgments about the earth and his life on it. Reason and logic – and the language which houses them – no longer work in Arsene's experience of nature and the human life it sustains. Watt undergoes an experience like Arsene's in his encounter with the Galls – "father and son" – who come "all the way from town to choon the piano" (p. 70). After this experience (and others like it), Watt finds not only objects within the house but also the "bushes,"

---

[5] Albert Camus, *The Myth of Sisyphus and Other Essays*, trans. from the French by Justin O'Brien (New York: Knopf, 1955; rpt. Vintage Books, 1960), p. 11.

"light," and "clouds" of the outside premises strange and unstable. He and Arsene would agree with Camus' claim that the rationality of science cannot explain nature, nor the supposed logic of language the human experience called life:

> I realize that if through science I can seize phenomena and enumerate them, I cannot, for all that, apprehend the world. Were I to trace its entire relief with my finger, I should not know any more.[6]

Thus nature in *Watt* becomes an ironic symbol for the total system of life – a life that refuses to be apprehended logically or named with the assumed rationality and systematization of language.

Watt is an unusual Beckettian hero in that he does not seem to exhibit the need to resolve a dichotomy between his flesh and his spirit. Unlike Belacqua and Murphy, who are torn between the sensory demands of the flesh and the mystical yearnings of the spirit, Watt projects all of his being toward Mr. Knott. In the passage I have already quoted as proof of Watt's obsessive need for Mr. Knott as a significant other, we discover that the hero's "heart," "hand," "mind," and "body" – however "little" this composite self may be – are sacrificed as a unit to the cause of "learning" Mr. Knott (p. 166). If, as the "Addenda" to *Watt* specifies, and as the language Watt uses in relating his experiences to Sam makes clear, this hero's spirit becomes a "dim mind wayfaring / through barren lands" (p. 250), his flesh follows suit. The last glimpse Sam gives us of Watt is of a forlorn and wretched figure striking against the trunks of trees and falling into clumps of briars and nettles as he stumbles toward the elaborate asylum that has become the "habitation" of both his broken flesh and his troubled spirit (p. 213).

No existential need that Watt does seek to have fulfilled is met. He gains no identity of the self, no significant and lasting union with another or with a community,[7] no permanent home that is a

---

[6] *The Myth of Sisyphus*, p. 15.

[7] If the argument is made that Watt attains unity with Sam as a significant other, I would reply: 1. Watt has not been questing for Sam, or Sam for Watt (as far as we know) in any fashion, and 2. whatever communication or kinship the

resting place, and no harmony with nature, or the system it represents. Watt's quest to make contact with an awesome and transcendent Other who, he assumes, could enrich his life with existential gifts fails. Ruby Cohn calls the failure of Watt's quest "the failure of Western man. *Homo sapiens* ponders the imponderable,"[8] and, we might add, seeks to grasp the ungraspable.

The God/sign or word/promise beckoning poor Watt toward a possible fulfillment of these needs is, of course, Mr. Knott. To say that Knott is a God/sign is not to state that he is a symbolic portrayal of divinity. On the other hand, neither can we say that Knott is not a symbolic portrayal of divinity. Perhaps nowhere else in Beckett's entire canon do we find characterization that so effectively fuses content with form. All the illogicality and irrationality of Watt's world, a world that stubbornly refuses to be comprehended or named, are epitomized in the shifting forms of this personage who is Knott (not) and yet who is, who suggests divinity and yet who does not do so. To try and contain Mr. Knott in any kind of descriptive formula is to allow Beckett to play cat-and-mouse games with us as readers and also to miss the mysterious essence of Mr. Knott's awesome and ridiculous presence. We can say that Watt's world revolves around the single reality of Mr. Knott, that Watt's only purpose in life is to learn of him and serve him, and that Watt conceives of him as holding the keys to the mystery of all being.

In fact, the pattern I have devised of the religious consciousness of the Beckettian hero can be applied to Watt in regard to his awareness of Mr. Knott. Arsene is speaking of himself but also of all Knott's servants, including Watt, when he states that it is at Knott's household that one "witnesses and is witnessed" (p. 42). Arsene elaborates on this Berkelian sequence of witnesses by explaining that the existences of the house and parlor maids, Ann and Mary (or Mary and Ann) depend not only on the perception of each for the other but also on the awareness of a third person,

---

two achieve eventually fades as Watt's strange styles of language become "so much Irish" to Sam, who, due also to the fact that his hearing now begins to diminish, can finally understand only "one half of what won its way past my tympan" (p. 169).

[8] *Back to Beckett*, p. 52.

on whose existence the existences of Ann and Mary depend (p. 51). Along with Watt, we conceive of Mr. Knott as the only possible ultimate perceiver in the world of the novel. Only Knott "neither comes nor goes" but "seems to abide in his place" (p. 57). As Rubin Rabinovitz explains, the "theological imagery" associated with Knott and the elaborate "causal chains" that Watt fabricates in his efforts to comprehend Knott "recall Descartes' search for God at the beginning of a causal series."[9] Rabinovitz also points out Beckett's use in the "Addenda" to *Watt* of a phrase from the Latin prayer "Agnus Dei, miserere nobis" ("Lamb of God, have mercy on us"). Beckett changes the phrase to "causa causarum miserere mei" ("cause of causes, have mercy on me").[10] To follow Watt to Knott as any kind of ultimate perceiver or cause, however, is to arrive with this misguided hero at the dead end of disillusionment and religious parody. Mr. Knott not only finds it necessary to have about him witnesses – of which Watt is one – to witness him so "that he might not cease" (p. 203), but also "is obliged to have someone . . . about him, to look after him" because he is "quite incapable of looking after himself" (p. 58). As John Chalker remarks in his essay in Katherine Worth's *Beckett the Shape Changer,* "the reader who is tempted to take Mr. Knott as a conventional godlike figure is essentially mocked." Chalker comments further, "Far from being a divine sustaining consciousness whose constant presence gives life to all created things, Mr. Knott is the incarnation of the irrational who needs a witness to sustain him."[11]

The preciseness and unalterability of Watt's service at the Knott household reveal the highly structured and rigorously determined behavior of all servitors in this establishment. The sequence of the comings and goings of the junior and senior retainers (pp. 56-57), the prescribed method of emptying the first floor slops (pp. 67-68), the elaborate procedure of concocting and

---

[9] Rabinovitz, "*Watt* from Descartes to Schopenhauer," in *Modern Irish Literature: Essays in Honor of William York Tindall,* ed. Raymond J. Porter and James D. Brophy (New York: Iona College Press, 1972), p. 267.

[10] Rabinovitz, "The Addenda to Samuel Beckett's 'Watt,'" in *Samuel Beckett: The Art of Rhetoric,* p. 219.

[11] Chalker, "The Satiric Shape of *Watt,*" in *Beckett the Shape Changer,* ed. Katherine Worth (London and Boston: Routledge and Kegan Paul, 1975), pp. 34-35.

serving Mr. Knott's meal "dish," and, above all, the incredible existence and arrangement of the Lynch family through several generations solely to provide a dog always hungry enough to eat Mr. Knott's meal scraps (pp. 98-111) offer, with a satiric eloquence, testimony to some all-determining power in charge of this strange household. As Watt contemplates the matter of the preparation of the meal "dish," he considers the possibility that Mr. Knott may not be the ultimate determiner of this procedure, that it may instead be "a past domestic . . . of genius" or a "professional dietician." The twelve permutations that Watt fabricates as he ponders this mystery dissolve into nonsense (pp. 89-90), and Watt decides that if Mr. Knott is not the power or force behind the determined systems of the household (which, at the moment, constitutes Watt's world), then it is a vague other "of whom all trace is lost" (p. 93). Whatever this power – and we assume it is Knott or someone acting for him or by his leave – it exerts almost complete control over Watt. His tenure of service at the estate –first on the ground floor, then on the first floor – is established (p. 132), and his moment of leaving – when Micks appears to take his place – is set (p. 216). We can assume further that the entire agonizing experience he undergoes has also been planned for him, since his final appearance is in the asylum where he relates his "story" to Sam – a place that seems to have been the point he has been moving toward from the moment of his first appearance in the novel.

Watt's sense of guilt is apparent throughout the novel and is directly related to his quest. This guilt, exhibited in an unquestioning acceptance of servitude and abuse, is evidenced as early as Watt's arrival at the train station. When Watt collides with the porter wheeling the milk can, he quietly waits to pick up his hat and bags until after the porter has finished verbally abusing him. The narrator informs us that Watt does "not feel at liberty" to retrieve his belongings until he has suffered the abuse (pp. 24-25). A sense of guilt and of deserved punishment is so much a part of Watt's consciousness that, when he later observes the porter wheeling cans from one side of the platform to the other for no apparent reason, he concludes that it must be "a punishment for disobedience, or some neglect of duty" on the part of the porter (p. 26). As Watt prepares the time-honored concoction for

Mr. Knott's meals, his experience of fear and responsibility is so intense that tears and sweat roll down his face and body (p. 88). Due to his intense dislike of dogs, after the first few weeks of his tenure at the Knott establishment, Watt becomes incapable of watching while the fabled dog (Kate or Cis), brought each evening by the dwarfs Art and Con, eats whatever meal scraps are left (p. 113). That this unavoidable "transgression" is not immediately repaid by some "thunderbolt" of punishment puzzles Watt: "And this was a great source of wonder, to Watt, that he had infringed, with impunity, such a venerable tradition, or institution" (p. 116). Watt finally concludes that it must be because he has never displayed an attitude of rebelliousness but instead has surrounded "his transgression with such precautions, such delicacies" that grace has been "counted to him" (pp. 116-17). As events progress, we as readers and Watt as character realize that little if any "grace" emanates from Mr. Knott to alleviate Watt's vague but overwhelming sense of guilt. The inaccessibility of Mr. Knott reminds us of the nebulous authority behind Joseph K's Court in Kafka's *The Trial.* Unlike Watt, Joseph K (Kafka's hero) cannot accept the fact of his guilt, although, like Watt, be recognizes his need to find grace at the hands of a power that remains obscurely hidden. Jean Onimus writes of Beckett's divinity as the "Hidden God," the *Dieu Caché,* who is at least partially resposible for man's frustration in not receiving grace to alleviate his guilt. This critic's observations could encompass the dilemmas of both Watt and Joseph K:

> Dieu ne réussit pas à donner sa grâce au bon moment et l'homme ne sait pas la recevoir quand elle s'offre à lui. Personne alors ne serait responsable, sinon ce sinistre malentendu qu'est l'existence elle-même.[12]

Watt is Beckett's first hero to be cursed with the continuation of a conscious existence that constitutes the ironic "eternal life" that is a significant segment of the typical protagonist's religious consciousness. A critic who describes Watt's pilgrimage in terms of different stages or states of existence is Gottfried Büttner, who

---

[12] *Beckett,* p. 105.

says that "Watt personifies the question of . . . the passage of the human soul through birth and death." The sojourn at Mr. Knott's is the time spent in death – here Watt is "no longer on an earthly plane" – and, in the train station (after leaving the Knott estate), Watt undergoes a "birth" back into life, coming out of the "womb" into freedom and a "new life journey." Beckett is able to create a character who has such experiences because he has "developed forces which enabled him to see into the world of the unborn and the dead." Apparently, for Büttner, both Beckett and Watt have "pushed forward into the boundary region between life and death to reach a new dimension, a new horizon of consciousness."[13]

The evidence at hand, however, not only in *Watt* but also in the other fiction, does not substantiate the optimism of Büttner's analysis. Like Swift's Struldbruggs, Beckett's heroes find the continuation of life a burden rather than a new freedom. As Sam relates Watt's stumbling backward through the hole in the foliage between his garden and Sam's, he implies that he and Watt will not "meet again (in this world)" (pp. 212-13). But we have no knowledge that Watt ever finds the surcease of physical death. Instead, the hallucinatory vision he has of himself as he leaves the Knott estate leads us to envision Watt as perpetually trapped in a continual coming and going, with no ending of his quest. The only "death" he undergoes is the "crucifixion" he experiences at the asylum as he attempts to relate the account of his quest-journey to Sam. We encounter Watt later in the fictional canon in *Mercier and Camier,* where he has undergone such a decided change of personality as to be, as he admits to Camier, "unrecognizable" (*Mercier and Camier,* p. 111). In the fiction that immediately follows *Watt,* the four *Stories,* the first-person hero/narrator deliberately tries to end the exile of life by finding a haven in death, but never succeeds. Like the Unnamable, these heroes cannot find "the place where one finishes vanishing," and can be said to echo his words: we "have all been here forever, we shall all be here forever, I know it" (*The Unnamable,* p. 293).

---

[13] Büttner, *Samuel Beckett's Novel* Watt, trans. Joseph P. Dolon (Philadelphia: Univ. of Pennsylvania Press, 1984), pp. 124, 126, 131, 136-38, 162, and 158.

We have examined Watt's journey considered as the macrocosmic quest to fill or have filled the five existential voids or empty circles of need. This examination has included an exploration of Watt's awareness of Mr. Knott in terms of the paradigm of the hero's religious consciousness. As I have pointed out earlier, however, the quest in *Watt* is best described as the search for Beckett's metaphysical zero, that enigmatic symbol used to gather all the voids of need into one empty circle. This symbol in Beckett's art represents the ever-beckoning but never-attained essence of knowledge and being in human experience. The three facets of this quest – a search for a mythical person, an effort to authenticate or fulfill the self, and a Promethean attempt to invade the sacred domain and appropriate the secret fire of knowledge and power – are actually deeper strata of the surface layers of the five existential needs of the hero. The search for a mythical person is the substratum of the need to unite with another – or a community – in love and of the need to find a place that is a true home, a resting place, for man's spirit. The effort to establish an identity of the individual self is the tip of the iceberg of the search to authenticate or fulfill human selfhood at its most profound level. The Promethean quest for sacred knowlege and power underlies the hero's desire for harmony with nature and/or the universal system it represents. The need to resolve the dichotomy between the flesh and the spirit can also be said to overlay the Promethean quest in that such resolution would be a solving of the ancient riddle of the relationship between spirit and matter. Thus, although the components of the quest for zero exhibit certain radical differences from the surface existential needs (i.e. Watt's search for the mythical Mr. Knott is not simplistically to unite with him in love), we can say that we are dealing with essentially the same quest described from a cosmic, philosophical rather than an individual, existential perspective.

However we define Watt's search for the mythical person of Mr. Knott (and however we define Mr. Knott), it is possible to say that this quest is like a person's journey or pilgrimage toward God, although, of course, the pilgrimage dissolves into ironic parody. The words Watt speaks in the asylum garden are those a pilgrim forsaking the world in order to approach God might use. With "emptied heart" and "emptied hands," with a mind ignoring all else, he accounts whatever "little" of worldly store he possesses as that which should be "reviled" "rejected," and forgotten in order "to find him [Mr. Knott]" (p. 166). Although these words are weighted with irony – Watt loses all and gains nothing – we are reminded of St. Paul's assertion that he has suffered the "loss of all things," counting them as "dung," in order that he might "win Christ" (Philippians 3:8).

In identifying Mr. Knott as the God/sign or word/promise, I have previously shown that Watt's world revolves around the single reality of this person, that Watt's only purpose in life is to learn of him and serve him, and that Watt conceives of him as holding the keys to the mystery of all being. That Watt is Everyman on pilgrimage is implied by Mr. Nixon's remarks concerning his knowledge of Watt:

> I seem to have known him all my life, but there must have been a period when I did not. (p. 18) The curious thing is . . . that when I see him, or think of him, I think of you Mr. Hackett, and that when I see you, or think, of you, I think of him. I have no idea why this is so. (p. 19)
> How I met him. . . . I really do not remember, any more than I remember meeting my father. (p. 23)

Like all pilgrims, Watt is "setting out on a journey" (p. 17). Like Dante in Canto 1 of *The Inferno*, Watt comes to himself (and to us) in a dark place: "Now it was quite dark, Yes, now the western sky was as the eastern, which was as the southern, which was as the northern" (p. 24). Like Dante and Piers Plowman (in *The Prologue* of *The Vision*), Watt becomes tired and sits down on the ditch or the bank of the road. Here he hears (for the second time) the mysterious voices of the "mixed choir" (p. 33). He has no Evangelist to guide him (as Bunyan's Pilgrim does), but is accosted by Mr. Spiro, the "neo-John-Thomist" who edits the Catholic monthly *Crux* (pp. 27-29). Like Bunyan's Pilgrim, Watt does pass through a wicket gate – as he climbs onto the platform of the train station (p. 24 compared with p. 224). Watt does not see Piers' "fair field full of folk," but is aware, as the train moves on, that he is passing the racecourse with its strands and people (p. 29). Lawrence E. Harvey recognizes the pilgrimage aspect of Watt's journey: "*Watt* opens with a symbolic departure from the city. Its structure resembles a three-stage *rite de passage* . . . the hero goes out, spends a period of initiation in a privileged locus, and returns. . . .[14] Beckett is mocking the literature of pilgrimage, but he is also writing it.

The mythical person Watt is seeking is a zero, a negative, a Mr. (k)not(t). Kenneth Burke, in his study *The Rhetoric of Religion,* deals with the conceiving of ultimate being as a negative or void, or the defining of God in terms of what he is not. He points out that the language ordinarily used to describe God uses negative suffixes—"immortal, immutable, infinite, unbounded, impassive and the like." Also, even positive terms such as "God is love" or "God is like a Father" have negative implications. God is not "merely human" love; he is not like a "literal" human father. In fact, the basic idea of God as supernatural is that he is "*not* describable by the positives of nature." Burke proceeds to explain that, in the Platonic dialectic, movement toward the Divine is described as movement toward "ever higher orders of generalization, toward the abstract," since it is "away from the realm of merely naturalistic positives, the objects of sheerly sensory experience." Also, Hegel's observation on going from "this being to that being and the other being, and so on, until you have a term for 'Pure Being'" is to reach "Nothing," since "there is not a single object that can be pointed to as an example of "'Pure Being.'" Burke also remarks on Heidegger's use of Nothing as the "contextual counterpart, or 'ground,' of Being."[15]

In reviewing Giovanni Papini's *Dante Vivo,* Beckett remarks that "Analysis of what a man is not may conduce to an understanding of what he is, but only on condition that the distinction is observed."[16] Then, in *Watt,* he speculates, tongue in cheek, that "the only way one can speak of God is to speak of him as though he were a man." Beckett is spoofing in this latter passage: "anthropologists have realized" that the only way to speak of man is to "speak of him as though he were a termite" (p. 77). Nevertheless,

---

[14] *Samuel Beckett: Poet and Critic,* p. 371.

[15] Burke, *The Rhetoric of Religion: Studies in Logology* (Boston: Beacon Press, 1961), pp. 22 and 25.

[16] "Papini's Dante," *The Bookman,* Christmas Issue, 87 (1934), 14.

the only way to begin to think of Mr. Knott is to accept the comment made by the narrator that "he was not" (p. 67). Since he also "was," we understand that we are locked in paradox, and are reminded of the group of critics I have surveyed in Chapter One who rest content with leaving the ambiguity of the question of God in Beckett's writings as a literary convenience that is best left unresolved. Mr. Knott is an excellent example of this paradoxical ambiguity. He is absent yet present, the object of the hero's quest and yet the power from which he eventually flees, and the instigator of promises of salvation (not spoken by Mr. Knott, to be sure, but implied by his characterization) and yet the annulment of these promises. As we shall see, the "notness" of Mr. Knott is a cipher for the emptiness or nothingness he comes to represent to Watt.

Beckett's quest for zero is not only a search for a mythical person but also an effort to authenticate or fulfill human selfhood at its most profound level. We have noted Watt's surface lack of identity in regard to the knowledge other characters have about him and in regard to his perception of himself. Watt's effort simply to name or identify himself as a "man" is outer evidence of profound need for self-understanding and authentication. Like the Unnamable, who is the clearest articulator of Beckett's search for the self throughout the entire fictional canon, Watt is not certain as to who he is, where he is, or what he is doing (*The Unnamable*, p. 404). The "no-self" of Watt is portrayed in two incidents occurring near the end of the text of the novel, in the closing pages of Section IV. (We must remember that, chronologically, Section IV precedes Section 111, which is, chronologically, the last section in the novel.) The first of these incidents reveals the failure of Watt in his quest to achieve any degree of self-understanding or knowledge. The second presents Watt as a no-self, practically invisible to those observing him. In the first, Watt does not recognize the hallucinatory apparition of himself that he sees on the road he has just traveled to the train station. As the figure, "human apparently," advances toward Watt, now standing in the station, he is uncertain whether it is a man or woman, wearing a "sack, or a quilt, or a rug." The description fits that given of Watt as the novel begins, and the figure exhibits Watt's characteristic gait, but this hero never recognizes himself. In spite of his deep concern simply to ascertain what the figure *appears* to be, he watches it grow fainter and fainter and finally disappear from view, still unrecognized (pp. 225-28).

In the second incident, Watt can be said practically to disappear as a person. He buys his ticket for the "further end" at the ticket window of the station, the train arrives, but it does "not take up a single passenger." Where is Watt? Mr. Gorman, Mr. Nolan, and Mr. Case, all of whom have been standing with him, walk out into the road and begin to take their separate ways. They each stop, turn, and ask, "And our friend?" But Watt (who, of course, is not their "friend") cannot be precisely located, either along the road, on the train, or in the text of the novel at this point. Our only clue that he might still be anywhere about is Mr. Nolan's question offered in reply to the general question, "And our friend?" – "Is it the long wet dream with the hat and bags? cried Mr. Nolan" (pp. 244-45). Watt reappears, of course, in the asylum garden (of Section 111), but at this point his non-appearance implies that he is a non-person.

Since modern literary notions of the self have been decidedly influenced by Sartre and Heidegger, we can with profit, at this junction, compare their ideas of selfhood with those of Beckett. In *Watt,* the picture in Erskine's room of the broken circle and the misplaced dot or "centre" (pp. 128-29) suggests numerous ideas dealt with in the novel. We become guilty of forcing specific symbolic meaning onto shifting figures if we say the picture represents any particular entity searching for some other. We do not know that it symbolizes Watt seeking Mr. Knott, language striving for meaning, or man questing for the essence of human selfhood. Any of these meanings (or none of them or various others) can possibly be assigned to this "circle and its centre in search of each other." Whatever the figuring represents, its non-connection is profoundly moving to Watt: as he contemplates the picture, his eyes fill with tears, which flow down his cheeks unchecked (p. 129). The next occasion on which Watt bursts into tears is on the evening when he leaves the Knott estate for the train station – the station where, as we have seen, he "disappears" as a person. In *Watt,* as throughout the Beckett canon, ideas of the self are conjoined with the concept of zero or nothingness – a circle with no indicated center.

In Sartre's thought, the self is conceived of as a nothingness, a conception based on the distinction of *en soi* and *pour soi*, the mutual contradiction of being and nothingness. Human consciousness is not an entity or being; only beings or objects other than the subjective self have an essence, gratuitously, in and of themselves. Since the only alternative to being is nothingness, the human self is nothing, simply a consciousness of whatever being it is contemplating, whether that contemplation is of a chair or of one's mother as an object. Because the *pour soi* is thus only a hole that leans on the edges of the beings it is conscious of, it can be said to depend on these beings for existence.[17] Nor is Sartre's nothing/self grounded in or derived from being. Negativity cannot come from being. Thus the self as mere consciousness cannot be explained by recourse to any *en soi* or being. Nothingness can only be produced by nothingness. Sartre never explains what is meant by nothingness as a source, except to call it the self's "own nothingness."[18] Sartre's diary novel, *Nausea*, relates the search of its hero, Roquentin, for the meaning of life, the self, or God. Rather than finding God, Roquentin discovers his absence, and the self he finally predicates is also conceived of as an absence.[19] To "find the self," Sartrean man would either have to die (become an object or being) or become God (be something that is an impossible blending of *pour soi* with *en soi*). Only in the extended interview given shortly before his death does Sartre forsake the absurd impossible implications of such a theoretical quest to embrace more social and practical philosophical goals. He speaks here of a "moral modality" that no longer wants "to be God, no longer wants to be *causa sui*." As Sartre expounds his last thoughts in terms of goals such as "seeking to live together like human beings, and to be human

---

[17] For an excellent comparison of Sartre with Beckett, see Livio Dobrez, "Beckett, Sartre and Camus: The Darkness and the Light," *Southern Review: An Australian Journal of Literary Studies*, 71 (1974), 51-63.

[18] For a discussion of these ideas, see Arthur C. Danto, *Jean-Paul Sartre*, Modern Masters Series, ed. Frank Kermode (New York: Viking, 1975), pp. 60-68.

[19] For a contrast of Sartre's diary novel with similar writings by Tennyson, Francois Mauriac, Goethe, and Georges Bernanos, see H. Porter Abbott, "Letters to the Self: The Cloistered Writer in Nonretrospective Fiction," *PMLA*, 95 (1980), 23-41.

beings,"[20] he departs from Beckett's individualistic, metaphysical concerns and becomes of less interest to us at this particular point.

We should be careful to note a basic distinction between Sartre's and Beckett's notions of nothingness. For Sartre, nothingness is simply a theoretical construct forming a part of the human structure of consciousness. For Beckett, nothingness is a plenum-void, a metaphysical "something" constituting the core of the self, of experience, and of outward reality. We can also recognize a basic difference between the two thinkers' concepts of freedom as it relates to their notions of selfhood. For Sartre, man is condemned to be free if he is to live an authentic existence – that is, to live without succumbing to manipulative shaping by his environment or by another. The particular terror of such authentic existence is that everything is permitted, and choices are inescapable. As Sartrean man chooses, he does so with the frightening realization that not only his choices but also the meaning he assigns to them are completely his personal responsibility. There is no direction available to him from either his inner or outer worlds. And, in view of the embarrassing fact that God does not exist, he is left with nothing to depend on, either within or without. This risky freedom, however, cannot be avoided: it is the sole condition of authentic existence.

To the contrary, Beckett's self, although caught in an illusionary web of making choices, has no significant freedom. The methods of Descartes for controlling reality certainly do not work for Beckettian man (Descartes himself admitted the illogicality of mind over matter). In fact, Beckett does not allow his hero even the microcosmic freedom the Belgian Geulincx describes as crawling eastward on a westward-bound ship (*Molloy,* p. 5). Instead, the hero is reduced to Malebranche's dependence on the continual intervention of God as the cause of all choice or action in an existence where God does not intervene. In spite of such reduction, the hero is compelled not only to choose mentally but also to act physically. Thus we have the Beckettian hero continually

[20] "The Last Words of Jean-Paul Sartre," interview between Sartre and Benny Lévy, *Le Nouvel Observateur,* 10, 17, and 24 March 1980: I have been unable to locate the source of the English translation of this interview. For a lengthy attempt to situate Beckett within the boundaries of Heideggerian philosophy, see Lance St. John Butler, *Samuel Beckett and the Meaning of Being: A Study in Ontological Parable* (London: Macmillan, 1984).

"going on" fettered with the chains of non-being. As Molloy ironically comments, "That is a great measure of freedom, for him who has not the pioneering spirit" (*Molloy*, p. 51).

Heidegger also incorporates the idea of nothingness into his analysis of human selfhood, but such incorporation is quite different from that of Sartre, although both can be said to begin with Husserl's definition of consciousness as an awareness of something other than itself. For Heidegger, man is *Dasein*, the self in relationship to his environment, a being-there in his world. Man does not first *be* and then *be somewhere;* he *is* or exists because *he is somewhere.* Thus the self is not an essence which also happens to exist: it is nothing but its existence, its being-in-the-world. Heidegger's thereness of man also includes a withness: man is similarly a *Mitsein*, a being-with-others. To say that man is an existence in the world, however, is not to say that he is at home in the world. As Heideggerian man experiences *Angst*, the everyday normality of his world collapses, and he becomes aware of himself as a void dependent for existence on an environment that has no intrinsic meaning, but which is simply "there" as an inescapable fact. *Angst*, then, is man's heightened consciousness of the nothingness of the self and of his world. Arsene's experience, which we have already examined, is an experience of *Angst*, as is Watt's entire experience, beginning definitively with the "non-event" of the Galls' visit to tune the piano.[21]

Beckett's thought is similar to that of Sartre and Heidegger in his portrayals of the human experience of selfhood as an awareness of emptiness and want and of the self as a depiction of nothingness seeking substance. In the "addenda" to *Watt* he offers certain questions in poetic form:

who may tell the tale
of the old man?
weigh absence in a scale?
mete want with a span?

[21] For an excellent comparison of Heidegger with Beckett, see Livio Dobrez, "Beckett and Heidegger: Existence, Being, and Nothingness," *Southern Review: An Australian Journal of Literary Studies*, 7 (1974), 140-53.

the sum assess
of the world's woes?
nothingness
in words enclose? (p. 247)

If the answer to these questions is "Samuel Beckett," it is because this writer resolutely refuses to portray absence, want, and woe as anything other than "nothingness."

To compare Beckett's thought further with that of Sartre and Heidegger is to depart from Sartre and proceed with Heidegger. The Being described by Heidegger as underlying and supporting all "beings" – *Sein* – is something other than the self's existence and other than the world. Being is that something beneath existence from which all things originate. Heidegger goes on to describe nothingness as that which paradoxically *is* the origin of things. Nothingness is identical with *Angst,* the void through which the world reveals itself through the agency of human consciousness. Thus, Heidegger does not, like Sartre, conceive of nothingness as the opposite of being. Instead, it is the same as Being, or *Sein.*[22] The similarities with Beckett's zero which is the essence of everything are apparent. Beckett's void or nothingness is a negative which is nonetheless impossibly there. This ultimate truth or core of the self is conceived of by the hero (as he is in his usual state of *Angst*) as being beneath the visible world of matter, beneath the speaking voice (as, for example, the voice of the Unnamable), and even beneath the surface layers of human consciousness (Murphy's various strata of selfhood). Although Watt's macrocosmic quest for the essence of selfhood is for the zero who is Mr. Knott, the quests of Moran for Molloy and of Malone for the language and characters of his stories shape themselves into ever more inwardly spiralling journeys toward the nothingness at the core of the human self.

The third (and final) element in Watt's search for the metaphysical zero of Being is the Promethean attempt to invade the sacred domain and appropriate the secret fire of knowledge and power. The sacred domain is the realm where the mythical personage resides, and the knowledge and power that Watt is seeking have to

---

[22] "Beckett and Heidegger," pp. 148-49.

do with language. Quite simply, he wants to name events, things, and people so as to understand, explain, and be familiar with them. Watt wants to make language work – at least on a superficial, if not a profound level – to articulate a sound as an auditory sign that meaningfully represents both his mental ideas of something and that something as object in the material world. Before his quest journey, Watt has assumed the adequacy of language, has taken it at face value. Unaware of any need for concern with "symbol" or "interpretation" in regard to words and their meanings, he has experienced no event of which, in retrospect, he has not been "content to say, That is what happened then" (p. 73). But once he arrives at the Knott estate and undergoes the initiatory rite of listening to Arsene's speech, the surface meanings of language start to elude him, and he begins to grapple, with increasing futility and desperation, with the linguistic problem in all of its ramifications and at its most profound level. That Watt is dealing with the use of language on such a deep stratum is something we know only from reading between the lines of the text. We are directly told of Watt's efforts only on the superficial level of his consciousness: he merely wants to name objects, identify persons, relate happenings, and locate causes. But the occasion of the Galls' visit resists being called an ordinary happening of two men coming to tune a piano in a country estate. In fact, this event refuses to signify anything and becomes "a mere example of light commenting bodies, and stillness motion, and silence sound, and comment comment" (p. 73). Watt's efforts are directed toward using language and logic as they have assumedly been used in the long tradition of Western rationalism – to define and assign order and meaning, not merely to the event of the piano tuners' arrival, or even to Watt's sojourn itself, but to the cumulative human experience. As Jennie Skerl states, "*Watt* is the story of modern man's confrontation with the basic irrationality of existence and his inability to comprehend or communicate this ultimate reality."[23]

Skerl and Linda Ben-Zvi are critics who analyze the linguistic problems in *Watt* within the framework of Fritz Mauthner's

---

[23] Skerl, "Fritz Mauthner's 'Critique of Language' in Samuel Beckett's *Watt*," *Contemporary Literature*, 15 (1974), 474.

Critique of Language.[24] An earlier study by Jacqueline Hoefer identifies Beckett's concerns in *Watt* with the language philosophy of Ludwig Wittgenstein's logical positivism.[25] Although Hoefer's linking of Beckett's thought with Wittgenstein has supposedly been proved false, her analysis of *Watt* remains valid. Morot-Sir applies a Manichean duality or dialectic (although not specifically to *Watt*) to Beckett's perspective on language,[26] and Angela Moorjani reveals the religious dimension of Watt's linguistic quest by explaining that Watt is in need of a "divine logos" to "satisfy" his "semantic need."[27]

My application of the adjective "Promethean" to Watt's linguistic quest is based on its religious dimensions. Certain aspects of this quest (or the Beckettian quest in general) are decidedly *not* Promethean. Charles I. Glicksberg correctly identifies Beckett as a "literary nihilist" and separates him from the humanism for which the Promethean myth has become a literary symbol. Although nihilists such as Beckett share with Promethean humanists the belief "that man is alone" and "reject faith in the supernatural," the nihilist does not proceed "to declare that man is the measure, the sole source and touchstone of value." Instead, he "repudiates all such man-made values as illusions, mere as-if-fictions designed to hide from human eyes the emptiness and futility of existence." The nihilist

> will not conceal from himself the desolating "truth" of human dereliction. He will proclaim far and wide his discovery that the idea of progress, like the romantic faith in the perfectibility of man, is a spurious myth. He harbors no revolutionary hopes; he does not look forward to the future for the redemption of mankind.

---

[24] Ben-Zvi's article is "Samuel Beckett, Fritz Mauthner, and the Limits of Language."

[25] Hoefer, "*Watt*," *Perspective*, 11 (1959), 166-82; rpt. in *Samuel Beckett: A Collection of Critical Essays*, ed. Martin Esslin (Englewood Cliffs, N. J.: Prentice-Hall, 1965), pp. 62-76.

[26] "Samuel Beckett and Cartesian Emblems," pp. 94-96.

[27] Moorjani, *Abysmal Games in the Novels of Samuel Beckett* (Chapel Hill: Univ. of North Carolina Press, 1982), p. 91.

Glicksberg further contends that the "mark of the nihilist . . . is that he realizes the self-defeating nature of his efforts, through the instrumentality of reason and art [for instance, Beckett's and Watt's constructions in language] to capture the ultimate meaning of life." The literary nihilist again takes on Promethean nuances when he "persists in striving even though he is fully aware that at the end of time the passion of his quest . . . will be swallowed up in oblivion."[28] It is in such descriptions as Glicksberg's that we isolate the Promethean characteristics of Watt's quest to master the mysteries of language and subdue it to his own purposes. Such characteristics are: a rebellion against things as they are, a commitment to a quest or action, a defining of the goal of the quest as self-authentication, an obsession with a mythical personage reminiscent of divinity, and the inevitability of suffering and/or defeat.[29]

Watt's Promethean effort to conquer the mysteries of language offers an example of the materiality of the Beckettian quest. In spite of the fact that Watt leaves the ordinary world and proceeds into the twilight zone of the Knott estate, he is searching for knowledge and competence that are related to the macrocosmic world of everyday human life. Although he is seeking abstract philosophical truth, he is not trying to attain mystical union with Mr. Knott in a spiritual realm. Instead, like Prometheus, he wants knowledge and power that, although they must proceed from a "divine" source, will enable him to function as he wishes in the human world. As we have mentioned, he wants to name himself (as a man), objects such as a pot, and events such as the tuning of a piano. Watt is Promethean and not Manichean in that whatever is good and desirable to him is inescapably attached to the macrocosm.

Studies which place Beckett's perspective on language into the frameworks of various linguistic philosophers are informative at this point. Hoefer explains that Wittgenstein's logical positivism

---

[28] Glicksberg, *Literature and Religion: A Study in Conflict* (Dallas: Southern Methodist Univ. Press, 1960), pp. 17, 29, and 31. Hugh Kenner (*Samuel Beckett: A Critical Study*, p. 69) also describes Beckett, along with Swift and Joyce, as one of the "great Irish nihilists."

[29] I have formulated and assigned these Promethean characteristics to the Beckettian hero in the paper entitled "The Promethean Quest of Beckett's Hero."

holds that language is capable of making truth statements about only empirical or scientific matters. Language used to attempt to make metaphysical or ethical statements is meaningless. Also, the so-called abstract operation of thinking is actually concrete: it is merely the process of using such empirical language.[30] Although we concede to the numerous critical exhortations that Watt is not a logical positivist,[31] we must nonetheless note that his efforts to use language are attempts to understand, explain, and speak of the empirical, material world. Skerl's placing of Beckett alongside Mauthner rather than Wittgenstein does not alter the element of empiricism in Watt's language quest. Mauthner agrees with the logical positivist that language is inextricably tied to the macrocosmic world. He not only claims that thinking and speaking are a single activity but also that language is nothing other than memory, which he defines as stored sensuous experience. Mauthner further insists that, since all language has its source in external reality, there is no language to describe man's inner world or consciousness, thus reducing Descartes' "I," the mind that creates language, from an agent with subjective interaction with the objective world to a no-self.[32]

Even if we assign a symbolic divinity to Knott, we must understand that Watt is "essentially a temporal being" and that he must therefore deal with the Jupiter who holds the needed knowledge and power "no where else but in this temporal reality."[33] Returning to a comparison of Beckett with Heidegger, we can say that man confronts (or is confronted by) nothingness (K(not)tness) only as *Dasein* or man-rooted-in-his-world.

A final Promethean aspect of Watt's quest for zero as an attempted seizure of the sacred fire is that the linguistic knowledge

---

[30] "*Watt*," p. 167.

[31] See, for instance, Skerl's "Fritz Mauthner's 'Critique of Language' in Samuel Beckett's *Watt*."

[32] See "Fritz Mauthner's 'Critique of Language' in Samuel Beckett's *Watt*," pp. 476-77; and Ben-Zvi, "Samuel Beckett, Fritz Mauthner, and the Limits of Language," p. 187.

[33] Nathan A. Scott, Jr. points out the inescapability of a confrontation between man and God taking place anywhere other than in the world where man is situated. See *The Broken Center: Studies in the Theological Horizon of Modern Literature*, p. 58. Scott is echoing Bultmann's ideas in his observations and is not, at this point, speaking specifically of Beckett.

and power he craves must come from a transcendent Other. This fact, of course, presupposes the ultimate failure of Watt's quest, a failure that can be succinctly stated as a syllogism: the desired gift must come from the Other; the Other is (K)not(t), or will (K)not(t) give the gift(s); the gift(s) cannot be received. The necessary presupposition underlying this logic is, as we have explained in Chapter One, the utter helplessness of Beckettian man to meet his own metaphysical needs. Watt is an example of such a man, a man described by Hugh Kenner as undeceived by the illusions of three centuries of the Enlightenment into entertaining "the fatal [Cartesian] dream of being, knowing and moving like a god."[34] It would be difficult to find in any literature a more ironic portrait of Enlightenment Man than Beckett's depiction of Watt in the asylum garden, pathetically and comically exhausting all of his mental, emotional, and physical resources in a futile effort to communicate to Sam the "eight states" of his stay at Mr. Knott's (pp. 164-69). The hidden irony of the use of the Promethean myth as symbolical framework for man creating his world in defiance of divinity comes into focus here: Prometheus is completely dependent on Jupiter's resources.

Beckett's use of Cartesian and Occasionalist philosophy is relevant in understanding Watt's impotence. The ability of Descartes' man to achieve any mastery of the macrocosm so radically split from his microcosm depends on that supposed point of interaction that he calls the pineal gland. But Murphy's pineal gland (his "conarium") has "shrunk to nothing" (*Murphy,* p. 6). The heroes who succeed him, including Watt, share, in all probability, in this biological disaster. The Occasionalists Geulincx and Malebranche, who follow Descartes, find no scientific or empirical interaction between man's desires and his abilities to enact these desires. Instead, the continued intervention of God, who mercifully acts as a kind of go-between linking the desire with its fulfillment, is the cause of all human competence. For Geulincx, man remains able to function on his own in the confines of the mind, but, for Malebranche, even mental activity rests on the enablement of God. As Livio Dobrez formulates, "The mind receives its ideas not from

[34] *Samuel Beckett: A Critical Study,* p. 132.

what is outside it but from God so that all its knowledge is a knowledge of things in God, and all its intellectual operations take place in the context of a continuing divine activity." Dobrez goes on to explain that the "disintegration of Watt's mind" and his reduction "to epistemological chaos" seem to occur in the kind of system Malebranche describes with one overwhelming and notable exception: the supernatural assistance which is absolutely required is never forthcoming.[35]

In contrasting the competency of man as defined by Sartre and Camus with the impotence of Beckettian man, David Hesla says that both of these existentialist thinkers "manage to transcend the condition of the absurd [with the word used here by Hesla to indicate the discrepancy between man's expectations of life with his experiences], the one by understanding it, the other by rebelling against it." Beckett, however, can neither devise a system nor choose a strategy that can enable his heroes to escape man's irrational and helpless condition. Instead, Beckett (and Watt) understands that because God is either dead or "unavailable" to humanity, man must "go on" knowing that "in the absence of the absolute . . . knowledge [and competency] is impossible."[36]

Since we have discovered that Beckett's notions of the human condition are closer to those of Heidegger than those of either Sartre or Camus, it is interesting to realize that, at this particular point, Beckett and Heidegger touch once again. In the interview Heidegger granted *Der Spiegel* (which he forbade to be published until after his death), he answers a question concerning the ability of philosophical thought and language to guide mankind through what he sees as the present-day era of technological disaster. He states that his answer is the result of "long reflection":

> philosophy will not be able to effect an immediate transformation of the present condition of the world. This is not only true of philosophy, but of all merely human thought and endeavor. Only a god can save us.

---

[35] Dobrez, "Samuel Beckett's Irreducible," *Southern Review: An Australian Journal of Literary Studies*, 6 (1973), 208-12.

[36] Hesla, *The Shape of Chaos*, p. 84.

Having made this statement, Heidegger moves away from Beckett by revealing the non-transcendent basis of his reflection. It is precisely by man's "thinking and poetizing" – that is, by human thought and language – that a "sort of readiness" for the "appearance of the god or for the absence of the god in the time of foundering" is to be achieved. Like Beckett, Heidegger seems to be saying that "in the face of the god who is absent, we founder."[37] But unlike Beckett, the philosopher conceives of human thought as the agent that can arrive at solutions to human incompetency: "I see the task of thought to consist in helping man in general, within the limits allotted to thought, to achieve an adequate relationship to the essence of technology."[38] The problem of Beckett's man is not a technological age *per se;* neither does he find hope for solutions in human thought and language. Instead, with Vladimir and Estragon, Beckett and Watt amuse themselves with playing language games as they desperately wait for Godot, who, alone, will be able to "save" them.

Watt is one of Beckett's most profound language games. By our extensive unraveling of the structure of Watt's quest, we have examined only the inner zero of a group of circles such as those made by a pebble tossed into a lake. The circle around Watt's language quest is the narration of Sam, the narrator of *Watt,* and the circle surrounding Sam's quest to relate the tale is that of the understanding (or bewilderment) of the reader who is confronted with the narrator Sam's flawed account of Watt's pilgrimage. The fourth circle that can be formulated is that of Beckett's creation of Sam and writing of the novel.

Sam does not refer to himself as narrator until the beginning of Section 11. At this point, he expresses the hope that certain "appearances of Mr. Knott" and the "strange impression they made on Watt" will be described in detail later. This authorical reference is summarily followed by a third-person designation of himself as narrator, as "his [Watt's] mouthpiece" (p. 69). Matthew Winston distinguishes "four separable but interrelated functions of Sam: he is a participant in Watt's experience, the recorder of Watt's story, the writer and arranger of a book, and a commentator on the

---

37 "Only a God Can Save Us," p. 277.
38 "Only a God Can Save Us," p. 280.

action."[39] Sam's quest, then, is also linguistic: he attempts to listen to Watt's recounting of his experiences and to record and comment on what he hears in the arrangement of words that becomes the novel *Watt.* Sam, however, finds his difficulties with language to be insurmountable to the extent that he is unable to construct any verifiable account of Watt's pilgrimage. By examining Sam's linguistic problems, we can arrive at an understanding of the futility of his quest. An initial difficulty reveals itself as Sam makes vague references to limitations on space and time in regard to his narration of events. The first footnote states that "valuable space has been saved" by omitting reflexive pronouns throughout the text of *Watt.* Exactly where such pronouns would occur and what "space" is being saved are problematical in the extreme,[40] especially when we find Sam devoting thirty pages to such episodes as Arthur's nonsensical account of the academic adventures of Mr. Ernest Louit (pp. 169-99). At least twice, Sam hurries on with a particular description after stating vaguely that he hopes to offer greater detail on the matters at hand in a somewhat nebulous future (p. 69). Such a future never materializes, nor do we hear anything more about the intentions of the statements.

A second difficulty that Sam seems aware of is the problem of whether or not Watt is intentionally or unintentionally withholding information from him. Sam acknowledges that it is "by no means impossible" that much of what has taken place may have been "left unspoken" by Watt (69). He also blames any inconsistency or incompleteness of his story on the possibility that Watt either "did not know a great deal on these subjects, or did not care to tell." The effort Sam makes to reassure himself on this matter is hardly reassuring – to Sam or to the reader:

> But he [Watt] assured me at the time, when he began to spin his yarn, that he would tell all, and then again, some years later, when he had spun his yarn, that he had told all. And as I believed him then and then again, so I continued to believe

[39] Winston, "*Watt's* First Footnote," *Journal of Modern Literature,* 6 (1977), 73.

[40] See "*Watt's* First Footnote" in its entirety for an excellent study of the implications of this footnote, pp. 69-82.

> him, long after the yarn was spun, and Watt gone. Not that there is any proof that Watt did indeed tell all he knew, on these subjects, or that he set out to do so . . . . (p. 125)

Whatever Watt's intentions are as to the truthfulness and completeness of his recitation, his personal difficulties in communication play havoc with the exchange of information attempted between him and Sam. Sam remarks on the "obscurity" of Watt's comments, the "rapidity of his utterance," and the "eccentricities of his syntax" (p. 75). In fact, Sam claims that he doubts whether any voice has ever ("except in moments of delirium, or during the service of the mass") been used by a man "*at once* so rapid and so low" as Watt's (p. 156). Watt's fatigue, whether mental or physical, also affects his relating of information to Sam. Watt informs Sam that, once, the telephone on the ground floor had rung and a voice, identifying itself as that of a "friend," had inquired as to Mr. Knott's well-being. When Watt states the incident – "A friend, sex uncertain, of Mr. Knott telephoned to know how he was" – he acknowledges that there are "cracks" in its "formulation." But Watt cannot repair this statement; he is "too tired to repair it" and dare not "tire himself further" (pp. 147-48). Order of events also becomes a communication problem between Sam and Watt. Watt tells the events of his sojourn in an order different from the order in which they have occurred or the order in which they appear as printed.[41] Watt's problems with grammar, syntax, pronunciation, enunciation, and spelling (p. 156) are given vivid and concrete form in the garbled and pathetic articulations he offers Sam of the eight stages of his stay at Mr. Knott's (pp. 164-69). Watt's basic problem in communication is that which we have already elaborated on in analyzing the events of the sojourn itself. Watt has been unable "to distinguish between what happened and what did not happen, between what was and what was not, in Mr. Knott's house" (p. 126).

What we may call the arena of communication complicates matters further for Sam, what he refers to as "the material

---

[41] For enumeration of these various orders, see John J. Mood, " 'The Personal System' – Samuel Beckett's *Watt*," *PMLA*, 86 (1971), 256-57.

conditions in which these communications were made" (p. 75). Apparently Sam and Watt are initially in the same "pavilion." Sam begins Section 111 by telling us that Watt has been moved to "another pavilion" (p. 151). Speculation leads us to guess that Watt's condition has worsened, but we cannot be certain as to the reason for his transfer. At any rate, the two deranged friends must now meet in the ten or fifteen acres of wilderness/garden that surround their mansions, Watt's area is separated from Sam's by two high barbed wire fences. Each clambers through the "large irregular hole" that occurs in each fence to pace and converse in the strip between the fences (pp. 156-63). Here much of what Watt says is "carried away" by the "rushing wind" and "lost for ever" (p. 156).

Sam's fifth difficulty is what he calls his "scant aptitude to receive" (p. 75). His hearing has begun to fail (p. 169), and he admits to "fatigue and disgust" in his efforts to incorporate the information Watt proffers into the novel *Watt.* As Winston remarks, Sam's difficulties "are part of *Watt's* central concern with how one may authenticate what is perceived and verify what is recorded." If, for Watt, to use language is to say nothing, for Sam, to "record is necessarily to falsify."[42]

The irony of Sam's linguistic quest is that his undercutting of Watt's account of the journey to Mr. Knott's is simultaneously an undermining of his own trustworthiness as a narrator. The reader's failure to find it possible to accept Sam's recording – the third encirclement of linguistic failure – is due not only to the difficulties we have examined which Sam is conscious of and which, as we have seen, he acknowledges, but also to subtle problems and ironic inconsistencies that Sam either does not mention or else does not fully explain. Where does the information come from that Sam includes in the novel that Watt could not possibly have known? *Watt* opens with about seventeen pages of an account of several characters interacting and communicating with each other before Watt is within earshot of them. Furthermore, other material surfaces throughout the novel that we cannot trace backward to its supposed source, from the printed page to Sam to Watt. How are we as readers to cope with Sam's claim that all that he offers us in

---

[42] "*Watt's* First Footnote," pp. 77-78.

Watt has come to him exclusively from Watt? If we arbitrarily disregard the question of the mystery of the source of this material, we remain bewildered by what is left. Winston points out that it is impossible for the reader to separate Sam's narration (supposedly straight from Watt) from Sam's comment and speculation on this narration; we cannot "distinguish between Sam and no-Sam."[43] For instance, whose conception of Mr. Knott is referred to in the account of Erskine and the bell (p. 120)? Sam's or Watt's? While it is true, as Winston reminds us, that we can be certain in *Watt* that we are reading the words of Sam, we often remain puzzled as to the origin of those words. Not only do matters which are never explained confound us as readers but also Sam's freely offered admission that he is an unreliable narrator undercuts his credibility as an author:

> And this does not mean either that I may not have left out some of the things that Watt told me, or foisted in others that Watt never told me, though I was most careful to note down all at the time, in my little notebook. (p. 126)

Is Sam's unreliability due entirely to his incompetence or does he at times deliberately mislead us? And why does he include the mass of obviously unrelated-to-the-plot material that bores us with its repetition and irrelevancy? Mood points out that at least a "third of the novel consists of material apparently only distantly related to the rest of the book."[44]

Our problems with Sam are not solved but multiplied when we realize that he is, if not insane, at least deranged. Both he and Watt are in an asylum – one of Beckett's favorite refuges from the madness of the ordinary world – when Watt relates his experiences to him. Winston notes, "Any single episode in the book, or all of them together, might have been made up by Sam. It is even possible that Watt never existed and that Sam's portrayal of him and relation of his adventures are the fantasy of a madman."[45]

---

43 "*Watt's* First Footnote," pp. 75-76.

44 " 'The Personal System' – Samuel Beckett's *Watt*," p. 257.

45 "*Watt's* First Footnote," p. 77.

The reader's problem, then, as he travels into Watt's world, guided by Sam, is also linguistic. As this world does not imitate the reality that we are accustomed to think we know, neither does the language of the text imitate the way we are accustomed to think language and logic function. Mood's analysis of the errors in *Watt* reveals numerous mistakes pointed out by the text plus twenty-eight more which appear to have crept into the work unawares.[46] If we concede that the text does not present any verifiable information about Watt and his experiences but offers instead a literary revelation of the "shape of Sam's mind or the nature of his psyche," we are again frustrated in our attempts to "read" the novel. As Winston explains, "Sam is not presented as a consistent character." Because "Sam is an illusion created through words," his "similarity to people is accidental and misleading."[47] As the Hamiltons succinctly summarize, "Watt's unwilling discovery that phenomena make no sense becomes the reader's discovery as well, as he grapples with the text before his eyes."[48]

We have thus far formulated and described three linguistic failures in regard to *Watt:* Watt's failure logically to comprehend his experience and explain it in words, Sam's failure successfully to relate Watt's experience, and the failure we as readers must cope with as we try in vain to decipher the novel as conventional literature. A fourth failure is Beckett's rendering of *Watt.* We have already explored – in Chapter Two – exactly what Beckett means by claiming that all art of value, including his own, is necessarily an art that fails. Astute critical efforts have been made to explain Beckett's successful failure which is the novel *Watt.* Winston ends his analysis with clear statements about the basic given concerning failure in *Watt* – *Watt* is a literary indictment and exploration of the irrationality and inadequacy of language:

> *Watt* deliberately evokes our awareness of how language does not correspond to reality. Words have only a very precarious and arbitrary relation to things. . . . Experience cannot be conveyed by words because there is no intrinsic connection

---

46 " 'The Personal System' – Samuel Beckett's *Watt,*" p. 263.
47 "*Watt's* First Footnote," p. 80.
48 *Condemned to Life: The World of Samuel Beckett,* p. 131.

> between events and the words which pretend to describe them; in the final analysis, all language is merely a fiction which aspires to an impossible identity with reality. . . . It [the novel] is self-negating because *Watt* embodies, although it does not assert, man's inability to affirm anything of significance.[49]

It is difficult to escape agreement with this basic given that *Watt* is an embodiment of man's failure to use language to affirm anything of significance. To accept this understanding of failure in regard to the novel, however, rather than resolving matters, leads to further problems. We can perhaps solve the problem of having to say that *Watt*, as a major work in language by Beckett, is seriously diminished in significance either because its entire premise is unfounded (man does have the ability to affirm significantly in language) or because its premise establishes its own insignificance (as a work in language, *Watt* is insignificant) by agreeing once more with Winston that the novel does not *assert* or *affirm* anything but instead *embodies* the impotence of language. But at this point, we are forced to ask whether or not Winston's essay on *Watt*, which certainly asserts and affirms numerous things in language, is itself an example of man's "inability to affirm anything of significance." If so, how has he been able to enlighten us about *Watt*?

Certain critics attempt to read *Watt* as an ironic satire which not only portrays the irrationality and inadequacy of language but also points in new directions for human understanding and communication. Thomas J. Cousineau, using Jacques Lacan's and Paul Ricoeur's frameworks of thought, suggests that the novel is about how "language allows a corrupt culture to seduce the individual with a distorted conception of himself." Watt *thinks* Mr. Knott is the key to the mystery of life, but Beckett as author and we as readers know that Watt is the victim of false assumptions foisted on his consciousness by a language that has become the instrument of a false God/culture.[50] To accept this reading, we would have to understand that Watt's world that does not work

---

[49] "*Watt's* First Footnote," pp. 81-82.

[50] Cousineau, " 'Watt': Language as Interdiction and Consolation," *Journal of Beckett Studies*, No. 4 (1979), pp. 1, 2, and 5.

and the self that cannot be named are illusions that can be unmasked. Such an understanding is foreign to any thematic premise undergirding Beckett's work as a whole, including *Watt*. Such a world and such a self are terrible realities, but they are realities. As Beckett renders so graphically in a later novel, Watt's condition of existing in a nothing/world as a no/self is *How It Is*.

Heath Lees, in his reading of *Watt* as ironic satire, deals at length with the music in the novel and suggests "that if Watt had accepted the invitations offered by music, all might have been well – or at least for the best possible." Lees goes on to say that "in *Watt* the failure goes deeper, for Beckett continues in a variety of ways to demonstrate that not even music is the ideal, purely musical language, intelligible yet undistorted. On the contrary, says Beckett [according to Lees], music itself is distorted and incomplete and, like language, forced to surrender its natural life on Western man's altar of systematic reason." What Watt should have done is to have gained "Attunement" with "a purely musical universe unsullied by the ordinary linguistic fidgeting with significance, systemization and sense . . . one which carries its own meaning within its own specially musical framework."[51] We are reminded of suggestions by various linguists (including Mauthner) that man can escape the limitations of language through transcending speech into the realms of music, laughter, or silence. Exactly how such transcendence could be achieved, however, remains unclear. As for Watt, we must remember that any linguistic solutions to his problems would have to work for man as Heidegger's *Dasein*, man rooted in his world of objects and others. In such a world, neither music, laughter, nor silence can serve as an adequate substitute for language. Arsene's cryptic categorizing of laughter is relevant at this point. There are three types of laughter: "The bitter laugh laughs at that which is not good, it is the ethical laugh. The hollow laugh laughs at that which is not true, it is the intellectual laugh." Most devastating of all is "the laugh of laughs," the laugh "that laughs – silence please – at that which is unhappy" (p. 48). Watt tries to use language as an instrument in gaining fulfillment of the empty circles of existential

---

[51] Lees, " 'Watt': Music, Tuning and Tonality," *Journal of Beckett Studies*, No. 9 (1984), pp. 6, 10.

need in his life. And laughter for him becomes, not a transcendent solution, but ironic comment on the failure of his efforts.

John C. Di Pierro sees Watt's individual selfhood as mirroring "the irrationality and chaos of our modern world." This critic, however, assigns a positive interpretation to Watt's deterioration of language skills, a deterioration exhibited most notably in Watt's conversation with Sam in the asylum garden, in which he is finally unable to join letters, words, or sentences together (p. 168). Beckett's intent here (says Di Pierro) is to show that "the super-rationalistic language of the twentieth century has reached the point where the 'reflux' to barbarism has set in. The Viconian language cycle starts afresh with primitive sounds and gestures. This is the theocratic and sacred historical stage where seers who are mad communicate the language of the gods which is incomprehensible except to the few. The 'mantic' language." Di Pierro thinks that Watt may be only "half-mad" but nonetheless "on the threshold of divine recognition." He is being reincarnated as a new Watt because he has glimpsed "the essence of an eternal cyclical process" and its "meaningless essence which is beyond time." This critic concedes that such a reading of *Watt* is possible only if we "approach *Watt* intuitively, like a poem or like a religious fragment, and absorb its complex essences."[52]

We have only to encounter Watt as the crucified Christ figure in the asylum garden or as the no-self in the train station – and the structure and tone of Beckett's language throughout the novel – to understand that, however we define the failure of Watt and Beckett, it is not an anticipatory prelude to the desirability of nonsensical speech. Watt and Beckett would accept the anguish and terror (though not the reason for this anguish and terror) that permeate the dining room at the fortress of Belbury in C. S. Lewis' *That Hideous Strength.* A breakdown in language similar to that which takes place in the story of the Tower of Babel occurs, and everyone begins to shout unintelligibly at everyone else. The resultant gibberish – "like the noise of a crowded restaurant in a foreign country" – becomes louder and louder until confusion, violence, and terror devastate the company of people.[53]

---

[52] *Structures in Beckett's Watt,* pp. 83-84, 90-93 and 103.

[53] Lewis, *That Hideous Strength: A Modern Fairy-Tale for Grown-ups* (London: John Lane the Bodley Head Ltd., 1945), pp. 429-35.

Jonathan Culler explains how ironic readings (such as these three critical assessments of *Watt*) can materialize, not in the text of a work itself, but in the expectations of a reader:

> At the moment when we propose that a text means something other than what it appears to say we introduce, as hermeneutic devices which are supposed to lead us to the truth of the text, models which are based on our expectations about the text and the world. Irony, the cynic might say, is the ultimate form of recuperation and naturalization, whereby we ensure that the text says only what we want to hear. We reduce the strange or incongruous, or even attitudes with which we disagree, by calling them ironic and making them confirm rather than abuse our expectations.[54]

Watt is indeed irony, but its irony is not focused on the character Watt. As Cohn insists, the "irony against Watt is blatant and pervasive, and yet Beckett evinces sympathy with Watt's heart-breaking, mind-breaking quest."[55] Beckett is no more satirizing Watt and suggesting what he *should* do than he is offering suggestions for escape from their calamitous world to Hamm and Clov in *Endgame.* As Cohn profoundly summarizes in regard to the meaning of failure in *Watt:* "*Watt* is a novel of the failure of a quest."[56]

Culler says that the "example of Beckett" (in general, not specifically in *Watt*) shows that "we can always make the meaningless meaningful by production of an appropriate context." He is referring to the meaninglessness or failure of language:

> If all else failed, we could read a sequence of words with no apparent order as signifying absurdity or chaos and then, by giving it an allegorical relation to the world, take it as a statement about the incoherence and absurdity of our own language.[57]

---

[54] *Structuralist Poetics: Structuralism, Linguistics, and the Study of Literature,* p. 157.
[55] *The Comic Gamut,* p. 94.
[56] *The Comic Gamut,* p. 68.
[57] *Structuralist Poetics,* p. 138.

In thinking of *Watt,* however, as a meaningful allegory of meaninglessness, we must confront ourselves with Beckett's insistence that genuine art is not simply "expressive of the impossibility to express." Instead, art must actually fail, it must be incompetent to express.[58] Mood concludes that *Watt* is "an involved and complex saga of a people falling to bits in every possible way, most especially internally."[59] We are, of course, playing with words when we say that Beckett's linguistic quest or effort to produce the novel *Watt* is a failure. Only when we accept his own definitions and perspectives can we understand that *Watt* is a mirror of man's failure to find any significance in his world that can be expressed as meaning in language.

In order to complete our study of *Watt,* we must now advance beyond analyses of structure and content and ask questions concerning Watt/Beckett's metaphysics. Why does Watt, as an example of the Beckettian hero, fail in his quest to find significance in his world? Why is he unable to express meaning in language? Beckett's portrayal of Watt (and of any other hero) is of Everyman, and Watt's world is not a particular culture or age but human experience in general. Thus Watt's problem is not unique to his personality or condition of being: it is indigenous to human life on the planet Earth as perceived by his creator, Beckett. Beckett's perception of the pain of imperfection in a consciousness only too aware of the potential of perfection remains suspended in his art from any rational or logical understanding or acceptance of this pain. This suspension of perception is reflected in a suspension or incompleteness of language. The multitude of words that Watt (or any other narrator or hero) uses to relate his impression of the suffering emptiness of life and consciousness fails to say anything about the why or the significance of this suffering. Thus we are prohibited from using the adjective "tragic" to define the failure of the Beckettian quest: such an adjective would imply some understanding or spiritual dimension gained from the experience of loss and failure – a gain that is not present in the experience of Beckett's hero. Instead, as the Unnamable laments, man comes "into the world unborn, abiding there unliving, with no hope of

---

[58] *Proust and Three Dialigues with Georges Duthuit,* pp. 120-22.

[59] " 'The Personal System' – Samuel Beckett's *Watt,*" p. 264.

death." We are "outside of life we always were in the end, all our long vain life long" (*The Unnamable,* p. 346). Human suffering is simply a meaningless given; it lacks any dimension of redemptive significance except Beckett's depiction of determined ongoing in the face of futility. Within the context of the fiction, this ongoing takes the form of the hero's continuing to quest without any real hope of apprehending the object(s) of the quest. Or, in the fiction of the quest as I have described it on level two, of the artist/hero's persisting in his efforts to fabricate the story without any valid anticipation of completing it. For Beckett, in the real world, the ongoing shapes itself into his persevering to produce the body of work that has become his canon, while simultaneously proclaiming this canon to be a "failure."

Since for Beckett's hero, the experience of life always includes suffering, and since this hero is preeminently rational man seeking a rationale for this experience, his failure to comprehend the reason(s) for the pain of life is the essential core of all other failure. As we have noted earlier, Beckett comments on the fact that the "light" (the desirable aspect of human experience) is always shadowed by the "darkness" (the undesirable aspect) in the interview with Driver. Beckett elaborates in this interview on the fact that Greek or classical thought offers a *reason* for suffering (a reason intrinsic to the adjective "tragic"). "The destiny of Racine's Phaedra is sealed from the beginning; she will proceed into the dark. As she goes, she herself will be illuminated." Beckett defines this drama as a movement of the heroine toward the dark so that she will eventually arrive at "complete illumination." Thus man (or in this case, woman) moves from light through darkness in order to come into a brighter and more lasting light. Traditional Jansenist thought (which is synonymous with Christian thought) offers a *cause* for darkness, epitomized by Beckett in the situation of the two thieves. Both are justly in darkness because of their sin. One, because of "grace given" is "saved" or moves by the fiat of God into the light. The other, because of "grace withheld," remains in damnation or darkness, also by the fiat of God, but fairly so, because he is receiving, as Luke phrases it, the "due reward" of his deeds (23:41). In Beckett's thought, there is no apparent reason why one thief receives grace and the other does not, except the arbitrary choosing of God. Having defined the "clarity" offered by these two modes of thought, Beckett rejects such solutions because he – and all of "us [that is, the modern world]" – are "neither Greek nor Jansenist."[60]

There is no "reason" for Watt's dark journey if we attempt to view it from the perspective of Greek tragedy. Although Watt resembles a tragic hero in his resistance to both an implacable universe and the frailty of his own mind and body, he realizes no potential godliness or stoic acceptance of transcendent ideals through his suffering. If "know thyself" can be defined as the psychological motto of the Greeks (the words inscribed over the temple of Apollo at Delphi) and insight into the self in regard to man's fate as the dominant aspect of "light" attained by the suffering of the tragic hero, Watt is no such hero. Rather than gaining any knowledge of himself, he loses the ordinary words he has once used simply to speak of himself as a man. Watt's "flaw" or *hamartia* is nothing other than that he is a man – even if he cannot describe himself as such – and, like other Beckettian heroes, seems to have little choice in regard to his inevitable progress into the "darkness." Beckett distances us as readers, by the ridiculous and pathetic aspects of Watt's characterization, so far from any sense his hero might have of the tragic nature of existence that we can hardly assign to Watt any grandeur of the human spirit in facing this existence. Watt's perspective is Greek, however, in that he feels no spiritual contact or sharing of understanding with the God apparently in charge of his fate. Thus Watt (along with Beckett's other heroes) has no sense of sin as an abstract and spiritual concept, such as that associated with the Christian idea of conscience. As we have seen, although Watt lives under a perpetual cloud of guilt, it is a free-floating guilt quite unconnected to any choice or action on his part.[61]

The only classically Greek characteristics, then, that we can isolate in a Beckettian hero such as Watt are the tenacity to "go on" in the face of an implacable fate steeled against him and the

---

[60] "Beckett by the Madeleine," p. 23.

[61] My summary of information on the Greek spirit and culture, including the literary understanding of classical tragedy, used in this paragraph and in succeeding paragraphs, is taken from two sources: *The World in Literature,* ed. Robert Warnock and George K. Anderson (Chicago: Scott, Foresman, 1959), pp. 90-94; and *A Handbook to Literature,* C. Hugh Holman, 3rd ed., based on the original by William Flint Thrall and Addison Hibbard (Indianapolis: Bobs-Merrill, 1972), pp. 531-33.

pervasive sense of guilt that arises, not from a conscious awareness of deserved punishment, but from the fact of the "crime" or "sin" of having been born to exist as a human being on the earth.[62] It is important to note at this point, that the milieu of Beckett's fiction is not that which has come to be thought of as classically Greek either. If the key to the Greek spirit was freedom – for man to explore himself and his world without restrictions – the key to Beckett's hero's spirit is what Molloy refers to as the "hypothetical imperative" (*Molloy,* p. 87), an urgent, all-controlling summons to the quest (or the wait) arising from both the microcosm and macrocosm. This summons so powerfully dictates the actions of Beckett's man that he almost seems to have no choice but to journey to Mr. Knott's, seek his mother, wait for Godot, or crawl though a mud-world to find some other. Man's freedom is as circumscribed as that described by Geulincx – to be left "free, on the black boat of Ulysses [which is traveling west] to crawl towards the East" (*Molloy,* p. 51). It is not necessary to offer examples proving that the Greek ideals of beauty of mind and body remain unrealized longings in Beckett's world. His heroes are neither handsome, agile in body, healthy, serene in mind, nor united with likeminded people in common pursuits. Nor do they enjoy a harmony of mind and spirit or find man's present experience of life to be so fulfilling that life after death assumes only a mythical significance. An exception to this general disparity would be that both the Beckettian and the Greek heroes sense a God (or Gods) who can be as evil and capricious as the heroes themselves are. That Beckett's hero does not find available to him a Greek or tragic reason for human suffering, then, is not surprising: he does not live in a world that operates as we expect the classic Greek culture to function in regard to its heroes.

Although Watt (and the other heroes) are no more Jansenists than they are Greeks, the world they live in is much more describable from the Jansenist perspective than from the Greek. The Jansenist movement in the seventeenth-century Roman Cath-

---

[62] Schopenhauer finds this "sin" in the works of the Spanish dramatist Calderon and quotes him in *The World as Will and Idea.* Beckett quotes Schopenhauer in *Proust,* p. 67, without acknowledgement, and finds (*Proust,* p. 75) the same kind of "sin" in Dostoevsky's *Crime and Punishment.* Pilling claims (*Samuel Beckett,* p. 213) that Beckett told Richard Ellmann that Joyce originally consolidated this idea.

olic Church was a revival of a form of Augustine's theology. Its basic emphasis is on God's determinism in the affairs of men. Without supernatural grace, no one can obey God's commands or be a recipient of his favor. Because it is impossible to resist God's grace, man logically becomes a victim of either natural or supernatural determinism. If God does not supernaturally ordain him to a state of grace or salvation, he remains naturally determined to damnation by God's non-ordination. The Jansenists were also advocates of a stringent moral asceticism.[63] Beckett's almost obsessive use of Augustine's two thieves crucified beside Christ becomes a symbol of his heroes' understanding of life. They have no choice but to experience the crucifixion of the flesh and to wait for God to decide whether to give or withhold grace. The fact that grace is never given, nor any understanding of why it is withheld, becomes the essence of the suffering associated with the failure of the quest.

We have previously described at length the Manichean traits of Beckett's fictional world. The Jansenist and Manichean characteristics overlie what is essentially, though not entirely, a traditionally biblical world system. A listing of certain traits of the milieu Beckett bequeaths his heroes will substantiate this claim. Some Other, not man, is responsible for the condition of life on earth. This Other (or "They") is the *Pantokratōr,* the All-Ruler, who is in control of all things and thus cannot escape the responsibility for the existence of evil and the determinism of humanity. The same kind of corporate principle that operates throughout the Bible, especially the Old Testament, appears to also be operative in Beckett's world: all men share in the "sin" of being a part of the generations of the earth and pass this quality on to their offspring. Nature seems to offer promises of beauty and life (and thus appears to be the "handiwork" of God), but often instead delivers the ugliness of decay and death. Man, though apparently possessing some potential for blessedness, has no chance of achieving this potential unless he experiences the serendipity of God's visiting him. Life in this world is one of suffering and uncertainty, and

---

[63] For information on Jansenism, see *The New International Dictionary of the Christian Church,* pp. 524-25; and *Handbook to the History of Christianity,* ed. Tim Dowley, et. al. (Herts, England: Lion, 1977); rpt., Grand Rapids: Eerdmans, 1977), p. 498.

man's longing for another life (after death) is shadowed by fear of its being even worse.[64] In Beckett's milieu, these traits are strongly overcast by Manichean presuppositions. The God who controls matters is evil or malign, and man, because he is trapped in the flesh, cannot escape his suffering. To propagate more misery through procreation is foolish if unavoidable. Flashes of light imprisoned in the darkness of matter cause man to continue to quest, lured on by a word that Beckett himself is fond of applying to the condition of his hero – the word "perhaps."

Reflection upon the descriptions we have just formulated reveals that Beckett's hero inhabits a world that possesses an intensification of negative biblical characteristics. From a biblical, but not a Beckettian, perspective, this transitory world outside of Eden is viewed as sharing the decay and death man has brought upon himself by his rebellion and sin against God. The world of Beckett's hero lacks, however, not only man's rebellion and sin but also the elements of grace that the Christian scriptures claim have been introduced into such a world through the person and work of Christ. Therefore, we can say that Watt and the other heroes are required to function in a world that has been cursed by God for some unknown reason and that never experiences his grace. The Hamiltons claim that Beckett, as "few others have done since the Enlightenment," has "accepted historic Christianity's view of existence as a vale of tears."[65] Were we to conceive of a world structured on biblical assumptions, and then to subtract from those assumptions all content that defines man as a deserving sinner freely offered, through the suffering and death of a Christ who is a Savior, salvation or redemption, both in this world and the next, we would have a caricature of Beckett's world. This caricature portrays man, not as a deserving sinner, but as an amoral protagonist, guilty of and suffering for he knows not what. Furthermore, Christ is no Savior/God but merely a pathetic archetype of man victimized by the Father/God. Thus salvation or redemption (as deliverance from meaningless suffering) cannot occur – man has no sin (that caused his suffering) to be saved

---

[64] For these descriptions of a biblical world system, see John W. Wenham, *The Goodness of God* (Downers Grove, Ill.: Intervarsity Press, 1974), pp. 25-26, 32, 42-44, 51, and 74.

[65] *Condemned to Life: The World of Samuel Beckett*, p. 40.

from, and he has no Savior (who suffered not only to deliver him eventually from suffering but also to give redemptive significance to suffering) to effect his salvation. Beckett's world is like the world of the Bible, but a world that lacks sin, grace, or redemption.

An examination of these deficiencies in the Beckettian world-frame will show why the hero cannot understand or explain suffering and why all the babble of words he sprouts forth fails to give any significance to a life of emotional and physical pain. Watt never clearly articulates his bewilderment as to what he has done or what he is doing that causes matters to go so badly for him, but this bewilderment permeates his consciousness throughout the novel. We can easily imagine him speaking certain words about sin and guilt that Beckett assigns to the Unnamable:

> Perhaps one day I'll know, say, what I'm guilty of. . . . Let them put into my mouth at last the words that will save me, damn me, and no more talk about it, no more talk about anything. But this is my punishment, my crime is my punishment, that's what they judge me for. . . . (*The Unnamable*, pp. 368-69)

Beckett's heroes, including the Unnamable and Watt, are Manichean in that they view as sin the condition of being spirit that is born as matter into the prison of a material body. This condition is itself a consciousness of guilt: "So long as it is what is called a living being you can't go wrong, you have the guilty one" (*Malone Dies*, p. 259). As he leaves the Knott estate, Watt envisions himself as the guilty one in that he is the one who has suffered loss without known cause:

> Of his anxiety to improve, of his anxiety to understand, of his anxiety to get well, what remained? Nothing. . . . He saw himself then, so little, so poor. (p. 148)

And what has Watt learned from this experience of failure? What has he gained in the way of understanding or spiritual enlightenment from his stay at Mr. Knott's? The answer is the same—"Nothing" (p. 148). The Unnamable summarizes the matter of sin and guilt in Beckett's world: "all here is sin, you don't know why, you don't know whose, you don't know against whom" (*The Unnamable*, pp. 403-04).

Unlike Milton's Adam and Eve, expelled from Eden into a fallen world, Beckett's protagonists cannot learn that they have chosen to act wrongfully and deserve their expulsion from Paradise. All of their actions and choices are made apart from any knowledge of good and evil, what they "should" have done, or "should not" have done. Therefore, Beckett's people are also unable to arrive at the self-insight and repentance of Racine's Phaedra, as she confesses in penitence to Theseus that the tragic culmination of violence and death that has occurred in Troezen is due to her lawless passion for Hippolytus.[66] Needless to say, Beckett's heroes also lack Adam's and Eve's assurance of grace, that Providence shall be their guide in their sinful state. They also lack the motivation of Phaedra to do away with themselves. Instead, they simply continue on in their "sin" of living and questing.

The logic apparent in Beckett's definition of "sin" (or "crime") and guilt is not flawed: to subtract sin as man's willful choice of moral wrongdoing and the need for and possibility of redemption from a biblically structured world does indeed render suffering totally inexplicable. The metaphysical construction of Watt's world is a Jansenist universe that lacks the two facts that Pascal (also a Jansenist) says the "Christian faith goes mainly to establish" – "the corruption of nature and redemption by Jesus Christ."[67] These two Christian premises do not solve the puzzle of the existence of suffering within such a world, but they certainly elucidate the matter. If man is not a sinner directly responsible for the fallenness of this world, and if God has not provided redemption, both for man and nature, through the suffering of Christ, then there is no dimension in human suffering, in a world such as that we have described, that renders it other than absurd or meaningless. We would join Beckett's heroes in assigning the greater sin, not to man, but to God himself. We can easily agree, in such a world, with A. E. Housman: "It is in truth iniquity on high/To cheat our sentenced souls of aught they crave." Housman's conclusion in the

---

[66] The ending of Racine's classical drama is actually heavily weighted with Christian overtones, due no doubt to the biographical fact that Racine began his adult life in the Jansenist movement at Port-Royal and later retreated from a worldly life and career to a pious domestic life within the Jansenist fold. It is interesting to note that Beckett chooses the use of this particular play as the setting for his example of a tragic heroine in the interview with Driver.

[67] *Pensées; the Provincial Letters,* p. 69.

poem where these words are found ("The Chestnut Casts His Flambeaux") is one that Watt and Beckett's other "sinless," "guilty" heroes would sanction: "The troubles of our proud and angry dust/ Are from eternity, and shall not fail."[68] Such "troubles" are static, having no cause of beginning nor hope of ending. As Wylie states in *Murphy:* "the syndrome known as life is too diffuse to admit of palliation. For every symptom that is eased, another is made worse. The horse leech's daughter is a closed system. Her quantum of wantum cannot vary" (p. 57).

The second deficiency related to the question of suffering in Beckett's world-view (given the definitions of this view that we have already formulated) is the grace that can be offered only by a divine Savior/Christ. I am using the quality of divinity here as a necessary element in the concept of any Christ capable of effecting redemption or salvation for men in Beckett's system of things. Such redemption may be conceived of in Beckett's world as primarily existential, rather than theological, in that it would assign significance to the broken expectations and suffering of the hero. Since the divine Christ not only overcame the experience of suffering and death by the resurrection but also made salvation possible precisely because of this experience, he assigns to suffering a profound and lofty significance that is lacking but sorely needed in Beckett's "fallen world." However redemption is conceived of, it would be like theological salvation in that it would effect forgiveness for the hero of the crime of being born and resolve him of the nebulous guilt of failure, meaninglessness, and nonsignificance that so pervade his consciousness throughout the fictional canon.

But redemption offered by such a Savior/Christ is not available in Beckett's world. Michael Robinson describes the complete humanization of Christ in Beckett's works and remarks that "To humanize Christ is to diminish his promise of salvation." In fact, "Christ become man has lost his power to save."[69] It is because of the biblical-world atmosphere that the Beckettian hero inhabits that the divinity of the person of Christ seems necessary for him. Such divinity is certainly not essential in many other literary

---

[68] See this poem in *The Collected Poems of A. E. Housman* (New York: Holt, Rinehart, and Winston, 1965), pp. 107-08.

[69] *The Long Sonata of the Dead,* pp. 114-15.

environments. Writers such as Emerson, Whitman, and Faulkner use a completely human, non-divine Christ as a symbol of archetypal man, a Christ whose qualities of spiritual strength, gentleness, love, and purity make him a fitting example and guide to struggling humanity. Beckett's Christ, however, is similar to that of Dostoevsky, Melville, and Hemingway. Lacking divine power to overcome suffering and death, he becomes the victimized clown/fool of the Father/God with whom man can identify in crucifixion but not in resurrection. The Hamiltons explain: "For Beckett, Christ represents the type figure of suffering mankind, lonely, mocked, and abandoned by his friends to bear the extremities of pain without hope of a reprieve. There is no suggestion that the Passion of Christ has any redemptive dimension, or that his death is followed by any resurrection."[70]

Beckett's description of Watt in the asylum garden is his most explicit depiction of such a Christ:

> His progress was slow and devious . . . for often he struck against the trunks of trees, or in the tangles of underwood caught his foot, and fell to the ground, flat on his back, or into a great clump of brambles, or of briars, or of nettles, or of thistles. But still without murmur he came on, until he lay against the fence, with his hands at arm's length grasping the wires. . . . His face was bloody, his hands also, and thorns were in his scalp. (His resemblance, at that moment, to the Christ believed by Bosch, then hanging in Trafalgar Square, was so striking, that I remarked it.) (p. 159)

This painting (*Christ Mocked* or *Christ Crowned with Thorns* by Hieronymus Bosch in the National Gallery in London) pictures a Christ being cruely mocked by four men. One, who is wearing a collar of thorns, has his arm around Christ as if he would pull him toward him (and thus against the collar), another seems in a position of derisive prayer, still another tries to grasp Christ's hand in mock sympathy, and the fourth is placing the crown of thorns on Christ's head. The expression on Christ's face is one of resigned, almost indifferent, very slight perplexity. The ephemeralness of his body and the non-involvement of his expression serve

---

[70] *Condemned to Life: The World of Samuel Beckett,* p. 41.

to remove him from the scene, so much so that the tormentors seem to be mocking a manikin. Bosch's meaning is probably that Christ is removed from the punishment of the immediate torture because he is undergoing universal punishment for the sins of all mankind.[71] Watt is like Bosch's Christ because he also is undergoing universal punishment, the crucifixion all men undergo for the sin Beckett defines as that of having been born into nature.

Such a Christ is found throughout Beckett's fiction. From the lingering death of Belacqua's crucified lobster (*More Pricks than Kicks*, p. 22) to the bloody and disheveled Watt in the asylum garden to the word images – "nails," "hair fallen," "scars invisible," "flesh torn of old" – of *Ping*[72] to the skulls of *La Falaise* and *Worstward Ho*, Beckett's writings abound in references to a crucified Christ who is man victimized by the Father/God. Such a Christ is in no way divine, nor is there any possibility that he might be a Savior.[73] Instead, he is the pathetic archetype of suffering humanity thrust unwillingly into life and betrayed by God into sacrificing himself for goodness and truth in a world where redemption and suffering are unrelated. Redemption is only a word-sign referring to nothing, and suffering is the meaningless and universal experience of inhabitants of the planet Earth. In Beckett's view, the philosophical repetitions throughout history to relate the two ideas in an interchangable cause-result relationship, most notably in Christian thought, have produced only confusion and disappointment.

Beckett's use of the Manichean mythology[74] is useful in understanding the Beckettian vision of Christ.[75] The Christ of the

---

[71] This description is of my own viewing of this painting in the Netherlandish room of the National Gallery. For reproductions of this painting, see Ludwig Von Baldass, *Hieronymus Bosch* (New York: Henry N. Abrams, 1960), p. 13 (color) and plate 110 (blk. and white).

[72] *Ping*, in *First Love* and *Other Shorts* (New York: Grove, 1974), p. 71. All other references to *Ping* are to this edition and are referred to by title and page number(s) in the text.

[73] For discussions of Beckett's Christ, see Michael Robinson, *The Long Sonata of the Dead: A Study of Samuel Beckett*, pp. 113-15; Alice and Kenneth Hamilton, *Condemned to Life: The World of Samuel Beckett*, pp. 40-43; and John Pilling, *Samuel Beckett*, pp. 120-23.

[74] For comment on Beckett's use of the Manichean mythology, see *Condemned to Life: The World of Samuel Beckett*, pp. 51-58; Alice and Kenneth Hamilton, "Samuel Beckett and the Gnostic Vision of the Created World," pp. 293-301; Pilling, *Samuel Beckett*, pp. 119-21; and Edouard Morot-Sir, "Samuel Beckett and Cartesian Emblems," pp. 81-92.

[75] No critic has elaborated on the Manichean subtleties of Beckett's Christ. Pilling (*Samuel Beckett*, p. 121) remarks that a "Manichean would be tempted to

gospels (Jesus in the days of his flesh) can be only an example of the suffering produced by the imprisonment of Light in the Darkness of matter. The Manichean disassociation between this fleshly (and therefore earthly and evil) Jesus and the completely spiritual "Jesus the Brilliant Light" parallels Beckett's separation of any element of divinity from the person of Christ. The weakness and foolishness of Beckett's Christ follow logically from the absurd and ridiculous notion (from a Manichean perspective) that God or Spirit would voluntarily be born into nature through a woman's body. In Beckettian and Manichean thought, *Incarnation* is a term of inherent contradiction. Voluntarily imprisoned in flesh or matter, Christ can be only human with no capability to redeem himself or others from such self-imposed darkness.

Jung's description of Christ as a symbol of the self[76] is both Manichean and Beckettian. The "traditional figure of Christ" is a "parallel" to the "psychic manifestation of the self" (p. 42). In spite of the "dechristianization of our world" psychologically (p. 36), "Christ is our nearest analogy of the self and its meaning" (p. 44). The problem with this Christ image in the modern sense is that it cannot account for the psychological totality of the self, for its evil or animal nature. St. Augustine denied the ultimate reality of evil (p. 49), but the Manicheans and moderns cannot solve matters so neatly. Therefore, Jung postulates the Antichrist or "shadow" of Christ as a necessary part of the archetype of Christ as symbol of the self: Christ

> corresponds to only one half of the archetype. The other half appears in the Antichrist. The latter is just as much a manifestation of the self, except that he consists of its dark aspect. Both are Christian symbols, and they have the same meaning as the image of the Saviour crucified between two thieves. (p. 44)

The two Manichean Christs and the Beckettian split Christ immediately come to mind, as does the mingling of human conscious-

---

stress the escapist aspects of the Crucifixion rather than its aspect of utter commitment."

[76] See C. G. Jung, *Aion: Researches into the Phenomenology of the Self*, 2nd ed., trans. R. F. C. Hull, Bollingen ser. XX (Princeton Univ. Press, 1959), pp. 36-71. Particular quotations from this work are referred to by specific page number(s) in the text.

ness as a fixed duality of darkness and light – of the undesirable and desirable aspects of human experience. In fact, Beckett's offering of the salvation and damnation of the two thieves on either side of Christ is a symbol of the inscrutable light/darkness, life/death, salvation/damnation of human experience and consciousness.[77]

Watt and the other heroes, then, live in a fallen world somewhat similar to the world portrayed in the Christian world view. But their milieu lacks the givens of this view that open such a world to hope through an understanding of suffering as potentially redemptive – the givens of the reality of sin as just cause for guilt, the grace offered by a Christ who is a divine Savior, and a salvation effected only through suffering and death. Needless to say, however, these givens of the Christian faith cannot function as keys to an understanding of the suffering of life for the heroes – or for their creator, Beckett. Since early adulthood, Beckett has rejected the Christian explanations for the human condition, and he has bequeathed this rejection to his literary creations. Such givens function only in a climate of faith, and neither Beckett nor his heroes are men of faith. The picture emerging, of course, is of a writer whose early world-view was strongly and permanently influenced by traditional Christianity, but who, as an adult, has moved away from this tradition toward the skepticism and unbelief of his age. This writer retains, however, an empty space where the metaphysics of Christianity would fit in a human consciousness that accepted such beliefs. This empty space is the void, the zero, the nothingness, that is the area toward which the heroes obsessively quest. The claim I have made, from the earliest days of my writing on Beckett's work, that only a God can fill this void, derives from this understanding of the Beckettian quest.[78] The hero must find an alternative to replace the traditional Christian metaphysics concerning the inevitable suffering of the human experience.

This understanding of the quest explains both the hero's obsession with Christian ideas of God and his blasphemous mockery of these ideas: the hero must find something or someone

---

[77] See Driver, "Beckett by the Madeleine," p. 23.

[78] See note 16, p. 284, " 'Coloured Images' in the 'Black Dark': Samuel Beckett's Later Fiction."

to be what the Christian God is supposed to be – in order to avail himself of needed grace or divine gifts – and he rages against a God who fails to be found to meet these needs. Furthermore, what is searched for must be divinely bestowed; as we have stated repeatedly, Beckett's man cannot arrive at answers or effect solutions on his own. The linguistic dilemma confronting us at this point becomes a matter of paradox: How can a God who is described as malign, absent, and/or non-existent proffer the grace of an understanding of the pain of life? He cannot, but logically, he must.[79] Therefore, Beckett and his heroes must quest or wait forever for an event of paramount metaphysical significance that can never occur, lured on by the word "perhaps."

This event would also be linguistic, the giving of a Logos, an offering of what Christ – in the fullness of his person, work, and word – is said to be in the Christian tradition.[80] Watt's preoccupation with language exhibits an obsessive need for such a God/Word spoken into the human realm, but, in his fallen world, he encounters only fallen language. Watt's lack of a Word that bestows significance on life and its suffering is the essence of his painful exile from existential fulfillment. Symbolically, Logos is a Word or Thought that is "light and the life, at once spiritual and material, which combats both death and night" by functioning as "the antithesis of disorder and chaos, of evil and darkness."[81] We should not be surprised that both Watt and Beckett conceive of man's deepest deprivation as the need for a divine Word. They agree with Heidegger that man's essential being is rooted in language:

---

[79] The yes/no structure of this sentence is thematically the basic structure underlying all of Beckett's other dialectical contradictions – "the screaming silence of no's knife in yes' wound" (text 13 of *Stories and Texts for Nothing,* p. 139).

[80] Helmut Thielicke's definition of Christ as the Christian Logos is informative at this point. The definition is from *The Hidden Question of God,* p. 116. "The exceptional character of Christ as the New Testament sees him is that he does not just represent a relation to meaning, or, as one might say, the logos. Instead, he is the Logos. The truth is incarnate in him. It is identical with him. Truth is what he is. The final reality which gives meaning is there in him, namely, the *pistis* or faithfulness of God which according to Romans 3:3 constitutes the truth of God and which is thus something which endures, on which one can rely, and which as righteousness stands opposed to man's falsehood."

[81] *A Dictionary of Symbols,* p. 191.

> In thinking Being comes into language. Language is the house of Being. In its home man dwells. Those who think and those who create with words are the guardians of this home.[82]

The Christian linguist Michael Edwards agrees with the non-Christian philosopher Heidegger on the foundational importance of the role of language in understanding the human condition. He writes of a "God who is the Word making heaven or hell depend on words, and the particular appropriateness of the Word himself [Christ] proclaiming it." Thus language

> is neither additional to the rest of our experience nor merely of extreme importance. It is within us and we are within it, rather as if language, like air, were the medium through which we move and which moves through us. It is our way, to ourselves, to another, and to God.[83]

In Watt's fallen world that lacks a Logos, language functions somewhat as the poststructuralist critics have claimed that language acts in everybody's world. Any influence on Beckett by Wittgenstein and/or Mauthner is evident in comparing the status and function of language in Beckett's literary universe with certain linguistic ideas of the poststructuralist Jacques Derrida. These ideas can serve as a point of reference in remarking on the incompetence of Beckett's language without a Logos. Derrida conceives of "writing" *(écriture)* as the kind of language that has priority over all others, but by "writing," he does not mean representational signs or marks in an alphabetical language system. Instead, he is referring to the most foundational language activity imaginable. Vincent B. Leitch describes Derrida's notion of such an activity:

> Writing is the most primordial 'activity' of differentiation. As this prevocal process operates, it inaugurates language, bestows consciousness, institutes being. These three emerge out of silence, the Unconscious, nonbeing, writing.[84]

---

[82] Heidegger, *Basic Writings,* ed. D. F. Krell (London: Routledge, 1978), p. 193.

[83] Edwards, *Towards a Christian Poetics* (Grand Rapids: Eerdmans, 1984), pp. 219-20.

[84] Leitch, *Deconstructive Criticism: An Advanced Introduction* (New York: Columbia Univ. Press, 1983), p. 27.

We immediately think of Watt's broken speech in the asylum garden or of the Unnamable's incoherent flow of words. For Derrida, as for Beckett's heroes, such "writing" offers meaning only as an interdeterminate enigma. Language cannot arrive at truth because the sign leads only to the sign. Edwards explains Derrida's no-exit interplay of language signs. The signifier or sound-image refers to the signified or mental concept. This signified or mental concept, however, does not refer to anything except the signifier or sound-image itself. Only if there were a transcendent entity or thing for the signified to depend on, could it refer to anything other than the sound-image. Such an entity or thing would have to be eternally present within some kind of divine Logos. Lacking such a Logos, the signified is cast "back toward the signifier, within a process of signifying from which there is no exit." Thus, significance, "being, truth, no longer exist outside of the sign, before language and independently of it."[85]

Derrida, unlike poor Watt, is not troubled by what he sees as the self-containment of language. Instead, he finds such a condition of language to be "a Nietzschean affirmation, the joyful affirmation of . . . a world of signs without the fault [of having fallen from some original mean], signs without truth, without origin, offered simply for our active interpretation.[86] Watt and his creator, Beckett, are much more pessimistic concerning such self-reflexive signifying. For them, such an understanding of language implies that man exists in a "contemporary version of hell, in a world un-named and incapable of being renamed." Language which cannot establish meaning must "yaw between aphasia, silencing or throttling speech in a silent and breathless world, and logorrhoea, streaming from a plethoric self abroad in a plethoric universe."[87]

Beckett would agree with Edwards' description of such language as all that is available for men on the earth, but not with the reasons Edwards offers for the lapsing of language from our expectations of it:

---

[85] *Towards a Christian Poetics*, pp. 220-21.

[86] This translation from Derrida's "Structure, Sign, and Play" in *Writing and Difference* is from Robert Langbaum, "Current Trends in Literary Criticism," *National Forum*, 60 (1980), 21.

[87] *Towards a Christian Poetics*, p. 222. I am assigning Edwards' description here to Beckett and his heroes.

> We do have a sense of language in an Edenic condition of efficacy and plenitude, at one with the world and with ourselves, fulfilling our desires as speakers and writers, and doing so with ease. We recognize it at times as a quite prodigious power. On the other hand, we also know, perhaps more clearly in our century than ever before, that language has been subjected, like the human and non-human world to which it belongs, to 'vanity' and 'corruption.' The Edenic harmonies being lost, our access to it – as to everything else – is troubled, and our engagement with it a form of our exilic labor. It no longer meets the world inwardly, and in our mouths and under our hands it falls short of evidence and necessity. Languages even die, through disappearing from use, and they half-die by altering, and so alienate us from their, and our own, pasts. Words, in Eliot's paradoxically memorable phrase, 'slip, slide, perish.'[88]

Such Christian speculation on the difficulties of language use is not limited to the present age. Isidore of Seville, in writing on Genesis, says that since the Fall, man has suffered a "loss in language of an essential 'bond' uniting a thing and its name" that was present at the Creation. Aelfric, Pope Innocent, and Wolfram von Eschenbach are a few of many Christian writers who agree that the "fragmentation of human speech signifies a deepening intellectual darkness in the fallen world." Such fragmentation is evident in the fact that man is "no longer capable of maintaining a right relation between knowing subject and known object which the original gift of language made possible."[89] Supposedly, from such a viewpoint, this condition of language is not new; it must date back at least to the era of the Tower of Babel.

As in analyzing the deficiencies of Beckett's metaphysics that are due to an absence in his world of divine grace, we must be careful not to conclude that the Christian Logos is what Beckett and the heroes are searching for. The Beckettian rejection of Christian concepts of sin, grace, and redemption is precisely a rejection of Christ as Logos. Nonetheless, the analogies between the undefined Logos so needed in Beckett's world and Christ as

---

[88] *Towards a Christian Poetics*, p. 11.

[89] "Appendix," Sample Article, "Babel," in *Dictionary of Biblical Tradition, Christianity and Literature*, 33 (1984), 59-60.

Logos are striking. Moorjani finds these similarities so great that she reads the account of Watt's quest as an attempt "to fit unto the unknown forces the figure of the biblical God, the Logos that mediates and totalizes reality." The outcome of this attempt, Moorjani explains, is Watt's realization that "the unnamable forces at play cannot be covered by the traditional figures of the divine." Such figures cannot serve as "mediator" or "logos." Having come to this realization, "Watt stages a ferocious attack on the anthropomorphic concept of divinity." This attack takes the form of violence against nature as Sam and Watt destroy the birds and the eggs in the nest, claiming that, by doing so, they come "nearest to God" (pp. 155-56). Thus these two "are the victims of a cruel God, with whom they identify as they in turn massacre and kill." Moorjani's reading assumes that Beckett's purpose in *Watt* is to reveal and dismantle the violence that man projects onto outdated images of God as he uses him as a scapegoat for his own cruelty.[90] I would suggest that the disappointment and rage that Watt experiences are Beckett's own, and that we are to read these qualities as expressions of metaphysical need rather than as statements about what Watt or men in general should or should not do. Watt is not – at any point in the novel – seeking for the Christian Logos, but he is questing for a Logos, a God/Word to answer his questions, affirm him as a person, and meet the needs of his spirit. Moorjani is particularly helpful as she writes of the failure of Watt's quest:

> Watt encounters instead of a divine presence . . . a dark mind, an empty heart, an extinguished fire in the soul. His is a word without grace. . . . Nor can the divine logos be replaced by a human one; no human name can satisfy Watt's semantic need.[91]

Morot-Sir confronts Beckett and Wittgenstein with Pascal's analysis of the fallenness of human language and the necessity of Christ as Logos. This linguist sees "confrontation" between the thought of Pascal and that of these two moderns as "fundamental": he does "not think there are many other ways to look for solutions

---

[90] *Abysmal Games in the Novels of Samuel Beckett,* pp. 90, 92, 93.
[91] *Abysmal Games in the Novels of Samuel Beckett,* p. 91.

to human problems, – many other linguistic possibilities." It is in Christ's existence as fully man and fully God that he "performs his function of semantic organizer for the human language." Furthermore, "any word, to be fully understood, should be referred to Christ," particularly to Christ on the cross:

> The role of the Cross is not to conjure away our poor and torn out situation. On the contrary it is to explain that it has to be so! It is the meaning of Jesus-Christ's double nature. In him converge divine and human languages. Those two languages coexist. . . . The Cross is the point of perspective from where we can understand the inevitable linguistic duality of God and man, and our ambiguous status, and the normality of our existential anguish. [92]

Morot-Sir is referring to the meaning that the basic paradoxes of the event of the Cross can confer on the "existential anguish" of the human experience. Freedom comes from submission, glory from suffering, and life from death. From a Christian perspective, to refer the word/sign "suffering" to the Person of Christ is to create the possibility of accepting these paradoxes and their significance to human life.

We cannot, however, assign such a Christian acceptance to Beckett and his confused and suffering Watt. Instead, we profit once more by comparing the Beckettian need for a Logos with Heidegger's understanding of the linguistic implications of man's need. For this philosopher, the primary matter facing man is not the ageless problem of why humanity suffers, but the twentieth-century dilemma of human society being uprooted from any tradition or home by technology. In the final statement of his thought, he insists (like Beckett) that "all merely human thought and endeavor" (including philosophy) are futile in meeting the needs of such an age. Instead, "Only a god can save us." By this statement, however, Heidegger does not mean that we can be saved by a return to Christian belief. He explains that the "traditional metaphysical mode of thinking, which terminated with Nietzsche, no longer offers any possibility for experiencing in a

---

[92] "Pascal Versus Wittgenstein, With Samuel Beckett as the Anti-Witness," pp. 215-16; 213-14.

thoughtful way the fundamental traits of the technological age." Exactly what he does mean is not clear, but his remarks lead to an understanding of a need for some kind of divine Logos spoken into this "time of foundering; for in the face of the god who is absent, we founder." Human language cannot bring about the presence of such a Logos, but it is the only means by which man can prepare himself to receive this god. "The sole possibility that is left for us is to prepare a sort of readiness, through thinking and poetizing, for the appearance of the god." For Heidegger, the "thinking and poetizing" are definitively linked to Hölderlin, to "dialogue" with this poet in the form of historical literary research. Whatever Logos Heidegger is awaiting will appear from the relationship of the German language (hence his emphasis on Hölderlin) with the language of the Greeks (his emphasis on the "truth" of pre-Socratic thought).[93] Thus it is in language as the house of Being that whatever God he is speaking of will appear, and God in the form of language is a Logos. Like Heidegger, Watt is questing for such a Word.

Although comparisons are useful in examining the mythical implications of the Beckettian quest for a Logos, none of them will serve as final parallels. Beckett does not remain at the level of Heidegger's phenomenological methodology and basic realism. Watt's quest is uniquely his own, and is similar in a large measure only to the quests undertaken by other Beckett heroes. Like Watt, these heroes seek identity or fulfillment of the self, a significant other or community, a home for the spirit, and harmony with nature or the universal system of things. These empty voids of existential need are symbolized by Beckett's zero, a metaphysical circle of emptiness. In *Watt,* especially, this zero of emptiness is a silence waiting for the speaking forth of a Logos – a divine Word that will signify, explain, and comfort. Watt labors in vain to hear such a Word:

> . . . how he had laboured to know what that was, to know which the doer, and what the doer, and what the doing, and which the sufferer, and what the sufferer, and what the suffering. . . . (p. 117)

---

[93] "Only a God Can Save Us: *Der Spiegel's* Interview with Martin Heidegger," pp. 277, 279, 281, 282.

But he is able, finally, only to stuff together what he hears and thinks at Mr. Knott's into a "pillow of old words" for his "head" (p. 117). Perhaps if he could lay his head on the stony pillow of his fellow sufferer Jacob, he might experience Jacob's dream of a stairway reaching from the earth to heaven and hear God speaking from its utmost height.

MALONE DIES, A STORY OF GRAVE PLAY

If Watt is waiting to hear a word, Malone is attempting to write many words. The second novel of Beckett's trilogy can be described as a watershed in the fictional canon in regard to the hero's situation and activity, which together constitute the overt literary nature of his quest. Malone is waiting in bed until he dies and, meanwhile, composing and writing stories. Previous heroes have been involved in the production of literary sounds or words. The hero of *Assumption* lives and dies in respect to the articulation of a particular sound, and Belacqua of *Dream of Fair to Middling Women* and *More Pricks than Kicks* is an aspiring poet. The adventures of both these heroes, however, are recounted by omniscient narrators. An omniscient narrator also relates all we know of the events of Murphy's life – fortunately for us, since Murphy is not given to reciting or writing words. In spite of his obsession with words and their meanings, Watt writes nothing (that we are aware of), and we have to depend for knowledge about his quest on the unreliable narrator Sam. The first-person recitations of the trilogy are prefigured in the *Stories,* where a hero's "I" rambles on about efforts he once made to find some kind of shelter that would serve as a physical or metaphysical home. The first hero of the initial novel of the trilogy, Molloy, self-consciously offers an account of his journey to his mother's room. Now in bed in this room, Molloy is writing pages, under the instructions of a man (or a group of men the man represents), describing his journey there. The second hero of this novel, Moran, admits that he is also engaged in writing a report, in his case, in response to an instructing voice. Supposedly, these pages or reports become the novel *Molloy*, a first-person recitation of quest/journeys that Molloy and Moran have completed before they begin to write. Perhaps Molloy/Moran is one hero, and the quest(s) a single one.

But, to the best of our knowledge, no pre-Malone hero deliberately makes up and writes down a story or stories about someone other (ostensibily) than himself. Nor does a hero write what H. Porter Abbot calls the "intercalated or nonretrospective narrative," that is, a story in which "the time of its writing is contained by the time of the events recorded."[1] Such composition is precisely what Malone is writing. Immobile in a bed in a room in some kind of non-institutional living quarters, Malone awaits his death, which he feels is imminent, and, to fill the interim time, writes stories about imagined characters. This protagonist, then, serves as a link between the earlier fiction, in which the hero – as a full-bodied person – is either narrated about by an omniscient narrator or narrates his own adventures after they have occurred; and the later, in which a more or less disembodied voice or immobile figure recites his present experience (i. e., *The Unnamable* and *Texts for Nothing*), or a figure inhabiting some kind of enclosure or limited landscape is described by an impersonal third-person voice (i. e., *Imagination Dead Imagine* and *Ill Seen Ill Said*).[2]

Thus Malone's immobility and literary task of writing what he openly states are fictional accounts make him the first hero to fit my descriptions of the protagonist in the role of the self-as-artist undertaking the microcosmic or second-level dimension of the quest. We have just defined Malone as the first hero who overtly states his quest to be the composition of stories.[3] We can locate him in a setting that is at least partially microcosmic by noting the

---

[1] Abbot categorizes *Malone Dies* as such a novel not only on the basis of this trait but also on the characteristic that the text we read "is written by at least one of its principal characters." See "The Harpooned Notebook: *Malone Dies* and the Conventions of Intercalated Narrative," in *Samuel Beckett: Humanistic Perspectives*, ed. Morris Beja, et. al. (Columbus, Ohio State Univ. Press, 1983), p. 71.

[2] *From an Abandoned Work* and *Enough* are exceptions to this division.

[3] If the claim is made that his primary purpose is to die and the writing of stories simply an interlude to fill the intervening time, I would reply that Malone is unable to die naturally on his own – dying is an event that may or may not happen to him. Also, if Malone were actively questing for death, he could commit suicide. Because writing stories is the action he chooses and carries out, this task must be defined as the quest he undertakes.

gradual transformation of the room he is writing in to an area resembling the skeletal enclosure of the human brain. In some strange fashion, the papered walls of the room ("a writhing mass of roses, violets, and other flowers") fade from view,[4] the floor whitens, he becomes aware of "a gleaming and shimmering as of bones" (p. 223), both he and the color in the room coalesce into a "kind of grey incandescence" (p. 221), and Malone begins to wonder if he is "in a head and that these eight, no, six . . . planes that enclose me are of solid bone" (p. 221). Although Malone speculates that he may actually be already dead and in a vault (p. 219), and continues to define his enclosure as a room ("let us call it a room," p. 235), the bed seems to swirl as if "caught up into the air," and the ceiling to rise and fall rhythmically (p. 283). Malone remains in a room – he surveys his possessions there and receives the strange visitor. But whatever else this description of his changing environment signifies, it also signals the beginning of a change taking place in regard to the mythical, twilight-zone landscape that first appears in *Watt*. Thus, although we must categorize Malone as generally situated in the same no-man's land between the macrocosm and microcosm that the heroes inhabit from *Watt* through *From an Abandoned Work*, we can discern an intensification of the inward movement of the protagonist that is first completely realized in the hellish microcosmic landscape of *How It Is*, a landscape that no longer resembles the normal human world. When, in some of the fiction written after the sixties (i. e., *Still* and *As the Story Was Told*), Beckett's soul landscapes begin once more to take on minimal resemblances to the outside world, they exhibit the same double dimensional quality that we have described in the setting of *Malone Dies*.

Malone Dies exhibits a double dimension not only in regard to setting but also in respect to the two levels of the quest as I am describing them. Malone is questing to write stories (the quest on the second level), but, by doing so, he is likewise engaging in the

[4] *Malone Dies* (New York: Grove, 1956), pp. 223-24. Other references to *Malone Dies*, the second novel of Beckett's trilogy, *Three Novels*, are also to this edition and are cited by page number(s) in the text of this chapter. This novel, originally written in French as *Malone meurt*, was begun in the winter of 1947, completed in May of 1948, and published in Paris by Editions de Minuit in October of 1951. Beckett's translation of the novel into English was first published by Grove.

quest for the fulfillment of the five existential needs and for whatever metaphysical quality it is that Beckett symbolizes with the cipher of zero – the quest on the first level. Just as Belacqua seeks relationships with women in order to meet his needs (both physical and metaphysical), and Watt journeys to Mr. Knott's to satisfy his, so Malone writes stories in his searching. Like Watt, Malone is also questing for Beckett's zero quality, a deepened understanding of what human life is all about. As the structure of Malone's existential and metaphysical quest assumes the artful form of writing stories, he becomes the bridge between the journeying selves-as-character of the quest on level one and the composing selves-as-artist of the quest on level two, who seek to authenticate the self and realize the absolute through art.

In the role of the self-as-character, Malone is searching for himself as profoundly as Watt, or any other hero. In fact, one of the most poignant laments for authentic selfhood voiced by a Beckettian hero is assigned to Malone:

> But what matter whether I was born or not, have lived or not, am dead or merely dying, I shall go on doing as I have always done, not knowing what it is I do, nor who I am, nor where I am, nor if I am. (p. 226).

We can make this claim although we understand that this hero is anticipating death and attempting to create surrogate fictional selves. In fact, his projected plans reveal the obsession with self-authentication that underlies his artistic quest. Malone's outlines of what he plans to write vary at different points in the text, but, basically, he hopes to describe his "present state," relate three stories, and put together an inventory of his possessions, all of which are with him in the room (p. 182). The first and last intentions – to describe his situation and inventory his possessions – obviously have to do with self-examination. Although Malone vehemently declares that the proposed stories will be divorced from the ugliness, beauty, fever (p. 182), suffering (p. 186), and earnestness (p. 194) of which he has discovered life in the outside world to consist, the exact opposite occurs. As numerous critics have noted, the fictional characters and events that Malone fabricates exhibit not only the precise qualities of life that he has announced his intention of avoiding but also characteristics of his own experience before he becomes immobilized in the bed in the room.

References to Malone's earlier life and to fictional characters he has created in the past abound in the three stories of Sapo with his family, Sapo with the Lamberts, and Macmann. Malone as author gives Sapo "eyes as pale and unwavering as a gull's," and then abruptly inserts the authorial comment: "I don't like those gull's eyes." We know why, when Malone ironically protests, in regard to Sapo, "Nothing is less like me than this patient, reasonable child." Sapo is obviously very like Malone, including having "gull's eyes" (pp. 192-93). In writing of Macmann's keeper, Lemuel, Malone has him watching "mountains," but quickly corrects the word to "hills." It was on the plain below these hills, Malone continues, that Lemuel (or Macmann?) was born – "in a fine house, of loving parents." When Malone then mentions that in these hills, once, the "hammers of the stone-cutters [would] ring all day like bells" (p. 286), we realize that he is incorporating his own boyhood memories into Macmann's story. Malone has specifically mentioned earlier that as a child he had lain in bed listening to the barking of dogs from "hovels up in the hills, where the stone-cutters lived" (p. 206). The scattered lights the child Malone remembers seeing on the slopes of these hills (p. 206) become the "faint fires of the blazing gorse" – the "absurd lights" that shine about the boat holding Macmann, Lemuel, and the "tangle of grey bodies" in the bay, after Lady Petal's fateful Easter excursion (p. 297).

When Malone as author refers to old stories and proceeds to state that his death will simultaneously be the death of all the "Murphys, Merciers, Molloys, Morans," we recognize that the many selves we are being confronted with comprise one self – or one no-self – a self we may call Macmann, Sapo, Malone, Lemuel, or Samuel Beckett. In fact, the gull's eyes belong originally to Beckett,[5] and the ringing of the stone-cutters' hammers and the lights of the gorse fires are autobiographical references from

[5] Charlotte Renner, in "The Self-Multiplying Narrators of *Molloy, Malone Dies,* and *The Unnamable,*" *Journal of Narrative Technique,* 11 (1981), note 17, p. 31, points out that Deirdre Blair, in her biography of Beckett, p. 376, reports Beckett's acknowledgement that Sapo's gull's eyes not only resemble the eyes of Malone, but his own as well. As Renner states (p. 13), "it is impossible to ignore the connections between Beckett's life and those of his characters" in *Malone Dies.*

Beckett's youth that appear throughout the fictional canon, for instance in *The End* (p. 72), *First Love* (p. 34), and *The Unnamable* (p. 399).

Critics who have recognized Malone's writing as a quest to answer "Who is Malone?" approach the question in various ways. Eric P. Lévy writes of the absence of selfhood for Malone within the context of the disappearance of the narrator. We cannot for certain identify the composing voice in *Malone Dies* and find ourselves left with an "irreducible absence at the core of narration."[6] Charlotte Renner views Malone as becoming the Unnamable (or "the Unnamable 'author'"), the ultimate hero of the trilogy as a whole, who begins his multi-vocal existence as Moran.[7] John Pilling writes of Malone's failure to achieve a synthesis of "the real and the fictional" – that is, to discover and identify the self (which we, of necessity, conceive of as the self of the past) in the present-tense act of fictionalizing. Thus Beckett is exposing the fallacy of Proustian notions of salvaging and freezing time – including a self not changed by each succeeding moment – by a merging of involuntary memory with art.[8]

Jean Yamasaki Toyama explores the matter of the connection between Malone's writing and his search for identity as thoroughly as any critic.[9] From her perspective, Molloy and Moran write in order to re-create the self as defined by the past, but Malone wants to create a fictional world divorced from himself, in Toyama's words, "to create a world unsullied by his presence" (p. 89). Malone is attempting to create a new self, a self not condemned to the false personality received from the real world (p. 91). As this false self continually threatens to invade the fictional world, Malone tries "to distinguish himself from his story" by piling up his possessions (p. 93). Complications with this plan ensue as Malone's self fractures not only into fictional and real but also into the other inside him (pp. 93-94) and an other outside him (p. 95).

---

6 Lévy, "Voice of Species: The Narrator and Beckettian Man in *Three Novels*," *Journal of English Literary History*, 45 (1978), 355-56.

7 "The Self-Multiplying Narrators of *Molloy, Malone Dies*, and *The Unnamable*," p. 29.

8 *Samuel Beckett*, p. 35.

9 Toyama, "Malone, the unoriginal centre," *Journal of Beckett Studies*, No. 9 (1984), pp. 89-99. Specific references to this article are cited by page number(s) in this paragraph of the text.

The problem, of course, is the matter of language. As Malone is creating the selves of his fiction, even so is Beckett creating Malone. But since an author does not control or create his text but is instead controlled by it, the author's self vanishes in the process of writing. Thus, what we commonly call the creative process is actually a destructive interaction between an author and his characters. Sapo and Macmann do not constitute Malone's alternate self but instead are no-selves because they are created entirely of Malone's words, just as Malone has no "real" self because he is fabricated of Beckett's language. And Beckett and Malone are robbed of selfhood because, instead of writing their texts, their texts "write" them: that is, the language they are forced to use and the meanings they intend to imply by its use are neither possessed nor controlled by them but are borrowed from others (pp. 96-97). Thus Toyama concludes that Malone, along with any other writer, cannot create a self: "He cannot be found among his words; he cannot be reconstructed from his ruins" (p. 97). Only a self "dependent" on "changeability" can be said to survive the ravages of time or "faulty memory" and the indeterminacy of language. Malone becomes Macmann, who survives only because he is being continually changed as he is created and destroyed by a writer's pencil (Lemuel's hatchet) (p. 99).

Obviously the tenuous self of Malone formulated by criticism such as Toyama's cannot bear close scrutiny, or it will disappear. For one thing its existence is dependent on Malone's manuscript, and, as Abbott points out in his description of *Malone Dies* as intercalated narrative, this manuscrit is continuously and radically threatened:

> . . . rarely has the document itself been so continually at risk. Its existence depends not on a pen but on a pencil – and one so used that its life is barely that of the writer. Sharpened at both ends, it is reduced by the last pages to a small piece of lead. As for the exercise-book, it gets lost, falls on the floor, at one point is 'harpooned' by Malone with his stick. [10]

[10] "The Harpooned Notebook: *Malone Dies* and the Conventions of Intercalated Narrative," p. 73.

Also, as we have noted in our comparison of Sartre and Heidegger with Beckett's thought as revealed in *Watt,*[11] the human self can be said to exist only as it relates to something other than itself. Thielicke speaks of this relating as "a final mystery of all anthropology":

> In every interpretation of man there necessarily shines through the reality of man another reality, an alien element, which decisively characterizes man. This is because man can never be described except as a being in relation, a being which reaches after something and stands related to it.[12]

If the existence of Sapo/Macmann depends exclusively on Malone's pencil and notebook, or on being related to the self of Malone, it is tenuous indeed.

Furthermore, although Beckett's manuscripts which house Malone and his created characters are not "threatened," they contain what Leo Bersani calls "their author's implicit disclaimer" in regard to them.[13] Implicitly in the works themselves and explicitly in his rare comments about these works, Beckett insists that his characters have emerged from some matrix of consciousness of which he is not fully cognizant or in complete control.[14] Therefore, as Bersani says, he creates a "particular drama of alienation and hostility between himself and his fictional world" in which his creatures refuse to be identified by their creator's imagination.[15] If Malone cannot derive his selfhood from Beckett, from what source can he derive it? And where does Malone's dilemma leave Sapo and Macmann?

Malone's efforts to define a self are apparent in his difficulties with names. These difficulties can be seen not only in his obsession with his inventory (naming his possessions) and in his efforts to categorize topics for his stories, but also in the assigning of names to his characters. He easily assigns his first character the

---

[11] See appropriate section of the chapter on *Watt* of this study.

[12] *The Hidden Question of God,* pp. 62-63.

[13] Bersani, *Balzac to Beckett: Center and Circumference in French Fiction* (New York: Oxford Univ. Press, 1970), p. 327.

[14] See the entire interview with Shenker in *The New York Times,* especially p. 3.

[15] *Balzac to Beckett: Center and Circumference in French Fiction,* p. 327.

name of Saposcat and the nickname of Sapo, but, at the loss for a "Christian name" for this person, abruptly decides that Sapo will not need one (p. 186). Becoming unable to "stomach" this name any longer (later in the text), Malone makes a change and settles on "Macmann," a name "not much better" than Saposcat, but one that will do as "there is no time to lose" (p. 229). Apparently, either Macmann or his name is vulnerable: two pages later, Malone breathes a sigh of relief, in referring to his "new" character – "But for Macmann, thank God, he's still there" (p. 231). Moll is already named Moll when we encounter her, but there is something strange about her being thus named:

> This woman was standing behind him, so that he could not see her . . . . Who are you? said the speaker. Someone replied, But it is Moll, can't you see, her name is Moll. The speaker turned towards this informant, glared at him for a moment, then dropped his eyes. To be sure, he said, to be sure, I am out of sorts. (p. 256)

Nearly all of Beckett's work exhibits names that are "out of sorts" but here, for the first time, we see the overt arbitrariness of assigning less names to characters. Beckett's people simply do not have what Thielicke calls "names to express their non-interchangeable identity,"[16] and, rightly so, since they have no such identity. The question is whether or not Beckett is celebrating the namelessness (and changeable identity) of his heroes and heroines or lamenting it. I, of course, am insisting that he is lamenting the no self-hood that prevades his work, that Malone is searching for himself and for a permanent name. In spite of much critical comment to the contrary, Iain Wright also reads Beckett as finding desirable in human experience "identity as fixed, pre-given, immutable." In regard to the namelessness of many (or most, if not all) of Beckett's narrating voices, Wright insists that "Beckett, as putative authorial presence, cares very much indeed who's speaking; and the whole strategy of these later fictions [*The Unnamable* and the fiction that follows] is to get us to address ourselves to

[16] *The Hidden Question of God*, p. 176.

that question: the problematic of the subject."[17] Thielicke explains the significance of a name. Someone's name is not a "designation"; isolated from the named person, it "says nothing." A name of someone unknown or known only by accounts of him carries no personal identity: a name "can normally be filled out and interpreted only by the one who bears it." Thielicke continues:

> For this reason, only the name can do justice to selfhood in its non-interchangeability. The one who bears a name is not defined but presented. He presents himself. That is, he opens a history with himself in which he discloses or hides his true self but in which this true self is always relevant. In contrast, mere mention of his name, as in a telephone directory, tells us nothing about him.[18]

Neither Malone nor his fictional avatars have names that are non-interchangeable, that present them as persons with histories that disclose what we may call reliable selfhood. Beckett's implication may be that such named selfhood is only an illusion or ideal in human experience – in the Revelation, John speaks of man's utopian state as one in which a person receives a "new name" (2:17). But Malone as author is searching for such an ideal. The "little creature" he is attempting to create is to be made "in my image," a phrase resonating with ideas of derived and immutable selfhood (p. 226).

It would be possible to explore Malone's quest in the role of self-as-character for each of the other existential needs in as detailed a fashion as we have examined his search for the self or identity. But because our primary concern with this hero is as a bridge into the artistic quest of level two, we shall present his other existential quests – for a home or place of belonging, a significant other, involvement in a universal system, and resolution of mind-body dualism – in much briefer fashion.

Immobilized in the seclusion of his room, Malone is questing for a home or existential place of belonging. This place of retreat

---

[17] Wright, "'What matter who's speaking?': Beckett, the authorial subject and contemporary critical theory," in *Comparative Criticism,* ed. E. S. Shaffer, V (Cambridge: Cambridge Univ. Press, 1983), 68 and 72.

[18] *The Hidden Question of God,* pp. 176-177.

from macrocosmic life, portrayed as a room, is a shelter that reminds the hero of life in the womb. As he sucks his pillow, he speaks of being "buried" in an "old world" that "cloisters" him. Whatever contentment this place or condition affords, however, is short-lived. Just as in nearly all the fiction that exhibits the retreat and creative endeavor of the quest on level two, the macrocosm intrudes into the secluded world, and Malone's consciousness is inundated with memories or visionary glimpses of the outside world:

> I go back again to the light, to the fields I so longed to love, to the sky all astir with little white clouds as white and light as snowflakes, to the life I could never manage. . . . The beasts are at pasture, the sun warms the rocks and makes them glitter. Yes, I leave my happiness and go back to the race of men too, they come and go, often with burdens. (p. 199)

Malone's retreat is hardly a place or condition of "happiness." Other than the bed, his belongings, the dish, and the chamber pot, the room he inhabits offers no comfort or security. Furthermore, the "Night, storm and sorrow" that have characterized macrocosmic life (p. 199) also invade the shelters of the stories he is writing. Sapo's home, the Lambert's farm, and Macmann's final refuge in the asylum called "the House of Saint John of God" are travesties of any kind of existential home for man's spirit. Accustomed to Beckett's religious irony, we are not surprised that the asylum is named for the Apostle John. It is in John's gospel that we read of "mansions" or rooms that Christ has gone to prepare in his Father's house (14:2). Whatever refuge Malone finds or creates in his stories becomes a replica of the insecurity and exile that he has experienced in the outer world. As he focuses mentally on settings for his characters (or for himself), he feels "lost in forests" or "whirled far out on the face of wind-swept wastes" and begins to wonder if he has "not died without knowing and gone to hell or been born again into an even worse place than before" (pp. 226-27).

Malone attempts by his writing to create another (or an other) for company and solace in his loneliness. Such company would consist of the characters he fabricates, or has fabricated in the past. "Yes, a little creature, I shall try and make a little creature, to hold in my arms, a little creature in my image, no matter what I say" (p. 226). The phrase "no matter what I say" refers to Malone's previous disclaimers of his imaginative creatures being made in his image. Although, as we have noted, they are so exactly in his image that they become surrogate selves, they can also be perceived as beings who might serve as significant others. Toyama comments on Malone's failure in this regard:

> . . . he always fails; he is always left alone. His art is not enough to create 'real' people who can join him and dispel his loneliness; they are only creatures. Their appearance paradoxically only emphasizes their absence in Malone's life. [19]

Although the strange visitor to Malone's room does anything but dissipate loneliness, Malone entertains the fleeting notion that this guest may be "the first of a series of visitors." If so, the hero plans to try and catch one with his stick, a "little girl for example." Perhaps he could force her to "kiss me, fondle me, smile to me, give me my hat, stay with me" (p. 273). No such visitor shows up, and, instead of being resolved by his imaginative plans, Malone's need for a significant other is intensified, an intensity that is increasingly apparent in his stories. The description of Mrs. Lambert in her "ruinous old house" surrounded by despair, incipient incest, and a total lack of interpersonal communication escapes Beckett's usual ironic tone, if not his irony, in its stark portrayal of human loneliness:

> It helped her, when things were bad, to cling with her fingers to the worn table at which her family would soon be united, waiting for her to serve them, and to feel about her, ready for use, the lifelong pots and pans. She opened the door and looked out. The moon had gone, but the stars were shining. She stood gazing up at them. It was a scene that had sometimes solaced her.

Whatever solace she finds is lost when her daughter reveals Sapo's plans to go away and not come back (p. 217). Macmann also suffers the loss of emotional "shelter, charity and human tender-

[19] "Malone, the unoriginal centre," p. 91.

ness" as Moll dies and the vicious Lemuel takes her place (pp. 265-66).

Malone's mind/body dualism is exemplified in his sensations of all the parts of his body being radically separated from his head. His feet "are leagues away"; at least a month would be required to "call them in." His fingers "write in other latitudes," and he does not expect to see his "sex" again with the "naked eye" (pp. 234-35). Toyama sees Malone as split into three selves: Malone, an other inside him, and one outside him, each separated from the other. "Although separate and strangers, these different selves or parts of the self seek out each other." The "method" Malone uses to attempt arrival at these other parts of himself is writing.[20] We are reminded of Murphy's three distinct zones of being, reproduced here with a separate self in each zone. No resolution of such duality or triangularity takes place between Malone as person, as author, and as character, nor between his body and his spirit. In fact, in his appearance in the opening pages of *The Unnamable,* he seems spiritless, merely an object. Rotating about the Unnamable, along with Beckett's other heroes (or containing them), he is "motionless" and wordless, retaining "little trace" of his former "mortal liveliness" (*The Unnamable,* pp. 292-93).

The quest for unity with a system finds expression in Malone's obsession with his possessions in the room. The earlier heroes Belacqua and Watt have exhibited attempts toward unity with nature, which they sense to be the outward form of some vast, universal system of things. Perhaps it is because Molloy and Moran journey through natural settings that constantly betray them (although Belacqua and Watt have been disillusioned by nature also) that their reincarnation Malone restricts his interest in the natural world to his room and whatever scenery appears through the window. An initial effort on Malone's part to create an affinity between Sapo and nature proves unfruitful:

> Sapo loved nature, took an interest in animals and plants and willingly raised his eyes to the sky, day and night. But he did not know how to look at all these things, the looks he rained upon them taught him nothing about them. He confused the

[20] "Malone, the unoriginal centre," pp. 93-95.

> birds with one another, and the trees, and could not tell one crop from another crop. He did not associate the crocus with the spring nor the chrysanthemum with Michaelmas. The sun, the moon, the planets and the stars did not fill him with wonder. (p. 191)

Malone later decides not to include description of the natural world in his stories and assigns "all this . . . scenery" to hell (p. 277). He is resigned to living, dying, and writing enclosed in the room or inner world of the imagination, "here, in the midst of my possessions" (p. 235).

In accord with his plan, Malone begins carefully to inventory these objects that fill his world and constitute his system of things. He commences to name each article, from the pencil (p. 246) to the photograph of the ass taken "at the edge of the ocean" (p. 251). But he soon encounters difficulties which make him despair of thus ordering this world. He may be naming things he no longer possesses and "reporting as missing others that are not missing." Also, he suspects there may be objects in the room of which he has no knowledge (p. 250). Apparently, Malone is not going to enjoy the order that Molloy achieves with his sixteen sucking stones. Malone's obsession with these visible phenomena does not abate; he plans, when "it is light enough to see," to take them all, by means of his stick, into bed with him (p. 251). But whatever hopes for achieving unity and order he has entertained by planning to include "my inventory" in his literary output (p. 184) are abandoned:

> I cannot account in any other way for the changing aspect of my possessions. So that, strictly speaking, it is impossible for me to know, from one moment to the next, what is mine and what is not, according to my definition. So I wonder if I should go on, I mean go on drawing up an inventory corresponding perhaps but faintly to the facts. (pp. 250-51)

Writing cannot achieve an empathetic entrance into or unity with the visible manifestation of Malone's life system.

Malone's quest, like those of Molloy, Moran and the Unnamable – the other heroes of the trilogy – can be described as a quest toward Beckett's zero, that symbol of the mystical essence of life.

However, Malone's search in such a direction is not as easily charted as theirs, nor its goal so readily defined. As Watt seeks for Mr. Knott, so Molloy searches for his mother, and Moran for Molloy. The Unnamable's quest is for the basic "I" of selfhood or the "true silence" (*The Unnamable,* p. 393) beyond words. Malone specifies dying and writing stories as his goals, but, as we have seen, such specification encompasses meanings not apparent on the surface of his claims. As he reaches for the fulfillment of the existential needs, especially the need for authentic selfhood, Malone expresses a sensing of a mythical someone or something vitally associated with these needs. In accord with his method of retreat and artistic endeavor, he also links this someone or something with the self or selves of the literary characters he is in the process of fabricating. "My concern is not with me, but with another, far beneath me . . . of whose crass adventures I can now tell at last" (p. 195).

Malone attributes this concern to a trait of his personality which he deplores, and which he has been unhappily aware of since childhood – the trait he calls "earnestness." Since his youth, he has been in the "toils of earnestness. That has been my disease. I was born grave as other syphilitic." Throughout his life, he says, "within me the wild beast of earnestness padded up and down, roaring, ravening, rending" (pp. 194-95). As David Hesla comments of Malone, "It was impossible for him to escape this disease. Even when he struggled to be grave no more, he struggled gravely not to be grave."[21] This hero has made desperate efforts to escape the gravity or earnestness, to play, to give himself to "jollity," "to live," "to invent," as others not afflicted as he. But each attempt to escape has been followed by a relapse into the same frame of mind, a return to

> darkness, to nothingness, to earnestness, to home, to him waiting for me always, who needed me and whom I needed, who took me in his arms and told me to stay with him always, who gave me his place and watched over me, who suffered every time I left him, who I have often made suffer and seldom contented, whom I have never seen. (p. 195)

[21] *The Shape of Chaos,* p. 107.

In this passage the trait of earnestness loses its total undesirability and undergoes a transformation by its association with qualities of personhood. We remember similar words spoken by Watt about Mr. Knott. Exactly what the "earnestness' is transformed into is not clear. Malone is probably referring to some mythic element of selfhood uncorrupted by the falsity and unhappiness he associates with macrocosmic life – an element that he hopes to discover by his descent toward the core of consciousness and readily symbolized by Beckett's zero. Although the hero tries to disassociate his writing from such serious pursuit, as we have seen, the stories become darkly earnest as they take on the spiralling shape of Malone's inward journey toward whatever is at the center of the self and its worlds.

Although we can no more equate Malone's core of everything with God than we can limit Watt's Mr. Knott to a similar definition, we can note in Malone's experience the four-point pattern of religious consciousness that we have observed in Watt and earlier heroes. If Malone senses his existence to be dependent on someone perceiving him, it would seem to be either the woman who feeds him and empties his chamber pot or the strange man who visits him, since these are the only personages we know of who see him. Although he realizes his physical dependency on the woman – without her help, he would starve to death – there are almost no metaphysical undertones to this dependency. Without her, he would starve, but he does not exist existentially because she perceives him. Nor can we rest Malone's being on the man who visits him. This man hits him on the head, watches him several hours, and probably meddles with his possessions, but his coming and going appear to have nothing to do with Malone's essential being. We come close to an awareness of some ultimate perceiver when we consider the mysterious "they" that Malone seems to think both the woman and the visitor represent. "They" may be trying (through the woman) to deprive him of soup and thus hasten his death (p. 255), and the visit may have been planned because it "amuses them" (p. 268). Thus we have the notion of Malone being observed much as the speaker of *How It Is* is watched by the witnesses. This notion, of an observing "they," however, is not developed in *Malone Dies,* but in the subsequent and last novel of the trilogy, *The Unnamable.*

Instead, Malone's dependence for being on a perceiver is best explored by noting his dependency on the characters he is engaged in creating. His being is dependent on his writing in the exercise book, and his writing in this book is the creation of his fictional characters and their lives. Thus his life is dependent on theirs: without them, he would not be an author, and there is no Malone except Malone the fabricator of stories. In order to think of Sapo and Macmann perceiving Malone, we have only to refer to the opening pages of *The Unnamable.* Here, this unnamed, egg-shaped hero sees Malone wheeling about him in orbit. Various critics surmise that Malone as narrator has become the voice of the Unnamable, and that the Malone in orbit is now Malone as character, a character whose creation we must now assign to the Unnamable. If, as Renner suggests, Malone as character contains all of Beckett's previous heroes (as the Unnamable says, "they are all here, at least from Murphy on" [*The Unnamable,* p. 293]), then the Unnamable as narrator is being watched or perceived by all his (or Beckett's) thus far created characters.[22] In a similar fashion, we can picture Malone in bed being given existence by the observation of his fictional creations. Such a picture fits well with the ideas of selfhood and ultimate consciousness that relate Malone to his avatars.

In writing of Malone as invented by someone else, Toyama sees his life as determined by this other:

> For although he plays the roles of creator and writer, Malone himself is a creature. He is someone else's invention. We may never hear the voice of this inventor, though we may glimpse him in the phrase: '. . . the business of Malone (since that is what I am called now)'. The passive voice, more evident in the English version [than in the French], indicates another who has named Malone. This 'other' is not actually present; his presence is marked by the passive voice, a sign of his absence. Malone points out that he has had other names at other times and admits that he has been manipulated by another.[23]

---

22 "The Self-Multiplying Narrators of *Molloy, Malone Dies,* and *The Unnamable,*" p. 26.

23 "Malone, the unoriginal centre," pp. 239-40.

Toyama describes this other as Malone himself in his role of creator and manipulator of fictional persons and/or Beckett who creates and manipulates Malone. But Beckett's familiar notions of some authoritative other being in charge of human affairs also appear in *Malone Dies.* As Malone ponders his present condition in the room, he wonders how he came to be left in it. Perhaps his presence there is "at the behest of one of the powers that be." He concludes that such is probably not the case, since he has been received and cared for in the room, and the attitude of "the powers" has previously been malignant rather than benign p. 182). Apparently Malone conceives of these others as similar to the mysterious "they" who throw the hero of *The Expelled* out of his room into the street, slamming the door afterward (*Stories and Texts for Nothing,* pp. 9-10). At any rate, both Malone and Macmann, his final created character, are almost completely under the control of whoever is "keeping" them. Beckett also includes in *Malone Dies* a reference to the motif of Augustine's two thieves, a motif that pervades both the fiction and the drama. Malone loses the stick with which he has been pulling his bowl of soup within reach, and becomes discouraged – about what is not clear, since he supposedly is longing for death anyway. He attempts to cheer himself by remembering that "one of the thieves was saved," and "that is a generous percentage" (pp. 254-55). The two thieves are visibly present in the novel as Moll's earrings (p. 263). Beckett's irony is blatant: Malone is certainly not being "saved," and the whole matter, as we have noted before, of why one thief is saved and the other lost remains a puzzle throughout the canon.

Of the four components of the hero's religious consciousness, guilt is Malone's strongest awareness. In speaking of his earnestness, Malone expresses a general sense of puzzlement and guilt in regard to his former life. Burdened since childhood with the sense of gravity, he has struggled to understand why and to escape the limitations such a trait has placed upon his life. As author, he assigns a sensing of guilt to both his minor and major characters. Mr. and Mrs. Saposcat feel responsible and guilty – although for no stated reason – for the financial straits and lack of life's material comforts that their family undergoes.

Macmann's experience in the pelting rain is one of Beckett's most graphic representations of man being crucified by nature and whatever or whoever created it. He lies on the ground, arms outstretched, while the stinging rain pelts down on his palms. He waits, expecting no help, remembering that in past experiences of distress, no one has helped him "avoid the thorns and snares that attend the steps of innocence" (pp. 242-43). Described with the usual markings of Beckett's Christ figures, he is overcome by a sensing of punishment and an awareness of guilt:

> The idea of punishment came to his mind, addicted it is true to that chimera and probably impressed by the posture of the body and the fingers clenched as though in torment. And without knowing exactly what his sin was he felt full well that living was not a sufficient atonement for it or that this atonement was in itself a sin, calling for more atonement, and so on, as if there could be anything but life, for the living. And no doubt he would have wondered if it was really necessary to be guilty in order to be punished but for the memory, more and more galling, of his having consented to live in his mother, then to leave her. And this again he could not see as his true sin, but as yet another atonement which had miscarried and, far from cleansing him of his sin, plunged him in it deeper than before. And truth to tell the ideas of guilt and punishment were confused together in his mind, as those of cause and effect so often are in the minds of those who continue to think. (pp. 239-40)

It would be difficult to find a more exact description of Beckettian guilt in the entire canon. Angela Moorjani sums up Macmann's suffering and distress:

> As wavering as Malone about life and death, Macmann cannot determine whether life is the sin or the punishment for sin, or again if birth is the original sin or the original expiation, or indeed if they are not part of an unending series of sinful atonements. [24]

Beckett's familiar ideas of life itself as a punishment for the crime of having been born are obvious here. As Malone comments later in speaking of Macmann's confinement in the House of Saint John

[24] *Abysmal Games in the Novels of Samuel Beckett,* p. 123.

of God, "So long as it is what is called a living being you can't go wrong, you have the guilty one" (p. 259).

Malone experiences unending life or a continuation of existence in two ways. As Malone the fabricator of stories, he never actually dies. Although, just before relating the last episode of the Easter excursion, he has some kind of death experience, this is not the end of Malone. "That is the end of me," he says, "I shall say I no-more." But, in the same breath, he has lamented, "My story ended I'll be living yet" (p. 283). We have only to turn the pages to the beginning paragraphs of *The Unnamable* to find him, still alive but more like an object than a person, orbiting about the Unnamable (*The Unnamable,* p. 295). Malone as the character Macmann does not die either. Tangled with the other gray bodies, two of which are dead, Malone's last surrogate lies in Lemuel's boat. But Malone as author reassures himself and us as readers that Macmann is not dead. "Macmann, my last, my possession, I remember, he is there too, perhaps he sleeps" (p. 287). Malone/Macmann may be sleeping, but he is not gone. True to the archetypal pattern of the Beckett hero's consciousness, his existence goes on and on.

Malone's continuing existence raises the pivotal question of exactly what is meant by his dying. If Malone is the first hero to withdraw decisively from macrocosmic life into the realm of the imagination to undertake the quest on level two – the quest to authenticate the self as artist – why is he simultaneously waiting to die? What is the exact connection between this hero's dying and his writing of stories? Is he, as he claims, simply awaiting physical death and filling the time until his death occurs by writing stories? Nearly all of Beckett's characters lie or tell half-truths, and the word/sign "death" echoes throughout the fiction with multiple soundings. I would suggest that the dying and the writing are the same – or nearly the same – undertaking, an undertaking that constitutes Malone's quest on the second level. Toyama equates Malone's dying and writing, and quotes Malone himself to prove her point. ". . . writing is not so much birth as a death, the death of the writer who gives birth to the text and dies in the writing. 'I [Malone] am being given, if I may venture the expression, birth to death' (*Malone Dies,* p. 114 . . .)." Her meaning, however, as we have previously seen, has to do with absence of authentic selfhood in the act of producing fiction, and assumes the "reward" of "oblivion" as Malone's goal.[25]

By our definitions, Malone is not seeking the oblivion of physical death or of a cessation of consciousness. Instead, his dying/writing is a predictable and recognizable stage of the Beckett hero's prolonged retreat from a macrocosm of disillusionment and unfilled needs towards the microcosmic realm of intensified consciousness and attempted creativity. We have already noted that Malone's room begins to appear to him as enclosed planes of bone, that is, as the interior of a human skull. The beginnings of such a retreat are abundantly prefigured in the earlier fiction – Belacqua toward the womb, the state of insanity, and death; Murphy in the direction of his rocking chair and the asylum; and Watt to the sanctuary of the Knott estate. The hero of *Stories* seeks serenity in a basement room, a hearse, a shed, and a boat. Both Molloy and Moran end their journeys in a quiescent condition – Molloy in his mother's bed and Moran in his garden. Furthermore, if we conceive of the heroes of the trilogy as developing stages of a single protagonist, we can describe him as progressing from mobility (Molloy and Moran) to quiescence (Malone) to interiority (the Unnamable). Malone's immobiblity in bed, pictured as the last stage before death, is separated only by the fixed interior voices of the Unnamable and the hero of *Texts* from the silent states of those frozen portraits Beckett offers in pieces such as *Imagination Dead Imagine* and *Ping*.

This understanding of Malone's "dying" explains why the title, first sentence, and last episode of the novel all deal with the idea of death. It also partially accounts for the numerous deaths or murders that occur throughout the novel – those of the Lambert's animals, Malone's earlier fictional characters (including whoever was killed by the bloody club), Moll, and the two sailors. In Beckett's *Stories*, a reference to the event of physical death serves as a metaphor for the estrangement of a hero from any metaphysical haven or home and the unending consciousness of such exile. Here the event of dying signals the hero's inward journey to escape the exile of macrocosmic life and reach the core of microcosmic consciousness.

---

[25] "Malone, the unoriginal centre," p. 97.

Other signals in the text alert us to such an understanding. Malone associates both his dying and his writing with stillness, darkness, and separation from the outer world of the macrocosm. Throughout the fiction, these qualities are used to symbolize retreat toward the microcosm. In speaking of his "present state" of immobility in bed as he writes, Malone describes himself as "Dark and silent and stale." He is "far from the sounds of blood and breath, immured"; such is his condition of dying (p. 186). Darkness pervades both Malone's consciousness and the atmosphere of his stories. Lying in bed, he expresses his fear of darkness, with the word used here to denote something that is either unclear or associated with suffering. "For I want as little as possible of darkness in his [Sapo's] story . . . it accumulates, thickens, then suddenly bursts and drowns everything" (p. 190). Unfortunately, darkness does accumulate in the stories he formulates. As he describes Sapo's place by the window in the Lambert's kitchen, Malone uses the adjective "dark" or "darker" eight times in the space of two pages, once describing Sapo, in spite of the natural light streaming through the openings into the kitchen, as situated in "the unconquerable dark" (pp. 202-03). As the "Words and images" of his stories "run riot" in his head, Malone's attention is fixed on a state beyond the "tumult" of life – both his own life and the life that constantly threatens to invade his stories – where there is a "great calm, and a great indifference" (p. 198).

Both of Malone's death spasms occur directly after authorial descriptions of retreat from the outside world or of suffering, which Beckett associates throughout his fiction with the approach toward inner consciousness or the core of selfhood. He is describing Macmann as representative of all men, including himself, as he describes retreat into a contemplative state:

> Bluer scarcely than White of egg the eyes stare into the space before them, namely the fulness of the great deep and its unchanging calm. But at long intervals they close, with the gentle suddenness of flesh that tightens, often without anger, and closes on itself.

Malone then briefly mentions physical death and, immediately, feels the first death spasm, an intimation that his "hour is at hand" (p. 233). This phrase introduces a long paragraph of several pages which consists of an interlude of personal speculation by Malone. As this artist/self resumes his story, he fabricates the lengthy scene of Macmann's painful lying in the rain contemplating guilt and punishment – a scene which, as we have noted, includes numerous images of Christ's crucifixion. Just after writing the paragraphs that make up this scene (pp. 238-46), Malone experiences the second death spasm (p. 246).

Dying is linked not only with a suffering retreat toward the inner self but also with writing. Malone makes the statement that this "exercise-book is my life, this child's exercise-book" (p. 274). When the book or writing is finished, apparently death will occur. What is happening is that Malone is withdrawing from life to the inward concentration of writing – a withdrawal that he describes as death.

This hero appears ignorant or naive in his initial attitude toward the writing of his stories. He approaches the literary endeavor as a game he intends to play, planning to exclude from the stories any intensity or earnestness that he has experienced in real life. His writing is to be a distracting and amusing way to escape the suffering and failure of the macrocosm. The stories are to be "almost lifeless, like the teller," and he resolves to "never do anything any more from now on but play" (p. 180). To carry out this happy plan, Malone is not going to write about himself or his own experiences, as previous heroes have done. Instead, he is going to make art into a game divorced from life and authorial selfhood. But Malone is whistling in the dark; he knows better. Previous attempts to play at life have proved futile (p. 180), "earnestness" has haunted his macrocosmic life, and he realizes that if he is to insulate the products of his imagination from the "fever" of real life, he must be "on . . . guard" (pp. 180-82). In spite of his plans, Malone is unsuccessful in such an effort; he cannot insulate his art from life or from the macrocosmic self. His own past experiences infiltrate the stories, and each major character he writes about becomes himself. He soon realizes fully the seriousness of his task, and the familiar darkness that has engulfed his life in the outer world (physical and emotional pain, and a lack of clarity as to what is going on) begins to ruin his stories also. As the plot of each story becomes a jumbled account of loss, suffering, or death, Malone struggles to keep his literary equilibrium: "For even as I said, How easy and beautiful it all is!, in the same breath I said, All will grow dark again" (p. 224).

The pattern in which the "darkness" invades the stories reveals the thematic structure I have described of the hero's response to a symbolic word/promise, a response that inevitably results in disillusionment. In each of the four examples that I shall describe, Malone experiences something in the present or remembers something from the past that seems to offer him an expectation of the fulfillment of his needs for love, security, and personal significance – needs that we recognize as those that the hero searches for in the macrocosm. In each instance, the "promise" of the meeting of such needs is depicted in language related to Christian symbols or activities, and the disappointment or failure of the need being met is a mockery or travesty of that language. Thus we have the familiar pattern of the hero responding to a "hypothetical imperative" embodied in language having connotations of divinity and finding no realization of his hopes. *Malone Dies,* however, is Beckett's first fiction in which the God/promise occurs in the macrocosm and its nonrealization in the microcosm, that is, in the stories Malone spins from his imagination. This pattern of the quest on the second level becomes repetitive in the fiction following *Malone Dies,* being fully developed, as we shall observe, in *How It Is.*

The first such promise occurs in the opening paragraph of *Malone Dies.* Looking forward to his death as a surcease of an unhappy life, Malone speculates on the probable date of its occurrence. For several days, he has had a definite "feeling" that "it will be the month of April or of May." If so, he will not be around for the religious holidays of Saint John the Baptist's Day, the Transfiguration, or the Assumption (p. 179). Whatever peace Malone anticipates by his death, however, is never experienced. Instead, he lives on as Macmann in the boat with Lemuel and his bloody hatchet, Beckett's final symbol of Malone's pencil, both of which become instruments of violence rather than peace. Malone has been granted a violent "resurrection" instead of a peaceful "death," but the event does indeed occur, as he had intuited, in April or May, in fact, during "the Easter week-end, spent by Jesus in hell" (p. 280). Earlier, Malone has wondered whether or not May has arrived, and why he believes that the word "May" is derived from the word "Maia" or "hell" (p. 234). Lady Petal's excursion becomes a travesty of Christian connotations associated with spring, Holy Week, and Easter – and Malone remains in the hell of Beckett's relentless continuation of consciousness.

The second promise reaches Malone in the form of a memory of and longing for the security he once experienced as a child in bed at night. The religious implications of this memory are derived from idealistic notions associated throughout the novel (and in Beckett's other fiction) with some final home as a haven or refuge from the ills of life. The association we have previously noted of Beckett's blending of the sounds of the stone-cutters with the blazing lights of gorse fires in the hills from his own childhood is in effect here also. Furthermore, Beckett's linking of light with whatever in human experience ironically seems good and desirable – in a manner similar to that of John in his gospel, but with the addition of the irony and with different definitions – serves to assign a religious dimension to these remembered lights. Malone reminisces about the comfort and security of hearing the barking dogs of the stone – cutters and seeing the lights of the fires:

> From the hills another joy came down, I mean the brief scattered lights that sprang up on their slopes at night-fall, merging in blurs scarcely brighter than the sky, less bright than the stars, and which the palest moon extinguished. (p. 206)

These lights occur as symbols throughout Beckett's fiction, each occurrence embodying ideas of childhood security and love. Here, in *Malone Dies,* they appear again later in the text, but this time in Malone's story of Macmann, and with quite different implications. Having concocted his "tangle of grey bodies" lying "in a heap, in the night," author Malone offers the comment that the "night is strewn with absurd." The gorse fires of childhood memories of love and security become part of this absurdity:

> . . . absurd lights, the stars, the beacons, the buoys, the lights of earth and in the hills the faint fires of the blazing gorse.

The lights the child Beckett watched from his window become a comforting and hopeful memory to Malone, but signs or symbols of betrayal and violence to Macmann (p. 287).

A third false promise is Malone's hearing of the choir as he lies in bed. Whether or not there actually is a choir to be heard is not certain, but Malone hears one, singing a song so familiar that when the sound ceases, it resonates in his mind. The song ends with a "triumphal cry," and Malone decides it is part of a rehearsal for Easter Week, and sung to the glory of Christ – who, for him, is no Savior (p. 208). The travesty of this Easter anthem is Lady Petal's Easter chorus, which she renders enthusiastically as she and Lemuel start on the celebrated picnic:

Oh the jolly spring
Blue and sun and nests and flowers
Alleluiah Christ is King
Oh the happy happy hours
Oh the jolly jolly – (p. 285)

The last sounds we hear from Lady Petal are not songs, but the moans and groans author Malone has her emitting as Lemuel knocks her down and deserts her on the island (p. 287).

The final promise, this one also including religious overtones of a refuge or haven for man's spirit, is Malone's room. In spite of his misery and immobility, this room is a refuge, reminding him of the security of his childhood. The woman meets his basic physical needs here, no one evicts him, and he feels (compare this verb with Malone's *feelings* about his death occuring on a Holy Day) that it is "not a room in a hospital or in a madhouse" (p. 182). Ironically enough, however, Malone/Macmann does end up in a room in a madhouse, an asylum weighted with descriptions exhibiting Beckett's ironic Christian symbolism, a mockery of the "rooms" Christ promises his disciples (again, in John's gospel, 14:2) are waiting for them in his Father's house. In this House of Saint John of God, Macmann's number is the number representative of mankind in John's Revelation – one hundred and sixty-six. As inmate, Malone is advised, "Fear nothing, you are among friends. . . . Take no thought for anything" – words echoing those of Jesus in the Last Discourse as given in John's gospel. The other inmates are "men and women dressed in white" (as the heavenly throng in the Revelation), and the speaker who welcomes him is a young man whose beard makes him resemble "the Messiah" (pp. 255-56). Such obvious use of ironic symbols lessens our astonishment on discovering that Moll – the pitiful old woman who becomes Macmann's "lover" – wears two earrings in the shape of the thieves on the cross and boasts a tooth (a "long yellow canine bared to the roots") which is "carved . . . to represent the celebrated sacrifice" of Christ on the cross (pp. 263-64). All that we have noted concerning Beckett's repeated use of Christ as a symbol of victimized mankind is apparent here.

Unlike Kafka, who, when questioned about the significance of the Christ story in human experience, bowed his head and answered, "That is an abyss filled with light. We must close our eyes if we are not to fall into it,"[26] Beckett attaches no awe or longing to the crucified Christ. Instead, he presents a Christ similar to the "mistaken" Christ C. S. Lewis rejects in *A Grief Observed:*

> He [Christ] had found that the Being He called Father was horribly and infinitely different from what He had supposed. The trap, so long and carefully prepared and so subtly baited, was at last sprung on the cross. The vile practical joke had succeeded.[27]

Malone's hope of a room or place as refuge turns into a violent practical joke as he lies in the bloody boat with Lemuel. Like Beckett's other artist/heroes, Malone uses the material of memories and events from real life to fabricate his stories. And, true to the patterns we have observed, the misery and nonfulfillment of life are transferred into the failure of the stories.

Particular evidence abounds that Malone's stories are indeed failures, that he has at hand no Logos to impart order and significance to his fabricated tales of Sapo and Macmann, although as Ruby Cohn states, "Of all Beckett's characters Malone is the most explicit creator of fiction."[28] Thus we can compare Malone as author with his author/creator, Beckett, who also claims to have produced literary productions that are failures. We have previously explored the term "failure" as applied to Beckett's work and understand that, in a very real sense, to use it is to play with words

---

[26] See Hans Küng, *On Being a Christian,* trans. Edward Quinn (Garden City, N.Y.: Doubleday, 1974), p. 146. Küng is quoting from G. Janouch, *Gesprache mit Kafka* (Frankfurt/Hamburg, 1961), p. 111.

[27] Lewis, *A Grief Observed* (New York: Seabury Press, 1963), p. 34.

[28] *Back to Beckett,* p. 99.

and their meanings. Beckett does not fail in his literary effort: he uses language exactly as he intends. Apparently, however, his creation Malone really does fail; that is, he is unable to use language as he wishes and plans, and fails to write the stories he intends, stories devoid of the misery and nonfulfillment of life. The exact connection between Beckett and Malone as authors invites an exploration that can yield new insight into Beckett's assigning of the term "failure" to his literary output and his creation of the artist/hero Malone.

Brian Wicker has tabulated and examined what he sees as the development of the deliberate and intended failure or deficiency of literary art in Beckett's fictional canon.[29] These deficiencies are defined as failure only when placed against the commonly held assumptions of Western literary practice up to the twentieth century. Thus the use of the term in regard to Beckett's or Malone's art would depend on the perspective of Beckett, Malone, or the critic or reader confronting the literature. We will proceed on the basis of Malone's clear understanding of his stories as failed effort, and on Beckett's repeated use of the term in regard to his work, remembering, in this regard, the qualifications previously offered in this study. Wicker claims that by the writing of the trilogy, the convention of plot has all but disappeared from the Beckettian *œuvre,* in two particular senses. One, the reader's privilege of "descent into the private life of a character" – a descent withheld from the character himself but conventionally offered the reader by an omniscient narrator – is denied. This ignorance of character motivation (the "vertical dimension of narrative") on the part of the reader results in a second disappearance, an absence that Wicker calls the "horizontal dimension of narrative art." The "causal connectedness which is the essence of plot" is missing, and the logic of the story is not that of "causality" but of "mere association" (Wicker, p. 65). That is, we as readers do not understand why a character does something, nor do we perceive why or how one event leads to another. T. L. Estress comments on this plotlessness of Beckett's later work in regard to style, by remarking that an "eclipse of conjunctions" often "implies lack of

---

[29] Wicker, "Samuel Beckett and the Death of the God-Narrator," *Journal of Narrative Technique,* 4 (1974), 62-74. References to this article are cited in this and succeeding paragraphs by page number(s) in the text.

linkage between events or impressions of life."[30] Certainly we can apply these definitions of plotlessness that Wicker assigns to specific stages of Beckett's fiction to Malone's stories.

Wicker notes also the absence of traditional setting of time and place in Beckett's fictional world, using *Malone Dies* as an example. Although Malone is in some bed in a room, "neither time nor place are [sic] clearly or consistently established." Malone tries to establish time and place by producing the stories, but they fail to rescue Malone from the "endless time without beginning or terminus" in which he "seems to be caught." Instead, the stories reproduce his timelessness (Wicker, p. 67).

Estress writes of the hero missing from Beckettian fiction. Like the narrator of *The Calmative,* Beckett's story-telling narrators and voices long for the ability to relate the tale of a traditional hero "with resolate purpose who effectively acts and who returns triumphantly."[31] Such a statement, on the surface, seems not to apply to Malone's intention of writing stories as a game, but our use and understanding in this study of the terms "hero" and "quest" can serve to qualify and explain it. If Malone's created character/hero could escape the misery and nonfulfillment of macrocosmic life by being transferred into the world of fiction, he would have achieved his author's purpose for him.

Wicker contrasts the difference between Beckett's earlier novels (such as *More Pricks than Kicks* and *Murphy*) in which a detached narrator manipulates and assesses the tragic/comic actions of the characters and the later works (such as *Stories,* the trilogy, and *Texts for Nothing*) which become monologues by a narrating voice consisting of "philosophical explorations of man's tragic predicament." What is lost in this transition is that "comic poise" which keeps the reader from being drawn into the abyss of the voice's situation. Without the God-Narrator to maintain distance or perspective, the problems explored by the novel – "the hero's quest for identity, security, peace, heaven" – become "not only insoluble: they are not even funny, except by accident" (Wicker, p. 66).

---

[30] Estress, "Inenarrable contraption; reflections on the metaphor of story," *Journal of the American Academy of Religion,* 42 (1974), 423.

[31] "Inenarrable contraption; reflections on the metaphor of story," p. 419.

It is difficult not to reply that certain scenes, at least through the writing of *Malone Dies,* are extremely funny (i. e., Macmann and Moll attempting to make love), but it is true that the humor depicted is much blacker than, say, even the scattering of Murphy's ashes on the saloon floor by Cooper (*Murphy,* p. 275). Also, we must recognize that such development on Beckett's part is not accidental but artistically deliberate, and has for its express purpose the disengagement of the reader with the hero. Christopher Lasch, in *The Culture of Narcissism,* speaks of the intentions of such writers:

> In the same way, experimental novelists have done whatever they can to alienate the reader, to make it impossible for him to identify with the characters in their works.[32]

Lasch continues:

> Novelists and playwrights call attention to the artificiality of their own creations and discourage the reader from identifying with the characters.[33]

In *Malone Dies,* both Beckett and Malone as author do dispense with the "comic poise" of omniscient narrators. No narrator who understands what is actually going on in the act of Malone's dying reveals the matter to us as readers. Nor does Malone know what his dying really is. Furthermore, Malone does not know certain things about his characters, and therefore cannot explain them to us as readers, for instance, the reason why Sapo is not expelled from school (p. 190). But the matter of effecting the reader's alienation from the desperate heroes remains ambiguous. We are repelled by Macmann's appearance and repulsive affection for Moll, but we understand quite well the needs for "shelter, charity and human tenderness" that drive him to her (pp. 265-66). Nonetheless, we can agree that a failure to maintain "comic poise" does diminish humor and empathy with characters in this novel, a failure apparent in Beckett's writing about Malone and in Malone's about Sapo and Macmann.

---

[32] Lasch, *The Culture of Narcissim: American Life in an Age of Diminishing Expectations* (New York: W. W. Norton, 1979), p. 161.

[33] *The Culture of Narcissism,* p. 175.

We have already explored the literary loss (both Beckett's and Malone's) in *Malone Dies* of identifiable names which signify reliable personality for a character. Wicker mentions this loss as a part of the failure of Beckett/Malone's stories. ". . . in *Malone Dies* the various names (Saposcat, Macmann, etc.) are patently the speaker's own inventions, mere persona for himself [Malone]. Even 'Malone' is only 'what I am called now' and has no absolute authority as a name giving permanent identity" (Wicker, p. 67). Judith Dearlove notes that many of Beckett's names evoke tentative psychological meanings for the reader but never fulfill the expectations of such evocations. "The motivations, anxieties, desires, and passions that give significance to the psychological terms are omitted."[34] Dearlove also comments on the failure of Beckett's names to connect his work with the entire tradition of Western literature:

> . . . instead of enforcing the connections between his tales and those of other times and places, the narrator's allusions enlarge the gaps. Joyce belonged to a tradition of artists that believed art could turn the surrounding chaos back into its proper order. His references to Greek mythology help connect Stephen's and Bloom's stories to each other, to the past, and to Western civilization. In contrast, Beckett's borrowings disrupt the past and diminish the present.[35]

Wicker writes of the Beckett hero's "unquenchable thirst for meaning," but points out that Beckett's world holds no "meaning except that which man can invent." Yet this critic insists that, for Beckett and his narrating heroes, to attempt to tell a story is to imply there should be a world that means:

> [literature] depends on there being that of which it is the meaning. It entails a dialogue between mind and object, between man and the world he confronts. If there is no such world and no such dialogue, then even the invention of meaning through the telling of stories becomes impossible, itself a contradiction in terms. (Wicker, pp. 68-69)

---

[34] Dearlove, *Accommodating the Chaos: Samuel Beckett's Nonrelational Art* (Durham, N. C.: Duke Univ. Press, 1982), p. 71.

[35] *Accommodating the Chaos*, pp. 71-72.

Here we have succinctly stated the reason that Malone's stories do not "mean" anything. Malone and his life have not meant anything either, and there is no dialogue between Malone and the world that houses him. Of course, this understanding can be rephrased as the pat formula often applied to Beckett's "meaningless" stories: an "aesthetic strategy which attempts to admit chaos into art" implies that no order in life (Beckett's "mess") must logically result in no story in art.[36] But we must remember that Beckett himself has repeatedly defined this aesthetic strategy as one of "failure."

As always, however, perspective is everything in linking this term with Beckett's writing. The developments that we have been describing as deficiencies can also be defined as gains, as advances that Beckett has achieved as he has attempted to shape his art to "accommodate the chaos" of human experience. S. E. Gontarski defines such developmental changes as freedoms that Beckett has won for himself as an artist:

> The 'formal concepts' from which Beckett has freed himself are the convention of the omniscient narrator (and author), a consistent voice, and the causality of psychological fiction, including the assumption of a unified ego.[37]

Gontarski's definitions are not only valid but also critically pivotal in assessing Beckett's incredible literary skill in paring down his art and shaping it to embody his vision of life. But Beckett's success in shaping an art that mirrors or contains human experience – described as lacking reliable knowledge of ourselves and others ("the omniscient narrator and author"), identity not subject to the ravages of time ("a consistent voice" and "a unified ego"), and some degree of cause-result in human events and relationships ("the causality of psychological fiction") – does not necessarily mean that he applauds these conditions as they exist in the human experience. As numerous philosophical and aesthetic remarks Beckett has spoken and written reveal, and as this study assumes,

---

[36] "Inenarrable contraption; reflections on the metaphor of story," pp. 441-42.

[37] Gontarski, "The Intent of Undoing in Samuel Beckett's Art, *Modern Fiction Studies*, 29 (1983), 12.

the very opposite is true. Such a human condition is what Beckett calls "the mess."

A final, but by no means least important, failure on the part of both Beckett and Malone is the failure to transmute the human experience of suffering into the high tragedy of art. We have already explored this facet of Beckett's writing, both in our descriptions of the quest on level two and in our writing on *Watt*. Beckett is greatly influenced by Schopenhauer, and in *Proust* seems to agree with this philosopher's "estimate of art as that human activity which frees men from the phenomenal world of causality to which their reasoning powers are chained."[38] As the Hamiltons note, however, we cannot equate Beckett's mature thought with Schopenhauer's ideas on art as described in *Proust*. Certainly, Beckett has rejected Schopenhauer's notions of art as "a disclosure of the eternal, changeless Ideas."[39] Both Beckett and Malone transfer the suffering of life into their art, but unlike the examples of suffering found in Proust or Schopenhauer, such distress is not transformed into the significance, beauty, and catharsis of literary tragedy. For Proust (or Marcel), the sight of three steeples perceived by an unhappy boy from a moving carriage inspires volumes of words describing life as essentially an experience of suffering, but also as a phenomenon that can be frozen by involuntary memory and the genius of the artist into a glimpse of an ideal world. Schopenhauer also envisions art as capable of disclosing the "underlying principle of the universe," which, although existing outside of time and space, expresses itself in certain forms which correspond somewhat to Plato's ideas.[40] For Beckett/Malone, however, this ideal world is forever beyond realization, existing only as a mocking echo, so faint that the artist/selves cannot reproduce its sound in the words they write.

At this juncture, we must advance – as we did earlier in *Watt* – beyond analyses of the structures of quest levels and ask questions concerning the metaphysics of the novel. The question here, however, becomes, not why a hero-as-character like Watt

---

[38] *Condemned to Life: The World of Samuel Beckett*, p. 47.

[39] *Condemned to Life: The World of Samuel Beckett*, pp. 69, 103, and 125.

[40] For a lucid explanation of Schopenhauer's complex thinking at this point, see Ernest Brennecke, Jr.'s study of Schopenhauer's influence on Thomas Hardy – *Thomas Hardy's Universe: A Study of a Poet's Mind* (Boston: Small, Maynard, 1924), p. 54.

cannot discover a Word that means, but why Malone in the role of the hero-as-artist cannot shape the words at his disposal into a Word that creates a significant story. Our sphere of action has shifted from the macrocosm to the imaginative realm of the microcosm, and our primary concern is not so much with words and their meanings (or non-meanings), as with the matter of Beckett's perception of literature as art. We have earlier explored Beckett's aesthetic theories and have now watched him create Malone, the protagonist and story-teller of *Malone Dies.* We can speak of the author Malone as having failed to write the playful and pleasant stories that he has planned, but we cannot describe Beckett in this fashion. To the best of our knowledge, Beckett has never planned to write playful or pleasant stories, and *Malone Dies* is supposedly exactly the novel he intended it to be. If not, he would have revised it; and besides, the novel takes its place as high artistic achievement, not only in the trilogy, but in the fictional canon as a whole. The matter of accounting for any literature is unpopular in critical theory – the literature (if we dare to use this designation) is there, and our critical duty is simply to describe it by breaking it down or undoing it. But we are like freshmen in a college English class and long to ask certain questions: what is Malone about as he undergoes the retreat from life he calls a "death," and writes his stories of loss and violence? What is the significance of Beckett's creation of such a hero? What does *Malone Dies* mean?

These important (or impertinent) questions are best briefly confronted by examining critical responses in regard to them. If we do not arrive at answers, at least we can postulate the theory that to ask such questions is neither nonsensical nor out of place. As Iain Wright insists, it is the business of criticism to be concerned with that "old-fashioned" term, Beckett's "vision" (Wright, p. 72). In his contribution (on the trilogy) to the 1983 special issue on Beckett of *Modern Fiction Studies,* Roch C. Smith deals with the oft-repeated idea that the Beckett hero's writing is a "labyrinthine quest for silence."[41] If much modern writing is no longer "the writing of a story" but instead "the story of a writing,"

---

[41] Roch Smith, "Naming the M/Inotaur: Beckett's Trilogy and the Failure of Narrative," *Modern Fiction Studies,* 29 (1983), 79. Specific references to this article are cited by page number(s) in this paragraph of the text.

then Beckett's trilogy is "a *fiction of failed narrative*" (R. Smith, pp. 78 and 79):

> Beckett's narrator does not seek merely to bare the word; he seeks to stop it. His goal is not to create novel fictional forms but to still the voice of fiction in order to say 'nothing.' (R. Smith, p. 79)

Whether referring to Beckett, the composite hero of the trilogy, or Malone, we can agree with Smith that the Beckettian writer is indeed seeking an end to the senseless flow of words in which he seems to be trapped. We can also agree that, as a writer, he is offering us as readers a chance to observe the process of an author failing to produce a story that connects him with life or gives significance to his personal or authorial identity. We understand that it is precisely this failure that forms the shape of the literature and constitutes the most concrete justification for the continuing existence of Beckettian writing, whether Malone's or otherwise:

> Increasingly, the narrator weaves the story of the impossibility of expression, but he does not stop weaving. Whatever hope Beckett's trilogy offers would seem to be found in this unbroken narrative line whose tensile strength barely resists, yet does not break, despite the tugs and pulls of despair. (R. Smith, p. 79)

There is, however, something logically, if not linguistically, tautalogical about such a justification: does an author keep writing simply *because* there is nothing to do but write? Why not stop? Surely Beckett could have stopped Malone (and himself) if he had wished. Smith leaves his essay open-ended with the observation that the narrator of the trilogy remains "uncertain" as to whether or not words may have "an ontological significance," that Beckettian narrative does exist in "the tortuous and tenuous space between logos and silence" (R. Smith, p. 80). Focusing on such definitions, we can say that Malone does not keep writing as a search for silence or death merely as an end in itself, but as a groping toward whatever ontological significance he intuits words should have.

Iain Wright reveals once and for all the falseness of Malone's claims that his writing is a game, that he is merely playing with words and the narration of stories. Wright is not dealing only with *Malone Dies* but with Beckett's work as a whole in his exposé of the difficulties involved in reading Beckett as a Nietzschean affirmation of joy in realizing that we exist in a world of language and being without inherent signification or meaning (Wright, p. 72). There undoubtedly are modern-day authors and critics who experience the indeterminacy of language, the nonrelation between life and art,

> This free-play in the flux of discourse, this deconstruction of the logocentric illusions underlying the whole of western man's utterance about himself since the pre-Socratics, this expunging of origins and foundations, this *mise en abîme*

as a "liberation, a discovery of erotic *jouissance*" (Wright, p. 71). But, says Wright, Beckett and his narrators are not of this company. Not that Beckett and his artist/selves (including Malone) are not engaged in "a deconstructionist activity." They are continually and obviously "foregrounding their own textuality, decentring the texts they inhabit, subverting subject-positions, denaturalizing language," but the product is not release and joy. Instead, the "issue is misery and meaninglessness, and that activity [of deconstruction] is what they seek continually but unsuccessfully to escape *from,* back into a world of solid foundations, solid signifieds" (Wright, p. 71). Wright is primarily involved with the matters of authorship and interpretation. He concedes that the origin of a literary work as the product of an author is never to be conceived of as something "single, simple, and unambivalent." Neither is it possible not to realize fully the "plural and contradictory" nature of the meanings of literature, particularly literature such as Beckett's. Nevertheless, not to take into account an author's intention(s) and not to attempt interpretation is to dehumanize the entire critical enterprise of writing about literature (Wright, p. 73). Malone would agree with Wright. In spite of his beginning illusions about writing being merely a game, he knows that *he* is telling *his* stories, and he is trying desperately to make the stories *mean something* about the experience of life.

Gontarski writes of Beckett's conflict with language and the experiences of life out of which the author forms his art. "Childhood memories, adolescent unhappiness, fears of mortality, wasted opportunities, familial and cultural alienation, memories of suicidal sweethearts: these are the elements Beckett's art needs and needs to undo as he struggles to make universal art out of personal neurosis."[42] No better summary of the life events of Beckett's heroes, including Malone, could be found; Beckett's art is formed of such memories, if, as Gontarski explains, "only by negation" (Gontarski, p. 23). This critic insists that Beckett does not perceive the artist's task to be that of explaining things, particularly what Beckett sees as the "mess" of the outside world. Gontarski also claims, however, that Beckett has a "*thematic* commitment" to the "fundamental *questions,* being, and *knowing,* to universal images of man's *predicament*" (Gontarski, p. 23). The italics in the preceding quotations are mine, and they are intended to raise a question of my own making. Given the "thematic commitment" spoken of by Gontarski and the obsessive rationalism of the Beckettian narrator/hero, how can we rest content with describing the creator of this narrator as having no need or desire to explain things? Is it not possible that the opposite is true? That both Beckett's and Malone's writings exhibit a stark and compulsive need to explain everything? What is Malone doing by writing if he is not trying to understand and explain his life?

A concern that Frederick N. Smith finds Dearlove assigning to Beckett in her book *Accommodating the Chaos* can also be attached to Malone. Smith says that Dearlove finds Beckett to be "an artist deeply concerned with accommodating the hypothesis that there may in fact be no relationship among the artist, his art, and the external world."[43] These are precisely the literary artist Malone's concerns, and his dying/writing is his quest to resolve them. Like Beckett at the close of his interchange with Georges Duthuit about the artist Masson,[44] Malone weeps (Malone speaks of his "tears, for I wept up to a great age" [p. 247]) at an understanding of the world as one in which language must be conceived of "as

[42] "The Intent of Undoing in Samuel Beckett's Art," p. 23. Specific references to this article are cited by page number(s) in this paragraph of the text.

[43] Frederick Smith, "Three on Beckett: An Essay-Review," *Modern Fiction Studies,* 29 (1983), 129.

[44] *Proust and Three Dialogues with Georges Duthuit,* p. 113.

expressing nothing more than its own capacity for going on unproductively."[45]

Leo Bersani attributes what he sees as Beckett's "deep resentment" of language to such a concern. Bersani links Beckett with Flaubert and describes them as expressing their resentment against language by a "retreat into silence."[46] This critic's definitions of Beckett's movement toward silence are more pessimistic than the associations with silence that Roch Smith formulates concerning Beckett and his narrators:

> Unable to believe that a viable existence can be successfully forged from words which can obviously never correspond exactly to a preexistent reality or inner essence, they would punish language for its inexpressiveness by beating it into insignificance. In his deep resentment of language, Beckett has striven to entrust less and less of what has been a powerfully individual talent and personality to the care and accursed inventiveness of words. His illusion of a self outside time has brought him to a willful ontological miserliness, to a retreat from life and literature, that is, from the uncertain futures to which time and language subject both the self and books. (Bersani, p. 330)

Bersani published these words in 1970, and since then it has become obvious that Beckett has not retreated from either life or literature. And we must remember that Malone does not die, but is reincarnated as the Unnamable, with his endless flow of words. In defining the Beckettian relation to silence, Bersani is closer to Malone's situation when he speaks of a "something before or behind language," something of which the artist/self dreams and which is connected both to reality and to his writing:

> There is something before or behind language and the novel; and the novelist's torture is that it is his use of language in order to write novels which nurtures his dream of a reality

[45] See Bersani's joining of Flaubert with Beckett in such an attitude in *Balzac to Beckett*, p. 330.

[46] *Balzac to Beckett*, p. 330. Specific references to this article are cited by page number(s) in this paragraph of the text.

> from which the novel is, by definition, a departure. (Bersani, p. 328)

The descent into the microcosm and the writing are retreats from reality for Malone, but they are nonetheless attempts to deal with that reality, to reach beyond its misery and nonfulfillment by assimilating its disorder and finding a Logos that will assign significance to its deficiencies.

If we concede that Malone as author is moving toward silence, playing games (by deconstructing his own words as he writes them), formulating objective correlatives of the "mess" of life, and attempting escape from the misery of past experience, we must insist that these definitions do not adequately encompass the total nature of his literary quest.

In spite of his clinging to his room as refuge and passion for his stories as directions away from the "mess" of life, Malone is in hell, both in regard to his personal location and to the settings of the stories, which reproduce the existential anguish of his situation. He wants to escape this hell by verbally going through his memories, robbing them of horror by translating them into pure fiction, and arrive at a state of heaven or Paradise, which we can define as the condition of having his existential needs supplied. These ambitions rest on the presuppositions of his initial literary plans, plans which assume some kind of link between the writing of pure fiction (i. e., stories minus the existential anguish of life) and the escape from the suffering of actual experience. The tone and structural movement of *Malone Dies,* as we have examined them, are evidence enough for this claim, but a particular bit of imagery serves to reinforce the general tenor of the novel in this regard. Malone is given to looking through his window, both physically and metaphysically. This single window is by his bed, and he lies "turned towards it most of the time" (p. 184). He remarks that watching this window, awaiting the dawn is something he has to do (p. 210). The stars he sees through it are real, "truly of mankind and not merely painted on the window-pane, but they tremble, like true stars" (p. 237). Malone's most human character, Mrs. Lambert, also finds solace by observing the night sky. She stands in the doorway, "gazing up" at the stars, a "scene that . . . sometimes solaced her" (p. 217). For some reason, Malone does not see the moon from his window: "how is it the moon where Cain toils bowed beneath his burden never sheds its light on my face?" (p. 221). We note the exactness of Beckett's imagery as we remember that the shining of the moon elsewhere in his fiction carries negative rather than positive connotations – for instance, in Belacqua's allusion in *More Pricks than Kicks* to Dante's moon branded with the stigma of Cain and his truss of thorns (*More Pricks than Kicks,* p. 12). At any rate, the glimpse of the night sky through Malone's window flickers like a faint promise of deliverance from his actual and literary hell.

The claim that Malone is in some kind of hell gains strong support by comparing the particulars of his condition (both actual and literary, as pictured in the stories) with Northrop Fry's descriptions of the sixth phase of tragedy or irony in his mythos of winter. We cannot, at this point, develop this analogy as far as it could be carried, and it could be carried quite far indeed. Instead, we will note that Malone inhabits Frye's demonic divine, human, animal, and vegetable worlds, that these worlds are defined as hell by symbols corresponding almost exactly to Frye's descriptions, and that Malone's quest is contained in Frye's questing movement through the center of hell and out the other side to the human world. The point of difference, of course, is that Malone only glimpses or intuits the existence of the other side; he never reaches it.

Frye's demonic divine world portrays an inaccessible, irrational nature or invisible, inscrutable fate, symbolized by a sky or heaven that seems distant or inaccessible to man.[47] Echoes of Beckett's absent or malign God/Power resonate in *Malone Dies* in such a portrayal. Sapo's alienation from nature (which we have already examined) and Macmann's betrayal by the beauty of the spring day of the picnic are instances of such demonic divinity in Malone's world. Also, Beckett includes in this novel a reference (repeated in *Company,* pp. 10-11) of a childhood memory of questioning his mother about the sky being much further away than it appears (p. 268). Whatever her exact reply, it is remembered as cutting enough to be included in the adult Beckett's fiction as evidence not only of interpersonal distance between mothers and sons but also

[47] *Anatomy of Criticism: Four Essays,* p. 147. References to this book are cited in this and succeeding paragraphs by page number(s) in the text.

of the cruelty and unconcern of a God far away from man somewhere in the distant sky.

Frye's archetypal demonic human world contains a society held together by a tyrant leader who sacrifices victims for his own pleasure or profit. It also includes images of the killing of divine kings, cannibalism, incest, and the tearing apart of a victim by a mob (Frye, pp. 147-48). The ruthless Lemuel is a tyrant/leader directing the group from the asylum; his victims are the two sailors killed with the hatchet and the helpless Lady Petal deserted on the island. Malone himself is a king being torn apart as he loses his life in sacrifice to his art – as we have noted, he senses a radical separation of his head from other parts of his body. Furthermore, he is a king who kills his subjects. In speculating on his earlier created characters – "the Murphys, Merciers, Molloys, Morans and Malones" – he asks, "How many have I killed, hitting them on the head or setting fire to them?" (p. 236). No instance of cannibalism occurs (we must wait until *The Unnamable* to find a hero tramping on the remains of his family), but echoes of such a phenomenon are present in the Lambert's killing and eating the white rabbit and the pet kid Whitey. Also, Malone's manner of relating Big Lambert's decision to kill Whitey connects the slaughter with incestuous feelings the father has for the daughter (pp. 215-16).

Frye's demonic qualities of the animal world (Frye, p. 149) are represented in the tortured animals of the Lamberts, and those of Frye's vegetable world (Frye, p. 149) in Malone's "forests of high threshing ferns." Malone remembers being lost (p. 227) in the wild, "ravening for earth and light" asylum garden (p. 275) – so reminiscent of that where Watt and Sam converse – and in the dead, "airless," "waterless" world "in the bed of a crater" that he holds in his memory (p. 201). The archetypal demonic burning fires (Frye, p. 150) appear as Malone's memories of the gorse fires, scattered on the hills of his childhood and mocking him with remembrances of youthful security. Rather than the purgatorial or cleansing waters of baptism, the demonic world contains waters of death, often associated with "spilled blood" (Frye, p. 150). What more demonic image of such a world does modern literature offer than Macmann in the boat with the dead sailors on the lake, huddled with Lemuel and his bloody hatchet – a hatchet at once Malone's own bloody club and his destroying pencil?

These instruments of death, Macmann's madhouse which becomes his prison, the final demonic scene on the lake, and numerous other images of horror identify *Malone Dies* unmistakably as Frye's "sixth-phase tragedy" which "shocks as a whole, in its total effect" (Frye, p. 222). Other parallels can be drawn. Frye's *desdichado* figures, characters linked to misery or madness, abound in Malone's real and fictional worlds. The strange visitor and Lemuel are servant giants, Big Lambert, a sinister parental figure, Lady Petal, a witch – a parodic figure of deity, who sings as she leads her troop toward death – and Moll, a travesty of Frye's "malignant grinning [so as to reveal her crucifixion tooth] female" (Frye, p. 238). The formulation of original sin as Beckett's vague, floating sense of guilt as it occurs in *Malone Dies* is another archetypal trait of the demonic worlds, as is the travesty of religious ritual we have already examined in detail in the Easter picnic episode (Frye, p. 238).

Most telling of all is Malone as the anti-hero, crucified in agony and humiliation as his character Macmann is by the pelting rain. His crucifixion results from Frye's "*tour abolie,* the goal of the quest that isn't there" (Frye, p. 239). The demonic motif of "*derkou theama* (behold the spectacle: get your staring over with)" (Frye, pp. 239 and 223) reveals itself in Malone's dependence for his miserable existence on the observing eyes of his readers and his created characters.

Malone fits Frye's patterns with astonishing exactitude, but he cannot follow the route Frye describes Dante and Virgil taking through the hell of phase six and out the other side:

> At the bottom of Dante's hell, which is also the center of the spherical earth, Dante sees Satan standing upright in the circle of ice, and as he cautiously follows Virgil over the hip and thigh of the evil giant, letting himself down by the tufts of hair on his skin, he passes the center and finds himself no longer going down but going up, climbing out on the other side of the world to see the stars again. (Frye, p. 239)

But Malone watches the starry sky from his window; he would like to find "a way out" from the "grey incandescence" of his hell into a world that the stars illuminate.

Wright, in asserting that "hope is always there in Beckett's texts," cites the words of the narrating voice of the ninth of Beckett's *Texts for Nothing,* in the French version, *Textes pour rien:*

> There's a way out there, there's a way out somewhere, the rest would come, the other words, sooner or later, and the power to get there, and the way to get there, and pass out, and see the beauties of the skies, and see the stars again. (Wright, p. 83)[48]

A similar hope or dream of Dante's escape from hell is in *The Lost Ones.* One group of the inhabitants of this hell, imagining a way out of their trap of a cylinder, dreams "of a trapdoor hidden in the hub of the ceiling giving access to a flue at the end of which the sun and other stars would still be shining" (*The Lost Ones,* p. 18).

Needless to say, none of the lost ones escape from this particular place of torment. Unlike Dante, Beckett leaves his characters stuck in hell, and his own literary forms fixed as tragic irony (or ironic tragedy). Beckett's ingenuity with literary form serves him well: by the creation of a demonic world such as that found in *Malone Dies,* he reveals himself to be an artist *par excellence.* But Malone does not fare as well as his author/creator. Stuck in his unique Beckettian hell, Malone quests for a power he senses to lie hidden in words, a Logos that might serve him as a *rite de passage* through hell into a better world.

---

[48] Wright's quotation, in his translation, is from Beckett's *Textes pour rien, Nouvelles et Textes pour rien* (Paris: Editions de Minuit, 1958), p. 117.

A *TRILOGY* OF SELVES, AND LARGE HOLLOW SPHERES

Analysis of Malone's withdrawal from the macrocosm into the confines of the microcosm (his "dying") in order to fabricate stories has demonstrated the pivotal significance of *Malone Dies.* Malone's quest, as we have seen, is to discover language capable of constructing a story that will define the hero as artist, and thus bestow selfhood upon his nebulous being. The status of this quest makes Malone the first Beckettian hero to exhibit overtly my paradigm of the microcosmic quest on level two. Malone fails in his quest and remains trapped in the hell of his imagination, unable to create a story that would qualify as art, and thus confer the identity of artist upon its creator.

Malone Dies is a single novel, but not a separate one, being preceded in Beckett's trilogy by *Molloy* and followed by *The Unnamable.* The other selves (or no-selves) of *Three Novels* advance toward and proceed beyond Malone, both in regard to descent into the world of the imagination, and in their efforts to manipulate the language of stories into the substance of selfhood. In fact, the Unnamable is, of all others, the Beckettian hero who most explicitly vocalizes the journey inward toward what we may call the core of consciousness. Furthermore, his frantic efforts to transcend the truncated nightmares of his stories by reaching beyond language for existential fulfillment and metaphysical significance make the novel that bears his name the key-work in Beckett's exploration of both the self and God. Continuity and progress characterize the development of ideas related to these concepts from *Molloy* through *The Unnamable,* with *Malone Dies* occupying the unique position we have described. By charting the course of this development through the trilogy, we gain new insight into the full meaning and power of Beckett's "failure," both in regard to art (the story) and the self – and its need for affirmation.

It would be possible to chart such a course by analyzing the thematic structures of both *Molloy* and *The Unnamable* as separate novels, according to the quest paradigms we have been applying to the individual works. We could chart the failure of the meeting of any of the five existential needs described throughout this study in either novel. Or, we could quest with Molloy, Moran, or the Unnamable for the elusive essence of the zero/symbol that beckons Molloy toward his mother, Moran toward Molloy, and the Unnamable toward a self not imprisoned and negated by language. Molloy and Moran quest on the macrocosmic level, and the Unnamable through the interior landscapes of the mind. Assertions by both Molloy and Moran that they are "authors," engaged in (Molloy) or planning to begin (Moran) the writing of accounts of their journeys, are made by heroes who are selves-as-characters. But the fact that these characters become story-tellers leads to Malone's identity of the self-as-artist. As the withdrawal of Malone's "dying" progresses into the Unnamable's deeper immersion of consciousness, the trilogy presents a hero whose quest as artist/self is to dispense with the deceptive shackles of fictional selfhood and reach beyond language for an essential self he intuitively senses to exist somewhere.

Such detailed analysis, however, would prove both tedious and unneccessary, since our concern – at this point – is to focus on the movement of the trilogy as it develops into the Unnamable's intensified ascesis through the territories of the mind. This hero's microcosmic descent becomes the most complex and significant parody in the fiction of Beckett's Cartesian Man Thinking, a parody which is schematized in a chapter from an early novel by Beckett not heretofore included for detailed examination in this study. This novel, *Murphy,* contains the famous (or infamous) Chapter Six, which delineates the interior of Murphy's mind as a "large hollow sphere." As we shall see, this description demonstrates Beckett's Cartesianism and raises the question of a Spinozist influence, not only on the structuring of Murphy's mind, but also on the states of consciousness and stages of thought of other heroes, most notably, the Unnamable. Beckett's heroes possess minds that engage in a peculiarly Beckettian mixture of isolation from the outer world, deductive reasoning, and imaginative fabrication. The functioning of Murphy's mind is an example of this mixture. The Cartesian basis of such mental activity is common knowledge. The influence of Spinoza – who considers himself to have "corrected" Descartes' metaphysics – reveals new ways of examining the labyrinthine territories of the Beckettian microcosm.

Molloy is exercising his mind in the opening paragraph of the novel that bears his name. He is writing pages of some sort, apparently an account of his recent journey to his mother's room, since his authorial prelude launches a description of his observation of A and C meeting on the road, the opening "action" of the novel *Molloy.* This hero encounters numerous difficulties in relating the account. He has decided that the traditional methods of storytelling don't really work, and he is struggling, after a lapse of literary inactivity (*Molloy,* pp. 7-8), to find language that describes his recent journey. The problem is that no matter what words he chooses to narrate the experience, it still makes little, if any, sense:

> But it is useless to drag out this chapter of my, how shall I say, my existence, for it has no sense, to my mind. It is a dug at which I tug in vain, it yields nothing but wind and spatter. (*Molloy,* p. 56)

As author Molloy continues, he decides to deal briefly with the most troublesome aspects of the journey,[1] hoping that his "story, so clear till now, may not end in darkness" (*Molloy,* p. 78). Whether this récit ends in "darkness" is a moot point, but it does close with Molloy lying helpless in a ditch, and the reader bewildered as to how the hero gets from the ditch to the bed in his mother's room, the place he occupies as he begins his tale.

Moran, the hero of the second section of *Molloy,* is also a writer of accounts – in his case, a "report" concerning the events that have transpired since he "received the order to see about Molloy" (*Molloy,* p. 72). Iain Wright observes that Moran begins his authorial task with a calmness unusual for a Beckettian teller of tales, writing in regular paragraphs and situating his account in a

---

[1] For an analysis of Molloy's storytelling, see Wright, "'What matter who's speaking?'" pp. 76-77.

somewhat traditional fashion as to setting and time. However, Moran also undergoes difficulties as to the relation of his past experiences to what he is writing: what tense shall he use, and what does the report mean, even if written successfully? Moran undergoes extreme trauma as he begins to wonder if perhaps he has only invented Molloy, a suspicion that causes the reader to suspect that *Molloy* is not really a novel at all but a farcical parody of one, as indeed it is. Moran despairs of the effort to tell stories – "Stories, stories, I have not been able to tell them. I shall not be able to tell this one" (*Molloy,* p. 137) – but continues his efforts with relentless perversity until Gaber orders him home.[2] When Moran arrives home, both Youdi and Gaber pester the disillusioned hero for the account which, apparently, remains unwritten. As *Molloy* closes, Moran, functioning in response to a "voice telling me things" (*Molloy,* p. 176), begins the writing of the report, which is supposedly the second section of *Molloy.* His infamous words – which constitute Beckett's enigmatic ending – subvert the entire enterprise of *Molloy* as anybody's narrative, either a hero's or Beckett's:

> Then I went back into the house and wrote, It is midnight. The rain is beating on the windows. It was not midnight. It was not raining. (*Molloy,* p. 176)

By the time we have journeyed through *Malone Dies* and observed Malone's troubled attempts to create fictional selves not engulfed by the darkness of his macrocosmic memories, we are not really surprised at finding the Unnamable. This egg-shaped hero seems unable to write; he has basic difficulties with simply speaking. Nonetheless, he describes himself as writing: "It is I who write, who cannot raise my hand from my knee. It is I who think, just enough to write, whose head is far" (*The Unnamable,* p. 301). In the preamble to his monologue, whether spoken or written, the Unnamable announces his purpose as simply being able to say "I," to speak about "me," and then to go silent. He scorns the previous narrators' obsession with fictional accounts of people and things. If necessary, a few "puppets" and objects will accompany his

[2] See "'What matter who's speaking?'" pp. 78-79.

"beginning," but he is reasonably certain that it will not take him long to "scatter them, to the winds, if I can" (*The Unnamable,* pp. 291-92). Even as he begins, this hero is at a much deeper level of descent into the microcosmic core of consciousness than Malone has been. Furthermore, his plans for communication are more confused than Malone's (and more bewildering to us as readers). He knows that word-play is no game, and he lacks Malone's comforting expectations of death. He is determined that neither fictive surrogates (Mahood, Worm), who assume existence and invade his monologue, nor the ubiquitous "they," who try to control his linguistic performance, shall hinder him from speaking of "me alone," of isolating and defining "me, for the first time" (*The Unnamable,* p. 303). The Unnamable foreshadows his failure in his opening paragraph. "I seem to speak, it is not I, about me, it is not about me" (*The Unnamable,* p. 291). The nature of the task defeats any possibility of its accomplishment. As Wright succinctly summarizes, language "is precisely that which prevents and blocks access to authentic selfhood."[3] The Unnamable reveals himself to be a no-self, beyond any Cogito, whether conceived of as "empirical, transcendental, or metaphysical."[4]

The literary efforts of these heroes reveal a breakdown of the possibility of story – a breakdown which is easily traced from *Molloy* through *The Unnamable.* In fact, in all of Beckett's fiction, this decline is the most comprehensive and definitive account of what we are calling the failure of language or story. A diminishment of characterization is a part of this breakdown. Both Molloy and Moran, for all their nebulous past experience and questionable transfusion of selfhood, qualify as characters if only because they function as grammatical subjects and objects. Each can say, "I did so and so." "This or that happened to me." What happens may be of no consequence, and the reaching of any goals may be symbolized most accurately by Beckett's empty zero, but nevertheless, both Molloy and Moran are able to use, if only in a contradictory fashion, the pronouns "I" and "me." As we have seen, Malone's

---

[3] "'What matter who's speaking?'" p. 81.

[4] Morot-Sir, "Grammatical Insincerity and Samuel Beckett's Non-Expressionism: Space, Subjectivity, and Time in *The Unnamable,*" in *Writing in a Modern Temper: Essays on French Literature and Thought in Honor of Henri Peyne,* p. 230.

problem is more acute than theirs. He is still able to say, "I am in this bed," "I am waiting to die," and "I am writing stories." But since his presence in the bed is almost entirely passive, since he does not die (or come any closer to death, as far as we know), and since his tales become, not composed fictions, but truncated and "dark" remnants of stored memories, his privilege to use "I" and "me" appears to be much more tenuous than that of Molloy and Moran. As we reach *The Unnamable,* the speaking voice acknowledges freely that he doubts his "own existence," in fact, has "no faith in it" (*The Unnamable,* pp. 590-91). Accordingly, the Unnamable recognizes the futility of his continued use of first-person pronouns.

A diminishment of characterization other than that of the heroes also develops as the trilogy progresses. In spite of the twilight zone which they inhabit and the uncertainty of the narrator in assigning them names, Molloy's police sargeant; Lousse; Ruth/Edith; the charcoal-burner; Moran's son, Jacques; Father Ambrose; the housemaid, Martha; the dim man; and the shepherd are at least facsimiles of "real" people. We know they are fictional creations of Beckett, and, as such, they seem on a par with Molloy and Moran. They have complete bodies, inhabit a somewhat recognizable space, move from one place to another, and react (except for the charcoal-burner/dim man) in predictable ways.

Malone's woman who cares for his needs is similar to the majority of these *Molloy* characters, and his strange visitor is reminiscent of the charcoal-burner/dim man. But a downward spiral begins with Malone's created surrogates. These surrogates are not "real," first-order, fictional people: Beckett creates Malone, and Malone creates them. But is Malone really in control of their creation, as, for instance, Chaucer's pilgrims control the characters of their tales? Malone knows that Sapo is named Saposcat, but he does not know if this is his Christian name. Nor does he know if Saposcat has any friends (*Malone Dies,* pp. 186 and 189), or why he has been expelled from school (*Malone Dies,* p. 190). The whole business of defining a character named Saposcat becomes "Mortal tedium" (*Malone Dies,* p. 217), and Malone renames him Macmann (*Malone Dies,* p. 229). Macmann's position in the text becomes increasingly slippery as his consciousness merges with that of Malone, whose actions in abandoning or killing off his characters blend his existence with that of the bloody Lemuel (*Malone Dies,* p. 288).

Confused efforts at characterization stretch into the opening pages of *The Unnamable.* Here, Malone as a character and the vague others who appear before the Unnamable have an existence so nebulous that the nameless narrator/hero seems to succeed in banishing them:

> There, now there is no one here but me, no one wheels about me, no one comes toward me . . . these creatures have never been, only I and this black void have ever been . . . . And Basil and his gang? Inexistent, invented to explain I forget what. (*The Unnamable,* p. 304)

But Basil reappears, whether by the Unnamable's intention or not is uncertain. Wright says that the Unnamable "fights against the new voice, Mahood [who is also Basil], who threatens to come to life."[5]

Morot-Sir points out that the effort to fabricate Mahood is an attempt "to create a person with a human nature (the essence of manhood)." The Unnamable's purpose is to impart to himself a "*subjective substance*" by fabricating a pseudo-self.[6] In the text, Mahood's appearance seems to be something that simply happens. The Unnamable sees himself "slipping . . . toward the resorts of fable," and notes that "Decidedly Basil is becoming important" (*The Unnamable,* p. 309). The forming of Mahood as character occasions both hope and despair. Perhaps, by speaking through him, the Unnamable can complete his pensum and reach the silence he desires. But, on the other hand, if Mahood usurps the Unnamable's voice, how can the Unnamable ever authentically utter "I" (*The Unnamable,* pp. 309-11)?

At any rate, the Unnamable (unlike Malone) is only too aware of the transference of characterization between himself and Mahood. He becomes increasingly uncertain as to whether he or Mahood is speaking, and finally decides to "scatter" this example of the "miscreated puppets" that "they" have shoved upon him (*The*

---

[5] "'What matter who's speaking?'" p. 80.

[6] "Grammatical Insincerity and Samuel Beckett's Non-Expressionism," p. 231.

Unnamable, p. 325). Mahood is slowly deprived of whatever characterization he has possessed as he loses arms, legs, sight, and any words of his own utterance. (If the words are neither the Unnamable's nor Mahood's, whose are they?) Worm, who shares the existence of both the Unnamable and Mahood, takes his place. And Worm is not a person or a character, but only a voice – the most shorn-of-identity voice to be found in the trilogy. The Unnamable describes him. He "says nothing, knows nothing." As to appearance, "He is nothing but a shapeless heap" (*The Unnamable,* p. 356). Indeed, he is an invention of "they": "he's an idea they have, a word they use" (*The Unnamable,* p. 366). But also, Worm is an invention of the Unnamable: "It is I invented him . . . since I had to speak . . . I couldn't speak of me . . . I invented my memories, not knowing what I was doing, not one is of me" (*The Unnamable,* pp. 395-96). So, says the Unnamable, Mahood and Worm are "me," and yet they are not "me." They are my only chance of saying "me" and yet, the definitive hindrance to my doing so. ". . . its the fault of the pronouns, there is no name for me, no pronoun for me, all the trouble comes from that" (*The Unnamable,* p. 404).

Elements of story other than first and third person characterization degenerate in obvious ways from *Molloy* to this final novel. The wandering journeys of Molloy and Moran become the limited movements in bed of Malone, which, in turn, become the fixed stasis of the Unnamable. Since fictional movement can be equated with plot, we can note also a gradual, but severe, reduction in plot, especially that limited to the actions of the hero apart from his surrogate selves. Place changes from wild forests, curving roads, strange cities, and nostalgic gardens to a single bed in some unidentified dwelling to whatever microcosmic space the Unnamable inhabits. Finally, the only visual places we can actually define are the spaces between words and in the margins of the text. Besides this obvious lessening of described area, a constriction of fictional field also occurs. Molloy and Moran are concerned with life, Malone is obsessed with art (his fictional stories), and the Unnamable is limited to the narrow sphere of his own self consciousness. The two early heroes' failures in life invade the art of Malone, whose physical withdrawal from the macrocosm foreshadows the final pattern of the Unnamable's desperate inward plunge into the core of consciousness.

Along with these changes in movement (or plot) and place, time – conceived of as some concept of past, present, and future – spreads itself into a tenseless forever. Molloy explains that he is presently in his mother's room, that he "was helped" there by some person or persons, and that he plans to "say my goodbyes" (write the account) and "finish dying" (*Molloy,* p. 7). Malone also plans to write and die, but he is more uncertain than Molloy as to exactly when (*Malone Dies,* p. 182). As for the Unnamable, he is situated in "forever" – "I have always been sitting here, at this selfsame spot." "I have been here, ever since I began to be." Furthermore, "Nothing has ever changed since I have been here." In regard to questions about the future, he has "no opinion on these matters" (*The Unnamable,* p. 293).

Reduction also occurs in what we may call the central subject matter of a novel – the web of relationships enmeshing the characters with society and with each other. By far, the most dominantly treated of such relationships in a conventional novel is the sexual/romantic involvement. In *Three Novels,* Beckett spaces his nightmarish vignettes of "love" with a subtle increase of both tragedy and comedy. Pilling remarks that "All Beckett's people abjure sexual involvement absolutely." This critic goes on, however, to comment on the continuing "resurrection" in the fiction of "encounters" between couples.[7] I would use the word "involvement" to describe various sexual bindings that occur throughout the writings, while emphasizing that desperation and disgust are the emotions most often displayed in such involvements. The love of Celia and Murphy (in *Murphy*) is a kind of a watershed in the fictional canon. We might say that from the affair of the hero of *Assumption* and his Woman through the episodes of Belacqua and his girls to the love of Murphy and Celia, we have a description of high expectations and disillusioned hopes. The relationship of Celia and Murphy is unique in that the irony attached to it does not overpower its pathos. After the affair of Celia and Murphy, nearly all depictions of romantic/sexual love are weighted with an irony signaling disillusionment.

In spite of Murphy's abandonment (or transcendence) of Celia, several of the passages Beckett uses to describe their love are

---

[7] *Samuel Beckett,* pp. 37-38.

lyrical in the finest sense. In the mortuary, Celia's eyes fasten on Murphy's remains:

> Celia alone seemed capable of giving her undivided attention to the matter in hand, her eyes continued to move patiently, gravely and intently among the remains long after the others had ceased to look. . . . (*Murphy*, p. 265)

Of course, Celia's attentive gaze is rendered ironic by her identity of Murphy's "birthmark deathmark" (*Murphy*, p. 267). But Beckett's employment of the pathetic fallacy in these events is almost without irony:

> Outside the horns of yew had the hopeless harbour-mouth look, the arms of two that can reach no further, or of one in supplication, the patient impotence of charity or prayer. (*Murphy*, p. 259)

As Celia has explained earlier, "I was a piece out of him that he could not go on without, no matter what I did" (*Murphy*, p. 234). *Watt* follows *Murphy*, and, from Watt kissing Mrs. Gorman the fishwoman to the narrator of *How It Is* stabbing Pim with the can-opener, we have a descending spiral of ironic portraits that are at once both disgusting and funny.

The classic episode of "love" in *Three Novels* is the involvement of Molloy with Ruth/Edith of the rubbish dump and rolling furniture. If this earliest romantic event in the trilogy surpasses the succeeding ones in repugnance and black humor, how can we describe Beckett's spacing of the episodes as increasingly degenerative, and thus mirroring the development of novelistic "failure" from *Molloy* through *The Unnamable*? The most simple answer is that Molloy and Edith/Ruth do achieve a circus-like sexual fulfillment, Malone and Moll struggle to partially overcome impotence, and Worm and Marguerite/Madeleine (who never speaks to him, "to the best of my knowledge" [*The Unnamable*, p. 344]) achieve no intimacy except her care for him in his jar as if he were an animal. A more subtle way to note the downward spiral of such involvements is to examine the accumulation of death imagery attending romantic incidents from *Molloy* through *The Unnamable*. We can recollect the plight – much earlier in the canon – of the unnamed hero of *Assumption* and the Manichean character of the Woman who visits him with death. Furthermore, death appears as the almost casual companion of lovers in *More Pricks than Kicks, Murphy,* and *First Love.* In the trilogy, where sexual attraction mushrooms into its full Manichean horror, we find a proliferation of death imagery.

Such imagery begins in *Molloy,* where the occasion of Molloy's meeting the temptress/sorceress Mrs. Loy or Sophie Lousse is his killing of her dog, Teddy, by running over the animal with his bicycle. As Lousse refuses to press charges and takes Molloy home with her, Beckett devotes several pages and much detail to Teddy's burial. In spite of Lousse's apparent friendliness, her sinister character reveals itself as Molloy makes the "grave charge" that she is adding poisons to his food and drink (*Molloy,* p. 53). It is, of course, the romantic undertones of his stay with Lousse that cause Molloy to recollect his most memorable experience of "love," the episode with Ruth/Edith. Her characterization blends with that of the mysterious Lousse, as Molloy reports that Ruth/Edith died "one black night" (*Molloy,* p. 58).

Macmann's loved one, Moll, exhibits death imagery in the form of ivory crucifixes (of the two thieves) for earrings and a tooth shaped like the crucified Christ. As the aging pair struggle for some physical expression of their attraction, they share an awareness of impending death. "For we shall soon die, you and I, that is obvious" (*Malone Dies,* p. 261). Malone, of course, is in the act of dying – on his own and in the character Macmann – and, as author, plots Moll's death as well: "Moll. I'm going to kill her" (*Malone Dies,* p. 264). Sure enough, on page 266, Moll does indeed die.

As we reach *The Unnamable,* Worm's final appearance is one of a living death. His only remaining bodily parts, the head and trunk, are encased in a jar reminiscent of an Egyptian canopic jar, a jar topped by a representation of either an animal or human head and holding the preserved viscera of a dead person. Such jars have often been buried with the mummy. The position of Worm's jar is on a corner in a city, near a slaughter house, clamorous with the "bellows of pain" of the herded cattle (*The Unnamable,* p. 341). Across the street is the chop-house of his "protectress," Madeleine or Maguerite, who cleans him from his "paltry excrements," makes him a nest of rags, covers him with a cloth in the snow (*The

Unnamable, p. 343), and hangs a Chinese lantern on his jar so as to take advantage of his strange appearance to advertise the meals (of meat from the slaughter house) prepared at her chop-house (*The Unnamable,* pp. 328-29). Thus we have moved from a meeting occasioned by the unexpected death of a pet dog to a relationship (or non-relationship) between a woman whose livelihood depends on the slaughtering of animals (a practice Beckett obviously regards with more distress than the ordinary person) and a man (?) encased in a death jar. All the ramifications of Beckett's Manichean ideas regarding human sexuality exhibit themselves in this negative progression. Love has become death, and this death is anything but the seventeenth-century literary notion of sexual ecstasy as a kind of "death."

The breakdown of the story, or of art, so apparent in the continuum of *Three Novels,* rests on the more basic failure of language itself. This failure, that we have detailed in *Watt* and in *Malone Dies,* assumes a particular form in *The Unnamable.* The Unnamable, as we have noted, struggles with a formlessness of first-person pronouns, an inability to use "I" or "me" with any adequacy of specific representation. This problem develops through the trilogy. Molloy and Moran say, "I journeyed"; "I am writing." The novel *Molloy* is a writing of their journeys, but the account is of circular movement, with the "I" (Moran) seeking the "me" (Molloy), but never achieving unified identity. Malone uses the pronoun "I": "I am dying," he says; "I am telling stories." But Malone's "I" gets lost in his stories, blending into the second-order fictional existence of his pseudo-selves, and disappearing into the negative existence of Lemuel, whose characterization Malone/Beckett negates with four repetitions of "not" and five of "never" in the last paragraph of the novel (*Malone Dies,* p. 288). The Unnamable's trapped "I" designates, not personal selfhood, but a voice responding to the controlling "they." He finally decides not to voice "I" again – "its too farcical" (*The Unnamable,* p. 355). But this nameless hero is addicted to chanting the pronoun, and he does so, on and on, through the last sentence of the trilogy. Therefore, we can say that *The Unnamable* is the key-work in depicting the Beckettian quest for speaking or writing capable of using first-person pronouns. In no other fiction by Beckett is the relation (or non-relation) between language and the self set forth more directly.

In order to categorize, we can describe the Unnamable's difficulty in specific ways – grammatically, linguistically, artistically, socially or politically, existentially, and metaphysically. I suggest that the "I" having no fixed referent grammatically or linguistically is the result of the absence of a metaphysical "I" in Beckett's novel.

Within the confines of grammar, the question as to the identity of "I" is answered by stating that "I" is the pronoun *I,* or by explaining that the nominative or subjective "I" corresponds to the objective "me." And, since "me" can neither speak nor act grammatically – is entirely passive – we still do not know who the "I" is. David Hesla surveys the grammatical problem with "I" from a slightly different perspective:

> For consider the problem which is the Unnamable's; and for the purposes of clarity, consider it from . . . the point of view of grammar. The Unnamable's task is to speak of himself. That is, the 'I' who is the Unnamable, or which the Unnamable is, is to speak of the 'me,' who is not the Unnamable or which the Unnamable is not. Concisely put, the Unnamable is not the same person or being in the objective case as he is in the nominative. It is impossible, that is to say, at least from the grammatical point of view, that I should speak of 'I'; for I can speak only of 'me.'[8]

Broadening the language sphere from grammar to linguistics as a whole offers little help with the question. As Allen Thiher asks, how "can 'I' be 'I' if every voice is 'I'?" Thiher continues, "To say 'I' – how can this confer being when it offers existence to every 'I' and thus to the pluralized no one?" This critic explains that, "Structural linguistics may point out that such a pronoun functions as a shifter, but this will bring little semantic succor to the speaker who feels that precisely such a semantic feature makes a mystification of the whole notion of personal identity."[9]

Morot-Sir carries the difficulty from its linguistic roots (or verbal-game status) to its logical implications in regard to literature or art:

---

[8] *The Shape of Chaos,* pp. 117-18.

[9] Thiher, "Wittgenstein, Heidegger, the Unnamable, and Some Thoughts on the Status of Voice in Fiction," in *Samuel Beckett: Humanistic Perspectives,* pp. 86, 88, and 86-87.

> Beckett does not try to find a theoretical answer to the question: What is the human self? He faces the problem that the writer has to solve: How can I create persons, characters, and, finally, how can I use the pronominal deictics of the first and second persons? In traditional literary criticism, this is known as the problem of characterization, i. e., the right, for the author and his/her creations, to say 'I' and 'you.' In *Un [The Unnamable]* Beckett, testing the spatial language, is also testing the psychological language, insofar as it has to be centered around persons. This is why *Un* appears to be an ***extreme attempt to create human beings with words,*** and it is the definite recognition of the failure of doing so.

Commenting further on the Unnamable's failure to assign character to Mahood or Worm, Morot-Sir describes the problem of a fictional world presumably made of things and persons being actually fabricated only of words – " if things [in the fiction] are words, *the reverse is not true.*" [10]

Numerous critics comment on the social/political ramifications of the Unnamable's difficulties with using the first-person pronoun, most often in regard to the ubiquitous "they" who are apparently in charge of the hero's discourse and against whom he rants with vehemence. The funniest incident in the novel concerning the efforts of the group known as "they" to determine the guilty hero's identity (as usual, he is uncertain as to why he is guilty – perhaps only because of the "pensum") is their insistence that he obtain or recognize his selfhood from looking at his photograph and "record:"

> But my dear man, come, be reasonable, look, this is you, look at this photograph, and here's your file, no convictions, I assure you, come now, make an effort, at your age, to have no identity, it's a scandal. . . . (*The Unnamable,* p. 377)

Hesla compares the swallowing up of the Unnamable's self by "they" in terms of Heidegger's "'Being-with-one-another,'" a "'Being-

---

[10] "Grammatical Insincerity and Samuel Beckett's Non-Expressionism," p. 230. See pages 230-34 for an analysis of linguistic pronominal breakdown in *The Unnamable.*

with'" by which "one loses one's own being to 'the Others.'"[11] Thiher also views the Unnamable's dilemma as related to Heidegger's "voice of *das Man,* the anonymous 'they' that speak, through inauthentic speech, the fallen logos of everyday existence."[12]

Thomas J. Cousineau compares ideas of lost selfhood in *Watt* and *Murphy* with Jacques Lacan's alienated self that is so distorted into a false objectivity by its culture, and the language of its society, that it cannot recapture a lost subjectivity. Speaking of Beckett's fiction in general, Cousineau says that the "implication which runs throughout the fiction is that alienation is merely reinforced by the acquisition of language; language allows a corrupt culture to seduce the individual with a distorted conception of himself."[13] As I noted in my chapter on *Watt,* numerous difficulties arise if we try to read Beckett's indictment of "they" (anywhere in the fiction) as a clearcut judgment of culture or society. Nevertheless, these ideas of a self formed by cultural pressures certainly hold sway in the Unnamable's monologue. Morot-Sir writes of the prevalence of such ideas in "modern sociology:"

> Collective consciousness, i. e., the *they,* teaches me how, where, and when to say *I.* My own language could be the product of a mystified *I* and of mystifying *they.*[14]

Both Hesla and Wright connect the "Others" or "they," not only with the Unnamable's "vice-existers" – Mahood and Worm – but also with the earlier gamut of Beckettian characters, and quote the Unnamable himself in support of this connection.[15] In Beckett's canon, however, the social/political remains subservient to the linguistic/literary.

---

[11] *The Shape of Chaos,* p. 127.

[12] "Wittgenstein, Heidegger, the Unnamable, and Some Thoughts on the Status of Voice in Fiction," p. 82.

[13] This quotation is from Cousineau's study on *Watt* ("'Watt': Language as Interdiction and Consolation," p. 2), which we have already discussed in the chapter on this novel. Cousineau's article on *Murphy* is "Descartes, Lacan, and *Murphy,*" *College Literature,* 11 (1984), 223-32.

[14] "Grammatical Insincerity and Samuel Beckett's Non-Expressionism," p. 233.

[15] See *The Shape of Chaos,* pp. 127-28 and "'What matter who's speaking?'" pp. 80-81.

While it is true that the inadequacy of the Unnamable's self exhibits itself primarily as a linguistic or literary problem, the existential need lies just beneath the surface of the text. As Wright summarizes,

> Beckett's texts . . . deconstruct all their authorial subjects, and the very possibility of being an author, and yet there is no modern writing in which the author, Sam Beckett, is so persistently present, directing us, always, relentlessly, back to the same problematic, badgering us, not to listen to 'language itself' – or not only to that – but to the problem of cognition.[16]

The Unnamable's linguistic difficulties with first-person pronouns reveal an urgent need for a selfhood that he nostalgically remembers or intuitively senses to be his birthright. As Livio Dobrez explains, in this novel, the descent of the self reaches such depths that a separation occurs between the speaking voice and the Unnamable's inner consciousness (thus leaving him a no-self), which, being beyond language, cannot be defined except as a further step toward the ultimate nothing that is impossibly there.[17] Dobrez designates the Unnamable as "Beckett's Irreducible" and describes this entity as follows:

> The Irreducible is that which is *beneath* consciousness, not consciousness itself. Descartes' *cogito*, for all its unlikeness to matter, is conceived as a thinking substance, a *res*, a thing. The Leibnizean monad, though immaterial, is also a substance. But Beckett's subject is nothing at all, a being utterly negative, impossible to define. Thus Beckett's Cartesian Reduction, his occasionalism and his monadology point in a direction which is uniquely Samuel Beckett, towards something that is not a thinking self nor even pure Thought but, if we may distort Kierkegaard's phrase, passionate absence.[18]

Dobrez transcends the existential and suggests the metaphysical as he writes of Beckett's absence or "void" as an "encompassing god-like presence beneath the eternal fretting of consciousness on

---

16 "'What matter who's speaking?'" p. 82.
17 "Samuel Beckett's Irreducible," pp. 216-17.
18 "Samuel Beckett's Irreducible," pp. 217-18.

its wheel of life."[19] However, a vague merging of ideas of the "I" or the self with notions of God is confusing here. We must remember that neither Beckett nor the Unnamable is a mystic. Nor do they embrace (to the best of our knowledge) modern theological/philosophical concepts of God as the highest essence of human selfhood. The Unnamable's perceptions of cosmic authority – guilt, experience of determinism, need for a witnessing authentication of being, and sense of unwanted immortality – are obvious throughout the novel. If this hero were to form a substantial thought of God, it would be of someone other than and separate from himself. Furthermore, as a true-to-form Beckettian hero, he would not seek the presence of the evil God formed by such thought. It is a reference point for his identity that he searches for in the depths of consciousness. But this reference point, this "*tour abolie,* the goal of the quest that isn't there,"[20] strongly suggests Dobrez's distortion of Kierkegaard's phrase – "passionate absence."

The Unnamable's quest strategy shows him to be an artist/self. He is trying to determine identity by telling the true story (not false fictions) of the "I" or "me" who is genuinely himself. This strategy explains the narrative movement away from fictional pseudo-selves toward the actual "me." It also accounts for the hero's severe withdrawal into the depths of consciousness, and for the proliferation of first-person pronouns in the latter part of the text. Perhaps the Unnamable thinks that if he voices "I" and "me" often enough, he will accidentally discover their reference point. But a pronoun relates to its reference point in somewhat the same manner as zero relates to a mathematical number: to write zero into infinity is never to write a number. A first-person pronoun is only a pronoun, and, as such, cannot be a reference point. The only possible reference point for a pronoun is a noun, the name of someone or something. The pronoun derives its name from the name of the noun.

So, the Unnamable is seeking a noun or name in order to determine his own name. But his title is not "no-name," or that which would have a name if he could find it. Rather, it is the

---

19 "Samuel Beckett's Irreducible," p. 221.
20 Frye, *Anatomy of Criticism*, p. 239.

Unnamable, or that which cannot be named. This hero is a passive being (or non-being), who, were he to obtain a name, would have to receive it, or have it bestowed on him. Once again, we encounter a hero who connects the meeting of a vital need with the withheld gifts of some malevolent authority. Just as existing depends on a cosmic witness, so naming requires a cosmic noun to bestow a name. This absent noun or point of reference corresponds to the Kierkegaardian distortion – "passionate absence" – that Dobrez identifies in the novel.

The false promise luring the hero on can be described linguistically. The noun "name" lurks within the expression "the Unnamable." The expression is preceded by the article "the" and begins with a higher case "U." If the prefix "Un" and the suffix "able" were discarded, the stem or root remaining would be the noun "nam(e)." If we could make these subtractions, retain the article "the," and transfer the higher case status of "U" to the "N" of "nam(e)," we would have "the Name." This noun suggests an ultimate or Platonic Name from which all other naming or names are derived.

The Hebrew tetragrammaton YHWA (Yahweh) is a Jewish absolute Name for God of this nature. In Exodus, Chapter Three, Moses responds to a voice from a burning bush by undergoing an identity trauma. "Who am I, that I should go unto Pharaoh, and that I should bring forth the children of Israel out of Egypt?" The threefold repetition of "I"in this sentence is not as desperate as that of the Unnamable, but it is urgent. At this point, the voice places Moses' identity into the objective case, three times also. "Certainly I will be with thee; and this [the future presence of the Israelites upon this spot of earth] shall be a token unto thee, that I have sent thee." Moses is no longer an "I" whose actions are uncertain; he becomes a "me" (or "thee") certainly acted upon by the source of the voice. But, more reassuring for Moses, this voice, which has already called Moses by his name – "Moses, Moses" – reveals itself as "Yahweh." The root of "Yahweh" is the Hebrew verb "to be" used in its simple stem – in English, "I AM THAT I AM," or "I am the God who will be there." To refer to this God in the third person is to adopt the form "He is," or, in Hebrew, the archaic spelling, "Yahweh." Thus Moses' personal name, and first-person pronouns used as referents to him, become ontologically based in the absolute "being there" of the Hebrew God.[21] The Unnamable, of course, would reject, not only Yahweh, but also any acknowledged Name for God as the source of his need. To need God would be to lose "all sense of decency" and to sink to "certain depths we prefer not to sink to" (*The Unnamable,* pp. 374-75). Curiously, a kind of reverse irony permeates the tone of this statement.

Were the Unnamable to receive a name for his "I," he would have a genuine identity that could deliver him from the surface assuming of whatever names float in his consciousness. Deciding he is not Malone, he tries being Mahood, but rejects this identity also. Pouncing on the name "Worm," he urgently tries to make it stick to whatever voice is saying "I":

> But it's time I gave this solitary a name, nothing doing without proper names. I therefore baptise him Worm. It was high time. Worm. I don't like it, but I haven't much choice. It will be my name too, when the time comes when I needn't be called Mahood any more, if that happy time ever comes. (*The Unnamable,* p. 337)

The name of a noun to serve as a reference point for his first-person pronouns, then, is the Logos or Word this hero is searching for. Because Beckett the author does not discover this name, nor the Unnamable the hero receive such a name, we the readers cannot know it either. It remains the unnamed mystery, or the Unnamable.

Focusing on the specific undertaking of the Unnamable as he quests to resolve this mystery discloses the uniquely Beckettian framing of the questions at hand. *The Unnamable* is a piece of literature that consists of words spoken by a solitary voice. Whether these words are being written as the voice speaks is unclear (of course, they have been written by Beckett, as one of *Three Novels*). But there is no question that the Unnamable is speaking, and the most acute observation of this event of speaking is that it is simultaneously an act of thinking. Although there does occur a fracture between the Unnamable's consciousness and the

---

[21] See Walter C. Kaiser, Jr., *Toward an Old Testament Theology* (Grand Rapids: Zondervan, 1978), p. 106, and J. Barton Payne, *The Theology of the Older Testament* (Grand Rapids: Zondervan, 1962), pp. 148-49.

rambling voice, the form of the literature (an audible interior monologue) presents this hero as thinking out loud. In reply to the question that naturally follows – what is he thinking about? – we answer that he is thinking about life and what it means (or does not mean). Whatever subject a Beckett hero thinks about, he relates that subject to the significance or non-significance of the human experience. The Unnamable's considerations about "dying, living, being born, unable to go forward or back, not knowing where you came from, or where you are, or where you're going" are thoughts about human life and what possible meaning it can have (*The Unnamable,* p. 370). Linda Ben Zvi has demonstrated the agreement of Beckett's thought with Mauthner's theory that thinking and speaking are one and the same activity; that is, that thinking is merely silent verbalization.[22] This agreement reinforces the assertion that the voice of the Unnamable, shut in the "hot cupboard" of the inner consciousness, is Beckett's most carefully drawn parody of the hero as Man Thinking.

This parodic portrait, then, presents The Unnamable as a particularly Cartesian hero. To consider the Unnamable (or any other hero) as Cartesian is to situate ourselves in the sixth chapter of *Murphy.* Here, in describing Murphy's withdrawal into the "hot cupboard" of his structured brain, Beckett depicts the space and mental activities of Man Thinking, or, perhaps a better expression would be Man Puzzling.[23] Murphy's visualization of his mind is as a "large hollow sphere, hermetically closed to the universe without" (*Murphy,* p. 107). Beckett's description of this visualization can serve not only as a graphic representation of Murphy's microcosm but also as a rendering of the area "inside" the

---

[22] "Samuel Beckett, Fritz Mauthner, and the Limits of Language," pp. 187-88.

[23] In *Beckett's Theaters: Interpretations for Performance* (Cranbury, N. J.: Associated Univ. Presses, 1984), pp. 12-16, Sidney Homan explores Murphy's three zones from a Beckettian aesthetic perspective. The artist mentally or imaginatively "moves toward" but "never reaches" the third or "'dark zone,'" Although the artist's efforts to express his "inner world" are, in any sense, "futile," the most useful strategy is the Proustain involuntary memory. This method is effective by chance; only about twelve instances occur in Proust's work. But Beckett "parts company" with even this much artistic optimism. For him, with his emphasis on "nothing," the endeavors of art are "all playing," only a "dream." Thus the artist's dictum is "I think; therefore I am not." Homan, however, finds such Beckettian futility to be "heroic, perhaps even romantic," but "not pessimistic."

Unnamable's "distant skull," where he "once . . . wandered" but now is "fixed." The Unnamable describes his head as likewise spherical – "a great smooth ball," in the shape of an egg (*The Unnamable,* pp. 303 and 305). The descriptions of Chapter Six allude pointedly to the methods of Descartes and the other seventeenth-century rationalist philosophers, who have so strongly influenced Beckett's writings. Here, Beckett borrows, rejects, and alters conclusions, as he does everywhere when making use of philosophical systems. In the process, he is more often given to parody than to pure emulation. As Pilling remarks of Beckett's use of Cartesianism, "The whole of Beckett's . . . philosophical thinking is determined by his acceptance of Descartes's methods and rejection of Descartes's consolations."[24]

Many aspects of Beckett's well-worn Cartesianism are evident in this sixth chapter, aspects which apply both to Murphy's mind and to the Unnamable's sphere of consciousness. Descartes' beginning stance is a skepticism that rejects as truth all evidence (such as tradition and sense experience) except that which issues from the thinking mind. Chapter Six opens with the assertion that Murphy's mind cannot be described objectively; it can be known only in terms of "what it felt and pictured itself to be" (*Murphy,* p. 107). *Murphy* as a whole reveals that Murphy's mind is the "gravamen" (significant part) of the novel itself, read as a grievance or complaint against the futility of life's struggles. The narrator remarks that, of all the characters in the novel, only Murphy is "not a puppet" (*Murphy,* p. 122). Thomas A. Warger, writing of madness in *Murphy,* says that the entire fictional world of the novel can be conceived of as "symptoms or outward signs" of Murphy himself; "everything leads to Murphy." As for the "dependent nature" of the minor characters, they are indeed "'puppets' that Murphy animates in the twin senses of putting into motion and imbuing with significance."[25] All is shaped by Murphy's mind. The Unnamable is trying to enable the "I" which is supposed to designate his selfhood to function in a Cartesian fashion by sifting out the invalid testimony of alternate false voices. He determines that only this "I" will speak. But he despairs of formulating his

---

[24] *Samuel Beckett,* p. 114.

[25] Warger, "Going Mad Systematically in Beckett's *Murphy,*" *Modern Language Studies,* 16 (1986), 18.

own thoughts; his words seem foisted upon him by the all-prevailing "they." Thus, his skepticism results in a rejection of almost all the "I" formulates because this formulation seems controlled by "they."

The unique ability of Descartes' *cogito* to formulate reality does not deny the actuality of the outside world. The description of Murphy's mind does not "involve Murphy in the idealist tar. There was the mental fact and there was the physical fact, equally real if not equally pleasant" (*Murphy,* p. 108). Thus, for Murphy, as for all Beckett's heroes, the macrocosm does exist, but it exists *as perceived in the microcosm.* Morot-Sir explains how inner and outer worlds exist simultaneously in a kind of Manichean dualism in Beckettian man's consciousness.[26] Murphy is aware of light (a symbol used often throughout the fiction to indicate the outer world) and darkness (symbolizing the state of inward descent), of kicks (the undesirable) and caresses (the desirable). Everything exists as either "actual" (that of which he has both physical and mental experience) or "virtual" (that of which he has mental experience only). "Thus the form of kick was actual, that of caress virtual" (*Murphy,* p. 108). Nothing exists, nor is there a term for, something that is merely physical. The outer world is real for the Unnamable also, intruding relentlessly into his consciousness and existing there in the nebulous "grey" which is a Manichean blending of outward "bright" with the inward "black" (or dark) (*The Unnamable,* p. 301). Thus the Cartesian dicta of ultimate reality residing in the awareness of the outer world as formulated by the reasoning mind, and of mind over (or before) matter are, if not exemplified, at least parodied, in the consciousness of both Murphy and the Unnamable.

The Cartesian/Beckettian split between mind and matter is so obvious for both these heroes as to need little elaboration. The Unnamable's split widens as his monologue lengthens. And, "Murphy felt himself split in two, a body and a mind" (*Murphy,* p. 109). The remedy for such anguishing partition is, as we have seen, one of the goals of the macrocosmic quest. A non-Cartesian element for Beckett's people is that they, unlike Descartes, accept empirical or sense evidence as valid data. In fact, the incongruence

---

[26] "Samuel Beckett and Cartesian Emblems," p. 97.

or incompatability of this data with the aspirations of the mind or spirit forms the basic conflict in the fictional canon. Like Descartes, the Beckett hero cannot learn truth from empirical evidence, but, unlike Descartes, his sense experience of this data is all the "truth" he knows. In fact, that is precisely his problem. Descartes claims that the existence of an outside world is mediated directly to him by God, and knowledge or truth about this world gained by rational thought. The seventeenth-century philosopher postulates the mysterious pineal gland as the physical agent of connection between microcosm and macrocosm. Beckett's heroes, including Murphy and the Unnamable, lack both a mediating God and a pineal gland.[27] Murphy accepts the "partial congruence of the world of his mind with the world of his body as due to some such process of supernatural determinism," but the "problem was of little interest" (*Murphy,* p. 109). As we shall note later, Murphy's notions of needed help from God at this point are more Geulincxian than Cartesian. The Unnamable is so frustrated with the intrusion of the outer world into the mental realm that he cannot bother to speculate as to how it occurs.

Both the Unnamable and Murphy employ, with varying degrees of difference, Descartes' method of pure thinking or rationalism in their pursuits of truth or knowledge about life. We have already observed the Unnamable in this pursuit. That what he produces is fiction should not surprise us; Hugh Kenner points out that what Descartes formulates is fiction also.[28] Like Descartes, the Unnamable insists on the desirability of reasonableness in regard to the outside world. Unlike Descartes, he does not discover this world to be reasonable. The relating of detail, the breaking down of situations and persons into parts or groups, the attempts for completion or exhaustiveness, the effort to rivet speculation (in what is almost a mathematical subtraction) to the subject at hand (the identity of "I") – all of these "methods" echo those of the great mathematician/philosopher. Murphy is not as skilled in method as the Unnamable, but he also formulates, breaks down, and figures. In this sixth chapter, as the narrator explains,

---

[27] When Neary remarks of Murphy that his "conarium has shrunk to nothing" (*Murphy,* p. 6), Neary is referring to this celebrated gland. The Unnamable finds no mediation between the world of "they" and the realm of the speaking voice.

[28] *Samuel Beckett,* p. 81.

Murphy divides his mind into three distinct zones and ascribes certain characteristics to each. Throughout his brief life, he relies, not on advice from lovers or friends, but on the "systems" of astrology and the fabricating mind.

For Descartes, truth that cannot be determined by such mathematical methods of reasoning must be given directly by God. Whether this bestowal is natural or supernatural is never made clear in his writings. The postulate itself is, supposedly, the result of reason. Man, who is merely human, cannot possibly, on his own, ascertain the existence of a cosmic Being such as God. The finite is unable to arrive at certain knowledge of the infinite. Therefore, if the mind ascertains God, God must be mediating the knowledge of his existence. Not to be confused with traditional ideas of divine revelation, this notion makes possible its corollary, that is, that God also gives assurance that the outside world actually exists. Descartes' problem is obvious: the thinking "I" is the sole arbiter of truth, but it can arbitrate neither God nor the world.

Neither the solutions of Descartes, nor of his followers – Geulincx and Malebranche – will work finally for Murphy and the Unnamable. Geulincx's speculations, however, can account for certain postures and assumptions found in both the sixth chapter of *Murphy* and in *The Unnamable.* Geulincx is called an "Occasionalist" because he rejects the interlocking of body with mind that Descartes postulates, and admits to both a greater skepticism and determinancy. We cannot know how – and therefore, if – the mind's willing a given movement results in that physical movement. Instead, experience gives evidence that many things willed in the mind occur in the physical world, but some, unfortunately (or fortunately), do not. God, then, must be in complete control in the outer world. Because he so wills, there is some congruence of thought with matter – not cause-result, but simultaneous occasion. Murphy is "content to accept this partial congruence of the world of his mind with the world of his body as due to some such process of supernatural determination" (*Murphy,* p. 109). Beckett parodies Geulincx in Murphy's understanding of the "actual" and "virtual" kick: Murphy knows how to think of a kick, and how to receive one (*Murphy,* pp. 108-09). Whether he can give one is not mentioned. Kenner describes the Unnamable's knowledge of the way he is seated, not as a posture the hero has achieved, but as one he observes.[29] The Unnamable's puzzlement as to how he is writing if he cannot "raise my hand from my knee" (*The Unnamable,* p. 301) might be a problem for Geulincx to ponder also.

Geulincx follows Descartes' convenience of assuming that whatever knowledge he entertains for which the efforts of his mind are not responsible must have been bestowed upon him, apparently by God. Murphy's knowledge of the accidental "collusion" between his mental and bodily selves is this kind of knowledge. It is "as unintelligible as telekinesis or the Leyden Jar"; he simply knows that this "collusion" exists (*Murphy,* pp. 110-11). The Unnamable wonders about similar matters in a more ironic vein, designating the crowd he calls "they" as the source of his knowledge:

> The things they have told me! About men, the light of day . . . But it can only have been from them I learnt what I know about men and the ways they have of putting up with it . . . . What puzzles me is the thought of being indebted for this information to persons with whom I can never have been in contact. . . .

The puzzled hero remarks that "they" are the ones who "also gave me the low-down on God" and "told me I depended on him, in the last analysis" (*The Unnamable,* pp. 297-98). The remark is weighted with irony.

The helplessness apparent in any such philosophy is a pervasive characteristic of the Beckett hero. In his many guises, he seems to wonder, with a kind of desperate resignation, exactly what his body and the rest of the material world are up to. Both Murphy and the Unnamable persist in their efforts to use the only freedom Geulincx's system does allow – a freedom confined to the realm of the mind. Molloy recollects an image of this limited freedom as he ponders whether he could have left Lousse earlier than he did. It is "old Geulincx" who leaves Molloy "free, on the black boat of Ulyssess, to crawl towards the East, along the deck" (*Molloy,* pp. 50-51). The boat, of course, is sailing West. The Unnamable indentifies himself with this kind of freedom: "I am he . . . who crawls between the thwarts, towards the new day that promises to be glorious, festooned with lifebelts, praying for rack

[29] *Samuel Beckett,* p. 84.

and ruin" (*The Unnamable,* p. 339). The limited freedom Murphy manages is in the first and second zones of his mind. As his rocking chair rocks faster and faster, he knows (or hopes) that "Soon his body would be quiet, soon he would be free" (*Molloy,* p. 9). In spite of the fatalism of such a system, Geulincx is the author of an *Ethics* (a copy of which the hero of *The End* has received in his past life [*Stories and Texts for Nothing,* p. 63]), and thus apparently holds to some kind of belief as to how to respond to the world he describes (or fabricates). Pilling designates this response by the verb "endeavor," and notes that both Lucky (*Waiting for Godot,* p. 29) and Malone (*Malone Dies,* p. 217) mention it as an act of "conation." Geulincx's "endeavoring" is the effort of a person to "transcend himself in a genuine activity that he has striven for without it being imposed from without."[30] As we note later, the verb is associated with Spinoza's thought also. For the Beckett hero, such action seems to consist of going on and on, doing whatever he can in spite of what he expects. The result is a kind of dogged, desert-father continuing of action (usually journeying, speaking, or writing) in the face of little hope of change for the better. Murphy continues his misdirected efforts to operate in both the big and little worlds, and the Unnamable ends his speaking/thinking with the much-quoted phrase, "you must go on, I can't go on, I'll go on" (*The Unnamable,* p. 414).[31]

Malebranche, who, along with Geulincx, "corrects" Descartes, gives up the concept of man's freedom altogether, accepting a complete dualism of mind and body, and curtailing Geulincx's freedom of mind to the extent of claiming that nothing happens any place, without or within, except by the direct intervention of God. In fact, all being is arbitrary in that it rests momentarily on God's intervention. The thought patterns of Beckett's heroes might well serve as modern-day examples of Malebranche's human mind minus the merciful interventions of God. With body divorced from mind, the self from God, and reasoning from truth, the bewildered heroes would not agree with Malebranche that to think of God (a process itself supposedly caused by God) is proof enough that he exists.

---

[30] *Samuel Beckett,* pp. 212, note 6, and p. 115.

[31] For discussion of Descartes and Geulincx in regard to Beckett, see "The Rational Domain," in Hugh Kenner's *Samuel Beckett,* especially pp. 79-91.

Certain characteristics of Murphy's mind suggest the theories of Spinoza – a seventeenth-century philosopher not ordinarily associated as closely with Beckett as are Descartes and his two Occasionalist followers. Of the thirteen chapters of *Murphy,* only two – Chapters Six and Nine –are prefaced by epigraphs. The epigraph of Chapter Six alerts us to the question of a Spinozist trend in Beckett's Cartesianism, as found in this novel and graphically depicted in this chapter.[32] The epigraph reads, *"Amor intellectualis quo Murphy se ipsum amat"* (*Murphy,* p. 107). In Chapter Nine, the narrator ironically admits the failure of Spinoza's conclusions for Murphy. This hero recognizes "the intellectual love in which alone he could love himself, because there alone he was lovable," but he is not able "to take the . . step of renouncing all that lay outside" this abstract verity (*Murphy,* p. 179). Spinoza's ideas of a Nature/God are abstract in comparison with Beckett's more concrete notions of divinity, but the concepts are similar in that both thinkers conceive of God as Being that is everywhere and yet nowhere.

Although Murphy feels an alienation between the mental and physical, Beckett's description of this hero's mind suggests Spinoza's premise that spatial objects and thought are not two entirely separate worlds but rather "two aspects of a single inclusive reality."[33] Spinoza argues that biological (Descartes' pineal gland) or theological (Geulincx's and Malebranche's interventions of God) speculations are not necessary to account for interaction between the worlds of thought and matter because the two systems are not distinct substances but two attributes of one and the same substance. Or, his thought seems to suggest, two conceptions of a single, unified entity. Taking as his point of reference the union of the single human mind with the individual human body, this philosopher asserts that all ideas in the mind have their corresponding *ideata* in the realm of matter. Thus the Cartesian concern with how thought is joined to object and/or energy does not arise. Correspondence between a thought and its extension in space is a

[32] This trend was pointed out to me by Edouard Morot-Sir, in comments concerning Chapter Six of *Murphy,* dated December, 1986.

[33] Stuart Hampshire, *Spinoza* (Baltimore: Penguin, 1951), p. 63. Information on Spinoza in this and succeeding paragraphs is from this source. Direct quotations are designated in the text by the author's name (Hampshire) and page number(s).

part of the premise. ". . . since there are both extended things and ideas of extended things, as Nature presents itself to us, and since both the extended things and the ideas must belong to the unique self-determining substance, there can be no ideas which are not ideas of extended things, or extended things of which there is no idea" (Hampshire, p. 65). The narrator of *Murphy* tells us that the hermetic closure of Murphy's mind to the "universe without" was "not an impoverishment, for it excluded nothing that it did not itself contain. Nothing ever had been, was or would be in the universe outside it but was already present . . . in the universe inside it" (*Murphy*, p. 107). Apparently, however, Murphy does not realize the full benefits of this plenitude of his mind with matter in the every-day events of life: "He neither thought a kick because he felt one nor felt a kick because he thought one" (*Murphy*, p. 109). Murphy's speculation on this problem advances in Spinozist directions. Perhaps the absence of correspondence between the mental and physical kicks is due to the hero's ignorance of a "non-mental, non-physical Kick from all eternity" that exists "outside space and time" and has been only "dimly revealed to Murphy in its correlated modes of consciousness and extension, the kick *in intellectu* and the kick *in re*." Murphy appears as Beckett's reasoning hero as he asks the question that logically follows: "But where then was the supreme Caress?" (*Murphy*, p. 109). Murphy, like Beckett's other heroes working with seventeenth-century philosophical systems, seems to have inherited notions and difficulties but no solutions.

The feeling Murphy entertains, more distinctly as he grows older, that "his mind was a closed system subject to no principle of change but its own, self-sufficient and impermeable to the vicissitudes of the body" (*Murphy*, p. 109) is also related to Spinoza's thought. Beckett's oblique allusions are to certain basics of Spinoza's vast metaphysical system. Murphy's mind as described here is not merely Cartesian. Descartes, Geulincx, and Malebranche all think that the mind can be changed, in varying degrees, by the action of God – quite logically, since, in their thought, the mind is the creation of God. For Spinoza, the human mind is a part of the "single, intelligible, causal system" which is God or Nature (Hampshire, p. 47). God has not created Nature (or the mind); God is Nature (or the mind), and Nature is God. True, only God, or the total system of Nature, can be described as a substance, that which possesses all its attributes as the deduction of its own essence and is determined by no cause – not even a First Cause – but can be defined as caused of itself (Hampshire, p. 36). The mind, because it is less than this total system, is acted upon by causes different from itself, but not directly. Instead, the "individual human mind is constituted by that set of ideas whose objects . . . are states of an individual human body." The body, "as a finite mode of extension," is constantly being affected by other bodies external to it, and these effects are necessarily reflected in the ideas of the body which constitute the mind. Spinoza is not saying that changes to the body produce changes in the mind. Rather, since the mind is the "idea" of the body, "every bodily change *is* a mental change and *vice versa*" (Hampshire, p. 83). Changes in the mind are the counterpart of changes in the body (Hampshire, p. 108). The language Beckett applies to Murphy's mind – "closed system, subject to no principle of change but its own, self-sufficient and impermeable to the vicissitudes of the body" – achieves added dimension from what Stuart Hampshire calls Spinoza's "most far-reaching proposition": "'In the nature of things nothing contingent is admitted, but all things are determined by the necessity of divine nature to exist and act in a certain way'" (Hampshire, p. 45, quoted from *Ethics,* Part I, Proposition 29). Is Murphy's mind, as Spinoza asserts of the human mind, a "part of the infinite intellect of God?" (Hampshire, p. 83).

Although we would agree with Murphy that the answer is "no," we can explore the question in depth by examining what the narrator refers to as "the three zones [of Murphy's mind], light, half light, dark, each with its speciality" (*Murphy,* p. 111). A particular advantage of such exploration – still within the context of what we are calling a Spinozist trend in Beckett's Cartesianism – is that certain questions raised in recent criticism on the tripartite structure of Murphy's mind can receive at least tentative answers. Cousineau advances beyond the standard critical readings of *Murphy* as basically revealing, in some negative/positive manner, Beckett's Cartesianism.[34] This critic poses the problem of

[34] "Descartes, Lacan, and *Murphy,*" pp. 223-32. As Cousineau acknowledges (p. 223), Samuel Mintz ("Beckett's *Murphy:* A Cartesian Novel," *Perspective,* 11 (1959), 156-65) first puts forth this reading, and has been followed in his basic premise by critics such as Ruby Cohn and Hugh Kenner.

Murphy's tripartite-structured mind not fitting into the pattern of Cartesian dualism. Is Murphy's sense of his mind's structure merely "perverse," an "idiosyncratic invention," or are we as readers to take it seriously "as a model which deserves respectful attention?" If Chapter Six is to be taken seriously, then how is its structure related to the obvious Cartesianism of the remainder of the novel? Cousineau connects these matters with the related question of the distance Beckett creates by the tone of the novel – what is the author's perspective on his hero, satire or empathy? Answering this group of questions by a Lacanian reading of *Murphy,* Cousineau compares the zones of Chapter Six with Lacan's three stages of development of identity, and concludes that Murphy is an ironic hero trapped by ignorance and a false sense of security in Lacan's imaginary stage, "where the self learns to identify with its objectified image." In other words, Murphy is afraid or unable to retreat into the dark or third zone of "primordial, undifferentiated experience," but unwilling to advance into the light or first zone of "the symbolic, constituted by language, social customs and institutions." Murphy needs to stop using his Cartesian theories as an excuse for alienating himself from the real world (remaining trapped in the mind) and risk achieving the only identification available to anyone, that of the "preexisting symbolic order" that both bestows life and initiates death. [35]

Lacan's stages will describe the development of almost any human mind, including Murphy's, and Celia would doubtless join Cousineau in admonishing the hero to come on out of his rocking chair and mind into the real, howbeit terrifying, world. But, in defining Beckett's relationship with any one of his heroes, dramatic or fictional, we must be on guard against assuming an authorial stance of satire. It is probably safe to say that Beckett has never even suggested a course of action a hero *should* or *should not* take. Each seems to be engaged in the only course of action possible under the circumstances. And, besides, as Cousineau himself points out, there can "be no question of a genetic relation between the novel [*Murphy*] and Lacan's theories since Lacan published his major work long after *Murphy.*" [36]

---

[35] "Descartes, Lacan, and *Murphy,*" pp. 224-29.

[36] "Descartes, Lacan, and Murphy," p. 225.

I wish to suggest that Murphy's three zones – which we will apply later to the Unnamable's sphere of consciousness – (1) do advance beyond the basic Cartesianism of *Murphy,* (2) are rough Beckettian approximations of Spinoza's three basic levels of knowledge, (3) are to be taken seriously, and (4) betray a tongue-in-the-cheek (but not satiric) stance on the part of the author. This suggestion is not a claim that either Beckett or Murphy is a Spinozist, nor is it an assertion that Spinoza even begins to equal Descartes as a major influence on Beckett. Beckett does, however, in his fiction as a whole and in *Murphy* in particular, display a fascination – which he bequeaths to his heroes – with the group of seventeenth-century rationalists dominated by Descartes and including Spinoza. As Hugh Kenner points out, Beckett and his narrators are naturally drawn to "so many homemade worlds, each hung from a simple principle,"[37] and, we might add, suspended by Beckett from some hero's brain.

If Geulincx and Malebranche attempt corrected modifications of Descartes' model, Spinoza alters the model radically. We have already explained Spinoza's theories of mind and matter as constituting a single substance called God or Nature, of the "truth" that for every idea, there is a corresponding entity in the world of matter, and of the changes the mind/body experiences as an extension in time – but not in the Total System of Things, which admits no cause, not even a First Cause, but exists as the sole cause of itself. We have alluded to Murphy's contemplation of his kick existing not only in the mental and physical worlds but also in some realm which is neither of and yet both of these. This realm would be, roughly speaking, Spinoza's third level of intuitive knowledge. No attempt is underway to explain Spinoza's metaphysics; we are, instead, laying a grid of his three levels of knowledge (as expounded in the *Ethics*) over the three zones of Murphy's mind. As we shall see, this grid not only enlightens us concerning Murphy's mind but also provides an excellent scale of descent for the Unnamable's journey toward the core of his consciousness.

Murphy's first zone is a zone of light, with light signifying, as throughout the fiction, the intrusion of the outer world into the mind. Here Murphy finds at his disposal "the forms with parallel,"

[37] *Samuel Beckett,* p. 81.

which are "the elements of physical experience," which are "the world of the body broken up into the pieces of a toy," which are "the docile elements of a new manifold." These elements of sense experience are malleable in the first zone. They can be relived as memory (the mental image of the physical kick) or rearranged in dreams of reprisal (the giving of a mental kick in the proper direction) – an activity the narrator also refers to as "spitting at the breakers of the world." In fact, Murphy is so free to rearrange these images in the first zone that he can make "the chandlers . . . available for slow depilation" and allow Miss Carridge to be raped by Ticklepenny (*Murphy*, pp. 111-13).

This first zone is Spinoza's level of imaginative knowledge.[38] At this level (Spinoza's model is not divided into zones), the mind receives ideas of what Spinoza calls the imagination – ideas resulting from the interaction of the body with other external bodies, sense perceptions of the changes of state in the body. These ideas are not active but passive; that is, they do not arise from the process of rational thought, but float into the mind via the body from the macrocosm. As in Murphy's case, they take the shape of memories, musings, or dreams. They can also appear as illusions, hallucinations, or mistakes in perception. These ideas of "confused experience" (Hampshire, p. 85) are true knowledge in that each has an actual counterpart in the outside world (the kick *in re* and the kick *in intellectu*), but they are less than true in that they do not relate to other ideas or objects in the total scheme of things. Nor, since they appear to be caused by some modified state of the body, do they reveal their connection with the totality of Nature as caused only by itself. Furthermore, these imaginative ideas are not connected logically with each other but are merely linked arbitrarily one to the other. Thus Murphy groups together remembered kicks, the chandlers in the park, sex, Miss Carridge, and Ticklepenny. Their order is not that of the intellect but of the "affections of the human body" (Hampshire, p. 91). Information concerning these ideas is conveyed by ordinary language. For Spinoza, such sense perception is not final, but speculative and uncertain, knowledge. For Murphy, impressions in this zone, although repre-

[38] I am again using definitions from Stuart Hampshire's *Spinoza.* Direct quotations are referred to by author and page number(s).

senting the "whole physical fiasco," can become a "howling success" (*Murphy,* p. 111). He obviously enjoys the apparent freedom of his first zone.

Murphy also feels "sovereign and free" in his second zone (*Murphy,* p. 112), where he finds "forms without parallel," that is, thoughts of which the material counterparts are not obvious. These forms are those of Spinoza's second level, the level of scientific knowledge. From our vantage point (twentieth-century psychology can really mess up seventeenth-century metaphysics), these ideas must also originate as sense impressions, but Spinoza would make a distinction here. Second-level ideas are not just perceptions but are abstract knowledge (such as mathematical equations), ideas of ideas (second-order reflections), and conceptual breaking down and placing of the individual within the whole (analysis). Murphy's chief pleasure in zone two is the "Belacqua bliss" of "contemplation" (*Murphy,* p. 111). If we are on the right track with our Spinozist comparisons, such contemplation (here) is not musing or day-dreaming (these activities take place in the first zone) but reasoning or rational thinking. For Spinoza, such reasoning must begin with "common notions" – self-evident truths available to all men – which serve as the "starting points" of "genuine reasoning" and "scientific knowledge" (Hampshire, pp. 95-96).

Murphy's comment that his second-zone "system had no other mode in which to be put out of joint" (*Murphy,* p. 111) refers to Spinoza's belief that reasoning on the scientific level avoids the errors in judgment made on the first level, where ideas too tightly knit to Spinoza's "mode" or "attribute" of extension into space (the material) are entertained. There, because the ideas are so closely bound to the material world and reach the mind through the senses, thoughts can easily be "put out of joint" (Murphy's words) by remaining inadequate, isolated, and affective. Spinoza uses the example of someone perceiving the sun as a small object far overhead as sense perception on the first level and an astronomical understanding of the actual position of the sun as scientific knowledge on the second level. Is Murphy's second-zone pleasure of lying beside the contemplating Belacqua, "watching the dawn break crooked" (*Murphy,* p. 112) an extremely subtle allusion to the fact that dawn does not "break" (nor the sun "rise") within the purview of Spinoza's scientific, second level? On this level, ideas of the modifications of our bodies become logically coherent, so that we can understand more fully the true causes of the modifications. Thus, we understand the vantage point from which we see the dawn "break," and we know that our perception of this event is "crooked."

In the "half light" (macrocosmic intrusions become more microcosmic) of his second zone, Murphy is able "to move as he pleased from one unparalleled beatitude to another" (*Murphy*, p. 112). Such movement may refer to Spinoza's logical linking of clear and distinct ideas. This linkage is different from the merely random association of ideas entertained in Murphy's first zone, or Spinoza's first level of imaginative knowledge. This train of logical ideas – beginning with one self-evident, scientific truth that cannot be other than it is – flows smoothly toward the optimistic belief Spinoza shares with other rationalistic thinkers of a coherence theory of truth. As we shall see, this theory – that if all particular mind and matter were truly and completely known, this knowledge would form itself into a rational and coherent understanding of the metaphysical whole – applies more to Spinoza's third level than the second. But the movement of ideas on Spinoza's second level is in this direction. And when Murphy comments that the movement of ideas in his second zone has "no rival initiative" (*Murphy*, p. 112), he may be referring to the mental delight of one true and logical idea initiating certain movement toward ultimate, coherent truth. That is, a particular scientific thought that initiates the movement of logical linking of ideas has no rival thought. A statement of scientific truth cannot be other than it is, and is apparent as such to every reasoning mind. This kind of thought would be a scientific verity which could initiate movement toward the true conclusion, which is a part of the coherence theory of truth. Surely, if Murphy could ever think in such Spinozist patterns, he would marvel at himself. On the other hand, as is true of Beckett's heroes in general, he would find such patterns highly desirable.

As Murphy realizes, logical movement from one idea to another, although potentially offering "bliss" and "states of peace," is essentially a method, and, as such, "introduced an element of effort" into his second zone (*Murphy*, pp. 112-13). Murphy's efforts here are not as fruitful as Spinoza's second-level descriptions imply. Murphy remains uncertain about both the possibility and usefulness of "scientific" (for him, astro-logical) methods. He certainly never arrives at any coherence theory of truth. In fact, it would be difficult to ascribe to Murphy very many clear and distinct ideas: his thoughts, even when supposedly logically formulated, seem to become more muddled in the process of reasoning. Perhaps he outreasons Spinoza. If all mental ideas are part and parcel of the modifications in space of the body, and if these modifications are determined by the order of Nature as total scheme, how can the mind reject the confusion of level one and initiate the logical method of level two? In spite of Spinoza's distinctions regarding language, a shift from ordinary language (that used on level one) to mathematical language (the language of level two) will not effect such a result. Spinoza allows no recourse to either Descartes' *cogito* or divinely-bestowed knowledge. Anything that is true is true, not because the "I" reasons it to be true, or because God imparts knowledge of it, but in and of itself. For Spinoza, Nature determines all thought, and all thought (that escapes confusion to become logical or true) leads inexorably to the final truth about Nature. Such formulations of metaphysical verity are weighted with tautalogy and determinism. Perhaps Murphy, beleaguered by the making of many decisions, finds such determinism attractive. By his own admission, the hero surrenders to "will-lessness," becoming a "mote" in the "absolute freedom" of the total darkness of his third zone (*Murphy,* pp. 112-13).

This "absolute freedom" is paradoxically an absolute determinism. Here Murphy can experience freedom from making any choices because decisions are not options. The hero enjoys this third zone more than the first and second (*Murphy,* p. 113) because he finds momentary release from choosing between Celia and the inmates of the Magdalen Mental Mercyseat (especially Mr. Endon). Spinoza's third level is the area of intuitive knowledge (*scientia intuitiva* [Hampshire, p. 104]), which is beyond choice because no change in space or movement in time occurs here. Realization exists that mankind cannot be other than it is, the existing state of matter is the only possible world, and logical reasoning must end in truth. This level is infinite, not finite, and, as such, is beyond time or alterations in space. By applying the adjective "eternal" to his third level of knowledge, Spinoza does not mean that it has no beginning or end (that it is "everlasting"), but rather that "no temporal predicates or tenses or time determinations or any kind can in principle be applicable to it" (Hampshire, p. 172). Furthermore, even the second-level movement from one logical idea to another is stilled here. The end result of such movement is the third-level awareness that all true reasoning leads to truth as the end of logical thought, where Nature or God is conceived of, not as First Cause, but as causeless, that which is caused in and of itself (*Natura Naturans* [Hampshire, p. 46]). Thus, this dimension of thought would encompass all change in its changelessnees. We can no more ask the question as to when or how the absolute logic of this dimension began or will end than we can inquire as to when and how the "three angles of a triangle" become "equal to two right-angles" (Hampshire, p. 172). Needless to say, the actual practice of thinking on this level of thought is always limited. Man could enjoy complete knowledge in this sphere only if his body adequately reflected the total order of causes in extended Nature as a whole. To do so, the body would become the world as determining and intelligible substance, and the mental result of such a complete extension in space would be the mind of God. Spinoza's determinism and pantheism are obvious.

Murphy conceives of his third zone as a place of nothingness (no "elements nor state") and perpetual non-movement (a "flux of forms, a perpetual coming together and falling asunder of forms"). His perception is of "nothing but forms becoming and crumbling into the fragments of a new becoming," an awareness of "nothing but commotion and the pure forms of commotion" beyond "any intelligible principle of change" (*Murphy,* p. 112). Beckett's language – "flux of forms," "perpetual coming together and falling asunder," "becoming and crumbling," and "pure forms of commotion" – is a parody of Spinoza's scientific nothingness. Neary's remark, on the occasion of Wylie's bringing to Neary and Miss Counihan the first news of Celia as a possible lead to Murphy's whereabouts, may be a hopeful, but ironic allusion, to Spinoza's example of the triangle. "Remember," says Neary, "there is no triangle, however obtuse, but the circumference of some circle passes through its wretched vertices. Remember also one thief was saved" (*Murphy,* p. 213). Perhaps Neary is saying that the order and logic of human events are not so fixed that no intervention or change can ever occur (we might find Murphy, after all). One thief was damned, but the other (outside of all probability) was saved.

Murphy's quest, which is the macrocosmic quest for the five existential needs, is apparent here as a search for this third zone of the mind as a home, or place of belonging. He spends "more and more and more" time in the third zone (*Murphy,* p. 113). His search for unity with the universal system (externally visualized by Murphy as astrology, and internally as the determinism of the third zone), also fits into the Spinozist description of his mind in Chapter Six. Spinoza formulates intuitive knowledge as the potential grasp of a single system of ideas reflecting the universe as a whole, including all persons, objects, situations, and thought. We have already described Spinoza's formulations of this system. Repeatedly, Spinoza (along with the other seventeenth-century metaphysicians) assumes that the universe is throughout rationally intelligible, and, as such, can be understood by reason and logic. If we could understand all causes, we would recognize the ultimate *causi sui.* Perhaps it is because Murphy appears unable to reason his way into this zone that he remains fascinated by it but removed from its benefits. His methods of getting into the depths of his little world are, by Spinoza's definitions, more like attempts of the imagination (thinking on level one) rather than efforts of logical thought (reasoning on level two). Rocking toward a partially insensible state in a chair and lying on the grass while conjuring up visual images are zone one, not zone two, activities.

Such methods may also impede Murphy's quest to resolve his Cartesian split. He simply escapes momentarily from his predelictions for Celia and ginger tea rather than analyzing his way through such desires. At any rate, the only method that finally works for Murphy – in regard to resolving his Cartesian split and becoming one with a system – is death, a death more final than any other Beckett bequeaths a hero. At least in death, whatever remains of Murphy's "body, mind and soul" is united, in the substance of the ash Cooper scatters on the saloon floor. But if he has become a part of Nature as a system, it is merely a physical blending – that of the ash with "the sand, the beer, the butts, the glass, the matches, the spits, the vomit" (*Murphy,* p. 275).[39]

---

[39] In a letter to Thomas McGreevy (July 17, 1936), Beckett expresses his concern that the content of *Murphy* which continues after the occurrence of Murphy's death is more than it should be. Beckett hopes that the "presence" of Murphy, as still permeating the novel, will save this content from becoming

Murphy's liking for physical enjoyment and emotional/imaginative sensation also hinders his quest for the self. In Spinoza's terms, individual personhood achieves significance only when a person "transcends his condition as a finite and perishing existence" by subordinating "all particular desires or passive emotions" to the thought processes of level three. By doing so, a person "re-creates in his own mind some part of the self-creative activity of Nature." Such subordination supposedly results from a genuine desire for pure scientific knowledge and dedication to a life of reason (Hampshire, p. 170). Only reason, neither the body nor the imagination, can grasp the notion of eternal substance (Hampshire, p. 173).

Such possibility entrances Murphy, and he returns again and again to the rocking chair, descending, whenever possible, into the third zone of his mind. Here he knows he must forego even the choice of movement, and become, in the narrator's words, "a point in the ceaseless unconditioned generation and passing away of line" (*Murphy,* p. 112). But problems other than a fixation on the pleasures of the flesh impede Murphy's finding "Murphy himself, improved out all knowledge" in the third zone (*Murphy,* p. 105). He fears the not-yet-experienced depths of this zone, referred to as "the deeper coils" (*Murphy,* p. 252). Again, a comparison of Murphy's fictional characterization with Spinoza's definitions provides insight. Murphy is addicted not only to Celia, ginger, and the emotional/imaginative practice of rocking in his chair, but also (unlike the Beckett hero in general) to making his own choices. The basic narrative conflict of the novel is between Celia's demands and his refusal to meet those demands. If Murphy does not want a permanent job, he probably will not take one, nor will he be found by the crowd of friends pursuing him in efforts to persuade him to conform to their wishes. Murphy is not only a character of free will (at least on the surface) but also of strong will. Consequently, he is afraid of deeper descent into the third zone of his mind. As we have explained, the "absolute freedom" of this "dark" (*Murphy,* pp. 112-13) is actually the absolute of an

---

"anticlimax." Beckett wishes that the reader share with him the feeling that Murphy "was liable to recur in his grotesque person until he was literally one with the dust." See "On Murphy (to McGreevy)," in *Disjecta: Miscellaneous Writings and a Dramatic Fragment by Samuel Beckett,* ed. Ruby Cohn (London: John Calder, 1983), p. 102.

all-determining Nature or God. To be a "mote" in this sphere is to embrace "will-lessness."

For Spinoza, unlike Murphy, such willessness is not inhibitory. The philosopher defines an action (or power) he terms *conatus,* a term that, for Spinoza, means the power toward self-maintenance of any particular thing in Nature. Any thing (or person) undergoes constant changes of its extension in space. To preserve its essence (whatever makes it what it is), it must "persist in its own being" (Hampshire, p. 122). For Spinoza, this persistence is *conatus* or endeavor, and can be observed as always taking place in regard to the body and the imagination as evidenced by human experiences of desire, love, and hate. *Conatus* is neither good nor bad; it is simply an observed condition.[40] Ideally, one should strive for understanding of this response to external causes. As such understanding grows, scientific knowledge of the inevitability of certain external causes increases, and one is able to achieve a disinterested, intellectual attitude toward all expressions of the body and imagination. This attitude is one of "power and freedom," not of "guilt and remorse" (Hampshire, p. 163). Thus, this stance is not one of self-abnegation or denial, but of deep self-understanding and acceptance. Such thought patterns lead to Spinoza's intellectual love of God, a mental condition possible only on his third level of intuitive knowledge. Here one knows that all is determined for the only possible best in the only possible world. Murphy's difficulties with an easy assimilation of *conatus* into an intellectual love of God are obvious.

Murphy does claim, in speaking of experience in his third zone, that the "sensation" is "pleasant," that he enjoys "being a missile without provenance or target, caught up in a tumult of non-Newtonian motion" (*Murphy,* pp. 112-13). But certain episodes gainsay his claims. The long gaze into Mr. Endon's eyes – eyes which for Murphy signify the brotherhood of madness as true sanity and serve as beckonings in his quest for the self and the other (Mr. Endon) – results in Murphy's "seeing himself stigma-

---

[40] Malone takes "counsel" on the "subject of conation" from an "Israelite." This Israelite, who is Malone's friend, and who is named Jackson, owns a parrot – a parrot who can say "Nihil in intellectu," but not one word more (*Malone Dies,* pp. 217-18). The Spinozist connection between *conatus* and the intellectual love of God is a problem for the parrot, Malone, and for Murphy.

tised in those eyes that did not see him." Tranquility flees as Murphy realizes that he is "unseen by Mr. Endon," a mere "speck in Mr. Endon's unseen." He withdraws abruptly, fearing lest this reflection might prove to be "the last Murphy saw of Murphy" (*Murphy,* pp. 249-50). Following this interchange of gazes, Murphy tries twice to regain solace by immersion in the world of the mind. In the first try, lying naked on the grass, he experiences a terrifying vision of violence, lust, and death (*Murphy,* pp. 250-52), a vision reminiscent of the subject matter of the fabricated stories of Malone and the Unnamable. The second try, in the rocking chair, is accompanied by the "superfine chaos" of the escaping gas (*Murphy,* p. 253), and soon Murphy is no more, his fate determined by forces beyond his control. Murphy has lost, not found, the other (Mr. Endon) and the self.

The delight Murphy often experiences during excursions into the world of the mind and the hopeful aspirations he associates with deeper immersion serve as false promises luring him on to this loss of the self. These beckonings can be defined as false God-promises by recourse to Spinoza's notions of God and the kind of awareness possible on his third (intuitive) level of knowledge. The fact that Spinoza is often referred to as a "mystical pantheist" and also, apparently in contradiction, as a "materialist and positivist" (Hampshire, p. 168) can help to summarize his concept of God. We have noted that ascent to the third level (of intuitive knowledge) is not marked by self-denial and inhibition but by vitality and power. The exact connection between Spinoza's *conatus* and the state of intuitive knowledge is not spelled out in his metaphysics, but it is a positive link. If thought is pushed off of level one (imaginative knowledge) and analyzed across level two (scientific knowledge), it becomes the intuitive knowledge of level three. Here man's strivings in the macrocosm are not judged or denied but rather assimilated into an understanding of and wisdom concerning the total expanse of the universe. This expanse is an area that includes, in the terms of modern physics, all matter, energy, thought, and substance. These entities, in their totality, are Nature or God, and interest in and love for God is to understand and identify with their existence as Truth. By such understanding, "the ideas which constitute my mind are identical with the ideas which constitute God's mind," and the individual becomes the Thought which is God (Hampshire, p. 170). The imaginative passions are transformed into the intellectual love of God. Such a state is of the greatest benefit for both the individual and society, resulting as it does in harmonious living. The route to this intellectual love is the logic of the reasoning mind, and Spinoza considers himself proving that the rational mind moves toward this kind of "love" of God. The assumption underlying such metaphysical models is that the universal system of things is both reasonable and suited to man described as a reasoning being. Murphy, along with all of Beckett's heroes, would approve of such a universal system but find it contrary to all experience.

Murphy's ironic quest into the mind, then, is not only a search for the meeting of the existential needs but also a quest for the essence of Beckett's zero, referred to by the narrator as "the accidentless One-and-Only, conveniently called Nothing" (*Murphy,* p. 246). The term is a mockery of Spinoza's description of Nature or God as *causa sui.* The first of Murphy's two final attempts to enter the little world – which we have already mentioned in regard to his quest for the other (Mr. Endon) and the self – is a reaching toward the willessness of the third zone to escape the harshness of macrocosmic reality. Murphy is seeking some kind of arrangement of the persons and events in his experience that will be better than the mess he has presently made of his life. Any determining of matters seems better than that he has effected. The sequence of events leading to this attempt begins with Murphy's duty of making night rounds at the Magdalen Mental Mercyseat. The hero wanders desolately through the wards of the asylum. Pondering the desirability of the mental state of those ordinarily known as insane, and considering such a condition for himself, he cannot form even an "illusion of caress from the world that might be" (*Murphy,* p. 240). After the disappointment and terror of the depths of Mr. Endon's gaze (or non-gaze), he heads for the garden area surrounding the male nurses' quarters. Removing his clothes, he lies naked on the grass and tries to use his imagination to escape from an unhappy reality. Murphy attempts to visualize loved people – Celia, his mother, his father – but can form no images of them. Instead, he forms a mental picture of the Christ-child being cruelly circumcised in a medieval painting – the *Giovanni Bellini Circumcision.* He begins to see eyeballs being scraped, and the eyeballs become those of Mr. Endon. He then attempts to imagine the likenesses of acquaintances, people in general, and, desperately, of animals. "He could not get a picture in his mind of any creature he had met, animal or human." We are again reminded of Malone's and the Unnamable's fictional nightmares – and of the viewer/narrator's difficulties with the cliff scene that fails to yield even a fragment of humanity in *La Falaise.* Murphy's final mental image is a colorcast of disorder, violence, mysterious movement, and geometrical confusion:

> Scraps of bodies, of landscapes, hands, eyes, lines and colours evoking nothing, rose and climbed out of sight before him, as though reeled upward off a spool level with his throat. (*Murphy,* pp. 250-53)

If this vision is of Spinoza's level three, the Nature/God in control there is the evil God of Manicheanisn.

Spinoza's formulas will not work for Murphy, but this hero would like them to. The problem, as is so often the case in regard to ideas of divinity in Beckett's fiction, can be defined in Manichean terms. Rather than relinquishing the material world, Murphy follows Spinoza's lead and tries to bring what is presumed to be a reasonable macrocosm into the microcosm. Here, as always in Beckett's world, macrocosmic experience continues to exist as images of confusion, bewilderment, and anguish in the microcosm. The result is Manichean: any connection with the material sphere is tainted with evil, for only pure spirituality is created by a good God. Murphy, true to form as a Beckettian hero, cannot search for the mystical as pure spirit – any more than Spinoza is a pure mystic. What the hero seeks is inextricably tied to the material world, and in this world, Murphy finds no reasonable evidence that goodness holds sway.

Exploring the landscape of Murphy's brain (as described in Chapter Six and as referred to throughout the novel) reveals that Beckett's Cartesianism becomes heavily overcast with Spinoza's "corrections" of Descartes. Beckett's authorial stance toward this hero so influenced by seventeenth-century metaphysics is, as he himself acknowledges, a "mixture of compassion, patience, [and] mockery." Beckett claims that his "sympathy" for Murphy goes "so far and no further," particularly "in the short statement of his mind's fantasy on itself."[41] Thus, we are right to take the phenomenon of Murphy's mind seriously, but we must realize that Beckett's descriptions betray a tongue-in-the-cheek (although not satiric) stance. Beckett is not wisely reprimanding Murphy for his futile methods of thinking and recommending changes – the heroes think in the only ways possible for them – but he is portraying Murphy's naiveté concerning choices and thought-processes during his brief life. And, whenever Murphy's thinking mirrors that of Descartes, Geulincx, Malebranche, or Spinoza, Beckett parodies their rationalism as well.

The Unnamable is not, like Murphy, a man thinking primarily about significant ways to love and live. He is an artist/self (if only negatively) trying to piece together his mental processes into some form of language that will become the authentic art of a genuine statement made by an "I" who is the actual self. The convoluted text of *The Unnamable* is a palimpsest – without erasure – of (1) the perception of sensory impressions, (2) the fabrication of imaginative constructs, (3) the (il)logic of deductive (or scientific) reasoning, and (4) the sensing of intuitive need. These strategies of the Unnamable's thought processes exhibit the Spinozist levels of Murphy's three zones, with the Unnamable's (1) and (2) combining into Murphy's zone one, which is, in Spinoza's terminology, the level of imaginative knowledge. None of the comparative categories fit neatly. Beckett is not presuming to describe exactly how anybody's mind works, either Murphy's, the Unnamable's, or his own as author. Supposedly, Spinoza thinks he has constructed an adequate model.

Murphy's late, desperate efforts lying naked on the grass seem to start as attempts to form comforting rearrangements of imaginative images – an activity belonging to zone one. Since Murphy cannot even fix the images in his mind, he cannot enjoy contemplation (analyzing the relation of such imaged persons to his total awareness) either, an activity of zone two. Instead, he seems to fall precipitously from the surface of zone one into the chaotic depths of zone three – which, for Murphy, is anything but Spinoza's third level of intuitive knowledge and self-understanding.

Macrocosmic sensory input, memory, and propaganda from "they" innundate the Unnamable's mental receptors. Reasoning

---

[41] "On Murphy (to McGreevy)," p. 102.

carefully, he determines not to fall into Molloy/Moran's and Malone's mental trap of fabricating this material into stories. His logic is valid – in no case, in the earlier novels of the trilogy, have the stories resulted in authentication of the artist's true self. Instead, he is going to escape imaginative fabrication and define the "I" of genuine selfhood through deductive, non-imaginative thought processes. But the Unnamable is not Descartes, and the imagined Mahood and Worm relentlessly invade his "pure" thinking. Furthermore, his sensory perception continues to be overpowered by the control of "they," who want him to suffer from his memories. As we have noted, the Unnamable's thought processes produce imaginative nightmares that can be read as a fleshing out of Murphy's confused and violent images. Any effort on the Unnamable's part to limit himself to pure reasoning results in thinking that becomes Mauthner's mere speaking–a ceaseless flow of words that say nothing. Neither the imagination nor reason will serve him.

The flow of words that the Unnamable produces will not shape itself into the order of art; therefore, he is no artist, and thus has no self. Needing a Logos to confer the significance of form to shapelessnees, he senses the need for intuitive thought that would discover some dimension of knowledge analogous to Spinoza's intellectual love of God or coherence theory of truth. But the Unnamable encounters only nothingness in his descent into consciousness, and this nothingness will not assume the order or significance that Spinoza attaches to his Nature/God. Linguistically, the nothingness becomes the empty spaces of the text, continually being blackened with words that say nothing.

Thus, the Unnamable's abortive quest becomes Beckett's magnificent "failure" which is *The Unnamable.* In this third novel of the great French trilogy, we have what is perhaps Beckett's most authentic art. For this author, art is not fulfillment or completion, but the failure of – or incompletness between – the need expressed and the need denied. This impossible point of tension – this place of nothingness –is the only valid signifier, both of life and of art.

HOW IT IS WITH JOURNEYS AND FISH

A journey from the Unnamable's place of nothingness into the hellish world of *How It Is* leaves all vestiges of the macrocosm as setting behind. As we have noted, this leave-taking begins in *Watt,* as the hero of this novel finds himself surrounded by a household and garden that refuse to exhibit the characteristics man reasonably expects of his domestic and natural environments. The settings of the trilogy – Molloy and Moran's various landscapes, Malone's room, and the Unnamable's fixed space – become increasingly mythical, and the voice of *Texts,* although making vague and disconnected references to earthly habitats, speaks from no stable and identifiable place. This gradual changing of setting from Belacqua's Ireland and Murphy's London is definitively realized in *How It Is,* which introduces a basic shift in situation that is maintained – with the exception of *Enough* – throughout the other fiction of the sixties.

In writing on Beckett's fiction of the sixties, I have described *How It Is* as introducing this basic shift in literary landscape that is generally maintained throughout the other fiction of the decade. We no longer have a situation in which the macrocosm serves as the setting for an alienated microcosm, a human consciousness so separated from the outer world that it has shed its body or even its voice. Instead, the landscape or setting *is* the microcosm, which is inhabited by the inner self, now split into a condition either of already being or of becoming a duality that conveniently may be described as the self-as-subject and the self-as-object. Thus the inner self, in alienation from its own body and voice and in retreat from the macrocosm, becomes the object of its own perception in the confines of the mind. The narrative movement of this situation is the retreat of the subjective self from the macrocosm toward the microcosmic core of objective selfhood. During this retreat, the self is assaulted with images of life as lived in the macrocosm, encapsulated in symbols of light and nature. Because the images become depictions of macrocosmic distress and because the ever-receding core of objective selfhood remains the empty circle of Beckett's zero, the retreat of the self can be described as a *via dolorosa* toward metaphysical crucifixion.[1]

The dominant task now before us is to discover within this basic situation the pattern that we are presently describing as level two of the quest. Is the split self the artist/self – depicted in *How It Is* as subjective self seeking to authenticate selfhood by producing narration about or from objective self? In what sense is the inability to "find the true self" the failure of the story or of art? Does art fail because life fails? Is the failure of art an indictment of God? If so, in what sense? Is there a Logos or God/Word needed but never given that would make the story work?

Before we embark on the difficult task of seeking possible answers to these questions, we can achieve a religious orientation in the reading of *How It Is* by identifying a God-consciousness on the part of the mud-crawler. Elements in this consciousness parallel the four-part paradigm of the religious consciousness of other Beckettian heroes with which we have been working. Within the content of the language structure, certain characters exist by virtue of being perceived by some other. All of the mud-crawler's "great categories of being" are dependent on the surveillance of the witness Kram and the scribe Krim.[2] In turn, the existence of these two is a "life" that "has been given" by someone (p. 18). Pim's existence is dependent on the "quickening" effected by the mud-crawler: "Pim never be but for me anything but a dump limp lump

---

[1] This paragraph is a summary of my treatment of *How It Is* in " 'Coloured Images' in the 'Black Dark': Samuel Beckett's Later Fiction"; see especially pp. 277 and 279-80.

[2] *How It Is* (New York: Grove, 1964), pp. 14, 18, and 80. Other references to *How It Is* are also to this edition and are cited by page number(s) in this chapter. Beckett began writing the French version *(Comment C'est)* of this work in 1960 and finished it eighteen months later. (See Bair's *Samuel Beckett*, pp. 435 and 522.) Editions de Minuit published it in Paris in 1961.

flat for ever in the mud" (p. 52). Our knowledge of Pam Prim and Bom is completely contingent upon the mud-crawler's awareness of them. Thus their fictional existence is dependent on the crawler's perception. Beneath this web of surface dependencies within the content of the novel lies the vast corporate dependency in the novel's structure described with such critical astuteness by Judith Dearlove. As she explains, "*How It Is* is only a voice speaking in the present and creating a universe." Everything in the novel – persons or objects – is created by and is dependent upon the "murmur in the mud." Only as we read the "voice's whey of words" does the identity or existence of these persons and objects come into being.[3] To be is to be perceived and, in *How It Is,* to be spoken forth in language.

The mud-crawler's recitation reveals a strong sensing of determinism on his part. Whatever happens to be in his life "this time" (i. e., in this particular fiction) has "been given to me this time" or "put in my life this time" (p. 11). The determinism becomes couched in more theological language as the crawler speculates on the "business of grace," that causes some sacks to burst or vanish while others, apparently of the same age and substance, remain in good shape (p. 61). In fact, everything, including the infinite number of meetings and departures by the multitude of crawlers and victims, is exactly as "our justice wills it" (p. 112). Justice has also willed that no one "knows" anyone else or himself (p. 123). Dearlove sees this "justice" as merely literary: it is nothing more than the "preservation of symmetry," that is, of the macabre order of the fictional structure of the novel. Dearlove also writes, however, of the determining of details of the mud-crawler's existence. "He can have no desires beyond those the voice grants him. He can make no judgments independent of the voice's evaluations."[4] All is determined then, by the narrating voice, whether it be structure or details of content. Beckett employs in *How It Is* the metaphor for determinism that he found in Geulincx and first used in *Molloy,* that of the "sadly rejoicing slave" who is "free" to crawl toward the east along the deck of a westward-

[3] Dearlove, "The Voice and its Words: *How It Is* in Beckett's Canon," *Journal of Beckett Studies* No. 3 (1978), pp. 60 and 74.

[4] "The Voice and its Words," pp. 62 and 64.

bound ship (*Molloy*, p. 51).[5] This metaphor embraces the entire universe of the mud-dwellers and thir witnesses.

Specific mentions of a sense of guilt are meager. Pam Prim, during the winter preceding her death, daily forgives her husband (the mud-crawler? Pim? both of these?) as she lies in the hospital. Supposedly the offense forgiven is the empty boredom of the couple's romantic or sexual relationship, that precipitates Pam Prim's falling or jumping from a window (pp. 77 and 91). Also, the mud-crawler voices a need for mercy, for someone somewhere "merciful enough" to reconstruct the Dantean mud-world that he inhabits (p. 143). But this mud-world and its inhabitants *per se* are the strongest evidences of guilt in the novel. Like the Greeks who are guilty because they suffer and Dante's unfortunates in the marsh of Styx in Canto VII of the *Inferno*,[6] the inhabitants of *How It Is* must have sinned greatly to have incurred the punishment of their habitation and circumstances.

The fourth and final component of the paradigm of the hero's religious consciousness – that of an experiencing of "eternal life" in the sense of a continuation of consciousness that does not cease even, most probably, in death – is also present in *How It Is*. Krim assures Kram that Pim and Bom can hardly be dead, in spite of their stillness, because "one doesn't die here" (p. 93). The question the crawler puts to Pim as to whether or not he thinks he "can die one day" is answered quite clearly and briefly with "no" (p. 96). Pim's brief response is extended one page further on:

> wishes to die yes but doesn't expect to no he expects to stay where he is yes flat as a cowclap on his belly yes in the mud yes without motion yes without thought yes eternally yes. (p. 97)

The mud-crawler, at one point, wonders if perhaps God might not be able to change things, to construct an alternate world that

---

[5] Ludovic Janvier notes the use of this metaphor in *How It Is* in "Place of Narration/Narration of Place," in *Samuel Beckett: A Collection of Criticism Edited by Ruby Cohn*, p. 107.

[6] Hugh Kenner in *A Reader's Guide to Samuel Beckett* (p. 138), Michael Robinson in *The Long Sonata of the Dead* (p. 216), and Alice and Kenneth Hamilton in *Condemned to Life* (p. 183), all remark on the similarities between Beckett's mud-dwellers in *How It Is* and Dante's damned souls in the mud of the Fifth Circle.

might be better than the present one. Any changing of the immediate situation, however, would have to take place "without ceasing to maintain us in some kind of being without end" (p. 139). Whatever alteration Beckett or God may devise will certainly not be a culmination of consciousness. All four elements, then, that we have ascribed to the Beckettian hero's religious consciousness are present in *How It Is*.

The quest pattern engaged in by the artist/hero on the second level is clearly discernible in the interaction of the three sections of this work. In fact, as several critics point out, *How It Is* is a novel primarily about the art of language.[7] The mud-crawler presents his narration as literary art. This statement is valid in spite of the fact that both the content and source of the narration remain uncertain. The narrating voice continually revises and contradicts itself: "The journey I made in the dark . . . I made that journey . . . and I didn't make it then again and I made it again" (pp. 126-27). The narrating mud-crawler claims the narration as his own, but he also attributes it to some external source ("I say it as I hear it murmur it to the mud every word always," p. 15) or foreign internal origin ("scraps of an ancient voice in me not mine," p. 7). Although we cannot be certain whose voice is speaking or what is being said, we know that a narrating voice is trying to tell a story, to give an account of something.

An understanding of the blatant, self-conscious offering of *How It Is* as narration or literary art explains the insistence of the narrating voice that the memories of Part One are not merely memories. Reference is made to the macrocosmic material contained in the flashes of light from "up above" as "past moments old dreams" that are "memories" (p. 7). Having described two such "memories," however, the voice insists that neither was a "dream" nor a "memory": "I haven't been given memories this time it was an image the kind I see sometimes see in the mud part one" (p. 11). The material for art that in *Malone Dies, The Unnamable,*

[7] The Hamiltons, in *Condemned to Life* (pp. 182-85) and in "The Process of Imaginative Creation in Samuel Beckett's *How It Is*," *Mosaic*, 10 (1977), 1-12, take this critical stance. John Pilling, in *Frescoes of the Skull* (p. 65), remarks that in *How It Is*, "Beckett is moving away from the visual and towards the verbal." Dearlove's "The Voice and its Words" is an examination of her conviction that *How It Is* "explores the fluid universe of the mind and its imagination" (p. 75).

and *Texts for Nothing* is presented as memories becomes here literary images – memories filtered through the artistic mind that are so separated from life that their substance is purely literary. To arrive at this knowledge makes it possible for us not only to agree with John Pilling that "Beckett sees the 'image' as a category distinct from the categories of 'dream' and 'memory,'"[8] but also to understand why the distinction holds.

The receiving of the memories as images occurs primarily in Part One. Within the boundaries of this section, the images contain only suggestions of suffering or unhappiness – suggestions connected with ideas of anxiety, confusion, resignation, and nostalgia. The various scenes that take shape in the mud seem to offer some promise of security, love, or happiness, but either the actual content or the tone of the passages negates the promise. Thus the images may be considered as stylized literary representations of the promises of happiness that lure the fictional self to engage in the quest on level one in the fiction preceding *Malone Dies.* The most detailed image is that of the boy and girl linked in romantic or sexual love. The description is one of nostalgia – for an episode of youthful love that occurs on a racecourse in April or May. The couple, with a small dog, walk on "emerald grass," eat sandwiches, and mouth endearments to each other (pp. 29-31). Nothing in the content of the image links it to suffering more intense than a nostalgic yearning for lost youth and love. Only the tone of the description of the couple as the image fades suggests the disillusionment and loss that the narrating voice associates with sexual love in Part Two:

> it is dusk we are going tired home I see only the naked parts the solitary faces raised to the east the pale swaying of the mingled hands tired and slow we toil up towards me the narrating mud-dweller and vanish. (p. 32)

In a similar manner, the image of the child instructed in prayer by his mother closes with a sense of confusion: "she stops her eyes burn down on me again I cast up mine in haste and repeat awry" (p. 16). Anxiety permeates the image of the child with his head and hand resting on the table as his mother stares at him only to

---

[8] *Frescoes of the Skull,* p. 64.

suddenly leave the room and run "to friends" (pp. 10-11). A dead crocus in a pot, dying in spite of having been often swung into the light, and tears behind hands supporting an old man's head on a table in a basement room lend gloom and resignation to a scene that is nonetheless resplendent with blue, gold, and green of sea, sky, and earth (p. 21). Beckett's false promises of happiness are habitually cloaked in scenes of nature.

Having received these images as the material for his art or "story" in Part One, the narrating mud-crawler finds Pim in Part Two and proceeds to extract from this alter ego of the artist/self art that is constructed from the stuff of the images.[9] The art extracted is bits and pieces of a "story" which is the novel *How It Is.* The methods of extraction are to score Pim's flesh with fingernails (p. 60), claw him in the armpit (p. 63), stick the blade of a can-opener in the rectum (p. 69), and thump him on the skull in a kind of Morse code (p. 76). Pim learns to respond to these varied stimuli by crying, singing, murmuring, or speaking. Only if the mud-crawler tortures Pim into response will he be able to name him (establish the self's identity as artist) and elicit a flow of words that will be a "story" (create language as art) (pp. 59 and 96-99).[10] Thus Beckett's theory of art is Proustian in that art can result only from suffering on the part of the artist. It is non-Proustian, however, in that whatever art is produced is not only non-redemptive personally and existentially for the artist (identity is never achieved) but also anti-literary in that it is an art of failure.

[9] Obviously, this particular interpretation of what is going on in Parts One and Two of *How It Is* is not "the interpretation." Multiple ways of viewing the activities, identities, and relationships of the narrator and Pim are possible. For instance, Pim may be viewed as any other significant "shaping" person in the narrator's past, as any fictional character the narrator might have created, or as a subconscious, previously unrecognized aspect of the self. Pim functions in the thematic structure I am describing in the novel as the part of the artist/self that is forced by the infliction of pain to recite bits and pieces of "the story." The story, of course, is the novel *How It Is.*

[10] In *Condemned to Life* (pp. 182-87) and in "The Process of Imaginative Creation in Samuel Beckett's *How It Is*" (pp. 6, 8, and 10-12), the Hamiltons emphasize this thematic concern in *How It Is:* art is produced only through suffering. They fail to explain, however, that, for Beckett, even suffering does not result in successful art. Also, their understanding of this concern as a "wholly new element" appearing in *How It Is* (p. 6 of "The Process of Imaginative Creation") is imprecise. Beckett's earliest fiction, *Assumption,* assumes such a linkage between suffering and art. Furthermore, the idea is implicit in nearly all of his fiction.

Pim is named Pim, but he is also Bom, and the narrator is Pim and/or Bom as well. As is most ordinary in Beckett's fiction, no one name identifies any particular person and any person may have various names. The self does not achieve identity as a person or as an artist. *How It Is* is a failure as art on the most elementary level simply because its narrative fails to tell how anything is, either being, art, or life.

A close examination of Part Two reveals that failure is not the result of a lack of artistic or literary effort. This section consists of at least three distinct efforts to create a story. Although, in one sense, as we have noted, there is only one cumulative narrating voice in *How It Is,* these three efforts are distinguished by three separate voices – the voice of the narrator, the voice, or, more precisely, the scribal recording of the witness Kram and the scribe Krim, and the tortured, responding voice of Pim, who is forcefully assigned the primary burden of relating the story in Part Two. From the very beginning of Part Two, the narrator has been "telling a story" in the sense that he continues the account (begun in Part One) of his encounter with Pim. It is possible, however, to differentiate between this continuing recitation and a somewhat definitive effort that he makes to "tell a story" based on the images described in Part One. As he initiates this effort, the narrator states that he is relating "samples" of his "life above," which also is "Pim's life." This relating voice, however, continues after a thump on the skull has apparently produced a "long silence" on the part of Pim (p. 76). Also, the style of the narration of this effort is identical to the narrator's style in Part One. It lacks the semblance of dialogue that characterizes the question and answer style of the effort that I am assigning to Pim. The "stories" produced by this first effort at narration are ironic negations of several images from Part One. The image of the boy and girl enthralled in romantic love is negated by the account of the narrator losing his wife, Pam-Prim, to a lingering death in the hospital. Her death results from a jump or fall from a window, which, in turn, results from sexual boredom and interpersonal alienation and bitterness (pp. 77-78). The images of the child with his mother are negated by an account of a father's untimely death due to a fall from or with scaffolding used in the building trade (p. 78). The image of the old man in prayer in the basement room containing the dead crocus is ironically balanced with an account of a mother – apparently the widow of the dead father – seeking consolation from the Bible but finding only a stark reassertion of her grief: man's days are indeed as transient as the existence of a flower of the field (p. 78). There is no one to one balancing in this ironic negation of images; many images of Part One have no particular counterparts in Part Two. Nevertheless, the balancing that does occur reveals that the images of memory of "life above in the light" from Part One become abortive, vague accounts of human anguish when rendered into literary form. As Susan Sontag insists, a particular genius of Beckett is his achievement of the "inseparability of form and content."[11]

The scribal recording which is the effort at story-telling undertaken by the witness Kram and the scribe Krim (pp. 80-87) is supposedly an account of the observation of the narrator as he crawls in the mud, forages in a sack, tortures Pim, and anticipates the arrival of Bom. The physical movements are reported by Kram and recorded by Krim in a blue notebook, the murmurs – or the little that can be heard of them – in a yellow notebook, and Kram's own comments or observations in a red notebook (pp. 81-82). The content of the blue notebook is a travesty of the word "story":

> one notebook for the body inodorous farts stools idem pure mud suckings shudders little spasms of left hand in sack quiverings of the lower [face] without sound movements of the head (pp. 81-82)

The murmurs that are to form the content of the yellow notebook can hardly be heard. Each "starts so sudden comes so faint goes so fast ends so soon" that "nine-tenths" of it is lost (p. 81). Sometimes Kram catches a "few scraps Pim Bim proper names presumably imaginations dreams things memories" (p. 80), but it may be only Kram's "fancy" that he hears anything (p. 83). Kram's primary concern is the third book containing his own comments, supposedly on the procedure he is undertaking.

It is this book that constitutes the "story" of Kram and Krim. The material in *How It Is* that purports to be "samples" or

---

[11] Enrico Garzilli quotes Sontag on Beckett in *Circles Without Center. Paths to the Discovery and Creation of Self in Modern Literature* (Cambridge: Harvard Univ. Press, 1972), p. 47.

"extracts" from their records is "more about me Kram than him the narrator" (p. 81). And what Kram/Krim records about his own "life" is a travesty of the task of a writer or scribe. He is a thirteenth generation witness/scribe whose forebears have all, like him, been entrusted with the task of witnessing and recording the activities of the mud-dwellers. He actually records almost nothing, however, except desolate bits of information that he has picked up about these forebears, not from observing the mud-dwellers, but from random reading in back numbers of the scribal notebooks. The bits of information have to do with death-wishes (p. 81), death (p. 82), madness (p. 83), and separation from loved persons (pp. 83 and 84). Thus Kram/Krim's "story" is as formless as the narrator's. As T. L. Estess observes in one of the studies devoted to Beckett's storyless stories, "in order to tell one's story, one must not tell a story."[12] Howard Harper sees overtones of a travesty of a "post-Biblical epic" in Kram/Krim's recording, a recording that becomes "an abortive attempt at witness in this wasteland of mud and darkness, where the only story possible is a gospel according to Kram."[13]

The third voice that attempts a story in Part Two is that of Pim. The narrator tortures this alternate self into responding to various signals and determines the content of the response by scoring questions with his fingernails in large Roman numerals on Pim's back. The general questions have to do with Pim's "LIFE ABOVE IN THE LIGHT," his "LIFE HERE BEFORE ME [the narrator]," and his feeling toward the narrator ("DO YOU LOVE ME?) (pp. 72, 73, and 90). Lesser questions have to do with Pim's journeys or quests in the macrocosm (p. 72), his arrival in the mud-world (p. 96), his memories, and his belief or non-belief in God (p. 97). Pim's replies – his "story" – are a confused medly of ignorance of the past (p. 79), partial knowledge of the same miserable existence depicted in the ironic counterparts of the images from Part One of sexual love and personal relationships (p. 85), obscure references to images from Part One not mentioned in Part Two (p. 85), and unrelated allusions to earlier works of fiction by Beckett – the "little heap [of bodies] in the stern" from *Malone Dies* and the dim

---

[12] "Inenarrable contraption; reflections on the metaphor of story," p. 429.

[13] Harper, *"How It Is,"* in *Samuel Beckett: The Art of Rhetoric,* ed. Edouard Morot-Sir, et al. (Chapel Hill: Univ. of North Carolina Press, 1976), p. 267.

lights, the mountain, and the current from *Stories* (p. 86). No "story" is forthcoming from the part of the artist/self that is Pim. Instead, dialogue between him and the artist/self who is the narrator reveals the bankruptcy of the story as a form of art in this particular version of Beckett's hell:

> but he can't affirm anything no deny anything no things may have been different yes his life here pause YOUR LIFE HERE good and deep in the furrows howls thump face in the mud nose mouth howls good he wins he can't. (p. 98)

What Pim cannot do is something that no one can do in Beckett's world – shape language into a story that becomes art.

Nothing significant in regard to the failure of art occurs beyond this point. The artist/self has failed in the basic task of authenticating the self by telling the story that would give credence to his identity as an artist. The "story" is a non-story, and its teller is the narrator Pim, Bom, everyone, and no one. Furthermore, the reason for the failure of art is the failure of life. No macrocosmic memory becomes a literary image that will serve in a "story." As Dearlove reflects, "The narrator is displaced in time, cut off from a causal world, denied an heroic past and a golden age." [14]

In *How It Is* Beckett implicates God as being ultimately responsible for each facet of this consummate failure more clearly than in any other fictional work. [15] Referred to as "one not one of us an intelligence somewhere," the divinity of *How It Is* finally disappears as the "story" of the novel disintegrates. But before his disappearance, God is charged with the distressful nature of macrocosmic life, the conditions of the microcosmic mud-world, and the failure of the story as art. The ironic conterparts in Part Two of the scenes of macrocosmic life in Part One indict God for the distress of "life above in the light." This indictment is overt in the ironic statement that Pam Prim's untimely death can be understood as "God calling her home" (p. 77) and in the account of the widow seeking comfort from the black Bible held in the

[14] "The Voice and its Words," p. 65.

[15] Beckett's drama *All That Fall* is an equally clear indictment of God for the misery of life, but the detailed interaction of life with art and of art with identity is not treated in that work.

black gloved hand so that only the "red gilt" edge is visible (p. 78). The verse that the widow contemplates is Psalm 103:15-16:

> As for man, his days are as grass: as a flower of the field, so he flourisheth. For the wind passeth over it, and it is gone; and the place thereof shall know it no more.

Thus God is implicated by the veracity of his own Word. No mention is made of surrounding verses in this Psalm that claim that God knows man's "frame" is "dust," that he pities man as a father pities his son, and that his mercy extends to future generations (verses 13, 14, and 17). The "muttering lips" in the "ivory pallor" of the widow's face mouth only the isolated verse.

A close examination of imagery in the Pam-Prim scene yields more subtle linkings of divinity with human sorrow. The "home" to which God is calling Pam-Prim is obviously a grave – a grave blasphemously associated with the "blue mound" of her pubic area (growing dark after having been shaved, p. 77). We are reminded of the bitterness and emptiness of the couple's sexual relationship that have precipitated Pam-Prim's death. Such bitterness and emptiness are easily ascribed in Beckett's world to a God who planned the intricacies of human sexuality. The flowers held before her face – "marguerites from the latin pearl" (p. 77) – resonate with ideas of suffering (the oyster's formation of a pearl) and religious ritual. The husband's "long icy toil" toward and away from the hospital throughout the winter of Pam-Pim's lingering death is along a road lined with "black boughs grey with hoar" and covered with "frozen slush." Because the dying figure toward whom he toils is forgiving "me everybody all mankind," we can define the repeated journey as a *via dolorosa* (pp. 77 and 91).

These comments on macrocosmic life are, as we have noted, parts of the narrator's effort to tell a story. Pim's effort includes comment on the image from Part One of the ten or twelve-year old daydreaming while sitting in the dust against a granite wall. Searching the sky for resemblances of human faces or animals, he imagines that he sees Jesus as a "beautiful youth with golden goatee clad in an alb" (p. 45). Pim's effort to use this image in story-telling results in a jumbled account of incidents obviously lifted from earlier fiction by Beckett. A current carries a boat out to sea. A figure, chained to the boat, crawls forward, uncertain as to exactly what voyage is underway (p. 86). The account alludes to *Murphy, The End* (from *Stories*), *Malone Dies,* and *Molloy.* Each incident alluded to involves suffering and/or death and contains language or imagery that refers to life as a crucifixion. Thus the golden-clad Jesus of the child's reverie becomes the suffering Man/God of the Passion. Pim describes the "sea beneath the moon" as having a "harbour-mouth" (p. 86), and we are reminded of Celia mourning the dead Murphy in a mortuary with yew trees outside:

> Outside the horns of yew had the hopeless harbour-mouth look, the arms of two that can reach no further, or of one in supplication, the patient impotence of charity or prayer. (*Murphy,* p. 259)

Any supplicatory prayer on the part of Celia is, of course, in vain. Murphy's remains are soon to be scattered as ashes on a saloon floor (*Murphy,* p. 275). The bitter humor of this early novel fails to negate completely the anguish of Celia's loss. Perhaps it is because she has invoked the God of astrology rather than the God of religion that her hopes have not been realized.

The hero of *The End* is alluded to in descriptions in *How It Is* of sea currents, dim lights on a mountain, and the "clink of chains" (p. 86). In *The End,* he has boarded and chained himself into a boat as into a living grave to be carried aimlessly out to sea while watching the gorse burning on nearby mountains. The lid he has made to cover himself is made of "stray boards," a "cross bar," and "two spikes" as "holds for my hands." We do not need the information that this hero would rather have heard "hammer strokes bang bang bang clanging in the desert" than the howling of the wind on the sea to recognize another Beckettian hero undergoing a crucifixion (*Stories,* pp. 68-72).

The allusion to *Malone Dies* refers to a mass crucifixion. The "little heap in the stern" from Pim's account (p. 86) can be easily identified as the "tangle of grey bodies" in the stern of a boat resulting from Lemuel's butchery on Lady Petal's picnic for the unfortunate inmates of St. John of God's asylum. This "little flock" has met unexpected horror and death at the hands of its group guardian, Lemuel. What was to have been an Easter excursion has become a week-end similar to that "spent by Jesus in hell" (*Malone*

Dies, pp. 280-84). The complexity of the interlocking of Beckett's imagery in various works of fiction is revealed by the fact that one of the inmates butchered by Lemuel is a "beautiful young man" with a "Messiah beard." The Jesus of the child's dream in the image from *How It Is* and the young "Messiah" of *Malone Dies* are interlocking Christ figures from different pieces of fiction.

The mere mention of "nails" (p. 80) in Pim's comment (with "nails" referring to those of the narrator's hand that "scores" the questions on Pim's back) can be read as an allusion to *Molloy* and another kind of nail. During his night in the canal ditch, Molloy lies "full stretch, with outspread arms," His situation and posture are more ludicrous than distressful, but Beckett's imagery subtly reveals that crucifixion is underway. Molloy has just sighted a barge, "a cargo of nails and timber, on its way to some carpenter," guided by a boatman with a "long white beard." Above the river, the horizon is "burning with sulphur and phosphorus" (*Molloy,* (pp. 26-27). Pim's "scene and words" (p. 86) connect him and his fellows in the mud with a numerous company from Beckett's earlier fiction who qualify as crucified "Christs" as they undergo various experiences of life on the planet Earth. The allusions to these experiences in the earlier fiction and the confused references to images of "life above in the light" in *How It Is* indict God as being responsible for the distressful nature of macrocosmic life.

Like the tailor in Nagg's story in *Endgame* (pp. 22-23), the inhabitants of *How It Is* have no problem with assigning the creatorship of the world they presently inhabit to God. Dearlove designates this divinity as "creator and trinity, 'the voice qua-qua from which I get my life . . . of three things one.'"[16] The "black air," the "couples," the "solitudes," the "journey," the "abandon" are all maintained at divine discretion (pp. 139-40). God is the one responsible for the deposition (or non-deposition) of the sacks and for the "unfailing rations [which are inevitably lost or sealed against use]" placed in the sacks (pp. 137-39). Positioned above the witnessing scribes, God becomes

[16] "The Voice and its Words," p. 63. Dearlove's quotation is from p. 113 of *How It Is.*

> an ear a mind to understand a means of noting a care for us the wish to note the curiosity to understand an ear to hear even ill these scraps of other scraps of an antique rigmarole. (p. 134)

Beckett's heavy irony is relieved somewhat by the narrator's speculation that the one responsible for the conditions of the mud world might "change some day" and "with profit revise us" (pp. 134-35 and 139-40). The speculation reminds us of Thomas Hardy's "Agnosto Theo." Unlike Hardy's stirrings of hope or hopes of stirring, however, Beckett's speculations remain tongue-in-cheek. A suggested change would simply transpose the parade of individual tormentors and victims into one "vast imbrication of flesh without breach or fissure" (p. 140). It is most unlikely that there actually exists "one perhaps somewhere merciful enough to shelter such frolics where no one ever abandons anyone and no one ever waits for anyone and never two bodies touch" (p. 143). Instead, God has decreed that existence in the mud continue as a suffering exercise in futility.

The ultimate failure of the quest on the second level is the radical failure of the story, recorded primarily in Part Three. This failure can also be assigned to God. The opening lines of *How It Is* contain an "invocation" – "tell me again finish telling me" (p. 7). Pilling says that this invocation is addressed by the narrator to himself, "so as to announce his 'vocation,' call himself into existence and constitute himself at the centre of the work."[17] Certainly the invocation serves to announce the narrator's vocation as literary artist. Nor can it be denied that the narrator is at the center of this work. It is hardly possible, however, that selfhood is authenticated or "called into existence" at this early point, or, for that matter, at any other point in the novel. Although God never achieves existence either, it can be argued that this invocation is more directly addressed to him. In the first sentence of *How It Is,* the narrator insists that he is quoting, that he is saying what he hears. The narrator "hears" the "past moments," the "memories" that he receives as images. As we have seen, God is responsible for the content of these memories. The memories are internalized in the literary mind as images, and the narrator explains that his source consists of "scraps of an ancient voice in me not mine"

[17] *Frescoes of the Skull,* p. 62.

(p. 7). Pilling concedes that the invocation is "also . . . a remark addressed to an Other."[18] By "Other," however, Pilling probably means Pim. In analyzing the ambiguity of this "ancient voice," Dearlove speaks of its "divinity": "The voice is prime matter and prime mover."[19] Dearlove also insists, however, that the narrator *is* this ancient voice: "Beginning with a voice which he locates externally, he goes on to construct a universe over which such a voice would be the divine intelligence, only to end by acknowledging the errors of his system and his own responsibility for the voice."[20]

Even though we cannot claim a clearly-defined assertion throughout the novel that the voice has a divine source, we can say that the narrator conceives, if only in a partial and imprecise manner, that the story he relates has its source in and is told for the ultimate benefit of God. The narrator's postulation of God is by means of logic. The unique arrangement and distribution of the sacks rule out the possibility that they have simply appeared by chance. There must logically be "one not one of us an intelligence somewhere a love [with the nouns used ironically] who all along the track at the right places according as we need them deposits our sacks" (pp. 137-38). In a similar manner, it is "at times not extravagant to impute that voice quaqua the voice of us all" to a cosmic other conceived of in terms of divinity (p. 138):

> there he is then at last that not one of us who listens to himself and who when he lends his ear to our murmur does no more than lend it to a story of his own devising ill-inspired ill-told. (p. 139)

Thus God is not only the deviser of the story but also its hearer. He is both originating source and listening ear of the murmurs in the mud. It is his voice that "tells us what we are as best he can" before "listening to us murmur what we are" (p. 139). If God later disappears, then logically the story should disappear with him. As we shall see, this is precisely what happens.

---

18 *Frescoes of the Skull,* p. 62.
19 "The Voice and its Words," p. 63.
20 "The Voice and its Words," p. 63.

The narrator speculates that this cosmic, verbal divinity might remedy matters, including the divinity's own absurd condition of existing because he deposits sacks and is the beginning and end of a "storyless story," if he could stop the vicious cycle of tormentors meeting victims (p. 139) or revise the entire system of life in the mud-world (p. 140). Since there seems to be no possibility of such a remedy on the part of God, the narrator introduces "a salvation more simple by far and by far more radical." This solution is to "eliminate him [God] completely and so admit him to that peace at least while rendering me in the same breath sole responsible for this unqualifiable murmur" (p. 144). Exactly how this elimination is to take place is not clear – the narrator, even as he is eliminating God and claiming sole responsibility for the recital, admits that he is still quoting (p. 144). The same kind of contradiction between what is asserted and what is apparently happening occurs in regard to Pim. If there is "only one voice here yes mine" (p. 145) and if there has been "never any procession no nor any journey no never any Pim no nor any Bom no never anyone no only me no answer only me yes" (p. 146), then why the blatant continuation of dialogue in the final paragraphs of the novel? Somebody is asking questions, and somebody is answering them. The narrator is asking, but, if Pim is gone, who is answering?

But consistent logicality has never been a characteristic of Beckett's writings, and, since God is not referred to again after his "elimination," we can safely assume – at least on the surface of things – that he does indeed disappear.[21] His disappearance signals the failure of the story in a most radical manner – the story that is the novel *How It Is* disappears with him:

[21] Logically, God not only does but must disappear. He exists merely as a postulate of the narrator's reasoning, and when this reasoning fails to adequately account for him, his existence becomes uncertain. In *The Hidden Question of God* (pp. 66-67), Helmut Thielicke comments on such a disappearance in regard to Descartes and Kant. "In both Descartes and Kant the I is the true reality, whether this be the ontological I of the former or the epistemological I of the latter. God is deduced from this primary reality of the I. It is not he who defines the I. . . . God is defined by the I. . . . God is not grasped in the force of an experience. . . . He is located on a continuation of immanent lines of certainty. . . . It is no wonder that in the light of this view of God Heine describes Kant as the father of the death of God theology."

> all these calculations yes explanation yes the whole story from beginning to end yes completely false yes. (p. 144)

With meticulous exactness, the narrator (and Pim?) concludes the novel by denying the validity of everything in it – macrocosmic or microcosmic – except for the single voice of a lone figure "flat on my belly yes in the mud yes the dark yes" (p. 146). Even the alter ego Pim can be said to evaporate as voice at this point. The narrator's most significant questions (with significance signalled by the use of higher case letters) receive no answers other than screams:

> HOW WAS IT screams good WHAT'S MY NAME screams good THAT'S MY LIFE HERE screams good I MAY DIE screams I SHALL DIE screams good. (pp. 144 and 146)

A novel that purports to tell "how it is" offers no answers as to the meaning of past or present experience, identity, or death. Only one question signalled by higher case letters in these last pages finally receives a definitive answer: "the arms spread yes like a cross no answer LIKE A CROSS no answer YES OR NO yes" (p. 146). The answer to the question as to whether a Beckett hero's arms are spread like a cross is most likely to be yes, even in a novel that fails to affirm much of anything else.

The problem of *How It Is* to affirm much of anything is a problem of language. Morot-Sir, in writing of Cartesian and Manichean influences on Beckett, explains that early on in his career as a writer, Beckett became "aware of the complacencies of the monist [or Christian] theory" of language. This theory is basically an assumption of the symbolic or allegorical nature of language, of the validity of a figurative meaning for words. A word or word group used as a symbol is a valid representation of the spiritual or metaphysical entity that it purports to symbolize. A word or word group used allegorically becomes a valid representation of the precise meaning that it holds in some particular structure of ideas. Thus the physical (or literal) and the metaphysical (or figurative) are bound together in a monolithic or unified system of meaning. The literal elements of narrative and their philosophical "meaning(s)" become a unified whole. Morot-Sir points out that "Western literatures, at one moment or another, fall into allegorical constructs" because they are written on such Christian and/or Platonian theories of language. It is this *theory* of language that Beckett rejects, although he does not reject the *use* of such langage. For whatever reason, Beckett consistently uses "words which belong normally to the abstract vocabulary of philosophy – the constant reference to universal statements on human destiny and cosmic involvements." Much evidence of "the presence of philosophy, with its problems and theories," abounds in Beckett's work. The writer's oft-repeated claim, however, that he is not a philosopher, is valid. Beckett does not believe that a proposition made in accordance with the rules of philosophical or allegorical language is capable of being false or true. Thus Beckett's theory of language is Manichean rather than Greco-Christian: metaphysical statements and/or symbolic word-groups refer only to themselves as language. They do not mean anything beyond their own linguistic forms. This theory is Manichean because of the eternal and fixed duality between the language used and the philosophical or symbolic "truths" the use of the language might suggest. Thus the continuing contradiction of affirmation/negation inherent in human language, that figures so prominently in Beckett's writing, is a denial of ever being able to assert anything as either true or false or to offer a linguistic sign that has a valid metaphysical meaning. It is possible to see the vacillating nature of Beckett's language as being itself a symbol of the Manichean duality to which he subscribes.[22]

The failure of the story in *How It Is* is precisely a failure of symbol and allegory. Symbol and allegory do not actually "fail," of course: they function precisely as Beckett intends. Therefore, the story is not so much a "failed story" as it is *a literary experience of the fatal failure of language signs.* If we go one step further and claim that the novel is a statement of such failure, we are forcing Beckett into the role of philosopher, a role which he consistently rejects.

The symbols or signs that fail in *How It Is* are, as in nearly all Beckett's work, distinctively Christian. In fact, a construct of the Christian symbols in the novel can be defined as ironic allegory. Immured in the water of the primeval mud, the narrator undertakes a journey while supposedly subsisting on the fish provided in

[22] "Samuel Beckett and Cartesian Emblems," pp. 91-96.

the tins in the sacks. Thus the symbols of water as baptism, cleansing, or rebirth; of fish as the spiritual sustenance that is Christ (*ichthys* as the primitive acronym for Jesus Christ Son of God Savior); and of the journey as religious pilgrimage are set forth emblematically as if they are to mean something. But a close examination of each of these symbols reveals an ironic negation of suggested meaning. Water that is a component of mud can hardly cleanse or baptize. Furthermore, any notion of cleansing is mocked by Beckett's deliberate use of four-letter words (pp. 11, 67, 78, and 96) and scatological language (p. 66). The Apostle John remarks on Jesus' quotation from the Old Testament in regard to the rebirth effected by the Holy Spirit – "He that believeth on me, as the scripture hath said, out of his belly shall flow rivers of living water" (John 7:38).[23] The mud-crawler of *How It Is* attempts to suck water from his environment but knows nothing of rebirth. Instead, his existence continues on and on as is – "flat as a cowclap on his belly yes in the mud yes" (p. 97). In "this immeasurable wallow," water effects a cleansing of neither spirit nor body.

The "manna" for this particular journey is fish contained in tins in sacks. The mud-crawler feels a devotion, even a reverence, for his sack. "I slip it under my head without letting it go I never let it go" (p. 10). "I . . . turn to it again clasp it to me again say to it thou thou" (p. 17). When the sack bursts (p. 46), God is blamed (p. 47). After all, God is in charge of depositing the sacks and is expected to supply replacements – "a celestial tin miraculous sardines sent down by God at the news of my mishap" (p. 48). The reason why some sacks become empty or burst and others do not is beyond the narrator's understanding. Is it possible that the "old business of grace" is in effect "in this sewer" (p. 61)? The reference to grace is to Beckett's notion of arbitrary salvation and damnation (existential, not theological) as it appears throughout his works, most famously perhaps in Vladimir's lines to Estragon on the two thieves, only one of whom was granted salvation (*Waiting for Godot,* p. 9b). The emptiness or bursting of sacks is of no great moment in the mud-world anyway: "there is more nourishment in a cry nay a sigh torn from one whose only good is silence . . . than sardines can ever offer" (p. 143). We can recognize in the irony of the symbol of the fish a parody of the Eucharist.

---

[23] Jesus' quotation in John refers to Isaiah 12:3.

The anguish of the movement of the journey as pilgrimage is quite apparent: "semiside left right leg right arm push pull flat on face curse God bless him beseech him no sound with feet and hands scrabble in the mud" (p. 47). The pattern of the journey is ironic in its futility – a lone crawler becomes one of a couple only to be abandoned to loneliness again. And who would not argue that aloneness is far better than the togetherness of these couples? The ultimate irony of the journey is its complete negation: "never any Pim never any Bom never any journey" (p. 127).

The disillusionment and suffering associated with the irony of each of these symbols are essential components of the meaning of the symbol that not only dominates Christianity but this novel as well – the cross. Only those familiar with Beckett's subtle shades of imagery will recognize the "snowy body" and "great black still spread wings" of the "frigate-bird" (p. 34) as symbolic of what Beckett sees as the Manichean duality of the cross.[24] That dying man should be God and that the instrument of death should become the means of redemption are mysteries that can be understood only as fantasies in Beckett's world. The fingernails of the eastern sage that pierce his own palms "through and through" at the "hour of his death" are symbolic of crucifixion (p. 53). The figure pattern of the connecting bodies of the narrator and Pim forms a Saint Andrew's cross (pp. 58, 88, and 90) as the narrator's nails claw desperate questions onto Pim's back and armpit (pp. 62 and 70). As we have noted, the final posture of the narrator, stripped now of all narrative elements except his own being in the mud, is to be "spread . . . like a cross" (p. 146). In fact, as the narrator observes at the beginning of Part Two, in this novel there are "indelible traces" of crosses "everywhere" (pp. 103-04).

Such images are sterile or ironic symbols of the Christian cross. The central meaning of the cross throughout the history of the church has been the paradox that suffering, even betrayal and death, can be redemptive in human experience. It is precisely this paradox that Beckett and his various heroes – including the narrator of *How It Is* – reject. Suffering for them is absurd, and logically so, because it is never redemptive. Therefore, Christ on the cross

[24] See Beckett's remarks on "darkness' and "distress" as contrasted with light in the interview with Tom Driver.

is not the divine Logos, God's Word of meaning on the necessity of suffering in human experience to effect redemption, of death to bring about life or resurrection.[25] Instead, the cross as symbol in *How It Is* is like the crucified Christ perceived by Prince Myshkin (in Dostoevsky's *The Idiot*) as he gazes at Holbein's *Descent From the Cross.* The crucified Christ of this painting is perceived by Prince Myshkin to be fully human – a victimized scapegoat whose only destiny is decay.[26] Obviously, such a Christ can never serve as a Logos, a Word that could make a story by imposing a redemptive meaning on the bleak memory/images and distressful journeys of *How It Is.* Because Beckett's symbols are non-symbols, his novel is a non-story – a precisely structured and artful quoting of mutitudes of words that never become a Word. What is missing is the Creative Logos, that the artist/self forever seeks but never finds.

---

[25] Morot-Sir writes of what he sees as Beckett's failure to understand the "supreme semantic role of Christ" in his Incarnation and death in the "divine language" which "can be but God himself as language" ("Pascal Versus Wittgenstein, With Samuel Beckett as the Anti-Witness," p. 212).

[26] See Michael Robinson's treatment of this Christ in Beckett's writings in *The Long Sonata of the Dead*, pp. 113-15.

MESSY MEMORIES AND ABORTIVE ART

STILL, *SOUNDS*, AND *STILL THREE*

How It Is is followed in Beckett's fictional canon by five short pieces also written during the sixties, although some were not published until the seventies. These works are *Imagination Dead Imagine* (1965), *Enough* (1967), *The Lost Ones* (1972), *Ping* (1967), and *Lessness* (1970). The fictional texts written and published after 1970 include *Still, Sounds, Still 3* (1973); *As the Story Was Told* (1973); *La Falaise* (1975); *For to End Yet Again* (1976); *Company* (1980); *Ill Seen Ill Said* (1981); and *Worstward Ho* (1983).[1] *For to End Yet Again* is best grouped with the texts of the sixties. The remaining six texts, however, can be grouped together not only because they are products of the same decade but also because they exhibit a very similar pattern of narrative movement. Because none of the texts published after 1970 has received extended critical attention, I shall examine the four of this group that I have chosen in detail as I reveal whatever structural patterns of God-consciousness and/or quest levels are found in them.

The question of narrative voice in *Still*[2] has been explored, to some extent, by Enoch Brater.[3] As Brater points out, an

---

[1] *Fizzles 1* through *6* and *All Strange Away* were also published after 1970. These pieces, however, appear to be abortive writings that are merely transitional or preliminary in nature – *All Strange Away* to *Imagination Dead Imagine* and *Fizzles 1-6* to all the post-*How It Is* fiction. For critical evaluation of *All Strange Away* and *Fizzles 1-6*, see John Pilling, *Frescoes of the Skull*, pp. 132-44.

[2] Beckett's published holograph of *Still* is dated June 17, 1972. *Still* was produced for a limited-folio edition that was illustrated with three engravings and

absence of "pronouns yields Beckett's familiar icon of uncertainty," in fact, to such an extent that the "responsibility for narration cannot be assigned." The usage of the verbs leads us toward assuming the first person, but without an "I" we cannot be sure.[4] Certain phrases also suggest the third person – "Always quite still [for] some reason"; "all quite quiet apparently" (p. 47, *Fizzles)* – and seem, as the brief fictional still life continues, to negate the suggestion that the narration is limited to the first person. In the two short texts that immediately follow *Still – Sounds* and *Still 3*[5] Beckett's familiar authorial imperatives ("Leave it so," [p. 156, *Essays in Criticism*]), speculations ("try dreamt away, saying dreamt away," [p. 157, *Essays in Criticism*]), and inclusion of five third person singular masculine pronouns ("he," "himself," "he," "his," "his," [p. 155, *Essays in Criticism*]) confirm our intuitions that the most probable narrative perspective of *Still* is a pronounless third person.

Still is a chameleon in that its significance varies in regard to where it is placed. If considered with the engravings and preliminary studies that Hayter produced to accompany *Still* (see note 2), it becomes the literary counterpart of these art works. If read in

---

three preliminary studies by Stanley William Hayter, an English engraver. Martha Fehsenfeld interviewed Hayter in the summer of 1976. She has stated, in a letter to me dated September 23, 1982, that Hayter did the engravings for the text, under Beckett's scrutiny, during 1972-73. Hayter had suggested to his friend Luigi Majro that Beckett be approached and asked for a text that Majro could publish showing a work at various stages of composition. Beckett agreed to the project sometime during 1970, and the limited-folio edition was published by M'Arte Edizione of Milan in 1974. *Still* then appeared in the *Malahot Review*, 33 (1975), 9-10. In 1975, *Still* was published in *Signature Anthology* by Calder & Boyars, London. In 1976, the piece was reprinted in *For to End Yet Again and Other Fizzles*, John Calder, London, pp. 10-20. Of this group of eight short pieces, *Still* is the only one originally written in English. The American edition of this collection is *Fizzles* (Grove Press), also published in 1976, in which *Still* appears as "Fizzle 7" pp. 45-51. My quotations are from *Fizzles* and are so designated in the text.

[3] Brater also examines verbal and grammatical structure, the interaction of form with content, and visual shapes in *Still*. See "Still/Beckett: The Essential and the Incidental," *Journal of Modern Literature*, 6 (1977), 3-13.

[4] "Still/Beckett," p. 13.

[5] *Sounds* and *Still 3* were not only written immediately after *Still* but are also connected with *Still* by titles. These two texts are published in *Essays in Criticism*, 28 (1978), 155-57, being reprinted from MSS 1396/4/50 and 1396/4/52 in the Beckett Archive of the University of Reading. They date from May and June of 1973. My quotations are from *Essays in Criticism* and are so designated in the text.

Fizzles, where Beckett placed *Still* as "Fizzle 7," following "Fizzle 6," it becomes a verbal portrait of a man contemplating death.[6] For our purposes, it is more feasible to place *Still* with *Sounds* and *Still 3* (see note 5).

In these three pieces, as in other very brief pieces by Beckett, the four-point paradigm of God-consciousness that I have described does not overtly appear. The pattern of the quest on the second level, however, can be clearly delineated in these pieces read as a group. In fact, this quest pattern of the artist/self's efforts to devise a story that will authenticate his identity as an artist, and thus as a person, serves as a key to unlock meaning.

All three pieces describe or comment on the single figure seated in the chair of *Still.* Three possible places or areas of experience are assumed in the pieces as a whole. These places may also be described as areas of tense – present, past, and future. The first (and the present) area is the room – probably the summerhouse of *Heard in the Dark 2* – where the figure sits in a wickerchair at an open window facing south over a valley (p. 48, *Fizzles*). At times he gets up to stand by a western (p. 47, *Fizzles*) or eastern (p. 49, *Fizzles*) window, staring out. Two further movements occur in this area. The first is the figure's coming to rest his head in his hand, as an effort to attain repose, relief, or "shelter" from some sort of disquiet or distress (pp. 49-51, *Fizzles;* pp. 155-56, *Essays in Criticism*). The second movement is the person's agitated and repeated catching up of a torch and going out and up a path toward a tree (pp. 155-56, *Essays in Criticism*), a beech previously sighted from the eastern window (p. 49, *Fizzles*). After standing under or against this tree, sometimes for hours, he returns to the chair. In this still room in this "stillest night" (pp. 155-56, *Essays in Criticism*), the figure, who is not actually still but trembling (p. 48, *Fizzles*), is engaged in listening for any faint "sound" and, as we shall see, in remembering and imagining. In this area, the figure corresponds closely to the person described as huddled in the dark in the fifteenth vignette of memory in *Company.* Both, like

6 In spite of my conviction that Beckett rarely writes of the direct and isolated experience of death – see my "Life and Death in Beckett's Four Stories" – I believe that "Fizzle 6" (*Fizzles,* pp. 41-45) is best read as a contemplation of actual physical death. Placing *Still* after "Fizzle 6" makes *Still* a still-portrait vignette of a person undergoing such contemplation.

numerous earlier Beckettian heroes, have retreated to repose and contemplation in a room and are attempting to devise stories from their memories. The room in *Still,* unlike the windowless room in *Company,* has at least two windows.

The second area of experience is the area of memory or of the past. This area does not differ topographically (as a similar area does, for instance, in *How It Is*) from the first area. Instead, reference to this area of memory is signalled throughout the three texts by the word "once." The word "once" occurs only in connection with this particular area. In *Still,* the reference is to "that beech in whose shade once" some incident or event of intense emotional impact occurred for the figure staring (in area one) at the tree from the window (p. 49, *Fizzles*). The fact that only this tree is viewed from the eastern window – all other objects and scenes are viewed from the western or southwestern window – probably implies life and vitality in contrast to ascesis and immobility. In *Sounds,* references are made to nightbirds which once came in great numbers (p. 155, *Essays in Criticism*), to someone's urgent leaving of the summerhouse (in the past, as in the present) to go to the tree outside (p. 155, *Essays in Criticism*), and to a loft where an abundance of sounds were once heard all night. In this loft, the wind was once loud, so loud that it muffled the sound of someone pacing to and fro and muttering "old words once got by heart" (p. 156, *Essays in Criticism*). In *Still 3,* reference is made to a mind in which certain questions – "where what how long" – once lurked "like ghosts" (p. 157, *Essays in Criticism*). As we shall see, these questions have to do with literary accomplishments.

The third area is a place, not of experience, but of non-experience. This area is Beckett's silence beyond words, an area or condition longed for by numerous heroes but achieved by none. Here the area appears as the hypothetical condition of the listening figure if he were to be "dreamt away":

> Or if none hour after hour no sound of any kind then he having been dreamt away let himself be dreamt away to where none at any time away from here where none come none pass to where no sound at any time no sound to listen for none of any kind. (p. 155, *Essays in Criticism*)

But the authorial imperatives – "try dreamt away, saying dreamt away" (p. 157, *Essays in Criticism*) – are ineffective, and the figure never reaches this area of soundlessness. Thus this area remains forever future.

The figure's interaction among these three areas of experience (or non-experience) can be described as the quest that I have defined. Seated in a chair, the stilled figure listens for sounds (p. 51, *Fizzles*). The "sounds" that he hears (as the "hearer" "hears" in *Company*) are memories of past life. The imagery that Beckett uses is that of a leaf that "sounds" or trembles in the night air ever so lightly. This "sound," however, is strong enough to reach the figure seated in the chair and to produce in him an immediate and urgent response. Catching up a torch, he rushes out and up the path to the tree (obviously the beech tree of *Still*) on which the leaf trembles (p. 155, *Essays in Criticism*). A decided change in the language at this point signals the figure's entrance into the vital area of memory – a return in mind to whatever once happened in the shade of the tree. We can note this difference in the following passage:

> . . . too still for even the lightest leaf to carry the brief way here and not die the sound not die on the brief way the wave not die away.
>
> For catch up the torch and out up the path all overgrown now as more than once he must up suddenly out of the chair and out up the path. . . . (p. 155, *Essays in Criticism*)

The change in the verb forms (infinitives to imperatives) and the use of the adjective "overgrown" and the adverb "suddenly" offer contrasts of action, wildness, and urgency with faintness and hesitancy. The language of the second sentence is reminiscent of the frenzied language of *From an Abandoned Work.*

It is possible that the figure as portrayed in *Still* does not actually undertake this urgent journey to the tree. Certain passages may imply that the distressful reposing of the head in the waiting hand in *Still* is the macrocosmic equivalent that denotes the microcosmic rushing out to the tree in *Sounds.* That is, the seated figure may simply relive in his mind past trysts at the tree as, in sadness and loss, the head sinks into the hand. The "self's [sound] when the whole body moves from its place as [if] to those leaves" may be simultaneous with "some part or parts [of the body] leaving the main [body] unmoved" and coming to be "at rest head in hand listening trying listening for a sound" (p. 155, *Essays in Criticism*). If this reading is valid, *Still* portrays the seated body, *Sounds* the imaginings of memory, and *Still 3,* as we shall see, imaginative efforts to construct literature from these memories. A sentence from the description of the hand moving toward the head in *Still* reinforces this possibility: "The right hand *slowly opening leaves* the armrest taking with it the whole forearm . . . (p. 49, *Fizzles,* my italics).

Whether actual or imagined, the journey to the tree encompasses all the "once" memories of area two.[7] The still figure has reentered in memory the vital but suffering world of the past (in a Proustian manner) as contrasted with the present condition of stillness and contemplation of the past.

The texts define this macrocosm of memory experienced in the microcosm of the imagination as a place of suffering in devious but convincing ways. The opening sentence of *Still* speaks of a bright gleam of light just before the closing of a dark day:

> Bright at last close of a dark day the sun shines out at last and goes down. (p. 47, *Fizzles*)

This light occurs in the landscape where the tree is. Such brief gleams of light followed by darkness as symbols of the brevity and misery of life are common throughout Beckett's canon. *Watt* opens with "failing light" (*Watt,* p. 7), as does *From an Abandoned Work.*[8] A "light goes on in the mud" momentarily for the old man bowed in prayer in the basement room of *How It Is* (*How It Is,* p. 21). In *Waiting for Godot,* night always falls suddenly, and birth is given astride of a grave – "the light gleams an instant, then it's night

[7] Although Brater contends that the beech tree "has . . . little to tell us about anything outside of itself" and that it "does nothing to answer our questions" – serving only to "excite our formulation of new ones" ("Still/Beckett," p. 15) – the precise opposite is true. The journey to the tree is the key to the meaning of these three texts taken as a group.

[8] *From an Abandoned Work,* in *First Love and Other Shorts* (New York: Grove, 1974), p. 39.

once more."[9] Such a gleam of light is a false promise offering hope but followed by non-fulfillment.

As I have pointed out, the resting of the head in the hand may be the physical counterpart of the mental journey to the tree. Distress in the form of a need for solace and shelter is epitomized in this meeting of head with hand. The tension of Beckett's detailed description of this movement leaves us wondering whether the "hand's need" or that of the head is "the greater" (p. 50, *Fizzles*). John Pilling speaks of "the head, seeking relief from its distress," reposing in the hand.[10] The text of *Still* obliquely states that it would be even more necessary to close the eyes completely against the dark if there were no sheltering of the head in the hand:

> As if even in the dark eyes closed not enough and perhaps even more than ever necessary against that no such thing the further shelter of the hand. (pp. 50-51, *Fizzles*)

The strongest indication that the memories are those of suffering is found in the description of the figure standing, in "certain moods," with his arms around the tree and his "head against the bark as if a human" (p. 155, *Essays in Criticism*). Such a posture suggests the painful memory of lost love: perhaps whoever the figure once met beneath the tree has been lost. Such a posture also symbolizes the almost universal identification of Beckett's heroes with the victimized Christ. A human head and outstretched arms against a tree occurring anywhere in Beckett's work certainly imply Christ against the cross, impaled there by his Father/God.

Still 3 depicts the artist/self attempting to create his story from the painful memories of area two. The attempt at the imaginative construction of these memories into a story must be assigned to area one – that of the contemplating figure in the still room:

> Back in the chair at the window before the window head in hand as shown dead still listening again in vain. (p. 156, *Essays in Criticism*)

---

[9] *Waiting for Godot* (New York: Grove, 1954), pp. 34, 52b, 57b.
[10] *Frescoes of the Skull,* p. 177.

But there are present in this room now what Brater calls "imaginary worlds far beyond the boundaries of the text."[11] A tree, nightbirds, and a loft full of wind and muttered words become objects from the past that stimulate the imagination profoundly. Pilling explains that "In 'Sounds' and 'Still 3,' the act of imagination, however sudden and however short-lived, cannot take place without external visual and auditory stimuli."[12] These external stimuli may, however, be those of the past incarnated in a present object. The tree seen from the window is the "beech in whose shade once . . ." (p. 49, *Fizzles*).

Like any good writer, the artist/self begins his efforts at creation by considering questions such as "Whence," "when," and "how it was." But the memories of area two become "faint," perhaps to the point of becoming "mere fancy": there is no "nightbird to mean night at least or day at least." Furthermore, even the "dim questions" begin to fade (p. 156, *Essays in Criticism*). In fact, as I have mentioned, such questions, lodged in the mind "once like ghosts," are a part of the now faint memories of area two (p. 157, *Essays in Criticism*). Apparently, these questions as they pertain to the present artistic effort merge in the consciousness of the artist/self with memories of past fictional achievement, that is, with the earlier fiction of Beckett himself. References are made to the "incarnation bell" of *Molloy* (*Molloy,* p. 15), Mother Calvert of *Texts for Nothing* (*Stories and Texts for Nothing,* p. 81), and the title of *How It Is* (p. 156, *Essays in Criticism*).

Because the memories fade, the place of the imagination becomes a "soundless place" (a place without vital memories), and there is "nothing to tell" (p. 157, *Essays in Criticism*). But the fading of the memories is not the only – or even the major – reason for the failure of the story. The suffering or pain of past memories suddenly invades the imagination:

> Till in imagination from the dead faces faces on off in the dark sudden whites long short then black long short then another so on or the same. White stills all front no expression eyes wide

[11] "Still/Beckett," p. 16.

[12] Pilling, "Review article: '*Fizzles*,'" *Journal of Beckett Studies,* No. 2 (1977), p. 98.

> unseeing mouth no expression male female all ages one by one never more at a time. (p. 157, *Essays in Criticism*)

Such chaotic reverie reminds us of Murphy's vain efforts to gain emotional solace from his memories:

> When he was naked he lay down in a tuft of soaking tuffets and tried to get a picture of Celia
>
> . . . .
>
> Scraps of bodies, of landscapes, hands, eyes, lines and colours evoking nothing, rose and climbed out of sight before him, as though reeled upward off a spool level with his throat. (*Murphy*, pp. 251-52)

For the artist/self of *Still 3*, as for Murphy, matters go from bad to worse. A particular face – "hers or his or some other creature's" – appears that is so painful that the authorial imperative is employed to try and remove it from the mind's eye:

> . . . try dreamt away saying dreamt away where face after face [disappears] till hers [disappears] in the end or his or that other creature's. (p. 157, *Essays in Criticism*)

But neither these efforts to relegate this particular face to the hypothetical area three of absolute silence or other authorial imperatives ordering it "back" ("try saying back") into the past (area two of memory) are effective. The face remains present to the still figure of area one (in the microcosm of imagination), persisting in the mind as large as life, at arm's length, with its eyes "not looking," and with its lips lacking any expression (p. 157, *Essays in Criticism*). The sterility of lost love is suggested. The art form produced in *Still 3*, then, is not a story successfully created from memory by the imagination. Instead, it is this face, persisting as "still" as "marble" in the mind until it finally goes "out," leaving soundlessness or no memory in the dark (p. 157, *Essays in Criticism*). Thus there is no story, no self as artist, and therefore no identifiable selfhood.

It is possible to conceive of the indictment of God as being due to his absence rather than to his cruel presence in these pieces. From this perspective, he becomes the missing Word, the Logos never given. The space of his absence is the area of soundlessness, of the silence beyond words.[13] This is the third area, that is always future: the figure in the wicker-chair is never "dreamt away" to this sphere. Therefore, he never finds the silence, the Logos beyond words, that would bestow meaning on language and make the story work.

The only art object maintained in the three pieces exists by virtue of metaphor: the figure seated in the wicker-chair is like the statue of the "old god twanged at sunrise and again at sunset" (p. 48, *Fizzles*). The "old god" is Memnon, the Ethiopian king of Greek mythology, whose mother, Aurora or Dawn, wept such dewdrops of grief that Zeus pitied her and made Memnon immortal. The statue of this God is the Vocal Memnon near Thebes in Egypt, a statue supposed to give forth a musical sound whenever struck by the sun, at dawn or at dusk.[14] The marble appearance of the painful face that blots out memory for the artist/self and makes any story impossible links the failure of the story to the marble statue of this God. Condemned to artistic failure by his painful memories and unable to construct a story that, in the Unnamable's words, will "find me," will "say me" (*The Unnamable,* p. 414), the seated figure sustains less identity as a self than the statue of the metaphor – Memnon of myth and stone. But Memnon as a God is blameless, a mere object of stone. The cruelly-present God (if God is conceived of as present rather than absent) who is to be blamed for the fact that the self cannot be created, because the story cannot be told, because life consists of meaningless suffering, is the Father/God of Christ, who impaled him and all men against the cross or tree to suffer for Beckett's original and everlasting sin – the sin of having been born to love and to lose.

---

[13] Morot-Sir speaks of an "absolute clarity" that is "beyond both language and silence, – in the glory of God": ("Pascal versus Wittgenstein, with Samuel Beckett as the Anti-Witness," p. 211). Morot-Sir sees Beckett's linguistic and semantic difficulties as being capable of resolution by recourse to Pascal's understanding of human language as derived from and dependent for meaning on God as revealed in Christ. Morot-Sir claims that his purpose in the essay is "not to extol Pascal's superiority on Wittgenstein or Beckett, but to prove that their confrontation is fundamental" (p. 215).

[14] See Dougald McMillan, "Samuel Beckett and the Visual Arts: The Embarrassment of Allegory," in *Samuel Beckett: A Collection of Criticism Edited by Ruby Cohn,* p. 135.

As the Story Was Told

Like *Still, Sounds,* and *Still 3, As the Story Was Told* (1973) is similar to nearly all of Beckett's fiction written during the seventies in that its meaning can be derived only from detailed examination of narrative structure. This work is an "occasional" piece that Beckett contributed to a volume published in memory of his friend, Günter Eich, the German dramatist and poet.[15] A narrating "I" relates, while lying in a hut, a story that someone else tells him. Using a paradigm of Chinese boxes, we can say that the communication of the original teller, of the someone telling the story or giving information to the first person speaker, is the outermost or first box. Pilling calls this original teller the "nameless interpreter."[16] The speaker learns of the location of the hut and of his situation in the hut from the teller. The hut is about two hundred yards distant from a tent in which some sort of "sessions" are being conducted.[17] The teller says that the speaker has been absent from this tent during the sessions, sessions which the teller describes in detail as being of a "harrowing nature."

The second Chinese box is the speaker's voice, the "I" relating the story or the circumstances and events told him as he lies in the hut. Both the first and second boxes are macrocosmic in nature. The hut housing the speaker is in a grove situated "among the trees" a given distance from the tent. The teller is not only a voice but also a physical presence in the hut or landscape. He responds by becoming silent to the speaker's raising his hand as a gesture requesting the cessation of information about the sessions held in the tent. The third box, however, is microcosmic – the imagination or inner consciousness of the speaker as he lies silently, with closed eyes, in the hut.

The voice we hear from the third box is that of the speaker devising an imaginative scene in the mind. Needless to say, this

[15] This volume is *Günter Eich zum Gedächtnis,* Frankfurt, Suhrkamp Verlag, Frankfurt-am-Main, 1973. *As the Story Was Told* is on pp. 10-13, in English and German.

[16] *Frescoes of the Skull,* p. 182.

[17] My references to *As the Story Was Told* are to the copy of MS 1396/4/14 in the Beckett Archive of the University of Reading. I quote no page numbers because the MS is a single page.

scene is of the speaker attempting to function as an artist/self, to tell a story of his own.[18] Thus we discover, even in this single-page, "occasional" fiction, the basic pattern of the quest on the second level. The devised scene begins with the speaker as artist/self describing the hut as it appears in his mind's eye:

> Lying there with eyes closed in the silence that followed this information [information about the distance of the tent from the hut] I began to see the hut, though unlike the tent it had not been described to me, but only its situation.

The speaker cannot see the hut – his eyes are closed. He has, supposedly, no factual knowledge of its interior. Having asked the teller where he is, he has been told of his location in the hut and of the hut's location in the grove of trees in relation to the tent, but nothing more. It is by virtue of his imagination that he describes the interior of the hut as having five log walls, colored glass panes, a narrow circumference, and a low ceiling. He then imagines himself as a literary artist seated in the hut that he has imaginatively described in a "small upright wicker chair with armrests." Sitting there, "very straight and still, with . . . arms along the rests, looking out at the orange light," he is interrupted (all within the confines of the imagination) by the appearance of a hand in the doorway. Apparently, the person whose hand appears has some connection with the proceedings going on in the tent: the hand appears "shortly after six," the hour at which the sessions close "puntually." If, as seems probable, the hand belongs to the teller, we must be careful to remember that we are examining a microcosmic scene and that the artist/self in the wicker-chair and the teller's hand at the doorway are imaginative constructs of the

[18] My contention that the speaker's devising of the imaginative scene is an attempt to tell a story rests on four observations. First, nearly every descent of the self into the microcosm that occurs in Beckett's fiction after *Malone Dies* is for the purpose of literary creation. Second, the speaker here is seated in a position and wicker-chair most similar to those depicted in *Still*. And the seated figure in *Still* is, as we have shown, engaged in literary fabrication. Third, the title (*As the Story Was Told*) and occasion (as a memorial piece written by Beckett for a dramatist and poet) suggest the construction of literature. And, fourth and finally, the exchange between the seated speaker and the teller, whose hand appears at the door, is an exchange involving a "sheet of writing."

third Chinese box. The teller's hand offers the seated speaker[19] a "sheet of writing," which he reads, tears in four parts, and puts "in the waiting hand to take away." Just after this point, box three ends as the imaginative scene disappears.

To find the Chinese box four, we must delve inside of box three of the imagination. Box four, as we might expect, consists of past macrocosmic events stored in the mind as memory and now transported into the imaginative microcosm of box three. This particular memory is of a summer-house, so strongly etched in the speaker's consciousness that he has described the interior of the hut as he remembers the inside of the summer-house. We cannot know whether the description is actually of either the interior of the hut or of the summer-house of the past. All that we know is that the speaker as artist/self imagines himself as seated in a hut whose interior is extremely similar to his memory of the inside of the summer-house.[20] As is usual in Beckett's depictions of the microcosmic quest to tell the story, the artist/self is drawing on memory to construct his art.

We cannot, within the confines of *As the Story Was Told,* define the memory of the summer-house as suffering or painful, although suffering is present in *As the Story Was Told.* The speaker reacts, in box two, with displeasure or disgust to the teller's descriptions of the sessions. He also reacts with violence in box three by tearing the sheet of writing in pieces. And the teller informs the speaker that the "man" succumbs "in the end to his ill-treatment."[21] But none of these reactions and the stimuli that provoke them have to do with the summer-house of past memory in this piece. It is only

[19] Beckett's manuscript substitutes "watched" for whatever verb he first chose to define the position of the speaker as the teller's hand appears at the door. (". . . for as I ▭ a hand appeared in the doorway. . . .") ('watched/^') The choice of the verb "lay" would have been incorrect: the figure lying in the hut *imagines himself as seated* in the chair when the imaginary hand appears in the door. The choice of "sat" would have been a dead give-a-way that the appearing hand is a part of the imaginative construct (box three, where the speaker sits) and not an element of the macrocosmic situation of the speaker lying in the hut. Beckett does not favor dead give-a-ways: he loves to puzzle his critics.

[20] The only difference between the interior of the hut as imagined and that of the summer-house as remembered is that the place where the speaker once sat in the summer-house was a window-seat, and, in the hut, he imagines himself as seated in a wicker-chair.

[21] After the speaker leaves box three of the imagination and returns to box two of the present situation, he refers to himself as artist as "the man."

by recourse to *Heard in the Dark 2* that we learn of alienation and rejection in love associated with the summer-house.[22]

Whether we associate suffering with the memory used for the imaginative scene by the artist/self or not, we have definite evidence that this fabricated scene fails or is unacceptable as literature. In fact, what Beckett has created in box three is the artist/self attempting to create a story and, instead, creating a scene of the rejection of himself as story-teller. The "literature" that the speaker as artist/self creates in the imagination is the "literature" of the negation of himself as literary artist. What he imagines, instead of a story, is the refusal of his story.

The reason for this refusal is locked in the mystery of the expectations of the persons participating in the sessions in the tent in regard to the speaker in the hut. Apparently, the speaker is expected to produce some sort of communique, perhaps a story, that is a report similar to the report that Gaber expects from Moran (*Molloy,* p. 175). We assume the sessions to be conducted by some superiors or persons in authority similar, not only to Moran's Gaber, but also to Malone's visitor (*Malone Dies,* pp. 269-72), Molloy's "superiors" (*Molloy,* p. 25), the Unnamable's "they" (*The Unnamable,* p. 358), and the Kram or Krim who is the scribe(s) determining the story of the mud-crawler of *How It Is* (p. 133). These others in authority expect the speaker to "say" something about the sessions, but he has no direct access to what is transpiring in the tent. He is placed far enough from the tent that he cannot hear even the "loudest cry," and he never goes near the tent during sessions. Instead, as we have noted, detailed information about the proceedings is given him by the teller.

This information is rejected twice by the speaker, once by his uplifted hand and once – in box three of the imaginative scene – by his tearing and returning the sheet of writing offered him at the door.[23] Like the Unnamable, the speaker as artist/self is not going

[22] *Heard in the Dark 2* appeared in the *Journal of Beckett Studies,* No. 5 (Autumm 1979), pp. 7-8. Beckett excerpted this piece from *Company* (the eleventh vignette of memory, pp. 38-42) and published it separately. The alienation and rejection in love here occur between the figure spoken of and a woman he once trysted with in the summer-house.

[23] Just as the seated figure's resting of his head in *Still* may be the macrocosmic equivalent of the figure's microcosmic journey to the tree in *Sounds,* so the rejection and tearing of the sheet of writing may be the microcosmic or imaginative equivalent of the macrocosmic uplifted hand silencing the teller's description of the sessions.

to fabricate his story according to the dictates of his superiors. Instead, he has retreated into box four of memory, the memory of the summer-house of his childhood. This memory, however, is nonproductive. The seated figure in the wicker-chair of the hut/summer-house imagines nothing more than the interior appearance of the hut. The remainder of the imaginative scene of box three consists only of the rejection of the writing the "others" are trying to impose upon him. Furthermore, we are not certain that the construction of a successful report or story has been possible. The speaker is told that he does not know what "the man" (the speaker as artist/self) is "required to say," whether he "would not" or "could not" say it. Ironically enough, the speaker possesses this information only because the teller relates it to him.

Such a parable as *As the Story Was Told* effectively comments, with a precise balance of empathy and commiseration, on what Pilling calls the "neglect and obloquy" that Eich received during his artistic life.[24] The descent into the microcosm of the imagination in order to fabricate a story, the recourse to memory, and the subsequent failure of the attempted art-work also, however, fit perfectly into the pattern of the Beckettian hero's quest on level two. So does the end result: no creation or authentication of the self as artist occurs, either for Eich or for Beckett's speaker. The speaker's statement that he cannot give the name of the man – although he would like to – is an admission that he does not know his name or identity as artist.

We cannot, as in *Company* and in *Still, Sounds,* and *Still 3,* indict God as being responsible for this failure because the macrocosmic memories the artist has to work with are memories of suffering. As we have seen, the functioning of memory is so brief that to detect any suffering in it we must revert to *Heard in the Dark 2* (see note 22). Nevertheless, a sensing of deity by the speaker subtly implicates God in the matter of the failure of the art-work and all that this failure implies. This sensing is patterned on the four-part paradigm of the Beckettian hero's religious consciousness that I have described: the speaker exists as perceived by some other(s), his freedom is decidedly limited by the determinism of this power, he experiences a sense of guilt or "sin" based solely on the fact of

---

[24] Pilling, "Beckett After *Still,*" *Romance Notes,* 18 (1977), 282.

his suffering – here as an artist – and he exhibits an awareness of consciousness that does not end with physical death.

The speaker's existence is dependent on what is told him by the teller, who represents the "others." The speaker's place of belonging or location is the hut. His function or *raison d'etre* is to "say" the report or produce whatever writing is required of him. His name or identity is dependent on the success of this writing. His community consists of those associated with the sessions in the tent. In fact, if the story is not told, there is no speaker: he is existentially and fictionally incapable of sustaining his own being.

The determinism shaping his being is extensive. His position in the hut, the distance of the hut from the tent, the material or information he is given to work with, the method of imparting this information – all details of his predicament are determined by another or others. The speaker's decisive rebellion against this determinism is, however, unusual for a Beckett hero. Perhaps Beckett is obliquely referring to some course of action in Eich's career. Beckett's run-of-the-mill artist/hero – for instance, the mud-crawler, of *How It Is,* who "says his life as it comes" (p. 20) – would be astonished at the speaker's rejecting and tearing the written sheet. Like his numerous counter-parts, the mud-crawler simply goes on attempting to create as best he can under the circumstances.

In spite of his rebellious gesture(s), the speaker's guilt is deep-seated:

> But finally I asked if I knew exactly what the man – I would like to give his name but cannot – what exactly was required of the man, what it was exactly that he would not or could not say. No, was the answer, after some . . . hesitation, no, I did not know what the poor man was required to say, in order to be pardoned, but would have recognized it at once, yes, at a glance, if I had seen it.

The Kafka-like helplessness of the speaker[25] who must ask if he knows what he as an artist was supposed to produce is rendered

[25] Pilling ("Beckett After *Still,*" p. 280) sees a Kafkaesque influence on *As the Story Was Told,* perhaps imposed on this commemorative contribution by Beckett because of certain similarities between the works of Eich and Kafka.

particularly Beckettian by the answer. Such knowledge of desired performance is not possessed, although this knowledge would be knowledge of the terms of pardon. The terms, however, do exist; in fact, they would be immediately recognized if seen. Who or what decides the terms, and why are they withheld? The speaker might well lament with the Unnamable: "If only I knew what they want, they want me to be Worm, but I was, I was, what's wrong?" (*The Unnamable,* p. 364).

The curse of a consciousness that does not cease with physical death is suggested in the statement made by the teller to the speaker that "the man succumbed in the end to his ill-treatment, though quite old enough at the time to die naturally of old age." Within the context of the piece as "occasional," the statement probably refers to Eich's death. As literature in its own right, the statement can be read simply as a prophecy that later on, "in the end," the speaker as artist will die. It is possible, however, to read the statement as implying the continuation of the self as speaker after the self as artist ("the man") dies. Whether "in the end" refers to the "end" of the man's long life or to the "end" of the story *As the Story Was Told,* the speaker is informed of this death as some kind of ending that has occurred. And the speaker does not "end," but continues beyond the boundaries of the last sentence of the piece in concern and puzzlement as to what he should have said – as artist/self – "in order to be pardoned." Like other Beckettian heroes, the speaker cannot escape a curse of unending consciousness that reveals itself as a continuing obsession with his story.

The speaker's awareness of dependence of being, determinism, guilt, and unending consciousness does not necessarily imply an awareness of divinity. We can no more define the one(s) in charge of matters here as God than we can deify Mr. Knott with certainty. But such an awareness, combined with a withholding of whatever word is needed to make the story possible, strongly suggests the pattern I have described of the quest on level two. The speaker as hero will never be pardoned for his failure, but the blame is not his. Whoever has sentenced him is to blame.

La Falaise

La Falaise (1975) also follows the pattern I have described of the quest on level two. Beckett has informed John Pilling that this piece was written as a *témoignage* for a Bram van Velde exhibition. Originally titled *Pour Bram,* it appeared with about two hundred and fifty other similar writings in a volume called *Celui qui ne peut se servir de mots* (Montpellier, Fata Morgana, 1975).[26] There is no puzzle in regard to narration in the twenty-one sentences of this text: a third-person voice renders descriptive comment on what we may assume is the experience of observing a van Velde landscape. Manuscripts of an early version reveal a preoccupation with the idea that the landscape may or may not have the appearance of being made by a man or a man's hands.[27] Beckett's emphasis is probably not only on the stylized or artificial quality of van Velde's painting but also on the primacy of the observer in the interaction between art object and viewer.[28]

In the final version, Beckett changes this question as to whether or not the landscape has a man-made appearance into a focusing on the observing eye's desperate search for some human element in the scene before it. The word "landscape" implies some area that is a recognizable habitat for man. But this scene – "*une falaise incolore*" – is hardly a landscape in any sense implying a human or earthly setting.[29] From any vantage point of the observing eye, the cliff appears to have neither crest nor base. Bordered on both sides with white patches of sky, the cliff thus becomes a merging of earth with heaven that seems to obliterate the space between them:

> Le ciel laisse-t-il deviner une fin de terre?
> L'éther intermédiaire?

---

[26] "Beckett After *Still,*" see note 2, p. 283.

[27] See Pilling, "Beckett After *Still,*" p. 284 and *Frescoes of the Skull,* p. 185.

[28] See "Beckett After *Still,*" p. 285.

[29] My references to *La Falaise* are to the copy of MS 1396/4/40 in the Beckett Archive of the University of Reading. I quote no page numbers because the MS is a single page.

We are reminded of Watt's sky and wasted earth, each meeting in a "dark colour" so much the same that Watt himself is engulfed in it ("Addenda" to *Watt,* p. 249). Such a "soul-landscape" is given fictional actuality in *Lessness:* "Little body same grey as the earth sky. . . . Ash grey all sides earth sky as one all sides endlessness" (p. 9).

In the air surrounding the cliff there is no trace of a seabird, no life in a living place. At this point, the observation becomes speculative: *Ou trop claire pour paraître.* Perhaps the bird is present but composed of white sky also, like a ghost. The abrupt question – *Enfin quelle preuve d'une face?* – reinforces our recognition that there is no evidence of a "face" in this scene. That is, there is no evidence of what a human look or glance would recognize and respond to as an earthly habitat – a human place for humans.

In writing of the treatment of nature in literature such as Beckett's, J. Hillis Miller speaks of a "change which transforms objects":

> Instead of being named, close, friendly, so much a part of man that their otherness is not even noticed, objects in this alien outdoor space turn away from man, withdraw into themselves, and lose all their historical, cultural, moral, and even utilitarian significance.[30]

This change is familiar to all readers of Camus. Beckett's description of the cliff might well be a stylized metaphor for Camus' world where "strangeness creeps in" – a world in which hills and sky "lose the illusory meaning with which we had clothed them" and become "more remote than a lost paradise."[31]

At this point in *La Falaise,* the pattern of Beckett's quest on the second level as I have described it becomes apparent. As Pilling states, the eye, "seeking to find human features" is "forced to abandon the idea and allow the imagination to take over."[32] The imaginative perception forces humanity upon the scene of the cliff. The result of this forcing is, as Pilling observes in his review article of *Fizzles,* a "recognizable simulacrum of the external

---

30 Miller, "The Anonymous Walkers," *The Nation,* 23 April 1960, p. 352.
31 *The Myth of Sisyphus and Other Essays,* p. 15.
32 *Frescoes of the Skull,* p. 185.

world."[33] But the (human) landscape imaginatively produced from sterile nature is one of human ruins ("*restes mortels*"), a landscape suggesting calamity and death. A ledge emerges, first in shadow but finally in distinct clarity. The cliff has been transformed into a human skull, seized on and separated by the imagination from the debris surrounding it:

> Un crâne entier se dégage pour finir. Un seul d'entre ceux que valent de tels débris.

Functioning somewhat as a telescopic lens, the imaginative eye closes in on the skull to examine the frontal or coronal bone and then the parietal bone. Actually, the imaginative perception is penetrating the vacant eye-sockets of the skull. The text suggests that some kind of gaze from the skull is returned: *Les orbites laissent entrevoir l'ancien regard.*

Suddenly the descent into the imagination ceases. The skull becomes once more the sterile cliff and disappears. And the observing eye retreats into whiteness: *Alors L'œil de voler vers les blancs lointains.* Or into nothingness. *Ou de se détourner de devant.*

Had we found *La Falaise* unsigned in some library, we might have guessed that Beckett wrote it. The self retreats from a macrocosm[34] of unfriendly strangeness into the microcosm of the imagination. Here, the artist/self attempts to construct, from the material of the outer world, an artistic little world to "shore against the ruins." But the imaginative artifact becomes one of ruin also, in fact, of more grotesque ruin because of the messy, human quality of its debris. As the human remains disappear, Beckett's familiar residue persist – the whiteness and emptiness of nothing. Like other Beckett briefs, *La Falaise* is a story of the failure of art, an art constructed as always out of the inadequate materials of the macrocosm, here, from the world of nature.

In *Sounds,* a human form against a tree suggests the Crucifixion. Here, in *La Falaise,* the imagination produces a Gehenna which

---

33 "'Fizzles,'" *Journal of Beckett Studies,* p. 99.

34 The argument can be made that the world retreated from is not the macrocosm of "real" life but the sterile world of art (van Velde's painting). I would reply that Beckett does not perceive van Velde's art as sterile but instead as valid representation of our perception of life. Furthermore, it is obvious that the cliff scene is expected to be a landscape – a setting for human experience.

becomes a Calvary – the place of the skull. This skull is that of Beckett's Christ, a Christ not divine but all too human. As Camus explains, as he describes the understanding of Kirilov, the engineer in Dostoevsky's *The Possessed,*

> Solely in this sense Jesus indeed personifies the whole human drama. He is the complete man, being the one who realized the most absurd condition. He is not the God-man but the man-god. And, like him, each of us can be crucified and victimized – and is to a certain degree. [35]

Such a Christ-figure, epitomized in *La Falaise* in the skull among the ruins of the skull-place, implicitly indicts whatever Father/God is in charge of crucifixions.

The particular crucifixion that Beckett seems to suggest in this portrait of an imaginative eye gazing into the sockets of the skull is mentioned by him in the interview with John Gruen:

> It is the weight of every man's fear and emptiness that produces this look [a look of 'hostility' which Beckett claimed to notice on the faces of New Yorkers]. Somewhere he must know that self-perception is the most frightening of all human observations. He must know that when man faces himself, he is looking into the abyss. [36]

From the sterility of nature to the ruined artifacts of the imagination to the emptiness of the inner self – such a journey is easily designated a *via dolorosa.*

---

[35] *The Myth of Sisyphus and Other Essays,* p. 107.
[36] "Samuel Beckett Talks About Beckett," p. 210.

DISAPPEARING *COMPANY* AND A MISSING WORD

The gaze of the viewer into the empty sockets of the skull/cliff in *La Falaise* becomes one of Beckett's most acute portrayals of human loneliness. To move from this portrayal to *Company* is to recognize that, for Beckett's hero, the presence of company (or other persons) does not necessarily dispel such loneliness. In *Company,* the narrating voice creates several "others," but loneliness, the lack of significant human communion, remains. Neither the hero's sensing of the divine presence/absence nor his literary effort in the role of the self-as-artist to create significant others as he engages in the quest on level two dispels the loneliness, associated here, as throughout the fiction, with the emptiness of the inner self.

Before we embark on efforts to discover God in either the heroic consciousness or the quest structure of this piece, we must define the structure in detail. Such definition necessitates that certain interpretive difficulties of this work be dealt with.[1] Enoch Brater has designated its two basic divisions as the "rhythm" or "voice" of "reason" and the "rhythm" or "voice" of "memory." The division of reason includes all the text that is not direct address by

---

[1] *Company* was published in 1980 by Grove Press. Beckett has excerpted and published separately two short texts from *Company* – *Heard in the Dark* and *Heard in the Dark 2. Heard in the Dark* was published by John Calder, London, 1979, in a collection of short fiction entitled *New Writing & Writers 17,* pp. 11-12. *Heard in the Dark 2* appeared in the *Journal of Beckett Studies,* No. 5 (1979), pp. 7-8. My references are to the Grove Press edition of *Company* and are cited by page number(s) in the text of this chapter.

the voice to the hearer. The direct address ("Use of the second person marks the voice," p. 8) is the division of memory. Brater's response to the interaction of these two divisions leads him to conclude that "just who is the narrator and who is the company really doesn't matter,"[2] but Judith Dearlove describes the narrator(s) and company as "four 'figures': the hearer (M) who lies on his back in the dark, the voice (W) which exists above and about the hearer, the characters in the scenes the voice recounts, and a Creator who fabricates it all for company." Dearlove also explains how these four "figures" blend, by the end of *Company,* "into a solitary being."[3] Angela B. Moorjani names the personae of *Company* as a "third-person narrator" who situates "his figments in a vaguely defined time and space," someone who lies in the dark on his back listening, a voice that speaks to the supine figure in the dark, and a hypothetical first-person narrator who exists only negatively in the first-person pronouns absent or missing from this work. She further identifies a "metanarrator" who is different from the other personae but who also contains them in his "various narrating/narrated roles." Moorjani sees this metanarrator as splitting into an infinite number of additional narrators as *Company* progresses.[4]

The designation of the divisions of reason and memory is basic and obvious, but the defining of the narrator(s) and company is perhaps even more basic and much more complex. In fact, *Company* is Beckett's first fiction in which the answer to the question, "Who is telling this story?" is emphasized by being developed progressively. To be sure, as Edith Kern has reminded us for some time, Molloy is probably the artistic self of Moran relating *Molloy,*[5] and Malone implies that there is someone in addition to himself having a hand in the events of his stories when he puzzles over the literary fact of Saposcat's not being expelled from school (*Malone Dies,* p. 190). But these matters are not really

[2] Brater, "The *Company* Beckett Keeps, or One Fabulist's Decay of Lying," Beckett and the Art of Allusion I, First Annual Symposium in the Humanities, *Samuel Beckett: Humanistic Perspectives,* Columbus: Ohio State Universtity, 9 May 1981, pp. 5-7, 10.

[3] Dearlove, "Allusion to Archetype," Beckett and the Art of Allusion II, First Annual Symposium in the Humanities, 9 May 1981, p. 12.

[4] *Abysmal Games in the Novels of Samuel Beckett,* pp. 133 and 137.

[5] Kern, "Moran-Molloy: The Hero as Author," *Perspective,* 11 (1959), 188.

in question. We have only to read the opening paragraphs of these earlier works to know that Molloy is writing his tale and that Malone is making up and attempting to write his stories. Brian Wicker points out that Beckett's "authoritative narrative voice" disappears after *Watt* (in which this voice becomes confused) to be displaced by the solipsist monologists of *Stories,* the *Trilogy,* and *Texts for Nothing.*[6] But these monologists, if they can be said to have any identities at all, are easily identified as those persons or voices who are relating the stories. If narrative dialogue, appearing once again in *How It Is,* implies uncertain voices reciting this journey in the mud, we as readers feel no compulsion to decide who says what. The victim, the torturer, Pim, Bom, the voice above in the light – whether they are one or the same – carry easily and indiscriminately the burden of recitation.[7] And in the fictional pieces following *How It Is,* the narrative voices of recitation or observation do not demand attention. The detachment and impersonality of these voices are an integral part of the literary stripping away that Beckett achieves in the minimal art of these late works. Paul A. Bové states that Michel Foucault sees Beckett as "the paradigm of the disappearance of the author from the stage of creation."[8]

We must not conclude, because *Company,* even on a first-time, cursory (and bewildering) reading, confronts us with the question as to who is telling the tale, that Beckett is backtracking into more conventional narrative structure. As nearly always, he is pressing beyond achieved frontiers. Rather than offering us, in *Company,* fiction in which the authorial voice is so detached and impersonal that it can almost be said to have disappeared, he presents us with *a literary allegory of the disappearing process itself.* Thus *Company* can be defined as what Foucault, in "What Is An Author?" calls "the writing of our day," writing which is "primarily concerned with creating an opening where the writing subject [or reciting or observing voice or author] endlessly disappears."[9]

---

[6] "Samuel Beckett and the Death of the God-Narrator," pp. 64-65.

[7] In a letter to Hugh Kenner, Beckett calls the narrator of *How It Is* the "narrator/narrated." See Ruby Cohn, *Back to Beckett,* p. 233.

[8] Bové, "The Image of the Creator in Beckett's Postmodern Writing," *Philosophy and Literature,* 4 (Spring 1980), 48.

[9] Foucault, *Language, Counter-Memory, Practice,* ed. and trans. Donald F. Bouchard (Ithaca: Cornell Univ. Press, 1977), p. 116.

A narrator relates to us, at the beginning of *Company,* that the "proposition" of the work is that of a voice telling of a past to "one [the hearer] on his back in the dark" (p. 7). These three are referred to grammatically as the second person (the voice), the third person (a "cankerous other," presumably, at least at this point, the narrator), and the first person (the hearer, if he could speak) (p. 8). The question is immediately raised (and tossed about, much as a dog would a bone) as to whether or not there is some other (or others) rather than the hearer to whom the voice is actually speaking. Apparently, this question is raised only to focus on the general matter of identity within the narrative structure. "Who is devising it all [the work that is *Company*] for company?" (first mentioned, p. 8). Is it the narrator constructing the book, the voice concocting the vignettes of memory, or someone else, and, if so, who? After several pages of text, in which the narrator focuses on his insight into and partial identification with the consciousness of the hearer and describes the voice in detail as it offers six vignettes of memory, the entire process of narration, what had "at first sight" seemed "clear," is decisively questioned. Is there, in the same dark as the hearer or in another dark, someone other than the narrator or voice devising the tale? And "What does this mean? What finally does this mean that at first sight seemed clear?" (pp. 22-23).

At this point, the first multiplication or fracturing of an utterance into mirror images of itself occurs. The narrator's "Why in another dark or in the same" is countered by "And whose voice [is] asking this." Then, "whose voice is asking this" splinters into "Who asks, Whose voice [is] asking this" (p. 24). Who and how many are the speakers and/or narrative selves that make up the company of *Company*? Who, if there is such, is the ultimate or final speaker of the narration? If there is "another still," can he be identified? Or is he "Nowhere to be found. Nowhere to be sought. The unthinkable last of all. Unnamable. Last Person. I" (p. 24)?

This splintering of the narrating voice is followed, almost nonchalantly, by a seventh vignette of memory. Then, quite abruptly, some speaker or deviser of the narrative other than the already functioning voice and actual narrator is overtly referred to:

> Deviser of the voice and of its hearer and of himself. Deviser of himself for company. Leave it at that. He speaks of himself as

> of another. He says speaking of himself, He speaks of himself as of another. Himself he devises too for company. (p. 26)

This deviser has been lurking in the story already, but now he appears as the one most directly responsible for the literary existence of the narrative that is being told or devised. In fact, as he appears, we are informed that he himself is responsible for his appearance as deviser in the narrative. He is the deviser not only of "the voice and of its hearer" but also "of himself." That is, he appears as the deviser who puts himself, as a character who is designated as "deviser," into the ongoing flow of the narration. As we are informed, "Confusion too is company up to a point" (p. 26).

The narrator continues to function, relating to us, as before, information about the voice and the hearer. But now he must also narrate information about the deviser whose imagination "is devising it all for company" and who also exists as an objective presence in the story. The following passage depicts the deviser in both these roles:

> Let him for example after due imagination decide in favour of the supine position or prone and this in practice prove less companionable than anticipated. May he then or may he not replace it by another? Such as huddled with his legs drawn up within the semicircle of his arms and his head on his knees. Or in motion. Crawling on all fours. Another in another dark or in the same crawling on all fours devising it all for company. (p. 27)

Here the narrator tells of the deviser imagining his own position and location in the story.

The presence of the deviser in the story is now more real or actual than those of the voice and the hearer. The narrator speaks of the deviser deciding on the composition of the place where the hearer lies. The deviser considers the merits of black basalt "as voice and hearer pall." Including himself in the deviser's imaginative process, the narrator refers to the place under consideration as "the place where our old hearer lies" (p. 33). Furthermore, it may be possible that the deviser will get rid of the images of the voice, the hearer, and his own presence as character in the story: he is not always in need of their literary company. At such moments, he experiences "Regret . . . at having brought them about" and faces the "problem" of "how [to] dispel them" (p. 31).

The deviser is said to assume literary prerogatives that the narrator has not yet exercised. Having exhausted his imaginative powers by having the voice relate two particularly long vignettes of memory (the two pieces Beckett published separately as *Heard in the Dark* and *Heard in the Dark 2),*[10] the deviser is "Wearied by such stretch of imagining" and "ceases." Returning to his task of devising, and feeling once more the "need for company," he experiences a resurgence of literary prowess to such an extent that he decides to name the hearer M and himself, as character in the narrative, W (pp. 42-43).

The deviser's appearance in the story is also signalled – other than by the narrator's direct and implicit references to his literary imagining and his presence in the story – by subtle changes in the tone or perspective of the narrative comment. The writing has been frankly self-conscious from the start; the narrator, for instance, names the grammatical persons being used and designates his own person as that of the third (p. 8). But, beginning with the disclosure of the deviser, the writing becomes blatantly and artistically self-conscious. The occasional self-questioning and answering on the part of the narrator develop into undisguised literary speculation. Whether the voice comes from the same or a different dark from that of the hearer has been considered from the beginning, but a difference occurs in this regard. Earlier, the question has been, "Which dark is the voice coming from?" (pp. 8 and 22). Now, the speculation is, "Which dark shall the literary imagination decree that the voice come from?" (p. 26). Other matters of speculation clamor for imaginative decision. What is the voice's position? If a given position is decided on, might that position be reversed (pp. 26-27)? Might the hearer be "improved" (p. 27), and how shall the place where he lies be described (pp. 32-33)? Also, the structure of the prose develops more definitively into a pattern of dialogue:

---

[10] See note 1 for publishing information on these two pieces.

> Might he [the hearer] cross his feet? On and off. Now left or right and now a little later the reverse. No. Quite out of keeping. (p. 28)

Such dialogue does not, as I have already made clear, imply two separate narrative voices, one of the narrator and one of the deviser. The narrator tells us, in the third person, what the deviser as narrating character says or expresses. Instead, the intensification of dialogue signals the presence of the deviser as literary mind deliberately imagining the direction that the narration shall take.

A third signal of the deviser's devising worked into the texture of the narration is the occurrence of the verb "imagine" and its derivatives ("imagining," "imagination," "imagined," "imaginable") before and after the appearance of the deviser. Before, the word "imagine" occurs only three times, once on page 7 and twice on page 19. After his appearance, "imagine" or a derivative of it occurs twenty-five times. What we have is the speculative imagining of a deviser who we might aptly designate as an artist/self appearing openly and beginning to function at a particular point in the text. Were we to plot simple diagrams of narrative method in *Company* before and after the deviser's appearance, we would have something like the following:

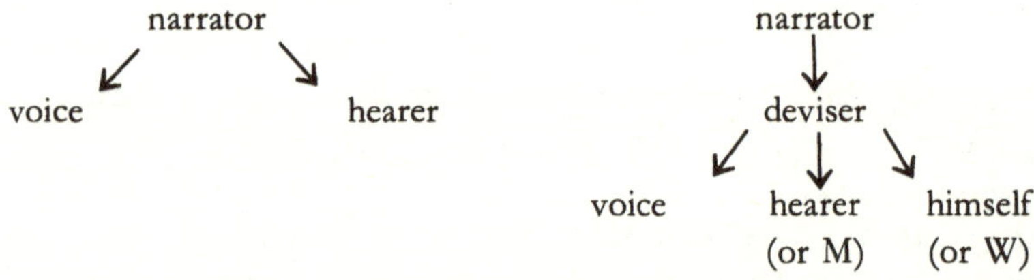

Just as we are becoming somewhat comfortable with this understanding of the narrating method in *Company,* the narrator jerks the rug from under us – or, more precisely, jerks the deviser from under us – by announcing that the deviser is a "Devised deviser devising it all for company" (p. 46). W, too, is a creature, a "Figment" of someone's imagination (p. 45). By association and logic, if W as character is a creature or figment, then the imagining deviser, who has named himself in the story as W, is a figment also. We must not think that we are simply being informed, as we have known all along, that the narrator exists behind the deviser as the speaker of the story. The narrator is speaking, in the third person, of someone other than himself when he refers to a "Devised deviser." The text is clear that we are once again confronted with the question, "Who is the ultimate narrating self that is devising all this for company?":

> W? But W too is creature. Figment. Yet another then. Of whom nothing. Devising figments to temper his nothingness. (p. 46)

With apologies for my own devising, I suggest the following paraphrase, with added words italicized:

> W? But W too is *a* creature, *a* figment *of someone's imagining. There is* yet another then. Of whom *we know and have said* nothing. Devising figments to temper his nothingness.

Or perhaps a better rendition of the second to last phrase would be:

> Of whom nothing *will be* said.

The deviser as a character does not depart the narrative at this point: he remains to be given the title or name by the narrator of "crawling creator" (p. 51). But he is removed at this point from his role as active deviser or imaginer of the story. As "creator," he does not create but begins to crawl and, possibly, to smell (p. 52).

Definite evidence exists, from the point in the text that the deviser is designated as a "devised deviser" (p. 46), that he is not the final or ultimate storyteller. He is said to be "imagined" about and to be "consigned" to a certain level of alertness by some "imagination" other than his own (p. 53). His role becomes much more that of a passive character in the narrative. Immediately following his appearance, the deviser is said, "after due imagination," to "decide" whether he is supine, prone, or crawling (p. 27). After his shift to the role of character only, he is decided about by another or others:

> Then let him move. Within reason. On all fours. A moderate crawl torso well clear of the ground eyes front alert. If this no better than nothing cancel. If possible. (p. 46)

The literary speculation no longer includes him as an active participant, and the title of "creator" becomes ironic.

Whatever participation in the imaginative process the deviser still holds becomes negative, passive, and subjunctive. He considers the question as to whether or not he can create while crawling in the dark and answers, no, he cannot (pp. 52-53). Falling, he experiencies the "craving for company," but only as a "need." He is no longer in charge of the voice, the hearer, or himself as character in the narrative (p. 55). The implication is that he might create, were he able to, but that he is not. Instead, he is last referred to as "Naked" and "Ghostly in the voice's glimmer" with only his own "bonewhite flesh for company" (p. 57).

Along with these developments in regard to the deviser, the narrative voice has multiplied or fractured again:

> What visions in the dark of light! Who exclaims thus? Who asks who exclaims, What visions in the shadeless dark of light and shade. (p. 59)

Thus, once again, we are confronted with the question as to whether or not there is "Yet another still devising it all for company" (p. 60). A hole or space seems to have developed that calls for some fabricator of the tale called the deviser of the deviser. A diagram of narration at this stage of our knowledge might be as follows:

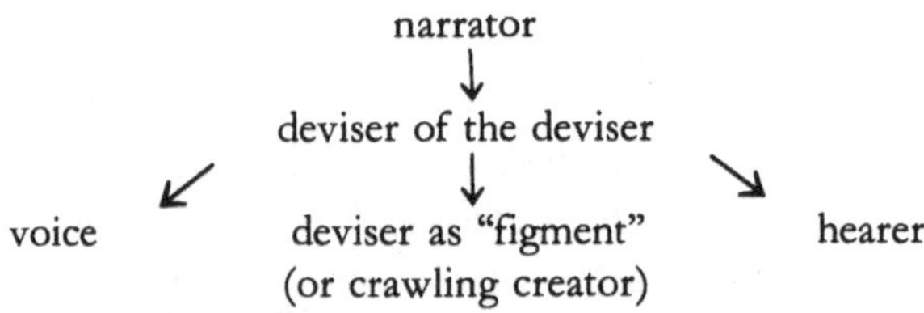

We know that there is a deviser of the deviser because he has been referred to by the narrator in the third person as someone other than himself, that is, as someone who devises the deviser but who is not the narrator (pp. 46 and 59-60). Thus the deviser has been displaced. What we are confronted with is Foucault's endlessly disappearing author. The narrator has abdicated in favor of the deviser, who has now been divested of authorship, and we cannot define the deviser of the deviser. All that we have is his location, the empty space(s) in the text vacated by the earlier fabulist.

The dilemma is explained (or the problem solved) and Beckett's incredible welding of structure with meaning exposed by recourse to a consideration of the fourth – the narrator is the first; the deviser, the second; the deviser of the deviser, the third – narrative voice in *Company.* This voice is the voice of memory, which (or who) has been trying, since the beginning of the tale, to animate the hearer by repeating over and about him various episodes of a life lived in the past in the macrocosm of the real world. Where we have been with our narrators and devisers is, of course, in the microcosm of the artistic imagination. This voice repeats fifteen vignettes of memory which offset the bleak, mechanical, literary speculation of the rest of the text with the suffering but vital life of humanity. The voice's goal seems to be to confer life or selfhood on the hearer by forcing him to claim the memories or past as his own. The voice desires the hearer to "confess," to say "Yes I remember," and thereby to become a person, a self who can meaningfully use the pronoun "I" (p. 16).

This voice of memory, that has been consistently functioning all the while that the other devising voices have been engaged in the mental gymnastics of their disappearing acts, exposes, in its fifteenth vignette, exactly who the ultimate fabulist of *Company* is. In spite of the fact that he has not yet, and does not at or after this point, have any quoted sentence, phrase, or word attributed to him,[11] this fabulist is the hearer. In the vignettes, the voice of

[11] The surface speakers of *Company* are, of course, the narrator and the voice of memory. Certain expressions, although not what we would think of as the equivalents of quoted dialogue in conventional fiction, do appear in the text as verbal statements attributed to the deviser. Some such statements are said by the narrator to be said by the deviser:

> Till feeling the need for company again he tells himself to call the hearer M at least. (p. 42)

Others are said by the narrator to be said by the deviser to himself of himself:

> He says further to himself referring to himself, When last he referred to himself it was to say he was in the same dark as his creature. (p. 43)

No verbal statements are attributed to the deviser of the deviser or to the hearer, as such.

memory informs the hearer ("now on your back in the dark") of certain incidents events, or activities of macrocosmic life that the voice insists are, or were, those of the hearer. In the fifteenth vignette, the event is that of someone sitting at home, "huddled in the dark," no longer able to tramp about the earth as he has previously done. As the voice speaks, we begin to recognize in this huddled figure the hearer, who is the fabulist responsible for the fable that is *Company*. The figure described commences, as he sits, to imagine that he is not alone, that is, to imagine as his companions the varied company that inhabits *Company:* "Huddled thus, you find yourself imagining you are not alone while knowing full well that nothing has occurred to make this possible" (p. 61).

The imagining process is interrupted by the figure's continual shifting between sitting and lying and lying and sitting:

> Supine now you resume your fable where the act of lying cut it short. And persist till the converse operation cuts it short again. So in the dark now huddled and now supine you toil in vain. (p. 62)

Finally, "supineness becomes habitual and finally the rule." On his back in the dark, "with face upturned for good," the figure in the fifteenth vignette of memory labors in vain at his fable:

> The fable of one with you in the dark. The fable of one fabling of one with you in the dark. (p. 63)

This figure in the vignette of memory is easily identified as the hearer, who has been lying on his back in the dark throughout the devising of the fable that is *Company*. Because the hearer is the subject of this vignette, we realize that he has been the original imaginer or deviser all along. Thus the hearer as fabulist supercedes even the narrator because what the narrator has expressed is what the macrocosmic, huddled figure of the vignette of memory – now identified as the hearer – has imagined.

In this manner, the hearer is not only identified as the final fabulist but also as the assimilation of all the narrating selves of *Company*. Like the narrator, he has produced *Company*. Like the deviser, he has imagined the circumstances of the tale. Like the deviser of the deviser, he has devised the deviser. Furthermore, admission is implicit in this final vignette that the voice of memory is indeed the voice of the hearer, thus uniting the selves of the voice and the hearer. The voice's narration must remain in the second person because the "first personal singular and a fortiori plural pronoun had never any place in your vocabulary," but the voice is the remembering of the hearer – his remembrance of things past out of which he fabricates *Company*:

> Thus you now on your back in the dark once sat, huddled there your body having shown you it could go out no more. Out no more to walk the little winding back roads and interjacent pastures now alive with flocks and now deserted. With at your elbow for long years your father's shade in his old tramping rags and then for long years alone. (p. 61)

Analyzing the structure of *Company* has disclosed its varied personae.[12] We are now in a position to explore the consciousness of these narrative selves or heroes in regard to theological aware-

---

[12] In *Abysmal Games in the Novels of Samuel Beckett,* Moorjani examines in depth and at length the question of the narrating persons of *Company.* She correctly notes that *Company* is the first work in which "the first person is excised from the narrative," with the second or third person being substituted "for the absent first." The reason that she gives for this absence is that the first person is "what cannot be" (p. 136). Moorjani sees this absence most definitively revealed by what she describes as an infinitely repetitive game in which a devised deviser devises a devised deviser who devises a devised deviser *and infinitum.* This game stretches "hypothetically" between "an ultimate narrator, an unreachable unnamable who would be 'I' on one end, and on the other, an unnamable hearer to whom this narrator could say 'I,' bridging the abyss." Having formulated this description, Moorjani then notes that if "the two hypothetical ends [could] coincide in perfect self-proximity (I am who am), the writer could create himself, be both his alpha and omega, the first and the last" (p. 137). Her language here describes a desirable state of two selves communicating with each other in such a way that one realizes self-identity because the other truly knows him as he actually is. Moorjani continues, however, to describe the two identities of the "unnamable deviser" and the "unnamable devised" as one self: "Like the Unnamable of the novel, this unnamable invents the fable that invents him" (p. 138). Thus she reaches the same conclusion that I have reached in regard to the hearer being the ultimate deviser who stages the entire cast of *Company* (p. 139). Moorjani does not explore in depth the philosophical implications of this structure of narrating selves – she notes that the "infinite company who address each other in the second and third person" do so "to mask the absence of the first" (p. 139). By implication, she is speaking of a covering of the empty place where the self should be with words. Thus her analysis reinforces my contention that the artist/self of *Company* seeks in vain to create himself with a story – a Logos/Word that means.

ness or a sensing of God, or of his absence. The first point of this God-consciousness in the paradigm I have formulated is an awareness that to be is to be perceived by some other, thus making human existence contingent on someone or something other than itself. Such an awareness is demonstrated in the "being" of the hearer. Flat on his back in the dark, the hearer exists in the macrocosm only in the perception of the voice. Apart from the experiences described in the vignettes of memory, the supine figure has no life or consciousness of life conceived of in what we might call human terms. In the dark place where he lies, he is able to breathe, open and close his eyes in response to the variations of light, enjoy "a certain activity of mind however slight" (pp. 8-9, 21), and, supposedly, to hear. But even this minimum degree of being is dependent on the narrating voices describing him in the microcosm. Even after the hearer is merged, in the last vignette, with the huddled figure of the macrocosm, his selfhood remains dependent on others. He is still unable to use "I," or to speak, for that matter. All that we know of him in this final disclosure of his identity is learned from the second person "You" address of the voice. The hearer is, as we have seen, the essential self and ultimate artificer of *Company,* but, in order to be, he himself must be narrated or fabled by others.

These others are, of course, the hearer's pseudo-selves or pseudo-narrators rather than God. But the degree of determinism that they exercise over the hearer's being is God-like. Another determines whether or not the hearer can speak (". . . he cannot. He shall not," p. 8), move (p. 20), cross his feet (p. 28), or think (p. 45). His exercising of the senses of sight, hearing, taste, touch, and smell is determined by the narrating voice (p. 51).

This determinism is, at its most obvious, not that of God at all but simply that exercised by a narrator over a fictional creation. It is only when the dependence for being and the determinism are joined with the two remaining elements that I describe in my paradigm of theological awareness that they begin to take on nuances of a God-consciousness. A sense of guilt or "sin" is experienced by the hearer at least four times, three times as related by the voice of memory and once as related by the narrator. A small boy's question about the sky being "much more distant than it appears" is punished by a "cutting report" from his mother. What is really distant is not the sky but the mother's face, and the punishment of her reply becomes guilt that is "never forgotten" (pp. 10-11). The same kind of guilt is implied in the mother's word to her neighbor that the child playing in the garden has "been a very naughty boy" (pp. 21-22). As in the Greek world, he is guilty only of being called naughty: his suffering and punishment are his sin. The "uneasiness" the child experiences after his kind attention to the hedgehog is the same kind of Beckettian guilt. The child has helped the animal, and he prays for it, but guilt becomes punishment in the sight of the "mush" and the smell of the "stench" (pp. 29-31). Like numerous Beckett heroes, the hearer is conscious of punishment but uncertain of its cause. As in Malone's circumstances, "God does not seem to need reasons for doing what he does, and for omitting to do what he omits to do" (*Malone Dies,* 245). For the hearer, to have a past is to be guilty of something that should be acknowledged (p. 34) and "confessed" (p. 16).

The fourth, and final, element I include as evidence of God-awareness in the hero's consciousness is found to occur as unmistakably in *Company* as in Beckett's other fiction. The hero experiences "eternal life" in the sense of a consciousness that does not cease. The voice of memory will never die, in spite of the hearer's hope that it will (pp. 17-18, 45). The imagining mind cannot cease; it is "Unstillable" (p. 23). In this Beckettian microcosm, as in others, no relief from consciousness is possible (p. 31). Words may be coming to an end (p. 62) and the company so tediously created shown to be figments, but the self, or the no-self, continues as it has always been – "Alone" (pp. 62-63). In his awareness of dependency, manipulation by determining forces, guilt, and the inescapability of consciousness, the hearer/hero of *Company* senses what we may refer to in an ironic sense as the presence of God.

The meaning revealed in the pattern of what I have described as level two, the internalized quest of the artist/self, emerges clearly from the intricate elements of Beckett's narrative structure in *Company.* Embedded in this pattern is a second disclosure of God. The artist/self becomes dominant as the macrocosmic body of the character/self is finally stilled in its supineness. Descending into the microcosm of imagination and memory, he undertakes the familiar Beckettian task of telling a story that will, if told, create a self, that will find the "unthinkable last of all," the "Unnamable," the "Last Person," the "I" of essential selfhood (p. 24). The story he tells is *Company,* but *Company* is a fable not told. The "process" of telling it is meaningless (p. 61), the artist/self labors and toils in vain to tell it (p. 62), the authorial voices endlessly disappear, and "in the end," the labor is lost for there is only silence (p. 63). The argument can be raised that *Company* is there, a story written. But the counter argument is, of course, that it is a story of a story not told – its title is *Company* and yet the self of the fable remains, as always, alone. *Company* (an ironic title) is a fiction of fictions, or, as the narrator says, of "figments" (p. 46).

Because the story is not told, the self remains uncreated. The sentence passed by the narrator in the opening pages of the tale that the voice of the first person "shall not" and "cannot" speak is carried out relentlessly to the end (p. 8). No "I" confesses or murmurs "Yes I remember" (pp. 16, 34). The past may belong, in fact, must belong, to the ultimate self, the artist/self, the hearer, but he cannot realize or acknowledge it (p. 34). We have been waiting for this self, as we wait for the Unnamable to "say I'm someone, to say I'm somewhere" (*The Unnamable,* p. 410), but we wait in vain as the split voices labor at the fable in vain. If the story-teller's art cannot create the self, there can be no self.

Here, as in all the fiction, the reason that the story will not work or be told is because life will not work. Without completion of the quest for fulfillment of the character/self in the macrocosm, the artist/self has no material out of which to construct a completed story and thus create himself. The memories of *Company,* like the fictions of Malone and the accounts of "rags of life above in the light" in *How It Is,* are those of alienation, separation, anxiety/fear, futility, loneliness, suffering, and death. Alienation exists in relationships between a boy and his mother (pp. 10, 21), a boy and his family (p. 25), a man and a loved woman (pp. 38-42), and a man and his father's ghost (p. 35). Anxiety/fear is found in accounts of a father fleeing the birth of his child (p. 12), a child attempting to jump into a sea that holds his father's face,[13] and a

[13] The child, from a vantage point high above the sea, sees his father's face as the "swell sways it under and sways it up again" (*Company,* p. 18). Although the face is a "loved trusted" one and although there are many calls to be a "brave boy" and jump, the child never jumps. Instead, the passage is filled with the anxiety of being poised in such a position but unable to move because of fear. Although the father's face speaks, it is far deader than the face of Ferdinand's father that supposedly lies "full fathom five" in Shakespeare's *The Tempest.* In

boy shutting a hedgehog into a box (p. 29). Futility is concretized in the second hand of a watch and its shadow "in their seemingly endless parallel rotation round and round the dial" (pp. 57-59), in an old man's tramping round and round the earth (pp. 14-15, 23-24), and in a fabulist laboring in vain at his fable (pp. 60-63). The vignette of a person standing, with closed eyes, alone, leaning on a staff, with his back to the sea, is the metaphorical quintessence of loneliness (p. 54), but loneliness is an ingredient of almost all the vignettes. Suffering is overtly depicted in the physical blindness, deafness, and poverty of the deranged beggar woman attempting to open the garden gate (pp. 16-17) and in the hunger of the boy going to bed without supper, but is implicit in other vignettes as well. Death appears in the "shade" of the ghost of the old man (pp. 14, 23, 35), the father's face in the sea (p. 18), and the decomposed hedgehog (p. 29). These categories of qualities of unhappiness in human experience that make up the vignettes of memory are not inclusive: other categories could be added, such as loss, failure, guilt, and scorn.[14]

Certainly we can agree that macrocosmic life does not "work" in *Company,* but is there a connection in *Company,* as there is generally in Beckett's fiction as a whole, between the failure of life and the failure of art? Such a connection is not explicitly stated in this work (what is?), but is basically and implicitly assumed throughout the fable. Two observations reveal this assumption. First, the only material for art in *Company* is this macrocosmic failure of life. Like Proust, Beckett conceives of the suffering of life as the only vital material out of which art may be constructed. Were we to remove the fifteen vignettes of memory from *Company,* the bleak mechanisms of narration that remain would be like a husk with the kernel of grain removed.[15] Second, the story or artwork that is dependent for material on these suffering memories of life

---

Beckett's world, there is no "sea change" to transform death into an element of comedy, or, for that matter, to assimilate death into the transcendence of tragedy.

[14] The twelfth vignette of memory is the only one of the fifteen that seem to be a happy memory. This memory is of the person addressed lying under an aspen tree with a girl who seems to share his love for her. There is nothing in this vignette that suggests suffering – a most unusual fact in view of the nature of the other fourteen vignettes.

[15] Enoch Brater comments on the literary dominance of the images of memory in comparison with the remainder of the text. See "The Company Beckett Keeps, or One Fabulist's Decay of Lying," pp. 8-9.

fails. Obviously, it is the story not told that fails, the narrative effort of Beckett's microcosmic hero. Beckett's story – the ironic fiction which is *Company* – is one of his most complex and brilliantly competent attempts to date to render the dilemma of the artist. With this distinction in mind, we can formulate the following equation: memories of failure in macrocosmic life equal the failure of art in the microcosm.

Careful examination of the vignettes of memory reveal that God is responsible for the suffering and failure of macrocosmic experience. The responsibility of God for the blindness, deafness, derangement, and poverty of the beggar woman at the gate is apparent in the irony of her "blessing" on the child helping her open the gate: "God reward you little master," and "God save you little master" (p. 17). This woman has perhaps incurred some of her misfortune by her efforts to fly from the first floor window of her house, but, like Mr. and Mrs. Rooney and the other wretched souls of Beckett's *All That Fall,* she can fault God for the "rewards" of her miserable existence. He does not, as his Word promises, uphold those who fall nor raise up those who are bowed down.[16] Irony also serves to implicate God in the mushy stench of the hedgehog's death. The emotion inspiring the child's putting the animal in the box is "pity" – an emotion God is reputed to have for his creatures, men. The child's prayer to God to bless all those he loves, including the hedgehog, is not answered or is answered with a terrible irony (pp. 29-31).

The hearer joins a large company of Beckett's heroes when the voice of memory identifies him with Christ:

> You first saw the light and cried at the close of the day when in darkness Christ at the ninth hour cried and died. (p. 55)

Such identification means, of course, that the hearer, along with nearly all Beckett's heroes (and all men in general), shares with Christ the experience of being a victim of the Father/God. Like Beckett himself, who claims to have been born on Good Friday,[17] a person needs no reason other than life on the planet Earth to

---

[16] *All That Fall,* in *Krapp's Last Tape and Other Dramatic Pieces* (New York: Grove, 1958), p. 88.

[17] See Pilling's, *Samuel Beckett,* p. 1.

claim identification as a co-sufferer with Christ at the hands of a vengeful God. The question posed by the narrator in *Company* as to whether "God is love. Yes or no?" receives the definite answer of "No" (p. 52).

The formulation of meaning revealed in the structure of *Company,* then, may be stated as follows: the self cannot be created because the story cannot be told because life consists of suffering because God cruelly refuses (for whatever reason – he is absent or malignant) to providentially care for mankind. Thus God can be said to "exist" negatively in the structure of *Company.* Like the disappearing authorical voices, he is located by negative evidence – the absence of a Logos, a Word that would redeem human suffering from meaninglessness and transform it into art. Beckett's quest on the second level – the internalized quest of the artist/self – is, in *Company,* as in the earlier fiction of the seventies, a quest for this missing Word.

CONCLUSION

Drawing back a distance permits a panoramic view of the questions examined in the preceding chapters. If Beckett is neither a philosopher nor a mystic, why are these nouns so often associated with the literature he has produced? In what way is the interweaving of the various religious stances that are apparent in the fiction – Buddhism, Christianity, Manicheanism, skepticism, blasphemy – a pseudo-mysticism? We know Beckett is a poet, and, less dominantly, a critic, even of his own literary achievement. What, if any, is the connection between his perspective and practice of art and the motifs of God and the quest revealed in the powerful substratum of narrative movements that we have discovered and explored in this study? Are these motifs related to his uniqueness as a poet, and if so, how?

The multiple facets of Beckett's professed bewilderment will not allow him to sit in the philosopher's chair. We should perhaps be more exact and follow his lead by agreeing that he is "working with impotence," even with "ignorance."[1] Recent attempts have used these negative qualities to compare Beckett's thought with that of modern language theorists whose dogma and practice serve as a methodology applied to all writing and speaking.[2] Such

---

[1] See Shenker's interview, "Moody Man of Letters," p. 3.

[2] Howard Felperin names Beckett in this sense in the same paragraph with Foucault, Barthes, de Man, and Derrida. See *Beyond Deconstruction: the Uses and Abuses of Literary Theory* (1985; rpt. with corrections, Oxford: Clarendon Press, 1986), p. 43.

attempts deny that Beckett is a philosopher in any older tradition, but at least imply that he shares the philosophical assumptions of this recent movement(s). It is true that Beckett's mode of writing exhibits a questioning and undermining of almost everything Western man has managed to put into language. In fact, it is possible to say that his literature is, in one sense, an exercise in such questioning and undermining. But, as we have explained, Beckett is a believer, in the older, traditional sense, in both language and literature, at least in regard to value. He conceives of literature as unique language which is distinct from ordinary discourse, and searches for a literary language that performs in a fashion superior to, not radically less than, that once so easily assumed to exist.[3] Nearly all critics, however, who align Beckett with modern linguistics/philosophy insist – and rightly so – that he is a poet who structures (or deconstructs) his art on modern theories of language rather than a philosopher *per se.*

What Beckett and his critics (including myself) usually mean by the assertion that he is not a philosopher has to do with traditional philosophy rather than modern literary theory. A traditional philosopher must at least define some consistent notions of ontology, epistemology, and consciousness. Beckett's literary rendering of shifting thought/forms defies such efforts at philosophical definitions. As Livio Dobrez points out, "in Beckett's universe collapse is the one staple ontological factor," characterizing both "personal development" and "human relationships."[4] Beckett's anti-philosophical pose, however, is exaggerated to the point of being radical. He has claimed not to understand Heidegger's and Sartre's ontologies: to speak of "being" is to "speak only of the mess."[5] Disowning even a belief in the "absence of system," Beckett limits himself to the observation that he sees no "trace of any system anywhere."[6] As we have seen, the puzzled heroes have no solutions to the formlessness of their lives but share a common

---

[3] See Oxenhandler's entire article "Seeing and Believing in Dante and Beckett." This critic's premise is that "the belief value of poetry for Beckett" stations him "*within* the great tradition rather than without" (p. 223).

[4] Dobrez, "To End Yet Again: Samuel Beckett's Recent Work," in *Transformations in Modern European Drama,* ed. Ian Donaldson (London and Basingstoke: Macmillan, 1983), p. 132.

[5] See Driver's interview, "Beckett by the Madeleine," p. 23.

[6] See Shenker's interview, "Moody Man of Letters," p. 3.

ontological insecurity. Our conclusions parallel Colin Duckworth's distinctions in this regard: "there is a great deal of difference between ontological insecurity and a basic existential position of ontological insecurity."[7] That is, the heroes's problems are not essentially psychological or psychiatric – they are existential, or, more precisely, metaphysical.

Beckettian insecurity is more epistemological than ontological. The heroes seen obsessed with an intuitive awareness that some undisclosed mystery undergirds the human experience. As Linda Ben-Zvi insists, Beckett does not assert "a total denial of absolutes," finding "negation with any certainty" to be impossible.[8] The difficulty is not only that we do not know but also that we lack any understanding as to why we do not know or how we could ever know. We have no reason, no strategy, and only the degree of hope embodied in Beckett's word "perhaps." Harry Blamires writes of Beckett's "aching yet farcical bewilderment which lacks even the clarity of doubt, the rudder of defined uncertainty":

> Here is a bafflement of the soul –an inner cluelessness prior to that state of organized interrogation at which one can ask: "What is the meaning of life? What is the purpose of anything?" Here is a primitive lostness which allows for nothing so confident as a question . . . . Here one fumbles for the very means of utterance. There is nothing so articulate as doubt.[9]

Indeed, in Beckett' world, even doubt is not articulated clearly, a fact that points to another disqualification of this writer as philosopher. He discounts the very possibility of meaningful philosophical comment. In her remarks on Beckett's agreement with Mauthner's insistence that the "only language should be simple language," Ben-Zvi explains the prejudice of both thinkers against abstract or philosophical speaking or writing. The use of simple words is man's only available means toward the possibility of an escape from the entrapment of language. Such use may aid persons in ordinary communication but proves "negligible" in "considering

---

[7] *Angels of Darkness,* p. 71.

[8] "Samuel Beckett, Fritz Mauthner, and the Limits of Language," p. 192.

[9] Blamires, *The Christian Mind* (Ann Arbor: Servant Books, 1963), p. 10.

the larger problem of the inherent mystery of life."[10] Morot-Sir writes of Beckett's denial of the possibility of either the validity or falseness of "philosophical language." For Beckett, "those who use the philosophical language and pretend that a proposition made in accordance with the rules of that language is capable of being false or true" are deceivers or deceived. The problem can be approached from a Manichean perspective. Metaphysical (or spiritual) truth cannot reside in human (earthly or material) language use. Thus human speech or words cannot function allegorically.[11]

The primary reason that the nouns "philosophy" and "philosopher" are so often associated with the *oeuvre* is that Beckett's writing has what Bradbury Robinson calls the "one characteristic which distinguishes writing that matters from writing that doesn't." This characteristic is an effort "to give some sort of answer to the only philosophical question worth considering: whether or not life has any meaning." Beckett's literature is at the forefront of that which "addresses itself to the question as to whether any of it [life] makes any sense." In reply to the critics who do not delve beneath Beckett's assertion to Harold Hobson that what matters in art is the "shape of ideas," Robinson retorts that, although the "shape . . . matters a great deal . . . it is not only the shape that matters. Even if he pretends otherwise, Mr. Beckett is very concerned with the sense too." Referring to a "grand design" in Beckett's writing, Robinson is sure that "Mr. Beckett is saying something, and obsessively saying it again and again throughout his work."[12] I would add that it is precisely by the medium or strategy of the "shape" or style that Beckett most profoundly says whatever he is saying. And what he is saying has to do with philosophical questions.

Such questions require, if not philosophical answers, at least thought/forms of a metaphysical nature. As we have repeatedly noted, the ultimate goal of the Beckettian quest can he defined only in (prohibited) language related to such thought/forms. Dobrez, in his several articles on Beckett's work, has formulated language

10 "Samuel Beckett, Fritz Mauthner, and the Limits of Language," p. 196.

11 "Samuel Beckett and Cartesian Emblems," pp. 93-94.

12 "A Way with Words: Paradox, Silence, and Samuel Beckett," pp. 255 and 252-53.

suitable for speaking of Beckett's quest. A recent formulation discloses the contradiction between Beckett's abjuring of philosophical language and his persistent use of it. Beckett's writing evokes "the mystery which sustains consciousness and which distinguishes itself from it as 'not I.'" Dobrez contends that there exists "no exaggeration" in saying that "all of Beckett's work has, from the beginning, sought to uncover this one mystery, this unnamable." The protagonists and dramatic characters engage in "a movement to a *deus absconditus* more remote than the 'spirit' which Teresa identified as the essence of 'soul,' in fact, to a point philosophically and experientially indistinguishable from nothing" . . . . Beckett retraces this path from the no-man's-land of his character to an aboriginal ground of being over and over.[13] Although Beckett is no philosopher, his writing is philosophical by virtue of its intense concentration on the nature of life.

Exploring what we may call the mystery of life calls forth the adjective "philosophical," but not necessarily the related adjective, "mystical." Perhaps the joining of Beckett's philosophical orientation with the sheer quantity of religious thought/forms, motifs, and imagery that he uses in the fiction explains critical tendencies to identify him as a mystic. As we have noted, Beckett creates a hero who assumes a consciousness and engages in a quest that exhibit an interweaving of several religious stances – Buddhist, Christian, Manichean, skeptical, and blasphemous. An example of such interweaving is the hero's response to his perception of macrocosmic existence as almost exclusively an experience of suffering. This aspect of consciousness is a combination of Buddhism's concept of the human experience as continuing cycles of unsatisfied desire, of Christianity's universal guilt of sinful mankind before a holy God, and of Manicheanism's definition of material or earthly existence as shaped by an evil deity. The hero's response is also religiously ecumenical. Lacking a Christian rationale for such a perception (no sin as moral accountability, no Christ as Savior, and no possibility of redemption), he attempts a Buddhist detachment from macrocosmic existence by immersing himself in the depths of consciousness. The failure of this withdrawal has Manichean

[13] "To End Yet Again: Samuel Beckett's Recent Work," pp. 144, 139, and 145.

overtones. Because the hero, in his asceticism, cannot escape the intrusion of the outside world, he cannot avoid its evil or suffering either. The Beckettian self is so rooted in macrocosmic experience that it never achieves pure abstraction or spirituality. The continuing perception of suffering and the futility of macrocosmic or microcosmic movement produce a skepticism that leads to Beckett's particular brand of blasphemy.

This obviously over-simplified example of profound states of consciousness and complex quest movements can underscore the inappropriateness of applying the adjective "mystical" to Beckett's hero. We cannot refer to the skepticism just described as a "skepticism of faith." The protagonist has not reasoned logically from or through various religious faiths or stances of belief. He has no interest in the religious labeling of strands composing his thought patterns. He is not non-religious, but irreligious, in the deepest sense. No religious explanations or consolations alleviate his acute experiential awareness of the strangeness and misery of life. Furthermore, the question as to whether Beckett has intentionally or inadvertently woven these (and other) strands together into this aspect of the hero's consciousness cannot be answered by exploring the literature. In addition, as my paradigms have demonstrated, Beckettian man seeks existential fulfillment and metaphysical knowledge, not union with any God. Most importantly, the purpose of the protagonist's inward descent is not spiritual or mystical, but aesthetic. As artist/self, he is attempting to create from human experience (or memories of this experience) and language a story that will authentically embody the undiscoverable and inexpressible mystery of being and life.

As a critic and practitioner of art, Beckett expresses certain ideas that, often ironically, attach a dimension of pseudo-mysticism to the artist's task. As art theorist, he is clearly in the European tradition of Schopenhauer and Proust. He is not, however, defined by or limited to this tradition. At the present time, neither he nor his critics have formulated a complete development of his unique theory.[14] Our purpose here is simply to isolate the elements in his comments and practice concerning art that can illuminate the

[14] For concise enlightenment on this matter, see the sections on Beckett as critic in Harvey's *Samuel Beckett: Poet and Critic;* Pilling's *Samuel Beckett,* pp. 13-24; and Ruby Cohn's Foreword to *Disjecta,* pp. 11-15.

question of God as it appears in the writings. Whether referring to other writers and painters, commenting on his own work, or creating the artist/selves who people his fictional world, Beckett seems more concerned with a quality we can call "truth" than with anything else. In fact, whatever words we use to signify this quality – a severe honesty, artistic integrity, a staunch determination not to falsify things as they are (or as he perceives them to be) – it has become the *penumbra* surrounding the writer Beckett and his work. Beckett's friend, the Israeli painter Avigdor Arikha, when hard pressed early in 1987 by the arts media to say something about Beckett, to offer some suggestion as to what the man and his writing "represent," refers to Beckett's obsession with "truth":

> All he wants is to tell the truth. That might be crazy in the last quarter of the 20th century, but truth is timeless . . . . I do not exaggerate when I say that is what his writing is all about. He questions everything. His writing is a perpetual questioning of what is true.

What Beckett is "doing," according to Arikha, is "being on the edge of being."[15]

On such an "edge," Beckett continues to reiterate the particular characteristics that he associates with "true" or authentic art. One reason that words such as "ignorance," "disintegration," "failure," "impotence," and "non-expressionism" have become so tired and vague as applied to the canon is that Beckett himself has used them repeatedly, and we, as readers and critics, have not comprehended fully what he intends by their use. Terminology such as "interrogation," "need," "rejection of a false clarity," and "inevitable unveiling" also occurs in his critical vocabulary. Whatever the nuances of these terms, they coincide with one of Beckett's less enigmatic statements concerning an artist he admires, the painter Jack Yeats, of whom he writes, "He is with the great of our time . . . because

[15] See Arikha's interview with art critic Michael Dobbs entitled "Waiting for Author of 'Waiting for Godot,'" in "arts and leisure," *The Mexico City News,* 20 January 1987, p. 18.

he brings light, as only the great dare to bring light, to the issueless predicament of existence."[16]

Presumably, such great art occurs – on the rare occasions when it does appear – as the creation of someone who recognizes and practices artistic integrity. Beckett applies this term to himself in the interview with John Gruen, saying that Joyce has had a "moral effect" on his work – "he made me realize artistic integrity."[17] Such integrity makes certain demands on an artist. He must recognize and acknowledge what Beckett perceives as the chaos of the human experience, he must refuse to disassociate this condition of life from his art, and he must not allow a deceptive artful form to cover or swallow up the chaotic formlessness of reality. Therefore, the artist must be committed to discovering the aesthetic form that can "accommodate" (Beckett's word) this chaos. For Beckett, the task is difficult, but not impossible. "Being has a form. Someone will find it someday. Perhaps I won't but someone will. It is a form that has been abandoned, left behind, a proxy in its place."[18]

To conceptualize the task of the artist as the discovery of this kind of artistic form is one of the easiest and most logical ways of thinking about truth in regard to Beckett's theories of art. But this conceptualization is not all that is present in Beckett's linking of art with truth. If it were, both Beckett and his fictional artist/selves would be classified as successful artists. In spite of the language of futurity and possibility that Beckett uses in describing this task of discovery, neither he nor his fabricated surrogates fail to produce art that "accommodates the chaos" of life. Nor does the form of Beckettian art – offered directly by Beckett himself or indirectly as the stories of the artist/heroes – falsely assimilate the chaos or "mess" into a deceptive order. Beckett's fiction is brilliantly stylized, but it displays an absence of any arrangement assuming cause/effect to be operating in human affairs. His own fiction and the stories of the artist/selves meet this particular qualification. What they do not – and cannot – achieve is an embodiment of any rationale, any understanding, any acceptance of the chaos.

This formulation of Beckett's artistic theory helps to explain the profundity and pervasiveness of the quest paradigms we have

16 "MacGreevy on Yeats," in *Disjecta,* p. 97.
17 "Samuel Beckett Talks About Beckett," p. 210.
18 Harvey, *Samuel Beckett: Poet and Critic,* p. 249.

described. And the disclosure of the paradigms leads to the formulation. The argument, however, is not circular, but evident, both in the literature and in Beckett's aesthetic, theoretical comment. The embodied clarity or truth is the Logos or Word that would inform the story, and remains forever beyond reach. No matter how deeply inward toward the core of the self the artist/self descends, no matter how many fictional selves or events he fabricates, and no matter how many words he contaminates the silence with, he never finds this clear or true Word. But its discovery is the goal of the microcosmic quest. Beckett refers to this purpose in writing of literary theory in a letter to Axel Kaun:

> It is indeed becoming more and more difficult, even senseless, for me to write an official English. And more and more my own language appears to me like a veil that must be torn apart in order to get at the things (or the Nothingness) behind it . . . . To bore one hole after another in it, until what lurks behind it – be it something or nothing – begins to seep through; I cannot imagine a higher goal for a writer today.[19]

Beckett's observation here has to do with rhetoric: he is insisting on a language that does not falsify the nothingness of life. But the reference is to more than rhetoric. Just as in the ancient world, rhetoric was a means to an end, and not an end in itself, so Beckett's serious and positive tone suggests a sense of something lurking behind the textuality of the rhetoric. Besides, if one genuinely wished to reach an aesthetic nothingness, to actually produce silence, he could – if he were Beckett – quit writing or publish blank pages of text. That Beckett continues to use words implies an existential/metaphysical sense to his theoretical observation.

The determination not to falsify the nature of life in art, and the desire to discover the truth embodied in a metaphysical Silence beyond words through the medium of art, combine into the essence of Beckett's artistic theory. Such aesthetic effort involves blood, sweat, and tears. In the piece of criticism entitled *Les Deux*

---

[19] See Martin Esslin's English translation of Beckett's German letter in *Disjecta*, pp. 171-72.

Besoins, Beckett writes of an urgency in the practice of art having to do with *rigueur, besoin,* the *chaos de vouloir voir,* the *question,* and the *procès créateur.* The work of art is *la série de questions pures.*[20] Whatever profundity underlies the text of this piece, Beckett is insisting on recognition and need, acknowledgement and quest. In her recent book on Emily Dickinson, *Lady in the Dark,* Cynthia Griffin Wolff writes of the attachment and obsession Dickinson exhibits in her interaction with language. Wolff suggests that Dickinson expects words to perform greater feats (existential and metaphysical) for her than the ordinary writer would expect. In reviewing Wolff's book, Christopher Benfry quotes Wolff as saying that Dickinson "was determined to construe writing as an heroic undertaking." Benfry defines Wolff's use of this language as meaning "a willingness to engage in a private wrestling match with God."[21] Perhaps we can say something of the sort of Beckett's expectations of art.

In Beckett's literature, this artistic expectation appears as a pensum to tell, not a false, but a true story. Furthermore, the impossible efforts to fulfill the pensum must be framed in art that truly represents the situation of this demand. Dobrez comments on this pensum as it appears in Beckett's dramas *That Time* and *Not I*:

> Seemingly, it is torment like that of the Ancient Mariner: the protagonist is required, by an obscure authority, to say something, to tell a story . . . . Obviously the punishment is eternal, just as the correct story is always out of reach.[22]

We have examined the theme of this pensum, or supreme artistic effort, in both lengthy and brief fictional works, for instance, in *The Unnamable* and *As the Story Was Told.*

An exploration of Beckett's artistic theory reveals both similarity to and distinction from the aesthetic ideas of Schopenhauer and Proust. We cannot, at this time reiterate this matter fully,[23] but

---

[20] *Les Deux Besoins,* in *Disjecta,* pp. 55-57.

[21] See Benfry's review of Wolff's *Lady in the Dark* (New York: Knopf, 1987), in *The New York Review of Books,* March 26, 1987, p. 47.

[22] "To End Yet Again: Samuel Beckett's Recent Work," p. 142.

[23] For comparisons of Beckett's aesthetic with that of Schopenhauer and Proust, see K. and A. Hamilton's *Condemned to Life,* pp. 47-49, 68-69, 105, and 213-14. See also Pilling's *Samuel Beckett,* pp. 14-16 and 126-27. Beckett's *Proust* is

will comment on it in regard to Beckett's artistic quest for truth. All three writers conceive of macrocosmic life as primarily an experience of suffering or of existential insignificance, and view an involvement with art as the only viable strategy for interacting with this experience. For Schopenhauer, immersion in art, whether for purposes of creation or contemplation, is the only possibility of escaping the macrocosmic hell of the "world as will." By such immersion, a person can find not only temporary respite from pain but also the fulfillment of glimpsing Schopenhauer's Idea or Thing-in-Itself. This vision of true reality (in opposition to the false, macrocosmic illusion of sensory experience) affords the only good in life, a good that is finally attainable solely by an absolute detachment from temporal life. Since Schopenhauer also discounts metaphysics and its language, the exact nature of the experience of art becomes problematical. The benefits of art are a part of his understanding of suffering as somehow purifying (aesthetically, not in the Christian sense) the human self. Beckett balks at any possibility of complete detachment from the world of the senses, nor does he assign any beneficial purpose to suffering. And, for Beckett, withdrawal into the microcosm intensifies existential pain. The general idea that truth or reality beckons man away from the ordinary world and into the depths of consciousness and an involvement with art are probably Schopenhauer's primary contributions to Beckett's artistic quest for truth.

Proust's aesthetic ideas are less philosophical than those of Schopenhauer. We are familiar with the French writer's condemnation of the ordinary dullness of habit and voluntary memory, and of man's illusory notions of reality residing in the apparent cause/effect and time sequences of macrocosmic existence. Proust's salvation is almost purely aesthetic. Only the unexpected bestowal of involuntary memory makes possible the transformation of the mundane flux of ordinary existence into the frozen and beautiful reality of art. The seizure of involuntary memory is an event of suffering, but this experience is desired, since the suffering is one with the salvation.

---

an expression of Beckett's interaction with the aesthetics of both the German and French writers.

Once again, truth (for Proust, the beauty and reality of art) beckons the artist into the sacred realm of the imagination. Schopenhauer conceives of descent into this realm as a transcendence of – or a moving beyond – the death-grip of the will, while Proust's definition is of something granted or bestowed gratuitously. Beckett's ideas are closer to those of Proust: his determinism is just as operative in the microcosm as in the macrocosm, where whatever good might be realized would have to be bestowed. For Beckett, however, macrocosmic existence is painful reality, not Proust's pipe-dream of habit and memory. And, while Beckett and Proust associate suffering with the artistic quest, for Beckett, the suffering does not result in salvation. Perhaps the reason is that Beckett's ideas of the quest for truth have a metaphysical dimension that Proust's existential aesthetics lacks. An important commonality for all three writers is the concept that withdrawal from the macrocosm, negation of sensory activity, commitment to the artistic experience, and suffering form the bedrock of the artist's *via dolorosa* toward whatever is perceived as truth.

At this point, we must risk redundancy by a reminder that Beckett's artistic rendering is a story of a quest for truth. The macrocosmic search for existential fulfillment (the meeting of the five needs) narrows itself to the journey toward the essence of Beckett's zero symbol, which, in turn, intensifies into the microcosmic descent into the realm of the imagination. Whatever the immediate object of any given stage in the developments of this narrative movement, the ultimate goal can be defined as a search for truth. The hero as character wants to find the person, place, or system where he truly belongs. He desires knowledge of who he truly is, in regard to body and spirit. As Beckett's settings shift into various twilight zones, the goal of the search objectifies and reduces itself to the Beckettian zero – an enigmatic cipher symbolizing a true understanding of the mystery of life. Correspondingly, the hero-become-artist descends toward the zero or core of consciousness in order to tell a story. As we have realized by now, this literary effort becomes the ultimate quest for truth. The story told cannot be just any tale; it must be *the true story* – art which embodies clarity and truth concerning the human experience. The puzzlement and inadequacy of the hero, the limitations of language, and the suffering of experience presuppose failure. But were this story told, truth as an ultimate absolute would be discovered.

If the "crime" of Beckett's man is that he has been born, the "crime" of Beckett's deity is that this unlocking of the riddle of life remains an urgent but apparently impossible feat.

We can say, then, that Beckett's aesthetic theory implies a quest for truth on the part of the artist, and his fiction relates a quest for truth by the hero. Bradbury Robinson draws a third circle of involvement with truth around these two circles of the artist as creator and the fictional character as quester. That circle is of Beckett himself as a unique poet:

> The . . . reason I would offer for suggesting that Mr. Beckett is important is that he is the only writer in this position to have had the courage and honesty to see that, if nothing matters, then the saying of this doesn't matter either . . . . The unique fact about Mr. Beckett is that he includes himself and his work in his own condemnation. This incredible and implacable honesty I find totally admirable, even ennobling.[24]

Beckett's artistic integrity involves all that he has said concerning the "failure" of his own art. A fourth circle of truth is Beckett's achieved engagement of the reader in the question of truth. Lawrence E. Harvey writes of Beckett's "exacerbating the reader's experience of need,"[25] and Bradbury Robinson considers the "effect on the mind and emotions [of Beckett's writings] unparalleled."[26]

Robinson's opinion leads to a consideration of the final matter, that is, of the relation of Beckett's uniqueness as a poet to the questions of God and the quest as they are raised in the fiction. Observations by Morot-Sir from two separate articles are relevant. This critic defines Beckett, in whatever genre he appears, as "fundamentally a poet who looks for the unique and rare meeting where words become at the same time music, meaning, and reference." (Is it possible to say that poetry *is* "music, meaning, and reference"?) Morot-Sir also writes of Beckett's "anguishing quest for an impossible *linguistic sincerity*," and notes that, as a poet, Beckett "finds himself at the heart of the most difficult questions

[24] "A Way with Words: Paradox, Silence, and Samuel Beckett," p. 258.
[25] *Samuel Beckett: Poet and Critic*, p. 412.
[26] "A Way with Words: Paradox, Silence, and Samuel Beckett," p. 258.

of modern philosophy."[27] An earlier insight of this critic pinpoints the matters at hand:

> Beckett's poems, novels and plays have more timeless qualities than have yet been granted them. I feel even that these works are destined to stand as they are, in their uniqueness and integrity, beyond the literary fashions and trends of their day . . . .[28]

Lawrence Harvey uses the term "evocative density" to describe Beckett's uniqueness as a poet, and elaborates as follows:

> To an extraordinary degree, he has the talent for giving to commonplace (and to not so commonplace) situations overtones that evoke man's conditon and destiny. Or to put it in terms of vision rather than making, he is able to see in nature, in people, in situations and events the signs of a single destiny. Such is the poet's gift.[29]

These critics are referring to the mythopoeic nature of Beckett's writings. As commonly used, this adjective has been employed to describe writers who recognize the non-existence of a viable myth in their milieu to undergird and order their creative efforts. In response, such mythopoeic authors deliberately devise their own mythic, alternate structures to embody their works. The term carries a positive connotation, in that such a writer assumes the role of a poet/prophet and expresses whatever universal truth(s) he sees as central in the present experience of his people or age. In a sense, then, we can say that mythopoeic writers create myths, although such modern myths are more limited and esoteric than widely-held myths of the past.

Nevertheless, certain mythopoeic literary constructions of the late eighteenth, nineteenth, and twentieth centuries can be described by language Michael Grant uses in his "Foreword" to discuss Graeco-Roman myths. Such mythic material, "in receptive conditions," can "generate and throw off potent, almost violent

---

[27] See pp. 224 and 225 of "Grammatical Insincerity and Samuel Beckett's Non-Expressionism." The difficult philosophical questions dealt with in this article are those of "Space, of the Self, of Time."

[28] "Samuel Beckett and Cartesian Emblems," p. 81.

[29] *Samuel Beckett: Poet and Critic,* p. 391.

flashes of inextinguishable, universal truths." This kind of truth can "impinge, sometimes with ungovernable force, upon the mind and feelings, and illuminate aspects of our human condition." Only the mythopoeic artist can offer such insight: "This particular brand of enlightenment is difficult or impossible to grasp by more logical and rational means, and would elude non-mythical presentation." Grant contends that the "images of myth, once they have stirred our perceptions, precipitate them into a new, unforeseen dimension outside time."[30] Blake, Arnold, Yeats, Joyce, and Hölderlin are mythopoeic writers whose literature can be described by such language as that of Grant. Each has achieved a more or less profound embodiment of the experience of a particular age in a mythopoeic *oeuvre.*[31]

Beckett is both similar to and different from these writers. The Beckettian quest – as defined in this study – and the often-acknowledged effect of Beckett's literature on the reader are evidences of his similarity. An examination of differences reveals Beckett to be unique in achieving a profound artistic rendering of man toward the end of the twentieth century. This is not to say that Beckett does not portray man in all ages and in all conditions. Like all genuinely mythic portrayals of the human condition, Beckett's depiction holds the past, embraces and emphasizes the present, and points to the future, however uncertainly. Paradoxically, the very qualities that characterize Beckett as mythopoeic also differentiate him from the other writers I have placed in this category. In fact, these distinctive qualities make problematical, in one sense, the application of the adjective to Beckett's writings. To contemplate either ancient or modern mythic literature is to entertain ideas that are positive, explanatory – at least to the extent of exploring and suggesting answers – and variously, although repetitiously, structured. A moment's reflection reminds us that Beckett's writings are negative, fabricated of questions with no answers, and contained in almost monotonously repeated structures.

A basic negativity of Beckett's canon is its assumed futility of language. How can literature mythically embody the spirit of an age if it lacks a functional language? All might be well if Beckett

---

30 "Foreword" to *Myths of the Greeks and Romans*, pp. xviii-xix.

31 For justification of the inclusion of Arnold in this list, see J. Hillis Miller's *The Disappearance of God*, pp. 262-63.

perceived this meaninglessness as normative and desirable, but, as we have seen, such is not the case. What does occur is that the Beckettian lament for a Logos that transcends meaninglessness, and perhaps even silence, becomes a mythopoeic essential of his art. The same can be said of the questioning underlying the actions and speech of all the heroes. The exploratory setting forth of questions common to all mythical literature pervades Beckett's writings, but this pervasion is implicit rather than explicit. On the surface of the text, no hero does more than perceive or experience, and then recite his perception of experience, or experience of perception. Explanations of what is happening become so ironic that we can say there is an absence of any offering of even tentative answers throughout the canon. Finally, the paradigms of movement we have found repeated in work after work, and the closed-in, "hodological" space described by Morot-Sir,[32] seem the opposite of the fanciful and various structures ordinarily associated with mythical writings.

The placing of negativity, questioning, and circular structural movement against the reader's expectations of the performance of such literature constitutes Beckett's uniqueness as the foremost mythopoeic writer of his day. Heidegger hopes and predicts that poetry such as that of Hölderlin might gradually provide answers to man's technological dilemma, might disclose a god who can save us. But Beckett halts with the language (or, for him, non-language) of myth shaped into an art (or the failure of art) that refuses to become more than an embodiment of repeatedly recited questions and laments, of reiterated emptiness and need. By such deliberate artistic creation, Beckett becomes a unique poet, a myth-maker, a prophet/seer of his age.

To perceive of Beckett as such a poet is to conceptualize him as the author of his literary works. Iain Wright cites Beckett's surrogate author – the Unnamable – as an "empty site traversed by discourses."[33] Like all authors, Beckett is not a non-contradictory, single-voiced, self-created authorial self. In fact, the closer to pure myth a body or a single work of literature moves, the more a "socially generative or productive power seems to operate above or

---

[32] See "Grammatical Insincerity and Samuel Beckett's Non-Expressionism," pp. 227-28.

[33] "'What matter who's speaking,'" p. 70.

beyond or through the individual author.[34] But Beckett's works are mythopoeic, not pure myth, and cannot be adequately understood apart from a recognition of what Wright correctly calls Beckett's "*authorial* discourse." This discourse, although it "nowhere speaks in the text," encloses the various and multiple textual discourses and "continually asks us to *frame*" them, and "to construct a mechanism for situating . . . them."[35]

This entire study has proceeded from my perspective and understanding of this authorial discourse. Within the amplitude of its large boundaries we have considered the matters of the quest and of God. In fact, only within this wide area can such matters be contemplated. Although we have been exploring the idea(s) of God as he inhabits the consciousness of the various literary heroes, we cannot adequately account for the Beckettian mythos of God by citing the language fabricating this consciousness as its sole source. This fictional habitation of perceptions about God is created, and, as such, arises from some ground other than itself. It has as source not only the textual consciousness of the heroes and the authorial framing of Beckett's thought, but also the collective human consciousness of actual experience as it waits in its poverty toward the close of the twentieth century. Beckett's most mythical dramatic heroes embody this waiting:

Estragon: I can't go on like this.
Vladimir: That's what you think.
Estragon: If we parted? That might be better for us.
Vladimir: We'll hang ourselves to-morrow. *(Pause.)* Unless Godot comes.
Estragon: And if he comes?
Vladimir: We'll be saved.

---

34 Felperin, *Beyond Deconstruction,* pp. 29-30.
35 "'What matter who's speaking,'" p. 72.

CLASSIFIED BIBLIOGRAPHIC LISTING

WRITINGS BY BECKETT EXAMINED AT LENGTH

Assumption. Transition, Nos. 16 and 17 (1929), pp. 268-71.

As the Story Was Told. MS 1396/4/14. Beckett Archive of the University of Reading. Reading, England.

Company. New York: Grove, 1980.

How It Is. New York: Grove, 1964.

La Falaise. MS 1396/4/40. Beckett Archive of the University of Reading. Reading, England.

More Pricks than Kicks. New York: Grove, 1972.

Murphy. New York: Grove, 1957.

Sounds and *Still 3.* In *Essays in Criticism,* 28 (1978), 155-57.

Still. In *Fizzles.* New York: Grove, 1976, pp. 47-51.

Three Novels: Molloy, Malone Dies, the Unnamable. New York: Grove, 1965.

Watt. New York: Grove, 1959.

ADDITIONAL WRITINGS BY BECKETT REFERRED TO IN THE TEXT

All Strange Away. London: John Calder, 1979.

All That Fall. In *Krapp's Last Tape and Other Dramatic Pieces.* New York: Grove, 1958, pp. 29-91.

"Dante . . . Bruno . Vico . . Joyce." In *I Can't Go On, I'll Go On: A Selection from Samuel Beckett's Work.* Ed. and introd., Richard W. Seaver. New York: Grove, 1976, pp. 105-26.

"Dortmunder." In *Echo's Bones and Other Precipitates.* Paris: Europa, 1935; rpt. in *Collected Poems in English and French: Samuel Beckett.* London: John Calder, 1977, p. 16.

Dream of Fair to Middling Women. Unpublished. MS in Beckett Collection, Baker Memorial Library, Dartmouth College, Hanover, N. H. Excerpts in *Disjecta: Miscellaneous Writings and a Dramatic Fragment by Samuel Beckett.* Ed. Ruby Cohn. London: John Calder, 1983, pp. 43-50.

Embers. In *Krapp's Last Tape and Other Dramatic Pieces,* pp. 93-121.

Endgame. New York: Grove, 1958.

Enough. In *First Love and Other Shorts.* New York: Grove, 1974, pp. 51-60.

"Fizzle 6." In *Fizzles,* pp. 43-44.

Footfalls. In *Ends and Odds: Eight New Dramatic Pieces.* New York: Grove, 1974, pp. 38-49.
For to End Yet Again. In *Fizzles,* pp. 55-61.
From an Abandoned Work. In *First Love and Other Shorts,* pp. 37-49.
"German Letter of 1937." In *Disjecta,* pp. 170-173.
Happy Days. New York: Grove, 1961.
Ill Seen Ill Said. New York: Grove, 1981.
Imagination Dead Imagine. In *First Love and Other Shorts,* pp. 61-66.
Krapp's Last Tape. In *Krapp's Last Tape and Other Dramatic Pieces,* pp. 7-28.
"Les Deux Besoins." In *Disjecta,* pp. 55-57.
Lessness. London: Calder and Boyars, 1970.
"MacGreevy on Yeats." In *Disjecta,* pp. 95-97.
Mercier and Camier. New York: Grove, 1974.
"On Murphy (to McGreevy)." In *Disjecta,* p. 102.
"Papini's Dante." *The Bookman,* Christmas Issue, 87 (1934), 14.
Ping. In *First Love and Other Shorts,* pp. 67-72.
[Rev. of] *Poems,* by Rainer Maria Rilke. *The Criterion,* 13 (1934), 705-07.
"Poetry is Vertical." [Beckett, et al.] *transition,* No. 21 (1932), pp. 148-49.
Proust and Three Dialogues with Georges Duthuit. London: Calder and Boyars, 1965.
Stories and Texts for Nothing. New York: Grove, 1976.
The Lost Ones. New York: Grove, 1972.
Waiting for Godot. New York: Grove, 1954.
Whoroscope. Paris: Hours Press, 1930.
Worstward Ho. New York: Grove, 1983.

WRITINGS OF OTHER LITERARY FIGURES, THEOLOGIANS, AND PHILOSOPHERS

Auden, W. H. "In Memory of W. B. Yeats." In *Selected Poetry of W. H. Auden.* 2nd ed. New York: Random House, 1970, pp. 52-54.
Augustine. *The Confessions of St. Augustine.* Trans. F. J. Sheed. 1943. rpt. New York: Sheed and Ward, 1965.
Blamires, Harry. *The Christian Mind.* Ann Arbor: Servant Books, 1963.
Camus, Albert. *The Myth of Sisyphus and Other Essays.* Trans. Justine O'Brien. New York: Knopf, 1955. Rpt. Vintage Books, 1960.
Dante. *The Paradiso.* New York: New American Library, 1970.
Eliot, T. S. "Choruses from 'The Rock,' X." In *The Complete Poems and Plays, 1909-1950.* New York: Harcourt, Brace and World, 1971, pp. 112-14.
———. *Selected Essays, New Edition.* New York: Harcourt, Brace, 1950.
Heidegger, Martin. *Basic Writings.* Ed. D. F. Krell. London: Routledge, 1978.
———. "Only a God Can Save Us." Trans. Maria P. Alter and John D. Caputo. *Philosophy Today,* 20 (1976), 267-84. Rpt. from *Der Spiegel,* 31 May 1976, No. 23, pp. 193 ff.
Housman, A. E. *The Collected Poems of A. E. Housman.* New York: Holt, Rinehart, and Winston, 1965.
Joyce, James. *A Portrait of the Artist as a Young Man.* 1976; rpt. New York: Viking, 1964.
———. *Ulyssess.* 1914; New York: Vintage Books, 1961.
Jung, C. G. *Aion: Researches into the Phenomenology of the Self.* 2nd ed. Trans. R. F. C. Hull. Bollinger ser. XX. Princeton: Princeton Univ. Press, 1959.
Kaiser, Walter C., Jr. *Toward an Old Testament Theology.* Grand Rapids: Zondervan, 1978.
Küng, Hans. *On Being a Christian.* Trans. Edward Quinn. Garden City, N. Y.: Doubleday, 1974.

Lewis, C. S. *A Grief Observed.* New York: Seabury Press, 1963.
———. *That Hideous Strength: A Modern Fairy-Tale for Grown-ups.* London: John Lane the Bodley Head, Ltd., 1945.
MacQuarrie, John. *Studies in Christian Existentialism.* London: SCM Press, Ltd., 1966.
Pascal, Blaise. *Pensées; The Provincial Letters.* New York: Random House, 1941.
Payne, J. Barton. *The Theology of the Older Testament.* Grand Rapids: Zondervan, 1962.
Sartre, Jean-Paul, and Benny Levy. "The Last Words of Jean-Paul Sartre." Interview. *Le Nouvel Observateur,* 10, 17, and 24 March 1980. I have been unable to locate publishing information for the English translation of this interview.
Thielicke, Helmut. *The Hidden Question of God.* Trans. and ed. Geoffrey W. Bromiley. Grand Rapids: Eerdmans, 1977.
Vahanian, Gabriel. *The Death of God: the Culture of Our Post-Christian Era.* New York: George Braziller, 1950.
———. "The Empty Cradle." *Theology Today,* 13 (1957), 521-26.
Wenham, John W. *The Goodness of God.* Downers Grove, Ill.: Intervarsity Press, 1974.

General Writings and Reference Works

"Babel." Sample Article from *Dictionary of Biblical Tradition.* In *Christianity and Literature,* 33 (1984), 59-60.
Borowitz, Eugene B. *A Layman's Introduction to Religious Existentialism.* Philadelphia: Westminster Press, 1966.
Cirlot, J. E. *A Dictionary of Symbols.* Trans. Jack Sage. 2nd ed. 1971; rpt. New York: Vail-Ballou Press, 1983.
Grant, Michael. *Myths of the Greeks and Romans.* N. d.; rpt. New York: New American Library, 1962.
Handbook to the History of Christianity. Ed. Tim Dowley, et al. Herts, England: Lion, 1977; rpt. Grand Rapids, Michigan: Eerdmans, 1977.
A Handbook to Literature. Ed. C. Hugh Holman. 3rd ed. Based on the original, William Flint Thrall and Addison Hibbard. Indianapolis: Bobs-Merrill, 1972.
McCasland, S. Vernon, et al. *Religions of the World.* New York: Random House, 1969.
The New International Dictionary of the Christian Church. Ed. J. D. Douglass, et al. Grand Rapids: Zondervan, 1974.
The World in Literature. Ed. Robert Warnock and George K. Anderson. Chicago: Scott, Foresman, 1959.
Zondervan Pictorial Bible Dictionary. Ed. Merrill C. Tenney. Grand Rapids: Zondervan, 1964.

Critical Writings and Interviews

Abbott, H. Porter. "Letters to the Self: The Cloistered Writer in Nonretrospective Fiction." *PMLA,* 95 (1980), 23-41.
———. "The Harpooned Notebook: *Malone Dies* and the Conventions of Intercalated Narrative." In *Samuel Beckett: Humanistic Perspectives.* Ed. Morris Beja, et al. Columbus: Ohio State Univ. Press, 1983, pp. 71-79.
Anders, Günther. "Being Without Time: On Beckett's Play *Waiting for Godot.*" In *Samuel Beckett: A Collection of Critical Essays.* Ed. Martin Esslin. Englewood Cliffs, N. J.: Prentice-Hall, 1965, pp. 140-51.

Bair, Deirdre. *Samuel Beckett: A Biography.* New York and London: Harcourt, Brace, Jovanovich, 1978.

Bajomee, Danielle. "Beckett devant Dieu." *Les Lettres Romanes,* 25 (1971), 350-57.

Baldass, Ludwig Von. *Hieronymus Bosch.* New York: Henry N. Abrams, 1960.

Barge, Laura. " 'Coloured Images' in the 'Black Dark': Samuel Beckett's Later Fiction." *PMLA,* 95 (1977), 273-84.

———. "Life and Death in Beckett's Four Stories." *The South Atlantic Quarterly,* 76 (1977), 332-47.

———. "Light in a Dark Place." *Christianity Today* (1973), 345-48.

———. "Forum." *PMLA,* 92 (1977), 1006-008.

———. "The Empty Heaven of Samuel Beckett." *Cithara: Essays in the Judaeo-Christian Tradition,* 15 (1976), 3-19.

Barjon, Louis. "Le Dieu de Beckett." *Etudes,* 322 (1965), 650-62.

Benfry, Christopher. Rev. of *Lady in the Dark,* by Cynthia Griffin Wolff. *New York Review of Books,* 26 March 1987, pp. 46-49.

Ben-Zvi, Linda. "Samuel Beckett, Fritz Mauthner, and the Limits of Language." *PMLA,* 95 (1980), 183-200.

Bersani, Leo. *Balzac to Beckett: Center and Circumference in French Fiction.* New York: Oxford Univ. Press, 1970.

Bové, Paul A. "The Image of the Creator in Beckett's Postmodern Writing." *Philosophy and Literature,* 4 (1980), 47-65.

Brater, Enoch. "Still/Beckett: The Essential and the Incidental." *Journal of Modern Literature,* 6 (1977), 3-16.

———. "The *Company* Beckett Keeps, or One Fabulist's Decay of Lying." Beckett and the Art of Allusion I. First Annual Symposium in the Humanities. *Samuel Beckett: Humanistic Perspectives.* Columbus: Ohio State Univ., 9 May 1981, pp. 1-10.

Brennecke, Ernest, Jr. *Thomas Hardy's Universe: A Study of a Poet's Mind.* Boston: Small, Maynard, 1924.

Burke, Kenneth. *The Rhetoric of Religion: Studies in Logology.* Boston: Beacon Press, 1961.

Butler, Lance St. John. *Samuel Beckett and the Meaning of Being: A Study in Ontological Parable.* London: Macmillan, 1984.

Büttner, Gottfried. *Samuel Beckett's Novel* Watt. Trans. Joseph P. Dolan. Philadelphia: Univ. of Pennsylvania Press, 1984.

Chalker, John. "The Satiric Shape of *Watt.*" In *Beckett the Shape Changer.* Ed. Katherine Worth. London and Boston: Routledge and Kegan Paul, 1975, pp. 19-37.

Clurman, Harold. *The Divine Pastime; Theatre Essays.* New York: Macmillan, 1974.

Coe, Richard N. "God and Samuel Beckett." *Meanjin,* 24 (1965), 66-85. Rpt. in *Twentieth Century Interpretations of* Molloy, Malone Dies, The Unnamable: *A Collection of Critical Essays.* Ed. J. D. O'Hara. Englewood Cliffs, N. J.: Prentice-Hall, 1970, pp. 91-113.

———. *Samuel Beckett.* New York: Grove, 1964.

Cohn, Ruby. *Back to Beckett.* Princeton, N. J.: Princeton Univ. Press, 1973.

Foreword. In *Disjecta,* pp. 7-16.

———. "Outward Bound Soliloquies." *Journal of Modern Literature,* 6 (1977), 17-38.

———. "Philosophical Fragments in the Works of Samuel Beckett." *Criticism,* 6 (1964), 33-43. Rpt. in *Samuel Beckett: A Collection of Critical Essays,* pp. 169-77.

———. "Preliminary Observations." *Perspective,* 11 (1959), 119-31.

———. *The Comic Gamut.* New Brunswick, N. J.: Rutgers Univ. Press, 1962.

Combs, Eugene. "Impotence and Ignorance: A Parody of Prerogatives in Samuel Beckett." *Studies in Religion/Sciences Religieuses,* 2 (1972), 114-30.

Coonin, Stuart Lee. "Samuel Beckett: The Eastern Influence." Diss. Michigan State Univ., 1974.

Culler, Jonathan. *Structuralist Poetics: Structuralism, Linguistics, and the Study of Literature.* Ithaca: Cornell Univ. Press, and London: Routledge and Kegan Paul, 1975.

Cousineau, Thomas J. "Descartes, Lacan, and *Murphy.*" *College Literature,* 11 (1984), 223-32.

———. " 'Watt': Language as Interdiction and Consolation." *Journal of Beckett Studies,* No. 4 (1979), pp. 1-13.

Danto, Arthur C. *Jean-Paul Sartre.* Modern Masters Series. Ed. Frank Kermode. New York: Viking, 1975.

Dearlove, Judith E. *Accommodating the Chaos: Samuel Beckett's Nonrelational Art.* Durham, N. C.: Duke Univ. Press, 1982.

———. "Allusion to Archetype." Beckett and the Art of Allusion II. First Annual Symposium in the Humanities. *Samuel Beckett: Humanistic Perspectives,* pp. 1-17.

———. "The Voice and its Words: *How It Is* in Beckett's Canon." *Journal of Beckett Studies,* No. 3 (1978), pp. 56-75.

Di Pierro, John C. *Structures in Beckett's* Watt. York, S. C.: French Literature Publications, 1981.

Dobbs, Michael. "Waiting for Author of 'Waiting for Godot.' " *The Mexico City News,* 20 January 1987, "arts and leisure," p. 18.

Dobrez, Livio. "Beckett and Heidegger: Existence, Being, and Nothingness." *Southern Review: An Australian Journal of Literary Studies,* 7 (1974), 140-53.

———. "Beckett, Sartre and Camus: The Darkness and the Light." *Southern Review: An Australian Journal of Literary Studies,* 71 (1974), 51-63.

———. "Samuel Beckett's Irreducible." *Southern Review: An Australian Journal of Literary Studies,* 6 (1973), 205-22.

———. "To End Yet Again: Samuel Beckett's Recent Work." In *Transformations in Modern European Drama.* Ed. Ian Donaldson. London and Basingstoke: Macmillan, 1983, pp. 130-46.

Driver, Tom F. "Beckett by the Madeleine." *Columbia Univ. Forum,* 4 (1961), 21-25.

Duckworth, Colin. *Angels of Darkness: Dramatic Effect in Samuel Beckett with Special Reference to Eugene Ionesco.* New York: Barnes and Noble, 1972.

Edwards, Michael. *Towards a Christian Poetics.* Grand Rapids: Eerdmans, 1984.

Estress, T. L. "Inenarrable contraption; reflections on the metaphor of story." *Journal of the American Academy of Religion,* 42 (1974), 415-34.

Federman, Raymond. "Beckett's Belacqua and the Inferno of Society." *Arizona Quarterly,* 20 (1964), 231-41.

———. *Journey to Chaos: Samuel Beckett's Early Fiction.* Berkeley: Univ. of California Press, 1965.

Felperin, Howard. *Beyond Deconstruction: the Uses and Abuses of Literary Theory.* Oxford 1985; rpt. with corrections, Oxford; Clarendon Press, 1986.

Fletcher, John. "Beckett's Debt to Dante." *Nottingham French Studies,* 4 (1965), 41-51.

———. *The Novels of Samuel Beckett.* London: 1964; rpt. New York: Barnes and Noble, 1970.

Foucault, Michel. *Language, Counter-Memory, Practice.* Ed. and trans. Donald F. Bouchard. Ithaca: Cornell Univ. Press, 1977.

Fraser, G. S. *"Waiting for Godot."* In *English Critical Essays: Twentieth Century.* Ed. Derek Hudson. London: Oxford Univ. Press, 1958, pp. 324-32.

Frye, Northrop. *Anatomy of Criticism: Four Essays.* Princeton: Princeton Univ. Press, 1957.

Garzilli, Enrico. *Circles Without Center: Paths to the Discovery and Creation of Self in Modern Literature.* Cambridge: Harvard Univ. Press, 1972.

Glicksberg, Charles I. *Literature and Religion: A Study in Conflict.* Dallas: Southern Methodist Univ. Press, 1960.

Gontarski, S. E. "The Intent of Undoing in Samuel Beckett's Art." *Modern Fiction Studies,* 29 (1983), 5-23.

Gruen, John. "Samuel Beckett Talks About Beckett." *Vogue,* 154 (1969), 210-11.

Hamilton, Alice and Kenneth. *Condemned to Life: The World of Samuel Beckett.* Grand Rapids: Eerdmans, 1976.

———. "Samuel Beckett and the Gnostic Vision of the Created World." *Studies in Religion/Sciences Religieuses,* 8 (1979), 293-301.

———. "The Process of Imaginative Creation in Samuel Beckett's *How It Is.*" *Mosaic,* 10 (1977), 1-12.

Hampshire, Stuart. *Spinoza.* Baltimore: Penguin, 1951.

Harper, Howard. *"How It Is."* In *Samuel Beckett: The Art of Rhetoric.* Ed. Edouard Morot-Sir, et al. Chapel Hill: North Carolina Studies in the Romance Languages and Literatures, 1976, pp. 249-70.

Harvey, Lawrence. "Art and the Existential in *En attendant Godot.*" *PMLA,* 75 (1960), 137-46.

———. *Samuel Beckett: Poet and Critic.* Princeton: Princeton Univ. Press, 1970.

Hesla, David H. *The Shape of Chaos: An Interpretation of the Art of Samuel Beckett.* Minneapolis: Univ. of Minnesota Press, 1971.

Hoefer, Jacqueline. *"Watt." Perspective,* 11 (1959), 166-82. Rpt. in *Samuel Beckett: A Collection of Critical Essays,* pp. 62-67.

Homan, Sidney. *Beckett's Theaters: Interpretations for Performance.* Cranbury, N.J.: Associated Univ. Presses, 1984.

Jacobsen, Josephine, and William R. Mueller. *The Testament of Samuel Beckett.* New York: 1964; rpt. London: Faber and Faber, 1966.

Janvier, Ludovic. "Place of Narration/Narration of Place." In *Samuel Beckett: A Collection of Criticism Edited by Ruby Cohn.* New York: McGraw-Hill, 1975, pp. 98-110.

Kenner, Hugh. *Samuel Beckett: A Critical Study.* New York: Grove, 1967.

Kern, Edith. "Moran-Molloy: The Hero as Author." *Perspective,* 11 (1959), 183-92.

Kroll, Jeri L. "Belacqua as Artist and Lover: 'What a Misfortune.'" *Journal of Beckett Studies,* No. 3 (1978), pp. 10-39.

———. "The Artist's Mind in Samuel Beckett's Fiction." *Journal of the Australasian Language and Literature Association,* No. 55 (1981), pp. 36-53.

Langbaum, Robert. "Current Trends in Literary Criticism." *National Forum,* 60 (1980), 20-22.

Lasch, Christopher. *The Culture of Narcissism: American Life in an Age of Diminishing Expectations.* New York: W. W. Norton, 1979.

Lees, Heath. "'Watt': Music, Tuning and Tonality." *Journal of Beckett Studies,* No. 9 (1984), pp. 5-24.

Leitch, Vincent B. *Deconstructive Criticism: An Advanced Introduction.* New York: Columbia Univ. Press, 1983.

Lévy, Eric P. "Voice of Species: The Narrator and Beckettian Man in *Three Novels.*" *Journal of English Literary History,* 45 (1978), 343-58.

McMillan, Dougald. "Samuel Beckett and the Visual Arts: The Embarrassment of Allegory." In *Samuel Beckett: A Collection of Criticism Edited by Ruby Cohn*, pp. 121-35.

Mercier, Vivian. *Beckett/Beckett.* New York: Oxford Univ. Press, 1977.

Miller, J. Hillis. "The Anonymous Walkers." *The Nation*, 23 April 1960, pp. 351-54.

———. *The Disappearance of God: Five Nineteenth-Century Writers.* Cambridge: Belknap Press of Harvard Univ. Press, 1963.

Mintz, Samuel. "Beckett's *Murphy:* A Cartesian Novel." *Perspective*, 11 (1959), 156-65.

The Month. Second New Series, 1 (1970), 7-8.

Mood, John J. " 'The Personal System' – Samuel Beckett's *Watt.*" *PMLA*, 86 (1971), 255-65.

Moorjani, Angela. *Abysmal Games in the Novels of Samuel Beckett.* Chapel Hill: North Carolina Studies in the Romance Languages and Literatures, 1982.

Morot-Sir, Edouard. "Grammatical Insincerity and Samuel Beckett's Non-Expressionism: Space, Subjectivity, and Tıme in *The Unnamable*," in *Writing in a Modern Temper: Essays on French Literature and Thought in Honor of Henri Peyne.* Ed. Mary Ann Caws. Saratoga, Calif.: Anma Libri, 1984, pp. 225-39.

———. "Pascal versus Wittgenstein, with Samuel Beckett as the Anti-Witness." *Romance Notes*, 15 (1973), 201-16.

———. "Samuel Beckett and Cartesian Emblems." In *Samuel Beckett: The Art of Rhetoric*, pp. 25-104.

Onimus, Jean. *Beckett.* Paris: *Desclee de Brouwer*, 1968.

Oxenhandler, Neal. "Seeing and Belıeving in Dante and Beckett." In *Writing in a Modern Temper: Essays on French Literature and Thought in Honor of Henri Peyne*, pp. 214-23.

Pilling, John. "Beckett After *Still.*" *Romance Notes*, 18 (1977), 280-87.

———, and James Knowlson. *Frescoes of the Skull: The Later Prose and Drama of Samuel Beckett.* London: John Calder, 1979.

———. "Review article: '*Fizzles.*' " *Journal of Beckett Studies*, No. 2 (1977), pp. 96-100.

———. *Samuel Beckett.* London: Routledge and Kegan Paul, 1976.

Rabınovıtz, Rubin. "The Addenda to Samuel Beckett's 'Watt.' " In *Samuel Beckett: The Art of Rhetoric*, pp. 211-23.

———. "*Watt* From Descartes to Schopenhauer." In *Modern Irish Literature: Essays in Honor of William York Tindall.* Ed. Raymond J. Porter and James D. Brophy. New York: Iona College Press, 1972, pp. 261-87.

Read, David. "Artistic Theory in the Work of Samuel Beckett." *Journal of Beckett Studies*, No. 8 (1982), pp. 7-22.

Renner, Charlotte. "The Self-Multiplying Narrators of *Molloy, Malone Dies,* and *The Unnamable. Journal of Narrative Technique*, 11 (1981), 12-32.

Robinson, C. J. Bradbury. "A Way with Words: Paradox, Silence, and Samuel Beckett." *The Cambridge Quarterly*, 4 (1971), 249-64.

Robinson, Michael. *The Long Sonata of the Dead.* New York: Grove, 1969.

Scott, Nathan. *The Broken Center: Studies in the Theological Horizon of Modern Literature.* New Haven: Yale Univ. Press, 1966.

———. *Modern Literature and the Religious Frontier.* New York: Harper, 1958.

———. *Samuel Beckett.* Series of Studies in Modern European Literature and Thought. London: Bowes and Bowes, 1965.

Shenker, Israel. "Moody Man of Letters." *New York Times*, 6 May 1956, Sec. 2, pp. x and 3.

Skerl, Jennie. "Fritz Mauthner's 'Critique of Language' in Samuel Beckett's *Watt.*" *Contemporary Literature,* 15 (1974), 474-87.

Smith, Frederick N. "Three on Beckett: An Essay-Review," *Modern Fiction Studies,* 29 (1983), 127-30.

Smith, Roch C. "Naming the M/Inotaur: Beckett's Trilogy and the Failure of Narrative." *Modern Fiction Studies,* 29 (1983), 73-91.

Sobosan, Jeffrey G. "Time and Absurdity in Samuel Beckett." *Thought,* 49 (1974), 187-95.

Swanson, Eleanor. "Samuel Beckett's *Watt:* A Coming and a Going." *Modern Fiction Studies,* 17 (1971), 264-68.

Sypher, Wylie. *Loss of the Self in Modern Literature and Art.* New York: Random House, 1964.

Szanto, George H. *Narrative Consciousness: Structure and Perception in the Fiction of Kafka, Beckett, and Robbe-Grillet.* Austin: Univ. of Texas Press, 1972.

Szasz, Fereanc Morton. *The Divided Mind of Protestant America.* University, Ala.: Univ. of Alabama Press, 1982.

Thiher, Allen. "Wittenstein, Heidegger, the Unnamable, and Some Thoughts on the Status of Voice in Fiction." In *Samuel Beckett: Humanistic Perspectives,* pp. 80-90.

Toyama, Jean Yamasaki. "Malone, the unoriginal centre." *Journal of Beckett Studies,* No. 9 (1984), pp. 89-99.

Trotter, F. Thomas. "Variations on the 'Death of God' Theme in Recent Theology." In *The Death of God Debate.* Ed. Jackson Lee Ice and John J. Carey. Philadelphia: Westminister, 1967, pp. 93-106.

Warger, Thomas A. "Going Mad Systematically in Beckett's *Murphy.*" *Modern Language Studies,* 16 (1986), 13-18.

Webner, Hèléne. "*Waiting for Godot* and the New Theology." *Renascence,* 21 (1968), 3-9, 31.

Wellershoff, Dieter. "Failure of an Attempt at De-Mythologization: Samuel Beckett's Novels." Trans. Martin Esslin. In *Samuel Beckett: A Collection of Critical Essays,* pp. 92-107.

Wells, Charles M. "The Transcendence of Life: The Positive Dimension in Samuel Beckett." Diss. Univ. of New Mexico, 1960.

Wicker, Brian. "Samuel Beckett and the Death of the God-Narrator." *Journal of Narrative Technique,* 4 (1974), 62-74.

Winston, Matthew. "Watt's First Footnote." *Journal of Modern Literature,* 6 (1977), 69-82.

Wright, Iain. " 'What matter who's speaking?': Beckett, the authorial subject and contemporary critical theory." In *Comparative Criticism.* Ed. E. S. Shaffer, Vol. V. Cambridge: Cambridge Univ. Press, 1983, pp. 59-86.

Zeifman, Hersh. "Religious Imagery in the Plays of Samuel Beckett." In *Samuel Beckett: A Collection of Criticism Edited by Ruby Cohn,* pp. 85-94.

INDEX TO WRITINGS BY BECKETT

GENERAL INDEX

NORTH CAROLINA STUDIES IN THE ROMANCE LANGUAGES AND LITERATURES

I.S.B.N. Prefix 0-8078-

Recent Titles

THE LIFE AND WORKS OF LUIS CARLOS LÓPEZ, by Martha S. Bazik. 1977. (No. 183). *-9183-5.*

"THE CORT D'AMOR". A THIRTEENTH-CENTURY ALLEGORICAL ART OF LOVE, by Lowanne E. Jones. 1977. (No. 185). *-9185-1.*

PHYTONYMIC DERIVATIONAL SYSTEMS IN THE ROMANCE LANGUAGES: STUDIES IN THEIR ORIGIN AND DEVELOPMENT, by Walter E. Geiger. 1978. (No. 187). *-9187-8.*

LANGUAGE IN GIOVANNI VERGA'S EARLY NOVELS, by Nicholas Patruno. 1977. (No. 188). *-9188-6.*

BLAS DE OTERO EN SU POESÍA, by Moraima de Semprún Donahue. 1977. (No. 189). *-9189-4*

LA ANATOMÍA DE "EL DIABLO COJUELO": DESLINDES DEL GENERO ANATOMÍSTICO, por C. George Peale. 1977. (No. 191). *-9191-6.*

RICHARD SANS PEUR, EDITED FROM "LE ROMANT DE RICHART" AND FROM GILLES CORROZET'S "RICHART SANS PAOUR", by Denis Joseph Conlon. 1977. (No. 192). *-9192-4.*

MARCEL PROUST'S GRASSET PROOFS. *Commentary and Variants,* by Douglas Alden. 1978. (No. 193). *-9193-2.*

MONTAIGNE AND FEMINISM, by Cecile Insdorf. 1977. (No. 194). *-9194-0.*

SANTIAGO F. PUGLIA, AN EARLY PHILADELPHIA PROPAGANDIST FOR SPANISH AMERICAN INDEPENDENCE, by Merle S. Simmons. 1977. (No. 195). *-9195-9.*

BAROQUE FICTION-MAKING. A STUDY OF GOMBERVILLE'S "POLEXANDRE", by Edward Baron Turk. 1978. (No. 196). *-9196-7.*

THE TRAGIC FALL: DON ÁLVARO DE LUNA AND OTHER FAVORITES IN SPANISH GOLDEN AGE DRAMA, by Raymond R. MacCurdy. 1978. (No. 197). *-9197-5.*

A BAHIAN HERITAGE. An Ethnolinguistic Study of African Influences on Bahian Portuguese, by William W. Megenney. 1978. (No. 198). *-9198-3.*

"LA QUERELLE DE LA ROSE": Letters and Documents, by Joseph L. Baird and John R. Kane. 1978. (No. 199). *-9199-1.*

TWO AGAINST TIME. *A Study of the Very Present Worlds of Paul Claudel and Charles Péguy,* by Joy Nachod Humes. 1978. (No. 200). *-9200-9.*

TECHNIQUES OF IRONY IN ANATOLE FRANCE. Essay on *Les Sept Femmes de la Barbe-Bleue,* by Diane Wolfe Levy. 1978. (No. 201). *-9201-7.*

THE PERIPHRASTIC FUTURES FORMED BY THE ROMANCE REFLEXES OF "VADO (AD)" PLUS INFINITIVE, by James Joseph Champion. 1978. (No. 202). *-9202-5.*

THE EVOLUTION OF THE LATIN /b/-/u̯/ MERGER: A Quantitative and Comparative Analysis of the *B-V* Alternation in Latin Inscriptions, by Joseph Louis Barbarino. 1978. (No. 203). *-9203-3.*

METAPHORIC NARRATION: THE STRUCTURE AND FUNCTION OF METAPHORS IN "A LA RECHERCHE DU TEMPS PERDU", by Inge Karalus Crosman. 1978. (No. 204). *-9204-1.*

LE VAIN SIECLE GUERPIR. A Literary Approach to Sainthood through Old French Hagiography of the Twelfth Century, by Phyllis Johnson and Brigitte Cazelles. 1979. (No. 205). *-9205-X.*

THE POETRY OF CHANGE: A STUDY OF THE SURREALIST WORKS OF BENJAMIN PÉRET, by Julia Field Costich. 1979. (No. 206). *-9206-8.*

NARRATIVE PERSPECTIVE IN THE POST-CIVIL WAR NOVELS OF FRANCISCO AYALA "MUERTES DE PERRO" AND "EL FONDO DEL VASO", by Maryellen Bieder. 1979. (No. 207). *-9207-6.*

RABELAIS: HOMO LOGOS, by Alice Fiola Berry. 1979. (No. 208). *-9208-4.*

When ordering please cite the *ISBN Prefix* plus the last four digits for each title.

Send orders to: University of North Carolina Press
P.O. Box 2288
CB# 6215
Chapel Hill, NC 27515-2288
U.S.A.

NORTH CAROLINA STUDIES IN THE ROMANCE LANGUAGES AND LITERATURES

I.S.B.N. Prefix 0-8078-

Recent Titles

"DUEÑAS" AND "DONCELLAS": A STUDY OF THE "DOÑA RODRÍGUEZ" EPISODE IN "DON QUIJOTE", by Conchita Herdman Marianella. 1979. (No. 209). *-9209-2.*

PIERRE BOAISTUAU'S "HISTOIRES TRAGIQUES": A STUDY OF NARRATIVE FORM AND TRAGIC VISION, by Richard A. Carr. 1979. (No. 210). *-9210-6.*

REALITY AND EXPRESSION IN THE POETRY OF CARLOS PELLICER, by George Melnykovich. 1979. (No. 211). *-9211-4.*

MEDIEVAL MAN, HIS UNDERSTANDING OF HIMSELF, HIS SOCIETY, AND THE WORLD, by Urban T. Holmes, Jr. 1980. (No. 212). *-9212-2.*

MÉMOIRES SUR LA LIBRAIRIE ET SUR LA LIBERTÉ DE LA PRESSE, introduction and notes by Graham E. Rodmell. 1979. (No. 213). *-9213-0.*

THE FICTIONS OF THE SELF. THE EARLY WORKS OF MAURICE BARRES, by Gordon Shenton. 1979. (No. 214). *-9214-9.*

CECCO ANGIOLIERI. A STUDY, by Gifford P. Orwen. 1979. (No. 215). *-9215-7.*

THE INSTRUCTIONS OF SAINT LOUIS: A CRITICAL TEXT, by David O'Connell. 1979. (No. 216). *-9216-5.*

ARTFUL ELOQUENCE, JEAN LEMAIRE DE BELGES AND THE RHETORICAL TRADITION, by Michael F. O. Jenkins. 1980. (No. 217). *-9217-3.*

A CONCORDANCE TO MARIVAUX'S COMEDIES IN PROSE, edited by Donald C. Spinelli. 1979. (No. 218). 4 volumes, *-9218-1* (set); *-9219-X* (v. 1); *-9220-3* (v. 2); *-9221-1* (v. 3); *-9222-X* (v. 4).

ABYSMAL GAMES IN THE NOVELS OF SAMUEL BECKETT, by Angela B. Moorjani. 1982. (No. 219). *-9223-8.*

GERMAIN NOUVEAU DIT HUMILIS: ÉTUDE BIOGRAPHIQUE, par Alexandre L. Amprimoz. 1983. (No. 220). *-9224-6.*

THE "VIE DE SAINT ALEXIS" IN THE TWELFTH AND THIRTEENTH CENTURIES: AN EDITION AND COMMENTARY, by Alison Goddard Elliot. 1983. (No. 221). *-9225-4.*

THE BROKEN ANGEL: MYTH AND METHOD IN VALÉRY, by Ursula Franklin. 1984. (No. 222). *-9226-2.*

READING VOLTAIRE'S "CONTES": A SEMIOTICS OF PHILOSOPHICAL NARRATION, by Carol Sherman. 1985. (No. 223). *-9227-0.*

THE STATUS OF THE READING SUBJECT IN THE "LIBRO DE BUEN AMOR", by Marina Scordilis Brownlee. 1985. (No. 224). *-9228-9.*

MARTORELL'S "TIRANT LO BLANCH": A PROGRAM FOR MILITARY AND SOCIAL REFORM IN FIFTEENTH-CENTURY CHRISTENDOM, by Edward T. Aylward. 1985. (No. 225). *-9229-7.*

NOVEL LIVES: THE FICTIONAL AUTOBIOGRAPHIES OF GUILLERMO CABRERA INFANTE AND MARIO VARGAS LLOSA, by Rosemary Geisdorfer Feal. 1986. (No. 226). *-9230-0.*

SOCIAL REALISM IN THE ARGENTINE NARRATIVE, by David William Foster. 1986. (No. 227). *-9231-9.*

HALF-TOLD TALES: DILEMMAS OF MEANING IN THREE FRENCH NOVELS, by Philip Stewart. 1987. (No. 228). *-9232-7.*

POLITIQUES DE L'ECRITURE BATAILLE/DERRIDA: le sens du sacré dans la pensée française du surréalisme à nos jours, par Jean-Michel Heimonet. 1987. (No. 229). *-9233-5.*

GOD, THE QUEST, THE HERO: THEMATIC STRUCTURES IN BECKETT'S FICTION, by Laura Barge. 1988. (No. 230). *-9235-1.*

THE NAME GAME. WRITING/FADING WRITER IN "DE DONDE SON LOS CANTANTES", by Oscar Montero. 1988. (No. 231). *-9236-X.*

When ordering please cite the *ISBN Prefix* plus the last four digits for each title.

Send orders to: University of North Carolina Press
P.O. Box 2288
CB# 6215
Chapel Hill, NC 27515-2288
U.S.A.

The Department of Romance Studies Digital Arts and Collaboration Lab at the University of North Carolina at Chapel Hill is proud to support the digitization of the North Carolina Studies in the Romance Languages and Literatures series.

www.ingramcontent.com/pod-product-compliance
Lightning Source LLC
LaVergne TN
LVHW041108080826

845145LV00007B/1734

9780807892350